# THE
# RETIREMENT
# NIGHTMARE

With best wishes,

Diane G. Armstrong, Ph.D.

January 2001

# GOLDEN AGE SERIES

*The Adventure of Retirement:*
*It's About More Than Just Money*
Guild A. Fetridge

*After the Stroke: Coping with America's*
*Third Leading Cause of Death*
Evelyn Shirk

*The Age of Aging: A Reader in Social*
*Gerontology*
Abraham Monk

*Between Home and Nursing Home:*
*The Board and Care Alternative*
Ivy M. Down and Lorraine Schnurr

*Caring for an Aging Parent:*
*Have I Done All I Can?*
Avis Jane Ball

*Caring for the Alzheimer Patient: A*
*Practical Guide,* Second Edition
edited by Raye Lynne Dippel, Ph.D.,
and J. Thomas Hutton, M.D., Ph.D.

*Caring for the Parkinson Patient:*
*A Practical Guide,*
Second Edition
edited by J. Thomas Hutton, M.D., Ph.D.,
and Raye Lynne Dippel, Ph.D.

*Eldercare: Coping with Late-Life Crisis*
James Kenny, Ph.D., and
Stephen Spicer, M.D.

*Geroethics: A New Vision of Growing*
*Old in America*
Gerald A. Larue

*Handle With Care: A Question*
*of Alzheimer's*
Dorothy S. Brown

*Long-Term Care in an Aging Society*
Gerald A. Larue and Rich Bayly

*My Parents Never Had Sex: Myths and*
*Facts of Sexual Aging*
Doris B. Hammond, Ph.D.

*On Our Own: Independent Living*
*for Older Persons*
Ursula A. Falk, Ph.D.

*Promises to Keep: The Family's Role*
*in Nursing Home Care*
Katherine L. Karr

*The Retirement Nightmare: How to*
*Save Yourself from Your Heirs*
*and Protectors*
Diane G. Armstrong, Ph.D.

*Taking Time for Me: How Caregivers*
*Can Effectively Deal with Stress*
Katherine L. Karr

*Thy Will Be Done: A Guide to Wills,*
*Taxation, and Estate Planning*
*for Older Persons,*
Revised Edition
Eugene J. Daley, Attorney at Law

*Understanding "Senility":*
*A Layperson's Guide*
Virginia Fraser and
Susan M. Thornton

*When Living Alone Means Living at Risk:*
*A Guide for Caregivers*
*and Families*
Robert W. Buckingham, Dr. P.H.

*Working with the Elderly:*
*An Introduction*
Elizabeth S. Deichman, Ed.M., ORT,
and Regina Kociecki, B.S.

*Where Did Mary Go?: A Loving*
*Husband's Struggle with*
*Alzheimer's*
Frank A. Wall

*You, Your Parent, and the*
*Nursing Home*
Nancy Fox

# THE RETIREMENT NIGHTMARE

## How to Save Yourself from Your Heirs and Protectors

*Involuntary
Conservatorships
and
Guardianships*

# Diane G. Armstrong, Ph.D.

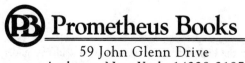 Prometheus Books

59 John Glenn Drive
Amherst, New York 14228-2197

Published 2000 by Prometheus Books

Inquiries should be addressed to
Prometheus Books
59 John Glenn Drive
Amherst, New York 14228–2197
VOICE: 716–691–0133, ext. 207
FAX: 716–564–2711
WWW.PROMETHEUSBOOKS.COM

04 03 02 01 00    5 4 3 2 1

Library of Congress Cataloging-in-Publication Data

Armstrong, Diane G.
   The retirement nightmare : how to save yourself from your heirs and protectors / by Diane G. Armstrong.
      p.    cm. — (Golden Age Series)
   Includes bibliographical references and index.
   ISBN 1–57392–796–1 (alk. paper)
   1. Guardian and ward—United States—Popular works. 2. Conservatorship—United States—Popular works. 3. Retirees—Abuse of—United States. I. Title. II. Series.

KF553.Z9 .A76  2000
346.7301'8—dc21                                                    99–087527
                                                                           CIP

Printed in the United States of America on acid-free paper

# CONTENTS

Acknowledgments                                                           7

Introduction                                                              9

1. The Graying of America                                                15

2. Frequently Asked Questions
      about Conservatorships and Guardianships                           27

3. Historical Roots of American
      Conservatorship/Guardianship Law                                   57

4. Individual Court Struggles for Freedom: Defeats                       77

5. Individual Court Struggles for Freedom: Victories                    117

6. Who Is Guarding the Guardians?                                       153

7. Alternatives to "Protective Proceedings"                             167

8. How Should Our Laws Be Changed?                                      179

9. Saving Yourself from Your Heirs and Protectors                       207

# APPENDICES

Appendix A. State Codes and Statutes     237

Appendix B. Costs Involved in Fighting Unwanted Protective
         Proceedings: One Example     323

Appendix C. Resources for the Elderly     325

         Major National Organizations     325

         National Legal Organizations     335

         Congressional Committees, Issues of Aging     337

         State Offices of Aging     338

         State Long-Term-Care Ombudsman Programs     348

         Related Websites     358

         References for Appendix C     360

Glossary     363

Bibliography     387

Index     393

# ACKNOWLEDGMENTS

*T*he *Retirement Nightmare* would not exist had it not been for the eighteen-month involuntary conservatorship battle waged against my mother by four of her seven children. To you, Mom, and to my remaining sisters, Cathy and Cynthia, I give my thanks. Let us hope this book will help others avoid the legal nightmare that befell our family. Ed Sezna, your wisdom and determination during the court hearings guided us all to safety. We shall never forget.

Roger Jellinek, agent extraordinaire, you were responsible for bringing this book to life. Your enthusiasm, your remarkable intelligence, and your rare editorial skills are invaluable gifts—generously shared—and I thank you deeply for your support. Editor-in-chief Steven L. Mitchell and the talented team at Prometheus Books, I thank you, too, for your dedication to this book. Kelli Sager, Entertainment Law specialist with Davis Wright Tremaine, you are a treasure without equal.

From beginning to end, the love and support of my family make all things possible. Bruce, Lorelei and Rebecca, mahalo! And a final mahalo nui loa to you, Lori. Armed with a can of chocolate frosting and a smile, you helped me focus on the stars during the darkest times.

I am also grateful to the following publishers and rights holders for granting permission to reprint from the works listed below:

The case of Glen Hawkins in chapter 1 is taken from S. Emmons, "Conservators' Reach Can Be a Surprise," *Los Angeles Times*, 23 November 1997, pp. A3, A29. Copyright © 1997 *Los Angeles Times*. Reprinted by permission.

"What to Ask a Lawyer" in chapter 9 is from "When You Need a Lawyer," © 1996 by Consumers Union of U.S., Inc. Yonkers, NY 10703-1057, a nonprofit organization. Reprinted with permission from the February 1996 issue of *Consumer Reports* for educational purposes only. No commercial use or photocopying permitted. To subscribe, call 1-800-234-1645 or visit us at www.consumerreports.org <http://www.consumerreports.org>.

# INTRODUCTION

*How sharper than a serpent's tooth it is*
*To have a thankless child!*

—William Shakespeare,
*King Lear* Act 1, Scene 4

Although newly widowed, sixty-two-year-old Mary Cummings was learning to make the most of her retirement years. Encouraged to do so by one of her four adult children, Mary purchased a modest home in Georgia and learned to manage a small family estate that generated $10,000 a year in interest. As her life as a fully independent widow began to unfold into a comfortable pattern, she even treated herself and two sons to a vacation in Florida. Unfortunately, Mary's financial independence was to last for only one year.

What happened to this unsuspecting widow? Did Mary fall prey to a fraudulent investment scam and lose her money, as some unwary seniors do? Did Mary remarry and voluntarily relinquish her independence? Did she become physically or mentally incapable of managing her affairs? No, not at all. What happened to Mary Cummings is something that is happening to far too many men and women across America. Mary's only daughter—who had not been included in the trip to Florida—filed a petition in Probate Court seeking appointment as guardian over her mother's estate. Were she to become her daughter's ward, Mary Cummings was warned, she would surrender many basic rights: to buy, sell, or otherwise dispose of real, personal, or trust property, to enter into business or commercial transactions, and to make contracts. She would no longer be permitted to spend her money as she pleased.

Mary was thrown headlong into a three-year nightmare of involuntary litigation that ended when the Court of Appeals found that "due to advanced age and perhaps mental disability" (although none was suggested or proven in court), sixty-five-year-old Mary Cummings was "incapable of managing her financial resources, which would be wasted or dissipated in the absence of property management." She was returned to the financial status of a child, doomed to ask her daughter's permission for every expense that exceeded a modest court-mandated allowance—all taken from her own retirement funds. And, with the cruel irony that colors all involuntary conservatorship/guardianship proceedings in America, Mary was also required to pay all legal costs relating to the protracted legal battle—then and henceforward.

Mary Cummings fell victim to little-known state laws that were originally intended to protect the rights of "infants and lunatics" only. These laws are our country's secretive conservatorship/guardianship statutes. Mary's story is but one of fifty-five that I have chosen to illustrate how such well-intentioned laws are being abused. Unhappy heir-petitioners and members of state agencies ostensibly charged with the care of needy senior citizens are using these "protective proceedings" to control the behaviors and/or testamentary dispositions of senior citizens across America.

One might assume that only the wealthy are victimized by the misapplication of conservatorship/guardianship laws, but this is far from the case. These court struggles are driven by two converging national trends: a rapidly aging population, and the anticipated transfer of almost $11 trillion from members of the World War II generation to their Baby Boomer children and relatives. Approximately 115 million men and women will be leaving bequests that average $90,000. Most of the involuntary conservatorship/guardianship cases filling America's probate courts today, however, are fought over surprisingly simple things—an old house, an average retirement account, a small family farm or business. Whether it is a modest savings account or a multimillion-dollar estate, that sum represents *everything* the targeted aging individual has accumulated to enjoy in his or her retirement years.

The number of elderly men and women who are now living as wards under state "protection" is variously estimated at between 500,000 and 1,250,000. As we shall see, however, the number cannot be quantified because none of our states know how many allegedly incompetent adults have fallen under their mantle of protection. Michigan reports that guardianship petitions have more than quadrupled since 1981, and courts in the state of New York acknowledge having appointed over 32,000 guardianships during 1997—more than double the number they granted in 1992. This legal epidemic has spawned a new growth industry of professionals involved in the business of servicing the needs of our burgeoning conservatorized population. The rising incidence of conservatorships and guardianships across America is an ominous trend for members of our country's successfully aging population.

Why have I written this book? My research on these oddly secretive laws was inspired by my mother who, as a fiercely independent woman of seventy-two, was forced to prove her personal and financial competence in California's Superior Court. Sadly, her legal nightmare was initiated by four of her seven children. The ensuing court battle consumed eighteen precious months of her life and cost over $1 million in legal fees. Unable to convince my siblings to withdraw their unnecessary involuntary conservatorship petition, she finally agreed to pay $100,000 to their attorneys to bring the litigation to an end. The unexpected and horrific legal battle split our family in two and, for my mother in particular, the resulting wound has never healed. She felt she had been betrayed by her children and betrayed by laws that were devised by California to manage the personal and financial affairs of incapacitated or incompetent adults. "It felt like abuse to me," she said after signing the settlement agreement that ended her case. What was worse, it felt like *court-sanctioned* abuse of the elderly.

As we age, each of us becomes increasingly vulnerable to the double-edged sword of these well-intentioned laws. It is important to understand this legal sword's power in order to avoid its sharp edge—or to use it well should the need arise. In a true twist of fate, as the last sections of *Retirement Nightmare* neared completion, I found it necessary to use the very laws that had brutalized my mother to weave a mantle of support around my increasingly fragile mother-in-law. Because I had studied these relatively unknown codes quite thoroughly, I was able to apply them in a moment of great need. The irony was not lost on anyone associated with this book.

Without a doubt, conservatorship and guardianship laws provide excellent tools in all states for helping elderly friends and relatives who, as a result of sudden illness or traumatic injury, can no longer make daily decisions concerning personal and financial matters. However, these statutes are being abused by calculating heir-petitioners to control the flow of inheritances and direct the transfer of family asseetes to themselves, all with our courts' blessings. They are being used by members of the social welfare community to determine how elderly men and women will live out their last years on earth—all too often against the express wishes of these capable but aging individuals.

*Retirement Nightmare* can help you neutralize these dangers. By focusing on how involuntary conservatorship/guardianship laws are being abused rather than used, this book will provide you with the knowledge and accumulated experience you will need to save yourself and your money from your heirs and protectors—be they neighbors, distant relatives, or social welfare agencies whose surrogate decision-making powers may one day be substituted for yours.

We will first identify the population most at risk of unwanted or involuntary conservatorship/guardianship proceedings. As we shall see, this group consists of men and women sixty-two years of age or older who, having accumulated assets for their retirement years, are being pulled closer and closer to a legal quagmire of litigation originally created by each state to safeguard the interests of those who cannot help themselves. We will also explore the origin of our states' involuntary conservatorship/guardianship codes and see how they actually function in and out of court.

Next, we will meet fifty-five men and women whose lives were changed forever by unwanted "protective proceedings." Their cases were drawn from superior, appellate, and state supreme courts across America, up to and including the United States Supreme Court. This material is very painful to read. In every instance, each individual suffers irreversible losses when forced to prove his or her mental competence in court.

Each case reflects the erratic and unpredictable nature of the courts' rulings—rulings which legally reclassify the elderly and transport them back to the status of dependent children for the rest of their lives. Incompetent "wards" and "conservatees," as they then become known, cannot spend their own money, make their own investments, decide where they will live, choose their own friends or caretakers, either vote or marry, or even avoid placement in a nursing home. The consequences of being adjudicated mentally or physically incompetent are grim indeed.

The book continues with some of the alternatives to conservatorships and guardianships that provide respectful assistance and legal substitute decision-making for people in need. Much of this information has been gathered from the local and state agencies that exist in every state in America to help the elderly with various aspects of daily living: balancing checkbooks and paying bills, shopping for food, preparing meals, keeping homes safe and clean, and even getting to and from necessary appointments and social events.

From a review of these alternatives to current conservatorship/guardianship arrangements, we will then look at specific ways in which our codes and statutes should be changed. This list of suggested changes has been culled from legal and mental health publications, from newspaper accounts of egregious cases, from discussions with experts in the field of elder law and, most importantly, from the personal knowledge I gained during my mother's remarkable $1,000,000-battle in California's courts. It is my fondest wish that legislators in every state will read this section and act. Modification of these codes is long overdue.

Finally, we will consider what each of us can do—while fully competent—to protect ourselves from future involuntary conservatorship/guardianship litigation. These recommendations flow from the pessimistic assumption that our state conservatorship and guardianship laws will not be changed in appropriate ways before they can be used against *you*. This last chapter contains the key legal protections you can and should put in place before anyone—*anyone*—challenges your capacity or competence to make personal or financial decisions during your retirement years.

# CHAPTER ONE

# ON THE GRAYING OF AMERICA

*To me, old age is always fifteen years older than I am.*
—Bernard M. Baruch

**D**uring each of the five years from 1973 to 1977, England placed an average of twenty-four adults under protective guardianships. In contrast, during the dozen months from 1976 to 1977, California alone—containing half the population of England—established guardianships for over 9,113 elderly men and women. By the year 1991, according to Kathleen Wilbur, Assistant Professor of Gerontology at the University of Southern California, approximately *half a million adults throughout America* were living in the velvet handcuffs imposed by these conservatorship/guardianship rulings.[1]

In its final report to the U.S. Administration on Aging in 1992, the Center for Social Gerontology increased this estimate to between 500,000 and 1,250,000 elderly men and women, an enormous population whose numbers are impossible to quantify because individual states themselves do not know how many aging adults they have agreed to "protect."[2] More recently, judges in the state of New York appointed over 32,000 guardianships during 1997, up from 15,000 in 1992, and Michigan's guardianship petitions in 1997 have more than quadrupled since 1981.[3] The greatest number of all of these petitions were filed by adult children seeking some form of control over their aging relatives.

In a trend that is ominous for all members of our successfully aging population, an increasing number of unwanted conservators and guardians are being appointed to manage the property and/or personal affairs of allegedly incapacitated elderly men and women. These individuals are not mentally ill. They are not incompetent. They are asset-rich and "old." The resultant legal epidemic is unparalleled anywhere else on the face of the Earth.

What has happened in America? When asked to comment on the growing problem, George Alexander and Travis Lewin, authors of *The Aged and the Need for Surrogate Management*, blamed this rising tide of litigation on the system created by our state laws.[4] Their words capture the flavor of how these surrogate decision-making proceedings—controlled by conservatorship and guardianship codes in individual states—are fundamentally flawed.

> It is not the fault of medicine or psychiatry; it is not the fault of institutions or of greedy relatives; it is not the fault of lax property management; and it is not the fault of corrupt judicial, legal or administrative officials. The fault lies with the system created by the law. We define the condition of incompetency in a way in which psychiatrists can give no meaningful assistance and then abrogate the decision-making power to medicine. We devise a system which operates only at the initiation of those who stand to gain by imposition of the procedure and then ignore competing interests which causally follow. We draft a procedure that insures a speedy institution of incompetency but fails to provide an equally expeditious method for restoration. We design a system of surrogate management in the belief that mischief will befall the unmanaged assets of the so-called mentally ill. Then we leave the determination and inauguration of incompetency in the hands of those benefiting from its continuation, magically believing that the basic beneficence of man will overcome his self-interest and greed.[5]

In too many states, any adult may initiate an involuntary conservatorship or guardianship proceeding simply by stating that the proposed conservatee or ward is old. The petitioner must then allege—allege, not prove—that the targeted elder is incapable of providing for his or her personal needs or managing his or her financial affairs. The allegation itself contains power in a legal system rife with references to "a loss of competency because of the 'infirmities of old age.' "[6]

Evaluating this problem in the *Hastings Law Journal*, Lawrence A. Frolik (Professor of Law at the University of Pittsburgh School of Law) and Alison P. Barnes (Senior Policy Analyst and Legal Counsel for the United States Senate Special Committee on Aging from 1989 to 1990) discussed the two ideals that form the bedrock of Western jurisprudence: individual autonomy and individual responsibility.[7] If individuals are accountable for their actions, then all should be permitted to choose the way in which they live—"even if that means the right to be irresponsible or self-destructive."[8] Unfortunately, our culture contains a pervasive and damaging myth of elder incompetence.

> Too often the elderly are treated as if they were aged children who need protection and guidance. The young adopt a paternalistic attitude toward the old and do what is "good" for them with little regard for the desires of the elderly. The view that the elderly, far from possessing the wisdom of their years, regress into irresponsibility is not new. Shakespeare expressed it at some length [in "As You Like It"] in Jacque's seven ages of man speech:
> "And one man in his time plays many parts, His act being seven ages. . . . Last scene of all, That ends this strange eventful history, Is second childishness, and mere oblivion, Sans teeth, sans eyes, sans taste, sans every thing."[9]

Obviously, much hinges on the issue of age in American law in general, and in our conservatorship/guardianship codes in particular. Ageism or discrimination based on age—and age is a criterion over which no one has any control—is alive and well in our courts. It is thus important to ask: How is America aging, and who is "old"?

## DEMOGRAPHICS ON AGING IN AMERICA

Demographics released on the Internet in February 2000 by the United States Census Bureau point out the relative newness of longevity in the twentieth century.[10] For people born in 1900, the average life expectancy was forty-seven years and only one in twenty-five reached the age of sixty-five. The biggest population group at that time was nine years of age and younger. By 1990, in sharp contrast, life expectancy had increased to over seventy-five. One out of every eight Americans was sixty-five and 1.2 percent of the population was 85 or over. By the year 2020, the sixty-five and above group will be the largest segment in America, and, by 2030, there will be more elderly than young people in our country. Twenty-two percent of all Americans will be sixty-five or older, and only 21 percent will be under the age of eighteen. In terms of percentage growth, individuals over the age of eighty-five—referred to as the "old old"—currently form the fastest growing population group in the United States.

In her capacity as director of the Aging Society Project for the Carnegie Corporation, Lydia Bront emphasized that "extraordinarily large numbers of people will have 20, 30 or even 40 years more of active life than they expected, and it will be time that is part of a normal adulthood rather than of old age."[11] This is a relatively new conceptualization of the human life span. Unfortunately, as we are reminded by Dr. James Birren, Associate Director of the UCLA Center on Aging, the new reality of an extended adult life span has not been embraced by society at large. "This century has given us the gift of long life, but we're still not used to the idea that mature people are the most populous group in our society."[12]

One of the consequences is that our laws have lagged far behind the new demographic realities of our graying population. In many states, the elderly can be declared incompetent or lacking in capacity on the basis of old age alone simply because the lawmakers who crafted our conservatorship and guardianship codes never considered the possibility that so many people could and would live well beyond sixty-five, seventy-five, eighty-five, and even ninety-five, and still have full control of their mental faculties.

In the conservatorship/guardianship arena, the precise answer to the question, "Who is old in America?" is surprising. "The statutes do not define advanced or old age," Gregory Atkinson writes in the *Journal of Family Law*.[13] What functional definition has the concept of old age been given by its actual use in the courtroom? "Most conservatees [or wards] proposed on the basis of age are over age sixty-two."[14] Is sixty-two "old"? Perhaps not, but remember: it was when these surrogate decision-making statutes were originally written and the average life span had not yet reached fifty years of age.

## WHY "OLD" AT SIXTY-FIVE?

How does one come to be called "elderly" or "old" in America, and at what age is one considered to be "old"? Why? Unlike the five developmental classifications of infancy, childhood, puberty, adolescence, and adulthood, which are defined by a cluster of specific physical and psychological characteristics, old age is just a social convention. It is a chronological categorization, pure and simple.

In fact, Germany's Chancellor Otto von Bismarck is credited with establishing sixty-five as the age at which one becomes "old."[15] In 1889, von Bismarck created the German social welfare system by setting seventy as a mandatory retirement age. In 1916 and needing support for the government during World War I, Germany reduced the age to sixty-five.

"This certainly is not the last time," Lawrence Frolik and Alison Barnes commented in *An Aging Population: A Challenge to the Law*, "that the onset of public benefits for the elderly was changed for political gain rather than as a result of a new insight into when people become old."[16]

Men and women who do nothing more than reach the age of sixty-five are put in a single group and labeled "elderly" or "old." Sadly, the categorization of individuals by age alone is a convention with harsh consequences. Consider the following example, again cited by Frolik and Barnes: "It is not by chance that if younger persons suffer a permanent physical or mental ailment, we label them 'disabled.' Yet, should a similar affliction strike older individuals, we are likely merely to identify them as being 'old.' "[17]

When all members of a remarkably diverse chronological group are labeled "elderly," the negative characteristics that are true of *some* individuals—qualities such as incompetence, feebleness, or vulnerability to the influence of others—are subtly assigned to *all* people in the group. Thus, all adults who are sixty-five and above become tainted with the problems of a very small minority.[18] It should not be so, but it is. One such projected myth is that all elderly people will develop dementia.

Statistics on the prevalence of dementia in our elderly population dispel this false notion. Dementia, an irreversible and progressive decline in emotional, intellectual, and motor skills over time, has well over sixty different etiologies. The most dominant cause of chronic dementia is, of course, Alzheimer's Disease.[19] Do most people develop dementia as they reach seventy, eighty, or ninety years of age? Not at all. It is true that most victims of Alzheimer's and other severe dementias are over the age of sixty-five. However, progressive dementia affects only one percent of all individuals between the ages of sixty-five and seventy-four, and only seven percent among those aged seventy-five to eighty-four.[20] Only 25 percent of those who live beyond age eighty-five suffer from any form of dementia.

More importantly, however, these statistics mean that a full 99 percent of all people between sixty-five and seventy-four years of age will *not* be afflicted by Alzheimer's disease or any other dementia. They mean that 93 percent of all individuals between the ages of seventy-five and eighty-four will *not* become demented, and that 75 percent of all people over the age of eighty-five will *not* develop dementia. Old age does not doom us to an inevitable senility.

There is also a tendency in our country to equate aging with institutionalization. It is a common but false belief that a large percentage of older Americans will live in nursing homes for an extended period of time. According to the 1990 census:

- Only 5.1 percent of people over sixty-five are in these institutions,

- Over 20 percent of seniors over age eighty-five are in nursing homes, and

- [Only] half of the 52,000 Americans who have reached age 100 live in a long-term care facility.[21]

Research conducted by the Washington, D.C. based Brookings Institution reveals that of those men and women who enter nursing homes, only 25 percent stay more than one year.[22] The average stay is just nineteen months. In the population group reaching eighty-five years of age, half will need help managing personal and/or financial affairs.[23]

Nonetheless, conservatorship/guardianship rulings continue to reflect a presumption of incapacity or incompetence oftentimes based only on the ill-defined concept of "advanced age" (whatever that might be). It is not always a subtle presumption. The following passage, written by Justice J. Leibson of the Supreme Court of Kentucky, forms part of a guardianship ruling rendered by the Court in 1989: "Medical science has extended the limitations on human existence to the point where many of us will now linger long in a twilight zone of incompetency and disability."[24]

On the contrary, our longer lives will also be healthier lives. Thanks to more careful lifestyles and better treatments for cancer and for chronic heart, lung, and liver diseases, each of us will have a good chance of living long enough to be classified as "very aged" or "old old." The alternative to this—of dying at a younger age from accident or illness—is not a happy one.

## THE ELEVEN-TRILLION-DOLLAR LURE

Just as these early legislators could not imagine a time when a typical life span might contain a "First Fifty" and a "Second Fifty," they would have had no way of anticipating an equally remarkable financial event that is now beginning to unfold in America. Starting in the 1990s and continuing for fifty years, an enormous flow of wealth—estimated at almost eleven trillion dollars—is transferring and will continue to transfer from one generation to the next. Emily W. Card and Adam L. Miller, coauthors of the 1996 financial handbook, *Managing Your Inheritance*, have clarified the two poles of a potential generational conflict created by this anticipated transfer of wealth:

One hundred and fifteen million Americans will leave bequests averaging $90,000 over the next decades, ranging in size from modest to multimillion-dollar estates. . . .

[Y]ou may be among the "new heirs"—baby boomer children of the first large-scale middle class in history—who stand to inherit almost $11 *trillion* from their savings-oriented, depression-era parents. These savings, combined with the twin effects of Reagan-era tax cutting and an economic boom in the 1980s, form the unprecedented projected transfer of wealth. . . .

Here's the problem: Unlike their frugal parents, boomers have exhibited the lowest savings rate in recent U.S. history, only about 3 percent of income. In addition, this generation—you know who you are—has amassed the highest debt in history, $722 billion, not counting mortgage and credit card debt. . . .

As the older generation's saving have begun to shrink—many attributing this change to the consumption of the savings for medical needs and the expenses of longer lives—their [adult] children watch their presumed inheritances dwindle.[25]

If our codes as they exist today are not changed in substantive ways, eleven trillion dollars will surely inspire a rising tide of involuntary conservatorship/guardianship litigation as alienated or envious heir-petitioners seek to direct this massive flow of accumulated wealth from an older generation to themselves before it vanishes. Aging relatives are easy targets in court. Once such a legal struggle for control is launched, what chance does the elderly person have to defend his or her right to an autonomous future? Based on statistical evidence, the outlook is bleak. It is estimated that 94 percent of all involuntary conservatorship/guardianship court battles are lost by the elderly respondent.[26]

The issue of money is without a doubt one of the most important factors driving many of these involuntary and unwanted proceedings. George Alexander and Travis Lewin studied over 400 guardianship cases in order to verify the courts' claim that conservatorship/guardianship hearings are held "to protect the debilitated from their own financial foolishness or from the fraud of others who would prey upon their mental weaknesses."[27] To no one's surprise, they discovered that only the financial interests of third parties—of hospitals, of dependents, of business partners and of heirs—were being protected.

The state hospital commences incompetency proceedings to facilitate reimbursements for costs incurred. . . . Dependents institute proceedings to secure their needs. Co-owners of property find incompetency proceedings convenient ways to secure the sale of realty. Heirs institute actions to preserve their dwindling inheritances. Beneficiaries of trusts or estates seek incompetency as an expedient method of removing as trustee one who is managing the trust or estate in a manner adverse to their interests. All of these motives may be honest and without any intent to cheat the aged, *but none of the proceedings are commenced to assist the debilitated.*[28] (Emphasis added.)

As you read these harsh words underscoring the seriousness of this unanticipated problem, are you aware of a sense of discomfort? Of dread? Does something not feel right? A small voice is whispering: "It will be different for me because *my* children and relatives are wonderful. They will be there if I need help—but I probably won't need help. I'll be fine." This thought process is almost a given. It is hard for each of us to imagine being physically or mentally infirm, and it is almost impossible to believe that the relatives we now love could turn against us in the future.

The issues that we confront in any discussion of aging and the law are uncomfortable and complex at a very deep psychological level. It is hard to imagine growing old enough to reach a point of physical frailty, yet we see the frail elderly around us every day and wish them well. It is even harder to contemplate changes to our mind, to the incredible sense of self that *is* our uniqueness in the world. Nonetheless, if we don't die fairly young, we shall cross that numerical threshold of sixty-five and become "old." Hard though it may be to accept, most of us will need help managing our personal or financial affairs in those very distant years to come.

If we can learn now how to dance around the land mines these conservatorship/guardianship laws have created, we can move one giant step closer to insuring that the years of our Second Fifty will be golden ones.

## AN ISSUE FOR WOMEN?

As we begin to look at the actual workings of America's current conservatorship/guardianship laws in our next section, we must keep one final fact in mind. Most of the over ten trillion dollars in accumulated wealth that is now controlled by America's senior citizens is transferring to women. Women, who generally outlive men, also form almost two-thirds of the large population of elderly individuals who are made wards or conservatees of court-appointed surrogate decision makers in America.[29] No one is safe from abusive involuntary conservatorship/guardianship litigation, but women are less safe than men. One reason for this disparity is because women outlive men. The elderly as a group are disproportionately female and disproportionately white.[30]

# THE CASE OF GLEN HAWKINS

The involuntary conservatorship battle that inspired this book (that of my mother, as described in the introduction) involved a woman of quite substantial means. Was this case a typical one? Given the demographics cited above, are only very wealthy females at risk of abuse in these proceedings? No. Although the estate in her contest was unusually large and she is unarguably female, my mother's case met the two more general criteria that attract most of this unwanted litigation, namely, she was older than sixty-two, and the financial trust she controlled was big enough to justify the attention of heir-petitioners and of professional conservators needing "adequate billings" to keep them in business. As the amount of money controlled by elderly individuals in America has increased, so, too, has the use these involuntary conservatorship/guardianship proceedings to control the ultimate disposition of that wealth.

To begin to appreciate the potential for abuse inherent in these "protective proceedings" for elderly men as well as for elderly women, let's look at a recent conservatorship drama printed in the pages of the *Los Angeles Times*[31] on November 23, 1997. The estate in this example, while not extraordinary in size, was quite comfortable. The would-be ward was both elderly and male. What happened to Glen Hawkins could happen to someone you know. It could happen to you.

Glen Hawkins, 89, had pedaled two miles from his Leisure World condo to his bank and was conferring with his investment counselor when he got the startling news. Without legal notice or a chance to object, Hawkins had been declared too feeble and addled to manage his financial and personal affairs. A Long Beach firm of caretakers had been called in because of Hawkins' allegedly hostile remarks to a social worker asserting that he had no relatives. The firm had petitioned a judge and had been awarded virtually total control of Hawkins' life.

He no longer had the right to touch his money, about $380,000 in all. He no longer had the right to make decisions about his medical treatment. And unless something was done quickly, he would no longer have the right to decide where and how he would live. If the firm believed that he belonged in a nursing home, that's where he would go. All his mail was being diverted to the firm, which would use his money to pay his creditors—including itself, for the firm was charging him $75 an hour. It already had racked up almost $1,200 in conservator and attorney fees.

That was in February [of 1997]. Since then, Hawkins has suffered a heart attack and a stroke and has trouble speaking. His relatives have spent an estimated $10,000 in legal and travel fees to wrest control of Hawkins' life away from the firm. They have succeeded, but a court battle remains over whether they must pay the conservators' legal fees.

In the process, they have learned what "conservator" means in California law.[32]

The Long Beach firm of professional conservators filed their case against Mr. Hawkins in Los Angeles County. Why in Los Angeles rather than Orange County—the county in which Glen Hawkins actually lived, as required by state law? Conservatorship/guardianship laws are rife with exceptions.

Nowadays, Los Angeles County courts are getting a lot of Orange County filings, attorneys say. Los Angeles County judges are more receptive to professional conservators and allow them to charge $75 an hour, which is about the average for urban areas. Orange County has a de facto $35-an-hour ceiling, too low for professionals to make a profit, they say.[33]

What had Mr. Hawkins done to attract the attention of a Long Beach firm of professional conservators? More importantly, how had a conservatorship been arranged over his person and estate without any notice to him or to his nearest relatives, as required by California's Probate Codes? Mr. Hawkins had angered the social worker who had just transferred his wife of sixty-three years into a nursing home against the wishes of both husband and wife. When Mrs. Hawkins died nineteen days later, refusing to eat because, according to the newspaper's account, she believed her husband had betrayed her, the social worker acted. She contacted professional conservators to protect the man she described as being "quite delusional and hallucinatory."[34]

Surely the grieving widower had done something unusual to merit this psychological assessment of psychotic behaviors. Not so. Because he believed that his money and his relatives were none of the social worker's business, Glen Hawkins had simply refused to discuss them with her. In spite of immediate intervention by Mr. Hawkins' relatives, who called the social worker and had been assured that no further steps towards a conservatorship would be taken, the system engaged gears and rolled on over another victim.

Unknown to Glen Hawkins or anyone in his family, a hearing was held in Long Beach on Jan. 28, and a judge granted a temporary conservatorship to [the firm of] Ellman & Gladstone.

Their petition stated that Hawkins did not need to be given legal notice because he was too ill to attend the hearing and too addled to understand what was going on. A standard court form filled out by Hawkins' doctor testified to his incapacity.

Regarding relatives, the petition stated that Hawkins' wife "died a few weeks ago and her relatives are trying to take over her affairs but [Glen Hawkins] has been married for over 40 years and he needs someone to preserve his rights in the estate. . . . [A] conservator should monitor Mr. Hawkins and make sure he is not being taken advantage of and his needs are met."[35]

Had Mr. Hawkins been forty-nine rather than eighty-nine, this involuntary proceeding would not have succeeded. As in Mary Cumming's case (briefly described in the Introduction), his two greatest crimes were in being at least sixty-two years old and in having money put aside for his later years. Months after the involuntary conservatorship was filed, Glen Hawkins described his reaction to the entire legal imbroglio. "Mentally, it has been hard on me," he said. "I'm still worried about it. I mean, it's hurting me right now. I want this thing out of my way. I want it understood that I don't need nobody."[36]

Mr. Hawkins had harmed no one, and he clearly was not a danger to himself. He conferred with investment specialists who helped him safeguard his assets and, at eighty-nine years of age, still bicycled for exercise and convenience. Glen Hawkins planned to live out the rest of his now-solitary golden years in his Leisure World condominium.

Unfortunately, his wish to be left alone led him into dangerous new territory—territory that is made unsafe by the legal reality that each state in America feels free to intrude into the lives of its elderly in ways that would be unthinkable if the objects of its intrusion were young. What are these so-called protective proceedings and how do they function? We shall continue with a review of some of the most frequently asked questions about our states' surprising involuntary conservatorship/guardianship codes.

# NOTES

1. K. H. Wilbur, "Alternatives to Conservatorship: The Role of Daily Money Management Services," *The Gerontologist* 31 no. 2 (1991): pp. 150–55.

2. The Center for Social Gerontology, *National Study of Guardianship System and Feasibility of Implementing Expert Systems*. Final Report to U.S. Administration on Aging (Ann Arbor, Mich.: The Center for Social Gerontology, 1992).

3. D. Starkman, "Guardians May Need Someone to Watch Over Them," *Wall Street Journal*, 8 May 1998, pp. B1, B2.

4. G. J. Alexander and T. H. D. Lewin, *The Aged and the Need for Surrogate Management* (Syracuse, N.Y.: Syracuse University Press, 1972).

5. Ibid., p. 138.

6. L. A. Frolik and A. P. Barnes, "An Aging Population: A Challenge to the Law." *The Hastings Law Journal* 42 (1991): pp. 683–718.

7. Ibid.

8. Ibid., p. 717.

9. Ibid.

10. See the United States Census Bureau's website at http://www.census.gov/.

11. J. Barry, "Redefining Aging: "Golden Years" Now an Extension of Middle Age," *Santa Barbara News-Press*, 16 February 1998, p. D4.

12. B. Beyette, "So, Do You Have a Strategy for Handling the New Longevity?" *Los Angeles Times*, 2 November 1997, p. E5.

13. G. Atkinson, "Towards a Due Process Perspective in Conservatorship Proceedings for the Aged," *Journal of Family Law* 18, no. 4 (1980): 825.

14. Ibid.

15. Frolik and Barnes, "An Aging Population," p. 687 (footnote).

16. Ibid.

17. Ibid., pp. 684–85.

18. Ibid.

19. J. Willot, "Neurogerontology: The Aging Nervous System," *Gerontology: Perspectives and Issues* 77 (1990).

20. A. P. Barnes, "Beyond Guardianship Reform: A Reevaluation of Autonomy and Beneficence for a System of Principled Decision-Making in Long Term Care," *Emory Law Journal*, 41, no. 3 (1992): 633–760.

21. R. Warner, "Your Chances of Needing Long-Term Care." Nolo Press: www.nolo.com, 1998.

22. Ibid.

23. S. Emmons, "Conservators' Reach Can Be a Surprise," *Los Angeles Times*, 23 November 1997, pp. A3, A29.

24. *Rice v. Floyd*, 768 S.W.2d 57 (Ky. 1989), p. 61.

25. E. W. Card and A. L. Miller, *Managing Your Inheritance: Getting It, Keeping It, Growing It—Making the Most of Any Size Inheritance* (New York: Times Books, 1996), pp. 3–4, 40.

26. K. Bulcroft, M. Kielkopf, and K. Tripp, "Elderly Wards and Their Legal Guardians: Analysis of County Probate Records in Ohio and Washington," *The Gerontologist*, 31, no. 2 (1991): 156–64.

27. Quoted in P. Tor, "Finding Incompetency in Guardianship: Standardizing the Process," *Arizona Law Review* 35 (1993): 761 (footnote).

28. Ibid.

29. Wilbur, "Alternatives to Conservatorship," p. 150.

30. Frolik and Barnes, "An Aging Population."

31. Emmons, "Conservators' Reach Can Be a Surprise," pp. A3, A29.

32. Ibid., p. A3.

33. Ibid., p. A29.

34. Ibid.

35. Ibid.

36. Ibid.

CHAPTER TWO

# FREQUENTLY ASKED QUESTIONS ABOUT CONSERVATORSHIPS AND GUARDIANSHIPS

*The only freedom which deserves the name, is that of pursuing our own good in our own way, so long as we do not attempt to deprive others of theirs, or impede their efforts to obtain it. Each is the proper guardian of his own health, whether bodily, or mental and spiritual. Mankind are greater gainers by suffering each other to live as seems good to themselves, than by compelling each to live as seems good to the rest.*

—John Stuart Mill (1859), *On Liberty*[1]

**B**ecause there is no federal policy governing how our conservatorship and guardianship codes work, there is a lack of any provision for national oversight to correct the problems that arise when involuntary and unwanted petitions are filed. Unfortunately, the potential for court-sanctioned abuse of the vulnerable elderly in such "protective proceedings" is great. As critics Lawrence Frolik and Alison Barnes have concluded, the laws as they now function are "procedurally inadequate, substantively archaic, demeaning to the elderly, and operated in a manner that permits widespread abuse and corruption."[2]

With funding from the National Institute on Aging, Professor Lawrence Friedman of Stanford University and Stanford J.D. candidate Mark Savage explored the law of conservatorship in California. Some of their conclusions pierce the heart of this complex issue:

27

Does the problem lie in the structure of the law? The *words* of the statute point toward a fair, flexible system, and ostensibly this is the goal. But fairness and flexibility are not self-executing. Wards are typically old men and women, in declining health, weak, and relatively powerless. Even when they are rich, they run the risk of losing whatever leverage their money once gave them. The system depends on the good will, competence, and understanding of judges and investigators, county by county. . . . The fate of elderly wards depends on strictly local contingencies. This is hardly due process at its best.[3]

What are these "protective proceedings" and how do they really function in our courts? Let's continue with a group of frequently asked questions about conservatorships and guardianships.

*What is a conservatorship or a guardianship?*

Every state in America (and the District of Columbia) has developed its own body of codes in an attempt to safeguard the well-being of its impaired elderly when they are deemed in need of assistance. These codes create protective arrangements for the elderly known as "conservatorships" and "guardianships." Thus, a conservatorship or guardianship is the official legal mechanism by which a state court appoints a substitute decision-maker to act in the best interests of an adult who has been declared incapable of or incompetent to make his or her own personal or financial decisions. The laws as written do have a beneficent function. However, the laws as they actually unfold in involuntary court actions across America are anything but protective.

*If "conservatorship" and "guardianship" refer to the same thing, why are two different terms used?*

Because each state creates its own laws concerning conservatorship/guardianship issues, there is no common legal language to describe the workings of such protective proceedings. Many states employ the term *guardianship*, while others prefer *conservatorship*. Some states follow model acts such as the Uniform Guardianship and Protective Procedures Act (UGPPA) or the Uniform Probate Code (UPC), which makes a distinction between proceedings relating to the care of the person (*guardianship*) and those relating to the care of property (*conservatorship*). In California, *guardianship* refers only to the protection of the person and/or estate of a minor (under eighteen years of age), while *conservatorship* refers to proceedings controlling the affairs of an adult. And, in contrast to the majority of states in which the court-appointed surrogate decision-makers are called *guardians* or *conservators*, some states use the terms *committee* or *curator* in their codes.

In this book, the combined form of *conservatorship/guardianship* is used to keep confusion to a minimum. It is important to remember that when the rights of the vulnerable elderly are being discussed, both terms are used to refer to the same court action. Be mindful of the fact that confusion—of terminology or procedure—serves the well-informed predator in this area of law. To see which terms are used in your state, please refer to appendix A. To find definitions for all legal terms used in this book, please refer to the glossary.

*What is the difference between a conservatorship or guardianship of the person and one of the estate?*

It is perhaps easiest to understand this difference by examining the consequences of the two different court rulings. Following a conservatorship/guardianship hearing in which the court determines that an elderly individual is incapable of managing financial matters (that is, a conservatorship/guardianship of the *estate* has been ordered), the new ward or conservatee immediately loses all right to manage his or her money, property, and investments. A court-appointed surrogate may even make financial decisions that are contrary to what the now-powerless ward would choose for himself or herself—if he or she had not been deprived of the right to make decisions.

To all intents and purposes, this determination of an inability to manage one's estate can prevent an adult from lending or borrowing money, making gifts, entering into contracts, receiving or paying money, or spending money frivolously (whatever "frivolous" is deemed to be by the surrogate decision-maker—typically a younger person who is often heir to the estate in question). It can also prohibit the ward or conservatee from hiring an attorney in an attempt to reverse the conservatorship/guardianship. The target of this litigation is well and truly trapped for the rest of his or her years, often on the basis of hearsay evidence presented in court by financially motivated or estranged relatives. The majority of conservatorship/guardianship cases are full or *plenary* conservatorships and guardianships, unlimited in power and covering both the estate and the person.

When a conservator or guardian of the *person* is appointed (and this is usually a male rather than a female appointee), the new conservator/guardian becomes responsible for almost every aspect of the newly created ward's personal life. Social contacts, reading matter, choice of food, clothing, shelter, medical care—all are determined by the appointed conservator/guardian. Thus, the conservator or guardian has the same power over the ward as a parent has over a dependent minor child. Depending on the statutes of the particular state, the ward can even be moved by this proxy-parent into a nursing home or board and care facility regardless of his or her wishes. The allegedly incompetent adult becomes a puppet dangling on court-sanctioned strings.

*Can these unwanted or involuntary conservatorships and guardianships be removed or terminated? Do the elderly have rights to due process?*

Surprisingly, criminals in America have greater due process rights (the right to be heard in court) than do the elderly in conservatorship/guardianship legal proceedings. Remember that once a person becomes a ward or conservatee, he or she is not permitted to make any of those decisions—either personal or financial—that might serve to *demonstrate* competence to the world. Once a conservatorship or guardianship is put in place, it can rarely be removed.

*Are the appointed surrogate decision-makers required to abide by the wishes of their elderly wards?*

Even in the best of cases this is not always so. It is important to keep in mind that newly created wards and conservatees have been deemed by the court to lack the capacity to make good decisions for themselves. Why should the court or surrogate follow the requests of an "incompetent, incapacitated person"? Research studies have shown that even those individuals who were selected by elders as their preferred guardians or conservators in hypothetical cases could guess the treatment the elderly individuals would prefer only 60 percent of the time.[4]

*What gives states the right to do this?*

These state statutes are driven by the underlying doctrine of *parens patriae,* literally "parent of the country." According to this doctrine, the state has the inherent power and duty to protect those who cannot protect themselves (originally, children and the insane). The power we call *parens patriae* was inherited from English law, where the Crown assumed "the care of those who, by reason of their imbecility and want of understanding, are incapable of taking care of themselves."[5] Our courts and court-appointed guardians and conservators use the *parens patriae* power to determine what is in an aging ward's or conservatee's best interests. In so doing, though, they also strip the protected individual of his or her personal and financial autonomy.

Writing in the *George Washington Law Review*, Professor Jan Ellen Rein strikes a cautionary note:

> As indicated, the protected person's well-being is the sole modern justification of the state's power as *parens patriae* to appoint a guardian or conservator of that person. There may occasionally be extremely vital, legitimate interests of third parties, society at large, or the state that justify overriding the individual's free will and liberty interests. In such cases, however, it is not the *parens patriae* power that justifies the unwanted or reluctantly received intervention. Our legal system should recognize frankly that whenever a court imposes guardianship or conservatorship over a proposed ward's objection or reluctance for the convenience, mental well-being, or financial interests of family members or other third parties, the court is going beyond the confines of the *parens patriae* concept to interfere with fundamental liberty interests, potentially including freedom from involuntary physical confinement.[6]

*Who files these conservatorship and guardianship petitions, and who pays the costs involved?*

Under existing codes, almost any adult may petition to have a conservatorship or guardianship established over another individual or over that person's estate. State officials appointed as public guardians regularly file petitions, often on behalf of nursing homes or hospitals seeking payment of overdue bills. Staff members in state mental health departments and social workers from both public and private agencies may petition for conservatorships or guardianships. Unfortunately, though, a large number of the petitions in our courts today are being filed by adult children who are seeking control of their aged parents—and, needless to say, of their parents' estates.

There is a tacit assumption in all of these cases that the petition would not have been brought to court unless the alleged incompetent truly needed help. In defining these actions purely in terms of a potential benefit to the elderly person while disregarding the motives of the petitioners, the courts continue to mischaracterize these "protective proceedings" as nonadversarial. Hearings are usually completed without any evaluation of the petitioners' motivation.

Anyone with assets to distribute and disgruntled relatives coveting those assets should worry. There are far too many attorneys who will take these cases without pay because this area of litigation has a kicker:

*ALL* ATTORNEYS' FEES (FOR BOTH SIDES), *ALL* EXPERT WITNESSES' FEES (FOR BOTH SIDES) AND *ALL* COURT COSTS ARE PAID OUT OF THE NEWLY CREATED WARD'S ESTATE IF THE PETITION IS GRANTED.

If, for instance, your estranged stepson succeeds in convincing a judge that your bequest to your favorite charity is proof of financial incompetence and a conservatorship or guardianship is established to conserve your assets, you will be forced to pay for this unwanted, unpleasant experience that has no beneficial outcome for you at all. The fees you will be required to pay will include your stepson's legal expenses incurred during the course of your protective proceeding.*

Adding insult to injury, if the petitioner (the stepson in this example) is successful, he will most likely be appointed as guardian or conservator of your estate. That is the plum, after all. Not only will he be paid a percentage of your estate as an annual fee for his services, but he also will be given control over everything you have amassed in a lifetime.

"Nightmare" is the word that adults targeted by involuntary conservatorship/guardianship litigation use to describe what these proceedings are like. It is a *nightmare*. Unfortunately, it is a *court-sanctioned* nightmare.

*Who licenses professional conservators, and how closely do the courts watch what the guardians or conservators do with their wards' investments and property?*

The courts rarely even know how many wards or conservatees they have under their jurisdiction, much less keep track of what conservators and guardians are doing. In chapter 6, we shall review fifteen cases under the heading, "Who is Guarding the Guardians?" In all too many cases the answer to that question is *no one*. Most professional conservators do not belong to agencies; they are independent operators, conducting business from their homes.

What is more, in too many states it is easier to become a professional conservator or guardian than it is to become a beautician. While writing about the case of eighty-nine-year-old Glen Hawkins (see chapter 1), Steve Emmons[7] investigated the current requirements for a conservator in California—a state noted by experts as having superior codes controlling these protective proceedings. His conclusions are disturbing.

"How do you become a professional conservator?" he asks. "It's easy. Just declare yourself one and register with the local Superior Court. The state, which regulates appliance repair and beauty shops, has no requirements for conservators, even though in California they control hundreds of millions of other people's dollars. Attempts to legislate standards for conservators have failed repeatedly and been vetoed once."[8] At present, a would-be conservator in California simply registers with the Superior

---

* Appendix B contains an itemized list of the actual costs incurred by one proposed ward in a bitterly contested California conservatorship case.

Court, where he or she is fingerprinted. A criminal records check is run, but even if the check reveals criminal acts the registration must be accepted. Don Green, former chairman of the State Bar of California's probate section, which has unsuccessfully attempted to regulate conservators, is concerned. "It's crazy to put people's welfare and their estates in the hands of private conservators who the state has screened less than it screens barbers."[9]

Does the court monitor the personal and financial well-being of the ward once a conservator or guardian has been put in place? Writing as Staff Director and Assistant Staff director of the American Bar Association's Commission on the Mentally Disabled, John W. Parry and Sally Balch Hurme point out the current guidelines—and the manner in which such well-intentioned requirements are disregarded:

> Most jurisdictions now require regular financial accountings and personal status reports, and many courts are becoming more active in supervising what happens after a guardianship is created. Statutorily, however, *only a few jurisdictions require the courts to review reports once they are filed.*[10] (Emphasis added.)

*How do these conservatorship and guardianship statutes define "old age" and "elderly"?*

As mentioned in chapter 1, state statutes do not define old age. In our culture, "old age" is simply a social convention, a label. Nonetheless, most of the individuals who are targeted by this type of litigation are sixty-two years of age or older. Keep in mind that these laws were written at a time when the average life expectancy was not even forty-seven years of age (as it was at the turn of the century) and that the laws are now being applied to seniors whose average life expectancy extends beyond the age of seventy-six. Combine this information with the fact that, in terms of percentage growth, individuals over the age of eighty-five currently form the fastest growing cohort in the United States, and you will see we have a problem. What is "old"? To quote from Bernard Baruch: "To me, old age is always fifteen years older than I am."

*Do conservatorship or guardianship petitions have to contain specific evidence to prove that an individual is incompetent or incapacitated?*

In too many jurisdictions, a petitioner may initiate these proceedings simply by stating that the proposed conservatee or ward is "old," and then alleging that he or she is incapable either of providing for personal needs or of managing his or her estate due to advanced age (sixty-two or above) or illness. Having made this initial allegation, the petitioner must then suggest the existence of incompetency, impairment, or lack of mental capacity. This is not too difficult a task, especially since many courts agree that impaired health can be used to prove an elderly person incapable of managing his or her estate or person, even though precluding an individual from making and executing decisions because of physical incapacity alone may be unconstitutional.[11] What is even more distressing is the fact that an elderly person can be placed under the court's protection *without a hearing*—immediately—on the basis of allegations and hearsay contained in a disgruntled relative's petition.

*If you are going to say that someone is incompetent or incapacitated in the eyes of the law, do you have to prove that he or she does certain odd things and that these odd behaviors mean he or she cannot manage by him- or herself anymore?*

Unfortunately, statutory definitions of competence or incapacity vary considerably from jurisdiction to jurisdiction. It would be nice if there were an agreed-upon checklist of criteria to be used by both sides in the ensuing legal battle, but there is not. There are *no* generally accepted guidelines followed by court-appointed experts in conducting competency evaluations or in giving "expert testimony."

What is even more unsettling for the targeted elder, of course, is the fact that the particular judge presiding over the hearing may decide which behaviors *in his or her opinion* constitute or even define incompetency—and dismiss any evidence to the contrary. As Humpty Dumpty said to Alice, words have different meaning to different people, after all:

> "When I use a word," Humpty Dumpty said, in rather a scornful tone, "it means just what I choose it to mean—neither more nor less."
>
> "The question is," said Alice, "whether you can make words mean so many different things."
>
> "The question is," said Humpty Dumpty, "which is to be master—that's all."

In her effort to stir statutory refocus and reform, Professor Jan Ellen Rein of the McGeorge School of Law expresses the opinions that are shared by many critics of current conservatorship/guardianship law: "Some judges, social worker, and court investigators . . . will conscientiously try to protect the autonomy interests of the proposed ward; others will not. The fundamental liberty interests of proposed wards and protected persons should not be left to the vagaries of how individuals at the grass-roots level choose to interpret the statutes."[12]

*Do the words "incompetence" and "incapacity" mean different things in the eyes of this law?*

They are supposed to have different meanings. The concept of incompetence was once applied to those who were incapable of defending themselves legally. It was thus used as a *legal* concept. In sixteenth-century England, this group of individuals consisted of the very young and lunatics "whose wit and memory had failed."[13] Although infancy is no longer a legal basis for lack of competence, our American statutes originally contained this language and rationale.

For better or worse, the term incompetence has come to imply mental illness even though "incompetence" and "incapacity" as legal terms have no precise medical meaning. Age alone (sixty-two and above) still creates a presumption of incompetence or mental illness in too many states.

Over time, revised state statutes such as those in states following the Uniform Probate Code (see appendix A) have shifted the traditional initial finding from *incompetence* to *impairment* or *incapacity*. Why? The change seems to have been made because a voice of compassionate reason finally intruded, suggesting that being labeled as mentally ill would inflict unthinking trauma on the vulnerable elderly. In theory, then, you need not be proven mentally incompetent to be deemed "incapacitated." In practice, however, the terms are being used almost synonymously in conservatorship/guardianship proceedings. " 'The system is just completely weighted against the proposed ward,' said Elise Donnelly, who studied guardianship in North Dakota for the State Department of Human Services. 'Once the petition is brought, you have to go in and prove you're not incompetent.' "[14]

*Is there a detailed list of exactly what constitutes impairment or incapacity in these revised state codes?*

You have probably already guessed that it is not so. The revised law requires that two facts be established before an elderly individual can be labeled as an "incapacitated person" in need of a conservator or guardian. The petitioner is supposed to prove that the targeted individual has a physical or mental condition (e.g., mental illness, mental deficiency, physical illness, physical disability, advanced age "or other") which causes an inability to manage his or her personal or financial affairs. This is a causal and directional link: the mental illness results in functional impairment. How is the second link in that chain of evidence (an inability or lack of capacity to manage affairs) supposed to be demonstrated? The elderly person is deemed to be incapacitated if he or she lacks the capacity to make or communicate "responsible decisions."

You can probably see the trap. Who determines whether or not a decision is "responsible"? Ultimately, the court—the judge—makes this determination. How so? If the proposed ward or conservatee's decisions seem to be "right" from the judge's point of view, the elder is said to possess capacity. If, however, the decisions are "wrong" according to the traditionally paternalistic bias of the judge, the individual lacks capacity. Far too often, the petitioner's *allegation* of irresponsible behavior is used in court as "proof" of the existence of the required "mental condition." The cart is placed before the horse—a subtle but devastating change.

*Can a poor decision be used in court as proof of an elderly person's mental incapacity or incompetence?*

Yes. Competency/capacity issues are assessed from an ageist perspective. "Ageist" means that the petitioners, judges, and attorneys often view elderly individuals through lenses that are distorted by powerful stereotypes about aging. Those who have merely reached a specific chronological age can be stripped of their autonomy because their decisions, while not necessarily incompetent or unreasonable ones, run counter to the prevailing cultural norms of the middle-aged adults who drive conservatorship/guardianship litigation.

*Is it true that a physical condition or physical disability can be used against a senior citizen in this kind of proceeding?*

Yes. The ailments which afflict many people over the age of sixty can be the basis for a successful petition. Any illness suffered by an aged person—be it pneumonia, diabetes, major or minor broken bones, and heart ailments, among others—may serve as the spark that ignites this legal conflagration. The targeted elder is usually vulnerable in some important way when his or her relatives file involuntary petitions.

*Where are these petitions filed, and where are the hearings held?*

In England prior to the middle of the nineteenth century, courts of the Church ruled much of the life of the laity—both spiritual and material.[15] Matters concerning the inheritance of goods and money were decided in ecclesiastical courts. Traces remain in America, where many states have special courts for the administration of inheritance. It is in these courts that all conservatorship and guardianship petitions are heard. Each such circuit court bears a distinctive, esoteric name: Probate Court, Superior Court, Surrogates' Court, Court of Chancery, Circuit Court, Courts of the

Ordinary, and Court of Common Pleas are examples. All petitioners and proposed conservatees/wards must follow the guidelines published by their particular local courts, county by county, parish by parish.

*When someone files a conservatorship or guardianship petition, how long does he or she have to get the initial paperwork ready? Can the petitioner be helped by an attorney?*

The petitioner may take as long as he or she likes and almost always has the assistance of an attorney. After all, the attorney has little to lose. Involuntary conservatorship/guardianship hearings are rarely brought against poor or impoverished adults and, when the petition is successful, the attorney will certainly be paid since the newly created ward must pay *all* legal bills generated by *every* attorney for *both* sides of the case. What is more, these petitions almost always succeed.

*What happens once the actual petition for a conservatorship or guardianship of the person or estate is filed?*

In general, the proposed conservatee or ward (the "respondent") must be served notice of the filing. In this notice, the targeted individual is given a specified number of days to prepare his or her objections and appear in court for a hearing on the matter. The time allotted to marshal a defense—to read the paperwork, contact and consult with a lawyer, arrange allies or character witnesses, and begin to understand the grave consequences of the looming court battle—varies from jurisdiction to jurisdiction. Many states do not permit enough time between the notice of the hearing and the date on which the hearing will take place even though adequate notice is a fundamental right protected by the Constitution of the United States.[16]

Some states give the respondent only three days to respond, while states following the Uniform Probate Code give fourteen days. California requires fifteen days. Be that as it may, keep in mind that a determined petitioner may have spent months or years preparing the assault on the elderly relative's freedom. This is not considered to be unfair because these protective proceedings are deemed to be "nonadversarial" in nature—brought only out of the goodness of the petitioner's heart for the benefit of the aging relative. In fact, if the petition claims that an emergency exists (alleging, for example, that the elderly individual will be harmed in some way or will dissipate his or her valuable resources without immediate court intervention), an emergency or temporary guardianship or conservatorship can be granted by the judge on the basis of the alleged emergency alone with *no* warning or notice to the targeted elder at all.

*What written warnings are given the elderly when conservatorship/ guardianship petitions are filed against them?*

The actual paperwork served upon the elderly varies considerably from state to state. In all fairness, it must be said that some states seem to be trying to make the process more understandable for the respondent. Many states have far to go. In Kentucky, for example, the minimal petition does not even warn the individual what is at stake in the proceeding. In California, the copy of the petition that is served on the proposed conservatee is supposed to state the nature of the litigation, all possible outcomes, and the standards upon which the determination will be based.

Again in California, a court investigator must also interview the individual in order to explain the petition and evaluate his or her condition for the court. State reforms passed in 1992 in New York, Rhode Island, and Pennsylvania all require that the judicial notice be in plain language and large type, and in West Virginia (as of 1994) the notice must contain a statement in large print detailing possible consequences of the hearing. Section §37.1-134.10(D) of Virginia's 1998 code, for example, requires that the notice given to the respondent must include the following statement "in conspicuous, bold print":

### WARNING

**AT THE HEARING YOU MAY LOSE MANY OF YOUR RIGHTS. A GUARDIAN MAY BE APPOINTED TO MAKE PERSONAL DECISIONS FOR YOU. A CONSERVATOR MAY BE APPOINTED TO MAKE DECISIONS CONCERNING YOUR PROPERTY AND FINANCES. THE APPOINTMENT MAY AFFECT CONTROL OF HOW YOU SPEND YOUR MONEY, HOW YOUR PROPERTY IS MANAGED AND CONTROLLED, WHO MAKES YOUR MEDICAL DECISIONS, WHERE YOU LIVE, WHETHER YOU ARE ALLOWED TO VOTE, AND OTHER IMPORTANT RIGHTS.**

A question should be raised at this point, however. How much legal material are the elderly capable of taking in and processing—be it in large print or even plain English—when they are emotionally overwhelmed just by seeing themselves described in official court documents (by people who know their strengths and weaknesses) as "incompetent and/or incapable of providing for food, clothing, and shelter"?

*Do the elderly who want to fight these proposed conservatorships or guardianships have the right to an attorney if they can't afford one, and do they have the right to appear in court and be heard?*

Not necessarily. Some states may argue that the interests of the petitioner and the proposed ward or conservatee are not adverse and thus refuse to appoint an attorney to represent the respondent's interests. Other states mandate the appointment of counsel in every case. Most make it clear that the elderly person has a *right* to legal representation, yet do not *require* the appointment of an attorney. Surprisingly, many states will not appoint an attorney even if the potential ward/conservatee appears without a lawyer because he or she cannot afford one. Although the targeted elder may chose to appear at the hearing, only a few jurisdictions mandate the respondent's presence in court. Judges may also excuse the proposed ward's absence if it is thought to be in the elderly person's best interests. "Thought" by whom? Thought by experts whose statements and affidavits are presented to the court by the petitioner. Thus, as Robert Brown states in *The Rights of Older Persons*, "Although the potential ward has the right to be present at the hearing in all states, in practice, he is seldom present. Considering the potential for loss of liberty and property, the ward's presence at the hearing is crucial for the protection of his or her interest."[17]

In general, constitutional due process rights are obviously being circumvented by conservatorship/guardianship statutes. It is odd, especially when one considers that the appointment of a conservatorship or guardianship of both person and estate is, as Parry and Hurme remarked, "tantamount to civil commitment."[18]

Ironically, though, in one landmark study in which they analyzed 1,160 court records from three jurisdictions in Missouri and Iowa and four in Colorado, Dr. Pat Keith and Dr. Robbyn Wacker concluded that proposed wards who had their own attorneys were more likely to have the petition denied.[19] However, having a *court-appointed* lawyer is not necessarily a good thing. According to Keith and Wacker, a full 97 percent of the 1,160 targeted elderly in their study who had court-appointed attorneys received full guardianships.

*If almost all elderly people who are assigned court-appointed attorneys have conservatorships and guardianships placed over them, does this statistic suggest the court system itself wants them to lose? If so, why?*

This is a tricky issue. One clear problem is that a court-appointed attorney is not really appointed as an advocate to vigorously defend the right of the individual to live as he or she chooses. Rather, the court assigns an attorney or guardian *ad litem* (who need not be an attorney) from an available pool of volunteers to function as a "guardian for the purposes of the lawsuit." As such, the guardian *ad litem* will make recommendations to the court based on the "best interests" of the proposed ward instead of the elderly individual's personal preferences.[20] "Without adversary counsel to advise the alleged incompetent of available rights, to prepare the best possible case opposing the petition, and to advocate his or her interests, the prospective ward is destined to lose."[21]

There is an even more insidious reason why many of these cases are lost by the proposed ward. The system itself, in far too many courts and in far too many states, is rife with a cronyism or patronage that borders on corruption. Guttmacher and Weihofen are more blunt: "There is some suggestion that even when a guardian *ad litem* is appointed, that appointment may simply be a 'political plum,' assuring only a formal appearance by counsel."[22] At the very least, our system of surrogate decision-making is antithetical to the well-being of the elderly precisely because it has become a fairly big business, and that business is built to a large extent upon money that has been put aside by aging Americans for the pleasures of their retirement years.

Each probate judge surrounds him- or herself with a group of lawyers or specialists who handle conservatorship/guardianship assignments from that judge, and that judge also approves payment of their requested fees. How do these probate or surrogate court attorneys get paid? Usually the only source of payment is the ward. As Robert Brown notes in *The Rights of Older Persons*,

> Payments to the guardian or conservator may be based either on a certain percentage of the value of the ward's estate or on the basis of what [the court determines] "reasonable compensation would be for the guardian or conservator's services." The court must approve all requests for payment, although such approval is routinely granted. The larger the ward's estate, the greater are the fees that can be paid, so there is rarely difficulty in finding a conservator or guardian for a ward with substantial assets.[23]

*What happens if the elderly respondent is truly incapacitated in a hospital, nursing home, or convalescent center, recuperating from a broken leg or heart attack, and cannot appear in court? Does the court come to the hospital?*

Under the Americans with Disabilities Act, every court should make whatever accommodations are necessary for those who cannot appear in court but wish to be heard. Does this happen in all states? No. In trying to appreciate how conservatorship/guardianship proceedings actually unfold in America, there is one key refrain to remember: it all depends on the particulars contained in your state's codes and on the judge who hears your case. According to a 1993 study published in the *Gerontologist*, fewer than 14 percent of all proposed wards were even *present* at their hearings.[24]

*Would a family attorney who has done work for the targeted elderly individual in the past and knows him or her quite well be able to help?*

Probably not. Unless the attorney is a specialist in the comparatively new field of Elder Law *and* is experienced in conservatorship/guardianship litigation, he or she should help in one way only. Namely, the family lawyer should refer his or her client to a competent elder-law attorney specializing in conservatorship/guardianship cases. The National Academy of Elder Law Attorneys—a group that has increased nearly sevenfold to 3,600 members between the years 1990 and 1998—can also be contacted for the names of local members. If you unwittingly choose an attorney who is unfamiliar with your state's conservatorship/guardianship codes and procedures, *you* will pay for your lawyer's subsequent but incomplete education in this field, expensive hour by expensive hour. In California, such fees can range from $150 to $450 an hour.

*Can witnesses be brought to court to prove an individual's competence to handle personal and financial decisions? Does testimony from psychiatrists or professional associates help? What about using so-called expert witnesses in court?*

Of course the proposed ward will want to have associates in court who will swear under oath to his or her various capacities and personal strengths. Such witnesses will expand the judge's awareness of the elderly person as a uniquely competent human being. An "expert witness," though, is slightly different.

As we shall see in our next chapter, an expert witness can be hired to provide "expert testimony" to educate the trier of fact (usually the judge, since a jury is rarely involved). For instance, you can hire a prominent forensic psychiatrist or psychologist to support your contention that the allegations contained in an unwanted petition brought against you are totally without merit. However, you can be sure that the adversarial relative-petitioner will find an equally powerful paid expert witness who will attempt to nullify or contradict the testimony of *your* expert witness. This

hostile expert witness will then do and say whatever is necessary to confirm your incompetence or incapacity.

*Don't expert witnesses have to swear under oath to tell the truth, the
whole truth, and nothing but the truth?*

Yes, of course. Unfortunately, the testimony of expert witnesses is driven
by the extremely adversarial nature of this judicial process. Your oppo-
nents will find *someone* with an impressive vitae who will, for a hand-
some fee, examine you and describe your incompetence in court.

   You can count on it. Expert witnesses—whose fees you will be
required to pay if a conservatorship or guardianship is established over
you and/or your property—are now permitted to present *opinions* as *evidence*, even if the opinions are based on hearsay.

*If enemies can make up anything they want about the vulnerable indi-
vidual, and hired experts can use opinions in court as though they were
facts, don't these laws actually force the proposed wards or conservatees
to prove their competence or capacity? Aren't we all presumed to be innocent or competent or capable until proven otherwise? Who has the burden
of proof?*

In theory, the petitioners bear the twin burdens of proof and persuasion.
In practice, however, these burdens are carried by the proposed
wards/conservatees. How can that be? Because the court considers these
to be "nonadversarial protective proceedings," there is a presumption that
a petition would never be filed unless a caring friend or relative had legit-
imate concerns about the safety and well-being of an elderly man or
woman. The type of proof usually submitted in the petition is unsubstan-
tiated and vague: letters suggesting that the elderly person has started to
behave in an unusual manner, a doctor's written opinion (in lieu of direct
testimony) that the unsuspecting elderly person has changed in a suspicious way, or testimony from relatives saying their uncle or aunt won't
talk to them any more. Unfortunately, courts will reach decisions based
only upon the evidence presented to them. The elderly person targeted by
an involuntary and unwanted conservatorship/guardianship petition must
make a vigorous attempt to prove his or her competence or capacity to
make reasonable or "responsible" decisions. As we have seen, the difficulty of this task is magnified by the fact that there are no agreed-upon
criteria used in court for determining incompetence, incapacity, or the
"reasonableness" of a decision. Furthermore, one of the many surprises
awaiting people as they attempt to shoulder this awkward burden of proof

is that their prudent financial decisions may actually be used *against* senior citizens in court to demonstrate their incompetence or unreasonableness.

*How can an elderly person's financial decisions be used in court to demonstrate incompetence or unreasonableness?*

Let's say that you have become estranged from two of your four children because they have caused significant problems for you over the last three or four years. Perhaps the two have been increasingly cold or neglectful toward you, or contacted you only when they wanted something from you. You decide to reward their behavior in kind by changing your will and leaving each estranged child a smaller inheritance than the two adult children who have filled your years with joy.

Your angry, partially disinherited children can use the conservatorship/guardianship courts to have your new testamentary wishes nullified even before you die. How? They can do this by claiming that your are mentally impaired because you lack the capacity to withstand the "undue influence" of others (in this case, of your favored children) and your mental impairment has resulted in a change in your once-loving actions toward them. No one will question the misplaced benevolence of the petitioners, and the conservatorship/guardianship proceeding will become the forum for an ante-mortem ("before death") will contest. If the judge is sympathetic to them, your least favorite children may even determine how you spend your money until and after the day you die. Avarice and anger are powerful motivators in these remarkable legal actions.

*"Undue influence" seems like such an artificial concept. Isn't it true that as we age, we tend to turn to chosen adult children or certain relatives who think the way we do for advice, for help?*

This is so, but the court in its wisdom pretends that a competent elderly person makes his or her important decisions without this consistent and loving input. "Undue influence" is, after all, just an ill-defined but currently popular theoretical concept. Physically or mentally debilitating illnesses, according to this theory, result in an unhealthy dependence upon a caretaker and increase an individual's susceptibility to influence. Lacking the capacity to resist undue influence, the vulnerable individual's decisions and behaviors can be unfairly guided or even controlled by the "undue influencer" (to use the court's jargon).

Keep in mind that there are no research studies that indicate which mental illnesses affect susceptibility to undue influence. Nonetheless, if the petitioners allege in court that a wealthy and aging relative relies on his only cousin for help with financial matters and personal needs and wants nothing to do with the petitioners (probably for good reasons), the strong possibility of undue influence is raised. This legal tactic is never an easy one for an elderly individual to fight.

*In order to prove that they are not incompetent or lacking in decision-making capacity, the elderly who are pulled into involuntary conservatorship/guardianship proceedings must convince judges that they can and do make all of their important decisions without any help from the people they trust, that all of their decisions are reasonable or responsible, that they can manage their financial affairs in a prudent way, and that they can provide for their own food, clothing, and shelter. Isn't that a tough burden of proof?*

It is. It is frustrating, too, since the burden of proof is supposed to belong to the petitioners. Sadly, though, the law as it actually unfolds in the courts today is, to quote a phrase, a "well-intentioned hypocrisy."[25] The petitioners make allegations supported by hearsay testimony and the allegedly incompetent/incapacitated elderly must then counter with proof of their competence. This is akin to assuming a person is guilty until proven innocent—a skewing of our legal system as we know it.

*If a conservator or guardian is appointed in spite of everything the elderly individual does, can that person fight the ruling by going to the Court of Appeals and getting the judgment overturned?*

He or she could try, although the right to appeal is limited. Most appellate courts will not hear new facts. What the appellate court will do is weigh the *evidentiary* basis for the lower court's ruling, evaluate procedural aspects of the hearing, and hear arguments concerning the constitutionality of your state's conservatorship/guardianship statutes.

> Generally speaking, the appeal can be based only on alleged mistakes of law made by the trial judge or on procedural irregularities. A "mistake of law" would occur if a judge allowed improper evidence such as second-hand hearsay testimony about a respondent's infirmities, for instance. It would be a "procedural irregularity" to conduct the trial on a specified day if the respondent had not been properly provided with the required advance formal notification of that date, time, and place of trial. Ordinarily, the appellate court will not overturn the trial court's findings of fact if there is evidence in the trial transcript to support those facts. Simply being disappointed over the decision by the trial court is not grounds for an appeal.[26]

Most of the elderly who are blindsided by these obscure laws suffer tremendous emotional and financial hardships during their initial court proceedings. The humiliating litigation may also become physically debilitating for the targeted elder. When told that they must go to a higher appellate court—a more expensive and time-consuming process than the first—in order to secure a chance to reverse the ruling, few elderly opt to continue the disheartening battle. Time and age serve the interests of the petitioners alone. As Senior Judge Field C. Benton of Colorado warned,

> Because of the large number of cases being appealed, this appellate decision probably will be handed down two years or more after the trial was completed. That delay is one reason for there being so few appeals in guardianship cases.[27]

Finally, if you have taken comfort in the belief that you could repel an involuntary or unwanted "protective proceeding" if one were lodged against you, pay special attention to the second of the two following statistics:

- A full 94 percent of all involuntary conservatorship/guardianship court battles are lost by the vulnerable elderly.
- Almost none of these cases are ever appealed.[28]

*What are the chances that a conservatorship or guardianship, once established, can ever be terminated?*

Remember that old saying, "I have good news and I have bad news"? The good news is that all conservatorships/guardianships will come to an end. The bad news is that they usually end only when the ward or conservatee dies.

> Zimny et al. (1997) reported that of 61 cases of guardianship of the elderly that were terminated over a 6-year period, 52 ended due to the death of the ward, 8 due to depletion of the wards' assets, and 1 due to the ward moving out of the court's jurisdiction.[29]

It is possible in theory to attempt to terminate a conservatorship or guardianship by means of a "restoration hearing." Although the elderly ward may file a petition for the restoration of his or her freedom/competence, it is a daunting task (which involves proving that the guardian or conservator is not acting in the elderly individual's best interests) and should be undertaken by an interested party who could retain an attorney. As you have already guessed, the elderly ward often has no right to a court-appointed attorney in these restoration hearings.

*Is an individual changed in a negative way in these "protective proceedings"?*

When any person comes under the control of a court-appointed guardian or conservator, he or she is profoundly changed. The individual is transformed into "the ward" or "the conservatee" of the state." Both of these words underscore the ignominious status accorded the human being who, in times of need, must be deemed incompetent or incapable in order to receive assistance. In too many states, if a conservatorship were appointed over Mr. X, for instance, he would be described in all subsequent legal papers as "X, Incompetent." Mr. X, independent adult, has ceased to exist.

After studying the demographic profiles of older wards in Ohio and Washington states, sociologists Kris Bulcroft, Margaret Kielkopf, and Kevin Tripp found much to criticize in contemporary conservatorship/guardianship statutes and their treatment of the elderly. "In particular, standardized and reliable assessments of competency are lacking; a family member's petition for guardianship is seldom challenged by the older person; and the primary goal of most guardianship cases is to preserve the estate of the older individual."[30] What is more, there is little or no research confirming the powerful premise that underlies these statutes—namely, that these elderly wards or conservatees are somehow incapable of making decisions concerning their personal and/or financial affairs.

*How many of these guardianships and conservatorships are terminated by this type of restoration hearing?*

Very few. After all, how does an elderly person who has not been *permitted* to make personal or financial decisions for months or years suddenly demonstrate to the court that he or she has regained the capacity to do so? The legal system works against the elderly once again.

*Is it easier to get the court to appoint conservators or guardians over elderly mentally ill or developmentally disabled patients since their mental or physical disabilities cause real problems?*

No. The competent elderly are more easily and more globally subdued in conservatorship/guardianship litigation than are the mentally and developmentally disabled. When evaluating mentally or developmentally disabled individuals in protective proceedings, the court follows one goal: minimal intrusion into the life of the disabled unless the person is dangerous to others or, as a result of a mental disorder, is unable to provide for his or her basic personal needs for food, clothing or shelter. When conservators or guardians are appointed, their tasks are tailored to fit the individual case. A double standard obviously exists.

Let me share with you one example discussed during my work as a predoctoral intern in the field of clinical psychology. It will illustrate the difficulty encountered in California when an attempt is made to secure a conservatorship over a truly needy mentally ill adult. Susan, a legless homeless woman in her mid-fifties, moved through a neighboring county in a wheelchair train. One wheelchair carried Susan and an abundance of possessions; a second wheelchair was overflowing with old clothing, paper bags, and small plastic baggies lashed here and there. The baggies contained her excrement.

Noticing that Susan was developing decubitus ulcers from her unsanitary living conditions, a mental health outreach worker enlisted the help of her county's psychiatric team to have Susan evaluated for a conservatorship. In court, the judge refused the county's petition. Why? According to the court, Susan's needs did not meet the criteria of the Lanterman-Petris-Short Act which governs involuntary conservatorship of the mentally ill in California. She was not a threat to anyone and, deep in the wadded jumble of her possessions, Susan had a can of tuna and seven dollars. She told the judge she had a place to park her wheelchairs each night and sleep. Having proven to the court that she could meet her needs for food, clothing, and shelter (as required by the codes), Susan was sent back to the streets, a free and independent woman.

*Can the conservator or guardian sell the new ward's home and make him or her move into an apartment or a nursing home?*

In many states, yes. You will soon learn that once they are appointed, most conservators and guardians (oftentimes family members) function with little or no oversight from the court and have carte blanche to do as they wish. Most state codes do not require any periodic review of a conservator's or guardian's actions, especially regarding personal matters. As summarized by Robert N. Brown of the Legal Counsel for the Elderly, "once appointed and unless the ward or a third party takes the affirmative step of seeking court review, a guardian [or conservator] generally has a free hand in determining what is appropriate with respect to the ward's life."[31]

The following sections from Florida's codes list the powers granted by the court to the plenary guardian or limited guardian of an incapacitated person's property. It is obviously an enormously powerful position. Because courts rarely read the reports filed by conservators and guardians (if reports are even required—or filed), the role is more all-encompassing than it appears in the stark black and white of the statutes.

**§744.444 Power of guardian without court approval.** Without obtaining court approval, a plenary guardian of the property, or a limited guardian of the property within the powers granted by the order appointing the guardian or an approved annual or amended guardianship report, may:

1. Retain assets owned by the ward.
2. Receive assets from fiduciaries or other sources.
3. Vote stocks or other securities in person or by general or limited proxy or not vote stocks or other securities.
4. Insure the assets of the estate against damage, loss, and liability and insure himself or herself against liability as to third persons.
5. Execute and deliver in his or her name as guardian any instrument necessary or proper to carry out and give effect to this section.
6. Pay taxes and assessments on the ward's property.
7. Pay valid encumbrances against the ward's property in accordance with their terms, but no prepayment may be made without prior court approval.
8. Pay reasonable living expenses to the ward, taking into consideration the accustomed standard of living, age, health, and financial condition of the ward.
9. Elect whether to dissent from a will under the provisions of s. 732.210(2) or assert any other right or choice available to a surviving spouse in the administration of a decedent's estate.
10. Deposit or invest liquid assets of the estate, including moneys received from the sale of other assets, in federally insured interest-bearing accounts, readily marketable secured loan arrangements, money market mutual funds, or other prudent investments. The guardian may redeem or sell such deposits or investments to pay the reasonable living expenses of the ward as provided herein.
11. Pay incidental expenses in the administration of the estate.
12. Sell or exercise stock subscription or conversion rights and consent, directly or through a committee or other agent, to the reorganization, consolidation, merger, dissolution, or liquidation of a corporation or other business enterprise.
13. When reasonably necessary, employ persons, including attorneys, auditors, investment advisers, or agents, even if they are associated with the guardian, to advise or assist the guardian in the performance of his or her duties.
14. Execute and deliver in his or her name as guardian any instrument that is necessary or proper to carry out the orders of the court.
15. Hold a security in the name of a nominee or in other form without disclosure of the interest of the ward, but the guardian is liable for any act of the nominee in connection with the security so held.

**§744.441 Powers of guardian upon court approval.** After obtaining approval of the court pursuant to a petition for authorization to act, a plenary guardian of the property, or a limited guardian of the property within the powers granted by the order appointing the guardian or an approved annual or amended guardianship report, may:

1. Perform, compromise, or refuse performance of a ward's contracts that continue as obligations of the estate, as he or she may determine under the circumstances.

2. Execute, exercise, or release any powers as trustee, personal representative, custodian for minors, conservator, or donee of any power of appointment or other power that the ward might have lawfully exercised, consummated, or executed if not incapacitated, if the best interest of the ward requires such execution, exercise, or release.

3. Make ordinary or extraordinary repairs or alterations in buildings or other structures; demolish any improvements; or raze existing, or erect new, party walls or buildings.

4. Subdivide, develop, or dedicate land to public use; make or obtain the vacation of plats and adjust boundaries; adjust differences in valuation on exchange or partition by giving or receiving consideration; or dedicate easements to public use without consideration.

5. Enter into a lease as lessor or lessee for any purpose, with or without option to purchase or renew, for a term within, or extending beyond, the period of guardianship.

6. Enter into a lease or arrangement for exploration and removal of minerals or other natural resources or enter into a pooling or unitization agreement.

7. Abandon property when, in the opinion of the guardian, it is valueless or is so encumbered or in such condition that it is of no benefit to the estate.

8. Pay calls, assessments, and other sums chargeable or accruing against, or on account of, securities.

9. Borrow money, with or without security, to be repaid from the property or otherwise and advance money for the protection of the estate.

10. Effect a fair and reasonable compromise with any debtor or obligor or extend, renew, or in any manner modify the terms of any obligation owing to the estate.

11. Prosecute or defend claims or proceedings in any jurisdiction for the protection of the estate and of the guardian in the performance of his or her duties.

12. Sell, mortgage, or lease any real or personal property of the estate, including homestead property, or any interest therein for cash or credit, or for part cash and part credit, and with or without security for unpaid balances.

13. Continue any unincorporated business or venture in which the ward was engaged.

14. Purchase the entire fee simple title to real estate in this state in which the guardian has no interest, but the purchase may be made only for a home for the ward, to protect the home of the ward or the ward's interest, or as a home for the ward's dependent family. If the ward is a married person and the home of the ward or of the dependent family of the ward is owned by the ward and spouse as an estate by the entirety and the home is sold pursuant to the authority of subsection (12), the court may authorize the investment of any part or all of the proceeds from the sale toward the purchase of a fee simple title to real estate in this state for a home for the ward or the dependent family of the ward as an estate by the entirety owned by the ward and spouse. If the guardian is authorized to acquire title to real estate for the ward or dependent family of the ward as an estate by the entirety in accordance with the preceding provisions, the conveyance shall be in the name of the ward and spouse and shall be effective to create an estate by the entirety in the ward and spouse.

15. Exercise any option contained in any policy of insurance payable to, or inuring to the benefit of, the ward.

16. Pay reasonable funeral, interment, and grave marker expenses for the ward from the ward's estate, up to a maximum of $6,000.

17. Make gifts of the ward's property to members of the ward's family in estate and income tax planning procedures.

18. When the ward's will evinces an objective to obtain a United States estate tax charitable deduction by use of a split interest trust (as that term is defined in s. 737.501), but the maximum charitable deduction otherwise allowable will not be achieved in whole or in part, execute a codicil on the ward's behalf amending said will to obtain the maximum charitable deduction allowable without diminishing the aggregate value of the benefits of any beneficiary under such will.

19. Create revocable or irrevocable trusts of property of the ward's estate which may extend beyond the disability or life of the ward in connection with estate, gift, income, or other tax planning or in connection with estate planning.

20. Renounce or disclaim any interest by testate or intestate succession or by inter vivos transfer.

21. Enter into contracts that are appropriate for, and in the best interest of, the ward.

*State legislators must believe that being moved into a nursing home might be in the new ward's or conservatee's best interest. What happens to the elderly once they are placed in nursing or convalescent facilities?*

Research shows that the survival rate of individuals who are institutionalized even for necessary personal care is lower than the survival rate of individuals who receive this care in their own homes—or continue at home without such care at all.[32] Sad but true, the mental health and well-being of the elderly will usually deteriorate when they are stripped of the right to exert control over their own lives and summarily placed in nursing homes.

This penultimate question brings to mind a warning given in court by Justice Brandeis of the Supreme Court of the United States:

> Experience should teach us to be most on our guard to protect liberty when the Government's purposes are beneficent. . . . The greatest dangers to liberty lurk in insidious encroachment by men of zeal, well-meaning but without understanding.[33]

Yes, of course a nursing home might be the most appropriate setting for an aging and impaired person. However, our states are permitting the institutionalization of too many elderly people whose major "impairment" is that they refuse to conform to the values of "concerned family members."

*What happens if an elderly impaired person really needs the help of a conservator or guardian but has no money to pay that person's ongoing fees?*

Since guardians' and conservators' fees are usually taken from the estate of the new ward or conservatee, it is harder to find a guardian or conservator to watch over the affairs of an impoverished incapacitated ward than it is to find a guardian or conservator to manage the affairs of a man or woman of means. Some states have attempted to solve this dilemma by establishing specific funds from which such surrogate decision-makers can be paid.

Other states have created offices of "public guardians" whose members are paid by the state to care for needy seniors. The largest and oldest such agency in the country is the Los Angeles public guardian's office. How is this system of public guardians faring? In their Pulitzer Prize winning year-long Associated Press investigation into guardianship of the elderly, Fred Bayles and Scott McCartney were able to shed some light on the actual functioning of our country's public guardians:

> Five social workers in the Los Angeles public guardian's office control the lives of 1,000 elderly people. The office also controls $200 million in assets and has run a hardware store, a plant nursery and an oil-drilling operation owned by its wards. . . . It's critics say it now turns away cases and favors moneyed wards over the indigent. . . . "We don't want

any more. We have too many," said Gordon Treharne, the Los Angeles
public guardian. "Everyone thinks we should expand and we're not.
We're retrenching."

And it's happening all across the country. Faced with a crush of
elderly who either outlive their relatives or live far from family, states
are setting up—and loading up—public guardians as a catchall for those
who have no one else. . . .

The public guardians take direct control of the lives of old people
and make the decisions any guardian makes—where the ward will live,
whether to pull the plug on life-support systems, how much money is
spent on groceries. . . . [But] meeting those needs is becoming increasingly difficult. In Phoenix, caseworkers have time to visit their wards
only four times a year.[34]

Bayles and McCartney estimated that just over two percent of all
people under conservatorships and guardianships may be wards of these
overworked public guardians. Law Professor Lawrence Frolik of the University of Pittsburgh sees danger in this added layer of bureaucracy. "The
last thing you want," he said, "is a state office whose existence depends
upon taking away the rights of others."[35]

*If estranged relatives come after an elderly man or woman in a conser-
vatorship or guardianship hearing and don't succeed, can't they just wait
and try again later at a time when that relative is finally having difficulty
managing?*

Yes, they can and they do. Time is always on the side of the petitioners.
You won't find any Fifth Amendment or double jeopardy protection here
against being prosecuted twice for the same offense because your offense
is simply that *you are getting old.*

*When all is said and done, what rights does an individual lose when he
or she becomes a conservatee or ward of the state?*

Depending on the sitting judge's rulings, an individual who loses his or
her fight for autonomy in a conservatorship or guardianship proceeding
suffers either a partial or complete removal of decision-making capacity
and surrenders almost all control over day-to-day affairs. Even if the
action is limited to the estate, the new ward or conservatee is instantly
reduced to the legal status of a child. He or she loses control of all property, be it a modest welfare check or a large estate—a catastrophe of
immense proportions to the aged individual whose autonomy is defined
by his or her right to make economic choices. He or she cannot acquire,

manage or obligate property, make gifts or contracts, create a trust or change beneficiaries of an existing trust or insurance policy, choose his or her residence, or enter into a joint tenancy. This subsequent loss of control over financial matters has many ramifications, as Gregory Atkinson described in "Towards a Due Process Perspective in Conservatorship Proceedings for the Aged":

> For example, if an aged person cannot make a contract, he cannot arrange for nursing home care, take a job, lease an apartment or buy a house. He cannot establish a joint bank account. His ability to marry may also be jeopardized specifically by statute or indirectly by his inability to create spousal property interests. The ability to write a will is unaffected as long as the conservatee has testamentary capacity.[36]

If the protective proceeding results in a conservatorship or guardianship of the person, the elderly man or woman loses his or her right to control his/her own destiny. The court's ruling unwittingly destroys the aging individual's sense of autonomy and self-efficacy. The new ward immediately surrenders a vast array of personal choices and decision-making about: living arrangements, clothing, friends, hobbies, meals, reading materials and movies, daily routines, education, and the right to consent to or refuse medical, psychiatric, or surgical treatments. In many instances, the court will extend orders determining incapacity and remove additional rights: to marry, to vote, to have a driver's license, to travel, to seek or retain employment, and to personally apply for government benefits.[37] Clearly, the conservator or guardian intrudes into an elderly person's privacy in a stunning manner. Although it is hard to imagine the resultant sense of degradation and meaninglessness suffered by the ward, the following passage captures one elderly conservatee's lament:

> I cannot tell you how much worse my mental condition is since I have been a "thing" of the court's without rights. I want to die, I pray to die. There is no happiness in life—my life is over. I would prefer death to living as a guardianship zombie the rest of my life.[38]

Conservatorship/guardianship codes were created to give states a legal tool to protect their vulnerable elderly. All too often, this tool results in their physical, emotional, and financial mistreatment. Where did our country's so-called protective proceedings originate? The answer to this question lies in centuries-old legal traditions begun in Europe during the Middle Ages, which we shall now review.

# NOTES

1. Quoted in J. E. Rein, "Preserving Dignity and Self-Determination of the Elderly in the Face of Competing Interests and Grim Alternatives: A Proposal for Statutory Refocus and Reform," *George Washington Law Review* 60 (1992): 1818–87.

2. L. A. Frolik and A. P. Barnes, "An Aging Population: A Challenge to the Law," *The Hastings Law Journal* 42 (1991): 698 (footnote).

3. L. Friedman and M. Savage, "Taking Care: The Law of Conservatorship in California," *Southern California Law Review* 61 (1998): 273–90.

4. Tomlinson et al., "An Empirical Study of Proxy Consent for Elderly Persons," *The Gerontologist* 30, no. 54 (1998): 54–64.

5. L. Shelford, "A Practical Treatise on the Law Concerning Lunatics, Idiots, and Persons of Unsound Mind 6," in N. N. Kittrie, *The Right to be Different* (Baltimore: Johns Hopkins Press, 1971). This book was nominated for the Pulitzer Prize in 1972.

6. Rein, op. cit., p. 1870.

7. S. Emmons, "Conservators' Reach Can Be a Surprise," *Los Angeles Times*, 23 November 1997, p. A29.

8. Ibid.

9. Ibid.

10. J. W. Parry and S. B. Hurme, "Guardianship Monitoring and Enforcement Nationwide," *Mental and Physical Disability Law Reporter* 15, no. 3 (1991): 304–309.

11. Rein, op. cit.

12. Ibid., p. 1880.

13. M. B. Kapp, "Legal Basis of Guardianship," in G. H. Zimny and G. T. Grossberg, eds., *Guardianship of the Elderly: Psychiatric and Judicial Aspects* (New York: Springer Publishing Company, Inc., 1998), pp. 16–24.

14. Quoted in Rein, op. cit., p. 1840 (footnote).

15. C. Rembar, *The Law of the Land: The Evolution of Our Legal System* (New York: Harper & Row, 1980).

16. R. N. Brown, *The Rights of Older Persons: A Basic Guide to the Legal Rights of Older Persons under Current Law*, 2d ed. (Carbondale, Ill.: Southern Illinois University Press, 1989).

17. Ibid., p. 343.

18. Parry and Hurme, op. cit., p. 304.

19. P. M. Keith and R. R. Wacker, "Implementation of Recommended Guardianship Practices and Outcomes of Hearings for Older Persons," *The Gerontologist* 33, no. 1 (1993): 81–87.

20. Ibid.

21. Quoted in Keith and Wacker, op. cit., p. 83.

22. Quoted in "The Disguised Oppression of Involuntary Guardianship: Have the Elderly Freedom to Spend?" *Yale Law Journal* 73 (1964): 685 (footnote).

23. Brown, op. cit., p. 338.

24. Keith and Wacker, op. cit., p. 84.

25. Rein, op. cit., p. 1819.

26. F. C. Benton, "The Courts," in Zimny and Grossberg, *Guardianship of the Elderly,* pp. 74–85.

27. Ibid., p. 83.

28. Rein, op. cit., p. 1880.

29. J. N. Kirkendall, "Judicial Process in Guardianship Proceedings," in Zimny and Grossberg, *Guardianship of the Elderly,* pp. 61–73.

30. K. Bulcroft, M. R. Kielkopf, and K. Tripp, "Elderly Wards and Their Legal Guardians: Analysis of County Probate Records in Ohio and Washington," *The Gerontologist* 31, no. 2 (1991): 156–64.

31. Brown, op. cit., p. 337.

32. G. J. Alexander, "Remaining Responsible: On Control of One's Health Needs in Aging," *Santa Clara Law Review* 10 (1980): 13–47.

33. *Olmstead* v. *United States*, 277 U.S. 438, 479 (1928) (J. Brandeis, dissenting).

34. F. Bayles and S. McCartney, "California's Public Guardians: Stewards of Elderly Beset with Cases," *Los Angeles Times*, 27 September 1987, pp. 28–29.

35. Ibid.

36. G. Atkinson, "Towards a Due Process Perspective in Conservatorship Proceedings for the Aged," *Journal of Family Law*, 18 (1980): 819–45.

37. See, for example, Fla. Stat. Ann. §744.3215(2).

38. Quoted in J. E. Rein, op. cit., p. 1836.

# CHAPTER THREE

# HISTORICAL ROOTS OF CONSERVATORSHIP/ GUARDIANSHIP LAW

*The law is the witness and external deposit of our moral life. Its history is the history of the moral development of the race.*
—Oliver Wendell Holmes Jr., Speech, Boston, January 8, 1897

In order to understand the purposes guiding proxy decision-making codes in America, it is helpful to understand the origin of our conservatorship/guardianship laws. To accomplish this goal, we must reach back through time to legal sanctions developed during the Middle Ages to deal with the acquisition, protection, and disposition of personal property, and back also to a key fourteenth-century English code protecting the property of "lunatics."[1] The two concepts—the individual's right to own and bequeath property and the state's right to manage the property and/or personal affairs of mentally disabled people—are the legal streams that flowed together over time to create our powerful river of involuntary conservatorship/guardianship litigation. Our historical overview will focus on several related issues: hereditary property rights and rights of testation; governmental intrusion into the lives of the incompetent; determinations of partial insanity, testamentary capacity, and undue influence; and the centuries-old use of expert witnesses to give meaning to undefined and oftentimes meaningless concepts in court.

57

# ON HEREDITARY PROPERTY
# AND RIGHTS OF TESTATION

The right to own property and to determine its dispostion following death began in the thirteenth century when the concept of an estate as "land in which parties have an interest and regarding which they have rights of enjoyment for a specified term (e.g., for life or for some number of years)"[2] first appeared in Western law. Feudal society contributed the concept of *real property* (realty), although real property was confined to a very limited number of people. The term *tenure* was used to describe the duration of ownership or controlled interest in the land.

Feudal lords had the right to grant their villeins (also called serfs) possession (*seisen*) of an estate. Villeins could, in turn, become functional "lords" by apportioning their holdings to others. In practice, the right to hold property for life and to confer this property on direct descendants in the form of a *fee* enabled freemen to function both as servants of A and as lords of B. The resultant stratification of society enhanced the durability of feudal hierarchies. In terms of this perpetuation of such rights of interest, feudalism ended with the *Quia Emptores,* an act passed by Parliament in 1290.[3] *Quia Emptores* vested the power of revocation in "the lord of all," and assured that the rights of ownership or interest remained with the tenant during his life unless these rights were revoked by the lord.

Two inevitable results flowed from *Quia Emptores.* Feudal hierarchies were replaced by a two-class system composed of a "landed" aristocracy and a growing population of tenant farmers.[4] Even more significantly, the number of legal owners of land (excluding females, who had no such rights) increased because many possessed rights of interest identical to those once held only by the villeins. Curiously, *Quia Emptores* also permitted the holder of a fee to sell it without the consent of his lord, an action that passed his lordly rights to the new grantee.

Following the historic custom of hereditary succession, the holder of the property "in fee-simple" could now bequeath his property to lineal descendants.[5] An incurred cost was the inevitable loss of status that heralded the breakdown of feudal society. By the year 1540, the right to pass such holdings on to strangers and exclude lineal descendants in one's will—the right to *disentail*—rose to prominence. Inevitably, threatened heirs sought legal remedies in the form of regulations against disinheritance. Issues that were at the heart of *postmortem* will contests in the past are now being argued in the thinly veiled *antemortem* will contests that characterize many conservatorship and guardianship proceedings today.

# STATUTE DE PREROGATIVA REGIS

In her research as consulting policy analyst for the Intergovernmental Health Policy Project at George Washington University, Alison P. Barnes studied the origins of our current conservatorship/guardianship laws.[6] She traced them back to a single English statute from the reign of Edward II: *De Prerogativa Regis* (the royal prerogative). Created at the beginning of the fourteenth century, *De Prerogativa Regis* permitted the king to manage the land and property owned by "lunatics" who had been declared incurably incompetent by an inquisition. The regent was also permitted to hold in trust the property and land of those who were considered to be "temporarily incompetent." The king under *De Prerogativa Regis* was required to return the protected property to the recovered lunatic or to his heirs and creditors following the lunatic's death—without taking any profits for himself.

Due process was initiated to curb the abuse inherent in this legislation, however, and committees were established to help administer to the estates and personal needs of incompetent people. How was "lunacy" determined? A jury would be impaneled to investigate the facts of each individual case and the magistrate would be guided by its ruling. It is clear to see that even in the fourteenth century the interest of the heir-apparent was a motivating force. "Because inquisitions were costly and rarely convened," as Alison Barnes discovered in her research, "guardianship applied only to a few wealthy persons whose relatives were interested in the preservation of hereditary lands and privileges."[7]

Early laws thus focused on both the property of the mentally ill and the hereditary interests of relatives in that property. Not until the Vagrancy Act of 1714 (to control "wandering lunatics") and orders written in 1744 by two justices of the peace to detain those who were "ferociously mad" did attention focus on the nonfinancial affairs of the insane.[8] The state's interest in the severely mentally ill sprang from a desire to protect others from their harmful behaviors.

# DETERMINATIONS OF PARTIAL INSANITY IN WILL CONTESTS

Over time, however, the issue of incompetency or mental illness had infiltrated the courtrooms where early postmortem will contests were being waged. As we have seen, men had been given the legal right to own property and bequeath their estates to chosen heirs. Similarly, they could bypass heirs-apparent by disinheritance—if they were of sound mind when drawing up their final testamentary documents. By the nineteenth century, the burden of establishing the mental capacity of a testator or testatrix (the male or female maker of the will) had become quite complex.[9]

In *Dew* v. *Clark and Clark* (1826), the concept of "partial insanity" was not only raised, it was ruled sufficient to overturn a will.[10] Mrs. Dew, the testator's daughter, argued that her father had developed an unnatural contempt for her as a child. His "delusion" caused him to bequeath the bulk of his estate to more distant relations, the Clarks—a final act of "groundless hostility" on the part of a shrewd, successful businessman. Arguing in their own behalf, the Clarks emphasized that the daughter's behaviors were directly responsible for the testator's enmity. The court was not convinced, and rendered a decision that connected the specific terms of the will to a "demonstrably insane delusion" as evidence of a diseased mind.

> The will propounded in this cause . . . being . . . the direct unqualified offspring of that morbid delusion . . . I, at least, can arrive at no other conclusion than that the deceased was insane at the time of his making the will . . . and consequently that the will itself is null and void in law. (*Dew* v. *Clark and Clark*, p. 455)[11]

Judicial rulings of partial insanity continued. In *Waring* v. *Waring* (1848), the lower or Prerogative Court of Canterbury nullified a will on grounds that the woman who made the will (the testatrix) was partially insane, "although no evidence had been presented to prove that this alleged insanity had entered into any part of her will."[12] In spite of their statement that "what is called partial insanity has never before been laid down in the Superior Court,"[13] the appellate court sustained the lower court's decision. The burden of proof grew heavier. By the year 1866, the court in *Smith* v. *Tebbitt* ruled that the fact that the testatrix had at some time experienced religious visions was sufficient cause to set aside her will.[14] According to Justice Wilde,

> I cannot reconcile the proved hallucinations of the testatrix in the matter of religion with the action of a sound and healthy mind on the one hand; and on the other, I find them to be just such as a diseased mind is known to engender. (*Smith* v. *Tebbitt*, p. 436)[15]

As witnessed in *Waring* and in *Smith*, the evolving determination of testamentary capacity in legal contexts was making it harder for an owner to dispose of personal property as he or she wished. A reaction to this can be seen in the English case of *Banks* v. *Goodfellow* (1870).[16] In *Banks*, a lower court ruling barred the use of "partial insanity" to overturn a will if the "disease" spares the faculties needed for an informed disposition of property. The decision was supported on appeal. Mental incapacity itself will not invalidate a will if

> it presents itself in such a degree and form as not to interfere with the capacity to make a rational disposal of property. . . . The standard of capacity in cases of impaired mental power is . . . the capacity on the part of the testator to comprehend the extent of the property to be disposed of, and the nature of the claims of those he is excluding. (*Banks v. Goodfellow*, pp. 555–56, 569)[17]

A similar case in America echoed this concern for the rights of ownership and disposition. In *Boardman v. Woodward* (1869), the jury was instructed that a proof of insanity is not sufficient to invalidate a will if two things can be shown: first, that the testator was aware of the nature of his act at the time of his signing, and second, that any delusions suffered by the testator did not play a significant role in the actual terms of his will.[18] Disregarding the argument that delusions are unerring signs of insanity, the appeals judge underscored his awareness that medical authorities held widely differing opinions concerning the nature of such afflictions as partial insanity, delusions, and moral insanity.

> We all have likes and dislikes among our acquaintances and even among our relatives . . . and yet are we all insane because we dislike somebody that someone else likes . . . ? Better make a law that all a man's property should be divided equally among his relatives, without regard to the peculiar views or preferences of the deceased owner, and prohibit the making of wills altogether. (*Boardman v. Woodward*, p. 139)[19]

The fundamental premise of the law of wills was stated succinctly in *Estate of McDevitt*, a California case settled in 1892. The premise is clear: "the right to dispose of one's property by will is most solemnly assured by law, and . . . does not depend upon its judicious use."[20] However, the testator/testatrix must be fully capable of forming the intent which wills law is designed to protect, and the wishes stated in the will must be truly the testator's own.

All of our state laws governing wills require mental or testamentary capacity. As variously described, a testator must have a sound mind, a sound mind and memory, or a sound and disposing mind and memory. The following passage from *Estate of McDevitt* is accepted as the legal standard of testamentary capacity in the United States:

> Testator must have sufficient strength and clearness of mind and memory,
> to know, in general, without prompting, the nature and extent of the prop-
> erty of which he is about to dispose, and [the] nature of the act which he
> is about to perform, and the names and identity of the persons who are to
> be the objects of his bounty, and his relation towards them.[21]

Many states do make additional requirements. California stipulates
that "the testator is also free of . . . delusions or hallucinations [which]
result in the person's devising his or her property in a way which, except
for the existence of the delusions or hallucinations, he or she would not
have done" (California Probate Code, §6100.5). Massachusetts adds "in
a general way" to qualify the criterion concerning "the nature and situation of his property."[22] Although most states require all three criteria—i.e.,
knowledge of property, knowledge of the act to be performed, and knowledge of the objects of one's bounty—some states require only one of the
three. Missouri, for instance, asks only that the testator have "recognized
his obligation to the objects of his bounty and their relation to him."[23]
Ruling in *Estate of Congdon* in 1981, Minnesota requires only that the
testator understand "the nature, situation, and extent of his property" and
be "able to hold these things in his mind long enough to form a rational
judgment concerning them."[24]

In general, once it has been determined that the testator meets the prevailing standard of mental capacity, his or her will must be carried out.
Although juries attempt to strike down wills of which they disapprove,
the testator's true intent set forth in a will may not be judged by others—
whatever its substance.

In a development with profound implications for involuntary conser-
vatorship/guardianship proceedings, courts can now consider the
bequests contained in a testator's will in making a determination of an
individual's mental capacity. Indeed, in some states, a will's provisions
*alone* may be sufficient evidence to raise the suspicion of incapacity.
When we are reminded that involuntary conservatorship/guardianship
proceedings hinge on the issue of "incompetence" or "incapacity," this
can be viewed as dangerous new territory, indeed.

If wills law is truly grounded in liberal individualism that honors personal values which may not be judged by others, it should not be possible
for a court to find lack of capacity by judging the individual testator's
choices. After all, can a competent testator who is free to be irrational be
judged incompetent when he/she makes an irrational disposition?

According to legal experts, there is a direct relationship between the
twin concepts of testamentary capacity and mental illness (or "partial
insanity") and that of undue influence. Writing in the *Bulletin of the*

*American Academy of Psychiatry and Law*, I. N. Perr describes that perceived legal connection:

> It requires much less influence to control the will of a person whose functional abilities have been severely impaired. . . . A demonstration of impaired mental powers or a clouding of intelligence of the testator makes it easier to establish a charge of undue influence.[25]

## CHALLENGES TO COMPETENCE: TESTAMENTARY CAPACITY AND UNDUE INFLUENCE

Legal remedies guarding inheritances have continued throughout the intervening centuries in the form of actual regulations against disinheritance. While challenges to the validity of a will or codicil (an amendment to an existing will) may take many guises, two have the clearest a priori relation to mental illness. Both issues are commonly argued by heir-petitioners in their involuntary conservatorship/guardianship actions.

The first challenge argues that the maker of the will lacked *testamentary capacity* at the time the disputed document was signed and could not have understood what he or she was doing. The second challenge reasons that specific contents of a will resulted from *undue influence* exerted by one or more interested or designing people.[26] Let's look first at the required legal component of testamentary capacity and then come back to the concept of undue influence.

Daniel N. Robinson, author of *Psychology and the Law*, points to the 1793 case of *Cartwright* v. *Cartwright* as a pivotal development of the concept of testamentary capacity.[27] In this case, Mrs. Cartwright's lineal descendants challenged specific previsions of her will on the grounds that she (the testatrix) was not of sound mind at the time the will was created. Because medical opinion had not yet entered the legal arena to assist in a determination of "mental capacity," the court based its decision upon its own understanding of the concept. The court concluded that:

> By herself writing the will . . . [she] . . . hath most plainly shewn she had a full and complete capacity to understand what was the state of her affairs and her relations. . . . She not only formed the plan, but pursued and carried it into execution with propriety and without assistance. (*Cartwright* v. *Cartwright*, p. 933)[28]

*Cartwright* v. *Cartwright* thus confined the issue of capacity to three questions. Did the testatrix have the power to promise the properties listed in her will? Did the terms of the will violate any law? And is the wording of the will clearly the language of intention? Because Mrs. Cartwright knew what was hers and knew who her relatives were, she was permitted to specify the manner in which relatives were to be treated regarding her properties.

In capacity rulings made in the mid-1930s and 1940s, the California court determined that the mental state of a decedent at the time his or her will was executed must be guided by the presumption that he or she was of sound mind.[29] The petitioner seeking to establish incapacity carried the burden of proof required to override that presumption, namely, a preponderance of the evidence.[30]

In addition to the premise of testamentary capacity, however, there is the second legal premise upon which a will challenge or involuntary protective proceeding may be grounded: that of undue influence. In their seminal work for the *American Journal of Psychiatry*, "Assessing Competency to Make a Will," James E. Spar and Andrew S. Garb warn that "undue influence is a more complex and less precisely defined concept [than that of testamentary capacity]."[31] Its use in court is always problematic. Its misuse in the context of involuntary conservatorship/guardianship litigation is inevitable. It is a legal entity lacking real definitions and it has no boundaries.

Nonetheless, a presumption of undue influence is recognized by many state courts in America if a certain combination of circumstances—which vary strikingly from jurisdiction to jurisdiction—can be demonstrated.[32] If undue influence can be proven (whatever that might mean), those sections of the will or codicil attributed to the results of undue influence are ruled invalid.[33] What is more, an insidious but powerful link is often made in conservatorship/guardianship proceedings between the assertion of ill-defined undue influence and the supposed existence of mental incapacity or incompetence that permitted the elderly to be influenced in the first place. This is treacherous ground, indeed.

The poorly defined legal concept of undue influence as it is used today requires the substitution of the desires of the "influencer" for those of the testator.[34] "Undue influence implies pressure brought to bear directly on the testamentary act with the purpose of procuring a testamentary disposition in favor of a particular person or persons."[35] There are four required elements of undue influence: (1) an individual who is subject to influence, (2) a disposition to exert undue influence, (3) an opportunity to exert undue influence, and (4) a result that indicates undue influence.[36] How are these established or excluded in probate court?

*Susceptibility of a testator* may be indicated in court by one of several factors: advanced age (remember, sixty-two or above), lack of intellectual capacity or of "firmness of character" (however that might be measured), and physical debility.[37] The testator's age becomes a crucial element in each case, as does his or her capacity or incapacity to withstand the influence of others. Supposedly, old age alone may not give rise to a presumption of undue influence in more enlightened state codes, but old age combined with an inability to handle business affairs may do so. Furthermore,

> evidence of the mental or physical condition of the testator, not too remote in time from the testamentary act, is admissible on the issue of undue influence. In this regard, physical suffering, especially of a long-standing, chronic nature, weakens the resistance of an individual and makes him more susceptible to influence than he would ordinarily be. In such cases, the withholding of slight favors designed to afford comfort may be sufficient to coerce the will of the suffering person.[38]

*Disposition and opportunity to exert undue influence* are required elements in a court's finding of undue influence, although evidence of either one alone is not supposed to support the inference.[39] Clearly, it is difficult to prove that a person was disposed to exert undue influence on another. This difficulty leads to the use of circumstantial evidence to provide indirect evidence. M. J. Coté describes the "solution by inference." "As a practical matter," he states in *Proof of Fact*, "if it is shown that an opportunity for a beneficiary to assert his influence existed, and that such opportunity was shortly followed by a will under which that beneficiary unduly profits, undue influence may be fairly inferred."[40]

Similarly, circumstantial evidence is generally used to show opportunity to exert influence. Because opportunity implies direct and undisturbed access to the testator for long periods of time, subsequent changes in the testator's relationships to family members or old friends—in favor of the influencer—may signal undue influence.

Thus, the nature of the relationship between the testator and the hypothetical influencer is of crucial importance in making the determination of opportunity to exert undue influence. Should the relationship between the testator and the person alleged to have influenced him or her be a confidential one (e.g., attorney and client, or trustee and beneficiary), such evidence may cause the burden of proof to shift or may give rise to an actual presumption of undue influence.

The fourth factor, or *result indicating undue influence*, incorporates the "unnaturalness" of the will itself.[41] By definition, a will is considered to be *unnatural* if "it provides a substantial benefit to one who has no natural claim to it or a benefit that is out of proportion to the amounts received by other persons having an equal claim to participate in the testator's bounty."[42] It should be noted that the unreasonableness of the will in itself should not raise a presumption of undue influence because each testator has the right to dispose of his or her property in any manner he or she deems proper—in theory.

*Prior wills or specific declarations of the testator* may be used to establish or refute claims of undue influence.[43] Earlier wills are admissible as evidence if they were executed at a time when undue influence does not appear to have been a factor and if their provisions conform either approximately or substantially to the contested will's provisions. If they support an inference that they represent the testator's thoughts at the time of the completion of the will, declarations containing evidence of the testator's state of mind and susceptibility to undue influence are admissible whether made before or after the execution of the will.

In general, the task of establishing a petitioning contestant's case of undue influence is a daunting one for lawyers and expert mental health witnesses alike. Although courts have identified several indicators suggesting the presence of undue influence in the crafting of wills, the concept itself remains poorly defined. According to Spar and Garb,

> to be considered undue, influence must contain an element of "coercion, compulsion or restraint." Mere appeals or arguments, or influence resulting from gratitude or affection, even if the acts creating these feelings were performed selfishly and were designed to affect the testamentary act, do not constitute undue influence. Rather, the testator's mind must be subjugated to that of another, the testator's free agency destroyed, or the testator's volition overpowered by another.[44]

When does the gold of loving support become legally transmuted into the lead of undue influence? How does one "subjugate" or "overpower" the mind and volition of another, particularly the mind and volition of a loved one? Lacking operational criteria for the expert witness or consultant, the concept of undue influence creates complex problems, indeed. Nonetheless, expert witnesses in the field of mental health are still called in to "educate" probate and surrogates' courts on these impossibly vague issues in contested conservatorship/guardianship proceedings.

## THE EXPERT WITNESS IN PROTECTIVE PROCEEDINGS

Expert testimony is introduced for the purpose of educating the trier of fact (in almost all protective proceedings, this is the judge since a jury is rarely involved) in areas which are beyond its understanding, bridging the gap between common knowledge and specialized knowledge.[45]

In contemporary American courtrooms, expert testimony has rightly or wrongly become an almost indispensable component in predeath will contests. As the Federal Rules of Evidence continue to relax restrictions on the admissibility of expert testimony, controversy concerning the intrusion of expert witness into the realm of the court in general has intensified.

It is fitting to comment, however, that while the context may be new (i.e., the expert witness in predeath will contests that are disguised as involuntary conservatorship/guardianship proceedings), the controversy is not. A 1897 *Harvard Law Review* quotes the following introduction to a nineteenth-century attorney's closing argument which is an often quoted outburst: "Gentlemen of the jury, there are three kinds of liars, the common liar, the d——d [*sic*] liar, and the scientific expert."[46] In 1858, Supreme Court Justice Grier said of expert witnesses:

> Experience has shown that the opposite opinions of persons professing to be experts may be obtained to any amount; and it often occurs that not only many days, but even weeks are consumed in examinations to test the skill or knowledge of such witnesses and the correctness of their opinions, wasting the time and wearying the patience of both court and jury, and perplexing instead of elucidating the questions involved in the issue.[47]

## History of Expert Testimony

The policy guiding the introduction of expert testimony to educate the fact finder in specific areas can be traced through centuries of legal tradition. As explained in *Buckley* v. *Rice-Thomas* in England of 1554, "if matters arise in our law which concern other sciences or faculties, we commonly apply for the aid of that science or faculty which it concerns."[48] Professor Wigmore (1923) defined experts as those having the "skill to acquire accurate conceptions,"[49] and proceeded to draw a distinction between experience and knowledge. Experience is the capacity to acquire knowledge on the facts at issue, and knowledge is the awareness or observation of the facts from which a witness draws his or her impressions.[50] Competence as a witness requires both experience and knowledge.

Since the eighteenth century, English courts have permitted the testimony of scientific men or those experienced in a particular area of interest to the trier of fact.[51] As highlighted by Wigmore, experience and knowledge form the criteria determining the admissibility of expert opinion testimony. In 1782 in England's *Folkes* v. *Chadd*, expert opinion based upon facts and upon the expert's own experience was determined to be admissible.[52] Fifty years later, *Ramadge* v. *Ryan* clarified *Folkes* by emphasizing that the witness must not only be an expert, he must also give testimony on areas beyond common understanding.[53] Contemporaneously with *Ramadge*, *Sills* v. *Brown* differentiated between speculation or opinion and education based on facts.[54] An expert witness was obligated to assist the jury in evaluating evidentiary facts but was not permitted to offer opinions upon those facts. Experts were, however, allowed to offer opinions and insights considered beyond the jury's capability.

## *The Opinion Rule*

Writing in 1923, Wigmore defined *opinion evidence* as "testimony which speaks on matters about which all the facts for judgment are already before the jury."[55] The witness is required only to have personal knowledge of the matter about which he or she is testifying. As described previously, common law opinion rules required the witness to testify only to facts and specifically excluded any biases, prejudices, or personal value judgments of the witness. Expert opinion testimony, which represents an exception to the rule excluding opinion testimony, does permit a witness to discuss matters in which he or she has either special knowledge or skill in areas concerning the issue to be tried. According to one key evidentiary treatise written in 1899, "on questions of science, skill, or trade, or others of the kind, persons of skill, sometimes called experts, may not only testify to facts, but are permitted to give their opinions in evidence."[56]

Although the trier of fact is free to accept or reject such testimony, opinion testimony remains an area of significant controversy. Critics fear it permits a witness to usurp the responsibility of the jury.[57] Supporters emphasize that expert opinions serve only to assist the trier of fact—not to limit them in any way. Opinion evidence is now considered to be both relevant and admissible when the expert is determined by the court to be more capable of evaluating the evidence than is the jury. As summarized by a federal district court in 1980:

> Opinions do not assist the jury when they are cumulative of evidence already before the jury, or when the expert has sifted through that evidence and reached a conclusion which, in effect, tells the jury how it should decide the case. Rather, the expert must utilize special knowledge, not ordinarily possessed by laymen, to reach an opinion which truly aids the jury in understanding the evidence or in determining a fact in issue. (*Zenith Radio Corp.* v. *Matsushita Elec. Indus.*)[58]

Thus, a lay witness can usually testify only to *events* that he or she has actually heard firsthand or seen, and any opinions or inferences are inadmissible.[59] An expert witness, on the other hand, may offer *opinions* and *inferences* which are "within the scope of his special training, skill and experience to interpret,"[60] and such opinions and inferences can be accepted as evidence in court. The expert is never a decision-maker or determiner of that which constitutes "fact" in the legal sense.[61] Rather, he or she functions to provide testimony that is relevant and useful to the court in reaching its legal decisions.

## Purpose of Expert Testimony

As we have seen, both the federal rules and common law permit the use of expert testimony only if it will aid the trier of fact.[62] The two differ in one key area, however: common law limits an expert witness's testimony to matters *beyond* the experience or understanding of the jury, and Federal Rule 702 allows expert testimony whenever it serves to assist the trier of fact—a difference permitting testimony on matters that are *within* his or her knowledge. Unfortunately, this provision has served to alter the function of experts who, according to some, "have become nothing more than additional advocates for the parties which hire them."[63]

> The adversary system compounds many of the problems associated with experts. Although the expert may wish to be an impartial source of information, the client, the client's attorney, and the expert's natural competitive tendencies pressure him to be a team player and help the client whenever possible. . . . Ultimately it is the attorneys who are responsible for questioning the witnesses and for seeing that the proper information is elicited from the experts. It would be unreasonable to expect an attorney to elicit information which damages his client's position, and the adversarial system calls for the attorney to attempt to keep out such information.[64]

Because attorneys hire expert witnesses to support a particular theory in a case, they obtain experts whose viewpoints will mirror their own. Thus, bias among expert witnesses is seemingly inescapable and, according to some, driven by the adversarial characteristics of the judicial process itself.

Wishing to counter the opposing testimony of "hostile experts," the witness often will reveal information which helps his or her client and conceal material which might aid the opposition. An additional form of bias results from the expert witness's unconscious adherence to a particular school of thought. Unfortunately, the use of impartial experts appointed by the court is permitted by Federal Rule 706. It is a questionable alternative, with theoretical virtues that quickly disappear in the actual arena of legal conflict. "Although court appointment of experts does tend to eliminate the 'hired gun' stigma, the impartial expert may be misunderstood by the jury, may be wrong, or may belong to a school of thought which favors one party over the other."[65]

## Mental Health Expert Witness

Clearly, anyone who, as a result of training, has knowledge or experience in matters not generally known by the average person, may serve as an expert witness.[66] In cases of mental illness which bear upon such legal decisions as civil commitment, competency to stand trial, and criminal responsibility, psychiatrists, or other medical specialists are usually the primary expert witnesses. In matters involving physical trauma, the witness is most often required to have a medical license, although the physician who testifies in psychiatric matters need not have psychiatric training. The question of which professional is qualified to testify as an expert witness in matters involving possible mental illness—and the legal determination of incompetence in our current conservatorship/guardianship proceedings—continues to stir much debate in American's courts.

> A lower court judge commented about a psychologist whom he did not permit to testify: "here is a man that comes in, glib of tongue, hasn't had a day's medical training at all, and he is going to qualify as an expert on insanity, when a part of the mental condition of legal insanity, as we know it in California, is a medical proposition; and I would like to see the Supreme Court tell me I am wrong." The California Supreme Court *did* tell him he was wrong. (*People* v. *Davis*)[67]

Nonetheless, different courts have accepted the expert opinion testimony of psychologists, social workers, sociologists, and hypnotists. Federal criminal courts have tended to accept psychologists as expert witnesses, while federal civil courts have been inconsistent in this regard. In numerous cases, the very failure to permit psychologists to testify on some aspects of mental illness or insanity has constituted reversible error (see *Rollins* v. *Commonwealth of Virginia*, *State* v. *Holt*, *Jones* v. *Williams*, and *People* v. *Davis*).[68] In other words, in some cases courts that refuse to let psychologists give expert testimony had their decisions overturned by higher courts on appeal.

*People* v. *Hawthorne* (1940) served as a pivotal case in deemphasizing the requirement of medical training for expert witnesses in American courts.[69] In Hawthorne, the prosecution's objection to the use of a Ph.D. psychologist as a defense expert on insanity was sustained by the trial court. This decision was reversed by the Michigan Supreme Court which rejected the argument that insanity is a medical matter about which *only* medical doctors can testify. The court affirmed that a psychologist's ability to evaluate issues of insanity and incompetence may actually be superior to the physician's ability if the particular psychologist has greater experience and training than that of the physician. A federal appeals court in *Jenkins* v. *United States* (1962)[70] similarly affirmed that the determination of a witness's qualifications to provide expert testimony concerning the presence or absence of mental disease or defect must be based upon the nature and extent of the witness's knowledge rather than on his/her title of "psychologist" or "psychiatrist."[71]

There is little agreement from jurisdiction to jurisdiction regarding the specific qualifications needed by a psychologist to satisfy the requirements of expert witness.[72] In *State of New Mexico* v. *Padilla* (1959), a witness who had worked for the state for eight years but who held only an M.A. degree was permitted to testify as a prosecution psychologist.[73] The subsequent conviction of an accused murderer was reversed in part because the witness lacked the following qualifications: a Ph.D. degree, a minimum of five years of postgraduate training in clinical psychology, and at least one year of internship at an American Psychological Association-approved mental hospital. Although licensing or certification does seem to be a key factor in obtaining expert status, case law also suggests that licensing may not be the controlling factor. Perhaps of greater significance is the precise nature of the legal question before the court.

## Effectiveness of Expert Testimony

Has this incorporation of expert witnesses into the courts of America succeeded in the goal of educating a jury or trier on complicated issues? Even though the evidence is mixed, it can be concluded that jurors do seem to reach just and competent decisions when expert testimony is introduced.

> Although several case studies which involved highly technical scientific evidence found that the jurors did not understand the expert testimony, the more convincing studies show that jurors do understand even technical testimony from experts. The most comprehensive jury study is the Chicago Jury Project, which compiled information from criminal trial judges comparing the jury verdicts with the judges' opinions about how the cases should have been decided. The research led to the conclusion that jurors usually understand the facts of the case (many of which involved scientific evidence) and that jury verdicts are usually in agreement with the weight of the evidence presented. Another study involving psychiatric testimony revealed that the jurors understood the evidence. Two noted psychologists, seeking to determine how individual

juror characteristics affected verdicts, found that "the studies are unan-
imous in showing that the evidence is a substantially more potent deter-
minant of juror's verdicts than the individual characteristics of jurors.[74]

Unfortunately, most contested conservatorship/guardianship proceedings take place in front of a judge rather than a judge and jury. Whether
or not a particular judge on a given day will be swayed by one hired
expert's testimony or another's seems too much of a gamble for the vulnerable elderly person whose personal and financial freedoms hang in the
balance in the court.

## *Influence of Expert Testimony*

An important last question to ask is: To what extent does expert testimony
influence the trier of fact? According to William E. Pipkin Jr., there are
three general components that are believed to have the greatest impact in
determining a witness's credibility: expertise, trustworthiness, and
dynamism.[75]

*Expertise* refers to the witness's training, knowledge, skill or experience, all of which may qualify him or her to testify on the issue of fact
before the court.[76] Both Federal Rule 702 and the common law affirm that
the actual determination of who is qualified as an expert witness is controlled by the court. One generalization seems to apply, namely, that the
expert who is found to have "the greater status or credentials is usually
the more persuasive or influential."[77]

*Trustworthiness* measures the expert's perceived candor, honesty, or
objectivity as a witness.[78] Of particular importance in trustworthiness is
the issue of bias or personal interest in the litigation's outcome. In an
article entitled "Source Credibility in Social Judgment: Bias, Expertise,
and the Judge's Point of View," Michael H. Birnbaum and Steven E.
Stegner explored the difference between the influence of trustworthiness
and the influence of expertise. They found that there is "a consistent trend
across all experiments . . . that an unbiased source of high expertise tends
to have greater weight than either biased source of the same expertise."[79]
The individual who is viewed as a disinterested, straightforward source of
information will be deemed to be trustworthy, and trustworthiness is considered by many to be the single most component of credibility.[80]

*Dynamism* refers to qualities of the expert witness's physical presence. How does he or she deliver relevant testimony? What is the witness's demeanor on the stand? This intangible component is arguably the
most influential indicator of credibility, yet it is also the most flawed. This
paradox was demonstrated by the famous "Dr. Fox" test:

An actor was hired to play the role of a medical expert and was supplied with a false but credible background. The actor practiced the delivery of a lecture about which he knew nothing. The lecture was composed of contradictions, vague generalizations, and double-talk, but was presented in a warm, confident, and experienced style. Despite the lack of substantive value, three well-educated audiences were so drawn in by the dynamic presentation that they gave the lecture favorable reviews.[81]

The implications of the importance of an expert witness's engaging demeanor and dynamic style of testimony are underscored by the following observation about medical experts: "The witness with the cultivated courtroom manner, rather than with the superior knowledge and greater integrity, may make the best appearance and carry the jury. The premium thus placed on personality and patter is so great that lawyers become more interested in retaining a good testifier than in retaining a good doctor."[82] It is a reality of tragic proportions that an expert witness with "personality and patter" can help petitioners prove the "incompetence" of elderly relatives in involuntary conservatorship/guardianship pleadings.

Involuntary conservatorship/guardianship proceedings thus represent an uneasy marriage of mental illness and the law. This alliance has grave and immediate consequences for older men and women in America. We have seen how our states came to deprive targeted elderly both of personal freedom and of management rights in their property under specific legal provisions that once protected the well-being of truly helpless infants and lunatics. In many states' conservatorship and guardianship codes, such lunacy provisions remain the prevailing legislation. Only the description of persistent intervention into the right of self-management of the elderly has changed. In too many states (and one state is "too many"), the elderly may still be declared incompetent on the basis of "the infirmities of old age" alone.

In America today, the procedural framework guiding conservatorship/guardianship litigation fails to protect the interests of the proposed conservatee or ward. As a consequence, the elderly are left far more vulnerable to the painful loss of personal and financial autonomy than they were even in Sophocles' day. The legal problems of the elderly are compounded by the inherently conflicting interests and values that drive heir-petitioners into courts—circuit courts, it should be added, whose primary function had always been the probating of wills and inheritances following an individual's death.

Conservatorship/guardianship law represents a potential violation of many rights we assume to be inviolate: the right to live where and as we wish, the right to spend our money as we wish as long as we harm no one, the right to vote or to marry, the right to due process in a court of law, and yes, even the right to make stupid mistakes. Each of us could lose all of these rights simply because we have grown old in America.

We shall now examine the cases of fifty-five men and women who were challenged by involuntary conservatorship/guardianship petitions in courts across America. The first forty cases (in chapters four and five) involve men and women who tried to avoid judicial determinations of incompetency and incapacity, to dance awkwardly away from the threat of being reduced to the status of a nonperson—a child—for the rest of their lives. Half were victorious, half were not. In a very real sense, though, no single aging American "wins" when forced to defend his or her competence in a court of law. These legal proceedings inevitably rob the elderly of time, money, happiness and peace of mind. My mother's "victory" cost her dearly: eighteen months of her life, one million dollars, and the violent splintering of her entire family.

The fifteen cases described in chapter 6 have been included to illustrate what can happen and what has happened when guardians or conservators are appointed and *no one* oversees their work. Removed from the beneficence of the courts where they have been transformed into "wards" and "conservatees," these fiftteen elderly men and women were set adrift in a system rife with abuse. Each story represents a unique betrayal of a vulnerable human being by the very laws that were designed to protect us as we grow old.

# NOTES

1. D. N. Robinson, *Psychology and Law* (New York: Oxford University Press, 1980).

2. Ibid., p. 91.

3. Ibid.

4. Ibid.

5. Ibid, p. 92.

6. A. P. Barnes, "Beyond Guardianship Reform: A Reevaluation of Autonomy and Beneficence for a System of Principled Decision-Making in Long-Term Care," *Emory Law Journal* 41 no. 3 (1992): 633–760.

7. Ibid., p. 651.

8. Ibid.

9. Robinson, op. cit.

10. Ibid.

11. Ibid.

12. Ibid., p. 94.

13. *Waring* v. *Waring*, 13 *English Reports* 715 (1848).

14. Robinson, op. cit., p. 94.

15. Ibid.

16. Ibid., p. 95.

17. Ibid.

18. Ibid.

19. Ibid., p. 96.

20. *Estate of McDevitt*, 95 Cal. 17, 30 Pac. 101 (Ca 1892).

21. Ibid., §12.21.

22. *Goddard* v. *Dupree*, 76 N.E. 2d 643, 645 (Mass 1948).

23. *Everly* v. *Everly*, 249 S.W. 88, 91 (Mo 1923).

24. *Estate of Congdon*, 309 N.W. 2d 261, 266 (Minn 1981).

25. I. N. Perr, "Wills, Testamentary Capacity, and Undue Influence," *Bulletin of the American Academy of Psychiatry and Law* 9 (1981): 16.

26. J. E. Spar and A.S. Garb, "Assessing Competency to Make a Will," *American Journal of Psychiatry* 149, no. 2 (1992): 169–74.

27. Robinson, op. cit.

28. Ibid.

29. *Estate of Finkler*, 3 Cal. 2d 584 (Ca 1935) and *Estate of Schwartz*, 67 Ca.App.2d 512 (2d Dist. 1945).

30. *Estate of Smith*, 200 Cal. 152 (Ca 1926).

31. Spar and Garb, op. cit., p. 170.

32. M. J. Coté, *Undue Influence in Execution of Will*, 36 POF 2d, §7.

33. A. Marshall and A. S. Garb, *California Probate Procedure*, 5th ed. (Los Angeles: Parker & Son, 1989), section 709.

34. *Duress and Undue Influence*, 25 Am.Jur.2d §36.

35. *Wills*, 79 Am.Jur.2d §392.

36. *Duress and Undue Influence*, op. cit., §36.

37. Coté, op. cit., §2.

38. Ibid., p. 115.

39. *Frazier* v. *State Cent. Sav. Bank*, 217 N.W.2d 442 (Iowa 1974), and *Hubbell* v. *Houston*, 441 P.2d 1010 (Okla 1967).

40. Coté, op. cit., pp. 115–16.

41. Ibid., §4.

42. Ibid., p. 117.

43. Wills, op. cit., §448.

44. Spar and Garb, op. cit., p. 170.

45. W. E. Pipkin, "Expert Opinion Testimony: Experts, Where Did They Come From and Why Are They Here?" *Law and Psychology Review* 13, no. 103 (1989): 103–18.

46. Ibid., p. 103.

47. Ibid.

48. *Buckley* v. *Rice-Thomas* (1554), 1 Plowd. 118, p. 124.

49. I. J. Wigmore, *Evidence* (1923), §555.

50. Ibid., §651.

51. Pipkin, op. cit.

52. *Folkes* v. *Chadd*, 3 Doug. 157, 160, 99 Eng.Rep. 589, 590 (1782).

53. *Ramadge* v. *Ryan*, 9 Bing. 333, 131 Eng.Rep. 640 (1832).

54. *Sills* v. *Brown*, 9 Car. & P. 601, 173 Eng.Rep. 974 (1840).

55. Pipkin, op. cit., p. 105.

56. Ibid., p. 106.

57. Ibid.

58. *Zenith Radio Corp.* v. *Matsushita Elec. Indus. Co. Ltd.*, 505 F. Suppl. 1313 (E.D.Pa. 1980).

59. C. M. Cook, "The Role and Rights of the Expert Witness," *Journal of Forensic Sciences* 9 (1964): 456–60.

60. Ibid., pp. 459–60.

61. R. L. Schwitzgebel and R. K. Schwitzgebel, *Law and Psychological Practice* (New York: John Wiley & Sons, 1980).

62. Pipkin, op. cit.

63. Ibid., p. 107.

64. Ibid., pp. 107–108.

65. Ibid., p. 112.

66. Schwitzgebel and Schwitzgebel, op. cit.

67. *People* v. *Davis*, 62 Cal.2d 791, 402 P.2d 142 (1965), p. 245.

68. *Rollins* v. *Commonwealth of Virginia*, 207 Va. 575, 153 S.E.2d 622 (Va. 1966); *State* v. *Holt*, 37 S.W. 2646 (Tenn 1969); *Jones* v. *Williams*, 246 A.2d 356 (Pa 1968); *People* v. *Davis*, 44 Cal. Rptr. 454 (Ca 1965).

69. *People* v. *Hawthorne*, 291 N.W. 205 (Mich. 1940).

70. *Jenkins* v. *United States*, 307 F.2d 637 (D.C. 1962),

71. Schwitzgebel and Schwitzgebel, op. cit.

72. Ibid.

73. *State of New Mexico* v. *Padilla*, 66 N.M. 289, 347 P.2d 312 (1959).

74. Pipkin, op. cit., p. 113.

75. Ibid.

76. Ibid.

77. L. Bank and J. Poythress, "The Elements of Persuasion in Expert Testimony," *Journal of Psychiatry and Law* (summer 1982): 173–85.

78. Pipkin, op. cit.

79. R. Birnbaum and J. Stegner, "Source Credibility in Social Judgment: Bias, Expertise, and the Judge's Point of View," *Journal of Personality and Social Psychology* 37 (1979): 48.

80. Pipkin, op. cit.

81. Ibid., p. 115.

82. Ibid.

# CHAPTER FOUR

# INDIVIDUAL COURT STRUGGLES FOR FREEDOM

## *Defeats*

*Plutarch and Cicero both wrote about the proceeding which Sopho-cles' sons brought against him while he was writing* Oedipus at Colonus. *To prove the aged writer's incompetency, his sons cited his preoccupation with the play. To prove his competency, Sophocles read from the play and asked the jury if that seemed to be the work of an imbecile. The jury rose, and amid shouts of appreciation and applause, declared Sophocles competent. Had Sophocles attempted this defense under contemporary statutes, his sons probably would have left the courtroom in control of his property.*
　　　　　　　　　　—Gregory Atkinson, J.D., *Journal of Family Law*[1]

**W**e shall now examine the stories of twenty elderly men and women whose lives were irreversibly diminished by contested conservatorship/guardianship proceedings. Their cases were drawn from trial courts, courts of appeal, and state supreme courts across America and, in all twenty instances, the proposed wards lost their battles for autonomy. Their stories illustrate the key problems that characterize involuntary "protective proceedings" when such litigation is pursued for less than altruistic reasons.

As we have already seen, there are tremendous liberty interests at stake when an elderly individual is forced into court to defend his or her competence or capacity in the eyes of the law. The remarks of legal analyst Annina M. Mitchell serve well to introduce the theme underscoring the twenty stories of defeat we are about to read:

> Lower court [conservatorship/guardianship] proceedings . . . [have] dramatically demonstrated the relative ease with which guardianship statutes can be used by virtually any individual to impose total control over another person (always in the latter's "best interests") by labeling that person as mentally incompetent.[2]

Even though almost all involuntary conservatorship/guardianship pleadings are driven by a complex array of statutory and/or procedural problems (to be discussed at length in chapter 8), each of the cases in this section has been placed under only one primary heading. Actual names of people and locations have been used as they appear in court records to serve as a reminder that this is real warfare, and it is being fought against the elderly in every state in America today. With the exception of specifically attributed material, all quotations have been taken directly from court documents.

Before focusing on these bitterly contested involuntary conservatorship or guardianship cases, let's briefly review how our court system functions in America today. The system reaches from the state level of trial courts where cases are initiated and up to the United States Supreme Court, which at its discretion may review decisions made by federal courts of appeal. Trial courts are divided into civil courts that hear cases involving common law and civil statutes, criminal courts that hear criminal cases, matrimonial courts resolve divorce proceedings, and surogate's courts that hear matters relating to the estates of incompetent and deceased people.[3] The names given these surrogate's courts vary from state to state, as can be seen in the state code summaries provided in appendix A (e.g., probate court in Los Angeles, surrogate's court in New York City, and county courts in Omaha).

Individual involuntary conservatorship and guardianship petitions are first heard in a lower court and cases that are lost can then be appealed to state courts of appeal. If unsuccessful at this intermediate appellate level, the case can be brought before the state's supreme court. In some states, however, the "Supreme Court" is actually not the court of last resort but an inferior court. New York's court of last resort is called the "Court of Appeals," and in Massachusetts it is called the "Supreme Judicial Court."[4] Beyond this highest state appellate court are the U.S. courts of appeal, which have jurisdiction over most cases decided by U.S. district courts. Decisions made by these courts of appeal are final except as they are subect to discretionary review on appeal by the United States Supreme Court.

In reading through these cases, it becomes apparent that contested cases are rarely black and white. In many instances, for example, the proposed wards *are* susceptible to being exploited by people who offer friendship and warmth in lonely times. Whether due to illness, disability, fear, or anxiety, these elderly men and women *may* be easily influenced and *may* make mistakes in judgment. As each case unfolds, however, the following question must be kept in mind: Should this vulnerability result in a loss of personal and financial autonomy for the elderly man or woman? There are many powerful and loving alternatives to the imposition of unwanted conservatorships and guardianships that support the right of the elderly to "age in place."

In his role as Hearing Officer for the Probate Court of Fulton County, Atlanta, Georgia, Judge James Brock deals primarily with cases pertaining to adult guardianship matters. His opinion on the assignment of legal surrogate decision-makers for the elderly, discussed in an essay entitled "Judicial Decision in Guardianship Cases," is clear:

> If the proposed ward is capable of making decisions, it [should not] matter whether the decisions are good or bad. For example, adult children of a proposed ward may feel a guardian is necessary because their elderly father is writing checks to a young woman. However, the physician or psychologist appointed by the court may determine that the elderly father is aware of his circumstances and is making rational, albeit foolish, decisions . . . [and] a rational person is allowed to make foolish decisions. If a guardianship was established for every person who made a bad decision concerning his or her own property, there would be few people who did not have a guardian and those few would be overburdened serving as guardian for numerous other people. Stupidity is not grounds for the appointment of a guardian.[5]

The major issues we shall discuss range from property-management tests that are biased against the elderly to the compromise of state and federal constitutional protections and due process rights in court and to the assumption that such proceedings are nonadversarial in nature. By following these court battles from the initial filing of the involuntary conservatorship/guardianship petitions to the ultimate court rulings of incompetence, you will gain a greater understanding for the forces driving surrogate decision-making litigation. The intense passion of the elderly to maintain their personal and financial freedom, the vested but unexamined motivations of the petitioners, the pervasive prejudices of judges and attorneys, and the oddly quixotic nature of individual judicial interpretations of these fatally vague state codes—all are factors coloring these unsettling stories of defeat. We begin with the case of Mary Cummings (described briefly in the introduction), a case in which a new widow's property management decisions become "evidence" of mental incompetence.

## COURT TEST OF PROPERTY MISMANAGEMENT BIASED AGAINST THE ELDERLY

*The case of* Cummings v. Stanford *contains no evidence of incompetence other than the court's suggestion that sixty-three-year-old Mary Cummings was incapable of managing her financial resources "due to advanced age and perhaps mental disability." In fact, the only psychologist who testified considered the proposed ward to be competent. In the eyes of the judges in both courts, however, issues of property management became "evidence" of mental incapacity.*

### Case 4.1. Cummings v. Stanford

Within one year of the death of her father in 1988, Marjorie Stanford filed a petition in Probate Court to be appointed guardian over the property of her newly widowed sixty-three-year-old mother, Mary Cummings. When Marjorie's petition was denied, she appealed the case to the Superior Court of Baldwin County, Georgia. The higher court reversed and granted the petition. Mary Cummings appealed the unwanted guardianship to the Court of Appeals. Both Mary Cummings and Marjorie Stanford were represented by attorneys during the subsequent appellate proceeding. What had happened in the year following Mr. Burns' death, and how did the Court of Appeals handle the plea of the now-sixty-five-year-old appellant, Mary Cummings?

According to court documents, prior to his death in May of 1988, Mary's husband had been in charge of household finances. The couple's estate was large enough at that time to generate over $10,000 a year in interest. Since her husband's death, Mary had moved into a $35,000 home she had purchased, while maintaining both her former residence and a house she had inherited from her mother. Mary also took an extensive (and presumably expensive) five-week vacation in Florida with two of her adult sons and "was unable to account for several thousand dollars she had spent." According to the court's summary, "the two sons who accompanied her on the Florida vacation, at the least, were not hesitant to exploit the appellant's resources; one of these sons lived with the appellant, and had suggested that the appellant buy the third house." The sons did not appear in an active role in their mother's defense.

A clinical psychologist testified that he did not consider Mary to be incompetent. He acknowledged, however, that he had not discussed with her the extent and management of her financial resources. On the basis of this evidence, why did Court of Appeals rule against Mary as it did?

*On the Court's Ruling.* The court's opinion of sixty-five-year-old Mary Cummings was grim, indeed. In its written ruling, the Court of Appeals found that "due to advanced age, and perhaps mental disability, the appellant [Mary Cummings] was incapable of managing her financial resources, which would be wasted or dissipated in the absence of property management." Daughter Marjorie was confirmed as guardian over her mother's estate.

In discussing *Cummings* v. *Stanford*, Professor Jan Ellen Rein commented that "the widow had plenty of money, but the court apparently did not consider that she was simply spending money on things that gave her pleasure."[6] Unfortunately, judges in conservatorship/guardianship hearings often measure the proposed ward's spending patterns and property decisions against the norms of middle-age men and women who must watch their capital carefully in order to build reserves for their retirement years. Declaring an older person incompetent because he or she chooses at last to begin spending more and saving less is a painful irony indeed.

# STATES' MISUSE OF THEIR POWER OF *PARENS PATRIAE*

*The cases of* Rice v. Floyd *and* Roberts v. Powers *illustrate the enormous power wielded by the state as "parent of the country,"* parens patriae. *As stated earlier,* parens patriae *is the legal doctrine by which each state assumes "the inherent authority and responsibility of a benevolent society to intervene, even over objection, to protect people who cannot protect themselves."[7] The next two cases demonstrate instances in which the state has elected to extend its power in surprising ways.*

## Case 4.2. Rice v. Floyd

In 1983, Mayme Floyd executed a comprehensive durable power of attorney appointing Guy Duerson Jr., a lawyer, as her attorney-in-fact. The document concluded that its durable powers "shall not be affected by disability." In 1986, Mayme became totally disabled and incapable of caring for herself. Although her daughter, Peggy Rice, petitioned in district court in Kentucky to become Mayme's guardian, the lower court dismissed the petition because Mayme's durable power of attorney made a guardianship unnecessary. Indeed, according to the district court, an attorney-in-fact "fulfilled all the purposes for which a guardian was sought by the petition."

Daughter Peggy submitted a motion for discretionary review of the case to the Court of Appeals and it, too, was denied. The circuit court's judge stated that the mother's personal and financial needs were "provided for in the Power of Attorney executed April 28, 1983." After all, both courts concluded, the durable power of attorney ensured that the appointment would survive Mayme's disability. Peggy Rice appealed the circuit court's ruling to the Supreme Court of Kentucky. Could this court actually rule that the existence of a durable power of attorney could *not* prevent the institution of guardianship proceedings?

*On the Court's Ruling.* Indeed it did. Kentucky's Supreme Court reversed the decisions of the circuit and appellate courts. It ruled that "the durable power of attorney [in Kentucky] is not a substitute for the appointment of a guardian. The existence of a durable power of attorney cannot prevent the institution of guardianship proceedings." Only one Supreme Court Justice dissented. He argued that when it created the durable power of attorney, the General Assembly had provided the means by which an individual, while competent, could arrange for the handling of his or her affairs should he or she become incompetent. According to the dissenting justice, an individual's decline into incompetence should neither automatically terminate a durable power of attorney nor mandate the appointment of a guardian.

> Medical science has extended the limitations on human existence to the point where many of us will now linger long in a twilight zone of incompetency and disability. Statutes such as KRS 386.093 were enacted to permit those of us who want some measure of control over what will happen in our lives when we can no longer manage our own affairs. If the legislature permits us such self-determination, as it has done at least in part by the durable power of attorney statute, there is no reason for us to force our courts into the "big brother" role by mandating guardianship for the disabled. First, the person seeking guardianship status should have to prove that such is necessary. KRS 387.605 gives preference to the daughter, Peggy Rice, as the person to be appointed if we force a guardianship on Mayme Floyd when such is unnecessary. It is quite possible that Ms. Floyd's purpose in executing the durable power of attorney was to prevent just such eventuality.

Surprisingly, the word "durable" gained a new conditional meaning when used in the context of a conservatorship or guardianship proceeding—at least in the state of Kentucky.

## Case 4.3. Roberts v. Powers

Lois LaRue Powers had resided in Oklahoma for sixty-eight years with her husband, George H. Powers, and the bulk of her substantial real and personal property was there. During a visit to sister Helen LaRue Roberts in Arkansas, Lois found herself the subject of litigation as her sister petitioned the Probate Court there to become guardian of her person and estate. Although Mr. Powers agreed that his wife's "mental condition unquestionably requires a guardianship," he bitterly opposed his wife's move to Arkansas and opposed the imposition of a guardianship in any state but her lifelong home state of Oklahoma.

The Probate Court in Garland County dismissed Mrs. Roberts' petition. Court records show that this decision was "based on the Court's finding that when Mrs. Roberts brought Mrs. Powers to Hot Springs [Arkansas], Mrs. Powers lacked the capacity to change her residence or domicile from Oklahoma to Arkansas." Undeterred, Helen LaRue Roberts appealed her case to the Supreme Court of Arkansas. How did the court rule?

*On the Court's Ruling.* In a decision rendered on November 16, 1992, the Supreme Court of Arkansas reversed the Probate Court's findings and ruled that the lower court could establish guardianships of Lois LaRue Powers' person and estate. Justice Newbern wrote:

> It is our view, that Mrs. Powers' mere physical presence in Garland County is a proper basis of jurisdiction of her person and estate. Jurisdiction to be exercised by a state through its courts of a person or property is established by mere presence. . . . That the General Assembly has not restricted guardianship jurisdiction to the domicile of the prospective ward makes sense. If an incapacitated person is in this State and in need of the protection of guardianship proceedings our courts should not have to decline jurisdiction due to the fact that the person in need is domiciled elsewhere.

At first glance, it would seem logical that the state of Oklahoma—the state in which Lois LaRue Powers had resided with her competent spouse—would have judicial control of Lois's personal and financial affairs when court intervention was deemed to be necessary. At second glance, this would continue to seem "correct," but it is not so. As this case demonstrates, the state in which a petition is filed may extend its power as *parens patriae* to establish guardianships over elderly people who are visiting from another state, even against the wishes of competent husbands or wives.

# PETITIONERS' MOTIVES OR COMPETING INTERESTS ARE NOT INVESTIGATED BY THE COURT—AND SHOULD BE

*There is one key assumption underlying involuntary conservator-ship/guardianship proceedings in America, namely, that no conservator or guardian will ever be appointed against the wishes of an elderly individual unless the appointment is in that person's best interests. In direct contradiction to this assumption is the reality that petitions may not stem from this benevolent motive at all, as is clear in the four cases which follow. In none of the four does the hearing judge evaluate the petitioner's motives or competing interests.*

## Case 4.4. In re Tyrell

Walter Tyrell, eighty-five, had diligently planned for his own personal security. He had prepaid his burial expenses and guaranteed his well-being by contracting with a rest home for his care until death. In the two years prior to the filing of involuntary guardianship proceedings against him, Walter had spent almost half of his remaining estate, including a $2,000 gift to a widow in need. Court documents confirmed his customary generosity to friends. Walter's remaining estate assets consisted of $12,000 worth of bank stock bequeathed in his will to his sister-in-law. However, when return of the stock was demanded, the sister-in-law instigated an involuntary guardianship proceeding against Mr. Tyrell.

A brief hearing was held. No independent inquiry by court-appointed physicians was conducted, although the court itself reported that Walter Tyrell had an exceptionally alert, keen mind and a good memory. Why did the court rule against him?

*On the Court's Ruling.* Evidence relating to Tyrell's demeanor held sway. According to the records, the court relied upon the testimony of the *petitioner's* physicians—men who had given Mr. Tyrell a fifteen-minute examination in the jury room just before the hearing. Their report was remarkable for its ageist bias: "[Walter Tyrell's] smile is at times not normal; his eyes do not focus properly at all times; his gait and reflexes are not normal; and . . . he is not laying his cane aside but dropping it."[8]

In spite of his astute planning for his own care, Walter's generosity to friends was found to be conclusive evidence of his incapacity to manage his own property. An analysis of this case in the *Yale Law Journal* went to the heart of the matter:

Since Mr. Tyrell had already provided for his own personal care, the only real function of the court-appointed guardian—another relative—will be to conserve the estate, thereby insuring a sizable inheritance. This result seems to contradict the premises of a doctrine couched solely in terms of benefit to the ward."[9]

## Case 4.5. *Cornia* v. *Cornia*

After her husband's death, eighty-one-year-old Fuchsia Fern Cornia moved from their ranch in Utah to a trailer adjacent to her son Jerry's home in Weston, Idaho. Although later testifying that she could not remember having done so, Fuchsia soon executed both a trust agreement and a deed to a lot given to her by her mother to two sons, Jerry and Don (two of seven adult children). On the same day, she executed a will leaving almost all of her property to Jerry and Don. Fuchsia explained her inability to recall the transactions by saying she was, at the time in question, "signing papers by the bushel" to settle and administer her late husband's estate. Lonely in Weston, Fuchsia visited a daughter in Arizona and ultimately moved to be near a second daughter in Utah. Her statement that she would rather live there in a rest home with other elderly people than return to live with her sons in Weston "appears to have given offense to her sons." Hostilities escalated.

"Before leaving for Arizona," court records affirm, "Mrs. Cornia [had withdrawn] approximately $9,000 from her savings account in Evanston after she learned that Mrs. Don Cornia had been making withdrawals without her consent. Upon her return from Arizona, Mrs. Cornia requested that her sons give her the certificates of deposit which were in their possession. This was refused and the sons instituted these proceeding to have a guardian appointed. . . ."

Fuchsia and her daughters opposed the guardianship petition. Two pieces of evidence were introduced: (a) testimony by a son-in-law that Fuchsia Cornia could be easily imposed upon by those in whom she had confidence, and (b) expert testimony presented by a doctor that Fuchsia was suffering from arteriosclerosis (hardening of the arteries), a disease that "normally increases as one grows older." Why did the court rule against Mrs. Cornia?

*On the Court's Ruling.* Fuchsia's doctor helped the court reach its decision by stating that "in his opinion Mrs. Cornia was senile to a greater degree than was normal for a person her age"—whatever "normal senility" might be.

He testified . . . that she was extremely hard of hearing, had poor eyesight, and suffered from arteriosclerosis, a disease which had a particular effect upon the brain and diminishes the ability to reason; and that this normally increases as one grows older.

The court held that the evidence of Fuchsia Cornia's "senility" was sufficient to warrant the appointment of a guardian to "safeguard the interests" of the elderly woman. The key issue raised and decided was Fuchsia's incompetency "in recent months and that particularly within the past two months by reason of her old age and physical infirmities." As Fuchsia Fern Cornia, Incompetent, she lost her right to personal and financial autonomy for the remainder of her days. The Supreme Court of Utah also reversed a lower-court ruling that had nullified the trust agreement that left almost all of her property to her sons—a document she could not remember having written or signed. No questions were raised concerning the son's competing interests in conserving Fuchsia Cornia's estate.

## Case 4.6. Conservatorship of Earl B.

Earl B., described by the court investigator as a belligerent, troublesome man, had focused much of his adult life on a seemingly endless lawsuit, and "his obsession with the case appeared to lead him into one difficulty after another." In 1984, he granted his daughter power of attorney to settle his nested lawsuits. He revoked the power within six months. Earl's daughter, fearing "that he will dissipate all of his assets in attempting to reopen the lawsuits," petitioned for a conservatorship. According to the California probate court's investigator, Earl was capable of managing his own care without assistance but seemed unconcerned with money and was confused or forgetful about his financial situation. The investigator recommended a conservatorship of the estate to protect the elderly man's assets.

The questions facing the court were complex. Did Earl B. need protection from himself? Should he be allowed to continue the obsessive pattern of litigation that had captured his fascination—and perhaps gave meaning to his life—for most of his adult years? Why did the court rule against Earl?

*On the Court's Ruling.* The court declared Earl B. to be an incompetent man whose capacity for financial decision-making was insufficient. His passion for litigation was abruptly and artificially extinguished by the ruling, but his daughter's inheritance was protected. A year later, according to the records, the probate court investigator looked in on then-eighty-year-old Earl B. and found a broken man who seemed confused, slovenly, and incoherent.

Pointed questions are asked by Lawrence Friedman and Mark Savage, authors of a study involving this case: "Would society decide to 'protect' him this way if he were twenty-five years younger? Are we really protecting Earl B. here, or his daughter and the estate?"[10] As Friedman and Savage conclude, "Does this mean that the original decision was correct? That allegations in the petition proved prophetic? Or did the process itself hurry Earl B. along on the road to ruin?"[11]

## Case 4.7. In re Estate of Liebling

Jeanne Gardner had successfully petitioned the Circuit Court of Winnebago County, Illinois, to have her father, Max Liebling, declared incompetent and incapable of managing his estate and person. According to material presented in extended hearings, Max was a controlled diabetic who had suffered several small strokes from generalized arteriosclerosis. Nonetheless, the alleged incompetent Max fought the lower court's ruling. His plea to the Appellate Court of Illinois was supported by the testimony of several business associates, two personal physicians, a trust officer who had known Mr. Liebling for many years, and the accountant who had worked for him for fifty years.

According to court transcripts, Max's accountant "testified as to her observations of the respondent over these years, including the recent months. Following the stroke in April, she had seen the respondent once in June and once in September and she was of the opinion that the respondent was capable of handling his ordinary business affairs." A second business acquaintance agreed.

> He testified that he consulted with the respondent in regard to the construction of a motel which the respondent had previously undertaken; that he came to Rockford nearly every weekend during the two-year period commencing in July, 1966, and saw the respondent on virtually all of these trips and discussed the project with him; that the respondent took an active part in all of these discussions; and that his memory was good and he was capable of managing his ordinary business and affairs as a prudent man.

Even though they were represented in the proceeding by Max's son Alvin as attorney, neither Max nor his wife nor his youngest daughter elected to testify. Their decision provoked the court's observation that "where facts material to the issues are within the knowledge of a party to the cause and the opportunity is afforded such party for the disclosure of such facts but is not availed of, a presumption arises that such evidence, if given, would have been unfavorable to him."

At the conclusion of most of the testimony, the court ordered a psychiatrist to examine Max and testify concerning his expert opinions. The psychiatrist, having seen the proposed ward *only once*, stated that

> the respondent was unable to answer certain types of questions, indicating to the witness that the respondent was suffering from a severe organic brain syndrome; that he was not suffering from any psychosis; and that the condition, as he, the psychiatrist observed it, was progressive and irreversible. It was his opinion that the respondent was not capable of handling his estate.

*On the Court's Ruling.* The long court hearings, lasting from June of 1968 through February of 1970, led to the judgment that Max Liebling was incapable of managing his estate and person. Max's incompetence was not proven by eccentric behavior, however, nor was it proven by any dissipation of his estate or by any demonstrated inability on his part to hire experts to help him manage his affairs. His incompetence was "proven" by his impaired health.

According to court records, the protective proceeding had little to do with Max Liebling, who alleged that "the petition was brought in bad faith, not to conserve his, the respondent's estate, but to thwart his wishes as to the manner in which his estate should be managed." The legal battle was waged over control of the wealth he had amassed. "The basis for the litigation was the dispute between the members of his family with reference to what was the appropriate manner of managing his estate."

# VAGUE OR NONEXISTENT DEFINITIONS OF KEY LEGAL CONCEPTS

*The following four cases illustrate the fact that the very concepts driving conservatorship/guardianship determinations are so vaguely defined as to offer little or no protection for the autonomy interests of proposed wards and conservatees. As emphasized by the United States Supreme Court in* Grayned v. City of Rockford:

> *A vague law impermissibly delegates basic policy matters to policemen, judges, and juries for resolution on an ad hoc and subjective basis, with the attendant dangers of arbitrary and discriminatory application.*

*Because the definitions of key legal concepts used in conservatorship and guardianship proceedings (such as "incompetence," "incapacity" and "undue influence") are too broad and too vague, judges now have*

*almost total discretion to decide whether proposed wards meet their per-*
*sonal conceptualizations of these terms. According to the U.S. Supreme*
*Court in* Connally *v.* General Const. Co., *when terms of a statute are so*
*vague as to compel "men of common intelligence" to guess at their mean-*
*ings and disagree about their application in court, the first essential of*
*due process of law is violated.*[12]

## Case 4.8. Guardianship of Mr. S.

Eighty-eight-year-old Mr. S. had accrued an estate valued at $153,000.
When he decided to give his money away to friends rather than to family
members, his stepson filed a petition for guardianship. The *ad litem*'s
report to the court confirmed the elderly man's ability to take care of his
financial affairs. "It is evident that Mr. S. does have a great deal of understanding of what is going on around him," the report began. "However,
he does clearly suffer from a lack of judgment."

What was the *ad litem*'s evidence to support Mr. S.'s "lack of judgment"? It was a simple statement from a nurse reflecting Mr. S.'s opinion:
"As the head nurse . . . indicated, he doesn't see why he shouldn't be
allowed to give away all his money since it is his." Mr. S. argued vigorously with the *ad litem* attorney and even submitted the name of an
acceptable guardian should one be deemed necessary, but the court ruled
against Mr. S. Why?

*On the Court's Ruling.* Court records did not provide specific details
concerning the manner in which the proposed ward demonstrated a lack
of capacity. Nonetheless, the court declared Mr. S. to be incompetent and
awarded full guardianship over the person and estate to his stepson. The
*ad litem*'s report, which mirrored the normative attitude that family members be given priority in matters of inheritance even if the transfer is
*against* the stated wishes of the elder, clearly won the day. In discussing
this case, Bulcroft, Kielkopf, and Tripp commented that they were

> struck by the general failure of the probate records or the courts to doc-
> ument incompetency. . . . Given the stated intent of the law to uphold
> individual rights, this is somewhat baffling. This case . . . serves to
> highlight the general level of competency of Mr. S. He was able to con-
> verse at length with the *ad litem* attorney, waive his own presence at his
> hearing, and make his preferences known concerning selection of a
> guardian. . . . Nonetheless, Mr. S was deemed incompetent by the
> court.[13]

As long as conservatorship and guardianship codes lack precise functional definitions of "incompetence" or "incapacity," the specific factors

leading courts to make surrogate decision-making appointments over the vulnerable elderly will not be documented.

## Case 4.9. Stangier v. Stangier

George Stangier filed proceedings in Umatilla County, Oregon, for the appointment of a full guardianship over his allegedly incompetent seventy-three-year-old father, George Stangier Sr. "The sole issue in this proceeding," the court stated, "is whether George Stangier is incompetent within the meaning of the statute authorizing the appointment of a guardian for the person and estate of an incompetent." George Sr. testified on his own behalf. He acknowledged that he needed physical assistance upon occasion as a result of two accidents: a knee injury suffered when he was sixty-seven, and a cerebral thrombosis that had paralyzed the muscles of one eye nine years earlier.

Evidence supporting George Sr.'s firm belief in his capacity to manage his own affairs was given by the attorney who had represented his ex-wife in a divorce proceeding during the year of the guardianship litigation. The attorney testified that "there wasn't any question in my mind, but what he was oriented. . . . My opinion is that he is able to manage his affairs." A psychiatrist who examined George Sr. also testified that Mr. Stangier was quite capable of managing his business affairs.

Conflicting testimony was presented by Mr. Stangier's long-time physician and his accountant:

> Mr. Stangier's accountant for almost thirty years testified that in his opinion Mr. Stangier could not "manage his own affairs by himself." Mr. Stangier's physician for at least thirty years, a man seventy-five years of age, testified to specific instances in which Mr. Stangier appeared confused concerning important affairs. His opinion was that Mr. Stangier was not "capable of carrying on ordinary business."

The circuit court determined that the evidence did establish George Sr.'s incompetence and appointed the petitioning son as guardian. In an attempt to have the unwanted guardianship overturned, the elder Mr. Stangier brought the case before the Supreme Court of Oregon and lost. Why?

*On the Court's Ruling.* In affirming the lower court's ruling, the Supreme Court stated that " 'Incompetent' includes any person who, by reason of mental illness, mental deficiency, advanced age, disease, weakness of mind or any other cause, *is unable unassisted to properly manage and take care of himself or his property*" (court's emphasis). The court thus focused on the knee injury which left Mr. Stangier "probably . . .

unable completely to care for himself physically." Because the evidence presented by each side was conflicting, the court relied upon the decision of the lower circuit court and found George Stangier Sr. to be incompetent within the meaning of the law.

It is curious that one of the two professionals who testified for the petitioner in this proceeding was the accountant Mr. Stangier had prudently hired to help him with his financial matters for three decades. How is it that an individual's wisdom in finding professional help when it is needed can be used against him or her in these "protective proceedings"?

As they exist today, most conservatorship/guardianship codes require that the elderly be capable of functioning *alone* in all areas of decision-making in order to demonstrate their right to personal and financial freedom. This is an unrealistic standard of autonomy—another destructively vague and artificially defined concept—which all too often permits heir-petitioners to successfully raise the fatal issue of "incapacity" or "incompetence." Judge James Brock warns about conservatorship/guardianship law:

> Since there is no precise definition [of standards of proof driving these incompetency determinations], the same evidence presented to two different judges may produce two different results."[14]

## Case 4.10. Matter of Nelson

Margaret M. Nelson executed a power of attorney in favor of her only child, Bill Nelson, in 1985. When, in May of 1993, eighty-six-year-old Mrs. Nelson realized she would require surgery for a colon obstruction, she opened a joint checking account to permit her son to "pay her bills and transact business while she was hospitalized." According to detailed court records, while Margaret Nelson was in the hospital, Bill took over her financial matters. He changed his mother's bank accounts to joint ownership with survivorship rights, asked her bank to mail all statements to his Texas home, inventoried her safety deposit box, removed all valuables from her farm home, and changed the locks on the house.

Again as described in court documents, when Mrs. Nelson was released from the hospital, Bill placed his mother in a nursing home against her will and refused her requests to be allowed to go home. On October 14, 1993, Margaret was able to sign herself out of the facility with the help of a friend, and quickly revoked her son's power of attorney. Having regained control of her bank accounts, Mrs. Nelson proceeded to organize her life, as court documents revealed:

She arranged for a woman named P. J. Phelps to live with her. She has a neighbor and friend, Sheryl Burnett, who visits her practically every day. Since Mrs. Nelson has poor eyesight, Mrs. Burnett has been assisting her with her financial affairs, and drives her to the bank, doctor's office, and other places. We gather from the record that Mrs. Nelson has several hundred thousand dollars of income producing assets. Even after her surgeries, she has dealt directly with her tax preparer and her stock broker.

Within a week of Margaret's return to her home, Bill Nelson petitioned the court to be named guardian of his mother's person and conservator of her estate. Mrs. Nelson filed a motion seeking to dismiss her son's application. The issues to be decided were those of *capacity*, which in Missouri "has to do with the ability to handle basic requirements for food, shelter, safety and health," and *disability*, which "has to do with ability to manage financial resources." After listening to contradictory testimony at the December 9 hearing concerning Mrs. Nelson's competency, the trial judge entered a judgment of partial incapacity and total disability and appointed the public administrator to be Mrs. Nelson's guardian.

Mrs. Nelson filed a motion for a new trial on December 30, 1993, and on March 7, 1994, filed a motion for reconsideration. Both motions were denied. Mrs. Nelson brought her appeal before the Missouri Court of Appeals, Western District. On January 24, 1995, the appellate court reversed the guardianship of the person, but concluded that a conservatorship over the estate was warranted. Why?

*On the Court's Ruling.* Documents filed with the Court of Appeals reveal that Mrs. Nelson had not suffered any difficulty caring for herself or living alone prior to her surgeries in May/June of 1993. Other than very poor eyesight, her health was fine. A psychiatric evaluation ordered by her son while Mrs. Nelson was convalescing in the nursing home suggested "some impairment of her judgment and insight." A second evaluation

found Mrs. Nelson at first to be articulate and knowledgeable, and then found further into the examination that Mrs. Nelson had a tendency to become confused and to lose focus when given matters of some complexity to think through. For instance, when asked to count backward from twenty, Mrs. Nelson was able to make it only to twelve before erring. Dr. Radom's conclusion was that Mrs. Nelson was suffering from moderate dementia, probably of the Alzheimer's type.

After Margaret Nelson had secured her release from the nursing home in October of 1993, she had asked to be evaluated by Dr. Emmanuel

Pardo, Associate Professor of Psychiatry at Kansas University Medical Center. His conclusions differed from those undertaken while Margaret was convalescing from multiple surgeries:

> Mrs. Nelson had been suffering from reversible dementia and delirium which resulted from her health complications, her pain, and the anxiety related to the surgery and the aftermath of the surgery. Dr. Pardo found her memory at the time he examined her to be no worse than that of others who are eighty-six years old and in similar situations. Although he found her to have memory impairment, in his opinion her impairment was not of such a degree that it interfered with her ability to evaluate her circumstances and make decisions in her best interest. . . . Dr. Pardo stated that he believed that as Mrs. Nelson continued her recovery from the trauma of surgery, her confusion was being resolved. Dr. Pardo testified in his opinion Mrs. Nelson is still intellectually capable of evaluating, receiving and processing information and making decisions in her best interest.

Testimony concerning Mrs. Nelson's financial prowess was offered by employees of her bank, by her stockbroker of nine years, and by Mrs. Burnett, the friend who helped her with certain money matters. The bank employees stated that Mrs. Nelson seemed dependent on Mrs. Burnett, had transferred substantial amounts of money between accounts, and had occasionally "cashed checks for significant amounts of cash. In one instance, she cashed a check for $1,000." In contrast, Kevin Bell, Margaret Nelson's long-time stockbroker, testified that "she always seemed to him to be capable of handling her financial matters herself." Mrs. Burnett also confirmed that Mrs. Nelson "was capable of taking care of her business herself."

When questioned in court late in the afternoon, a very tired Mrs. Nelson explained the prudent reason for her financial transfers between bank accounts: "to keep all account balances below the $100,000.00 figure for which federal deposit insurance is provided." She was familiar with her stock holdings and with the fact that trusts had already been established for her son and grandson. According to the appellate court records, "her testimony [in earlier proceedings] was fully consistent with the proposition that she is able to make her own health care decisions and understands her needs from a health standpoint."

Unfortunately for Mrs. Nelson, the trial court decided to focus on the lack of trust that seemed to run between mother and son and between Bill Nelson and Mrs. Burnett, his mother's trusted friend. As noted by the Court of Appeals,

the trial court is reluctant to leave Mrs. Nelson in a position where she
is vulnerable to Mrs. Burnett or others. . . . The trial judge was very
uncomfortable with the fact that Mrs. Burnett was reluctant to testify as
to certain matters . . . and her response was to invoke her right to remain
silent under the Fifth Amendment.

The appellate court ruled that the evidence in the trial court transcripts established by clear and convincing evidence that Margaret
Nelson suffered from "some mild to moderate interference with her
powers of reasoning and comprehension as to sophisticated matters, and
matters beyond the routine of daily life."

*On the Court's Ruling.* In affirming the finding of disability, the Court
of Appeals shared the circuit court's concern that others might "take
advantage of Mrs. Nelson in complex financial matters by virtue of her
mild dementia and her poor eyesight." The appellate court, however, disagreed with and reversed the lower court's finding of total disability—a
finding by which the trial court had voided Mrs. Nelson's right to contract, to make inter vivos or testamentary transfers, and to make dispositions of property. They also believed that the trial court had erred in limiting Mrs. Nelson to a personal spending allowance of only $250.00 a
month.

We conclude that the evidence supports a personal spending allowance
of $2,500.00 per month, which Mrs. Nelson should use for the payment
of bills, household expenses, vehicle maintenance, groceries, grooming,
veterinary care for her animals, yard care, colostomy bags, prescrip-
tions, entertainment and other expenses. She should also be entitled to
make gifts to others from her spending allowance. . . . Allowing her to
pay her own regular expenses . . . will allow Mrs. Nelson the dignity of
being able to control the financial affairs of her everyday life.

Ironically, in spite of having thus affirmed that Mrs. Nelson was
capable of managing a complex array of day-to-day financial affairs, the
Court of Appeals declared Margaret M. Nelson to be disabled in terms of
managing the bulk of her life's savings. The Missouri court's 1995 decision is in direct contrast to a Nebraska court's ruling some ten years earlier (see *In re Estate of Wagner*, case 5.1 in chapter 5).

## Case 4.11. In the Matter of Wurm

Martha Wurm was seventy-seven when she and her husband moved from
their Indiana farm so he could enter the hospital and she could live with
her daughter and son-in-law, Marilyn and Aloysious Molargik. Just after

they moved, Martha Wurm and her husband signed a general power of attorney giving Marilyn and Aloysious control of their property and "allowing the Molargiks to dispose of their 160-acre farm and take care of their other personal assets in the same capacity as themselves."

According to court records, Martha's husband soon died and, after the funeral dinner, five of their seven adult children pressured Martha into signing documents naming an Auburn bank as the guardian of her estate. Her assets at the time consisted of the farm, several buildings, an automobile, furniture, personal possessions, and some cash. In a vain attempt to forestall legal difficulties with her own children, Martha entered a petition in court to enjoin the filing of any guardianship action over herself "naming as defendants the aforementioned children and their counsel."

Four days later, as court documents show, three of her sons filed a petition for the appointment of a guardian for the person and the estate of their mother. After consolidating the two separate petitions, the court ruled that Martha Wurm was "incompetent and accordingly incapable of either managing her property or caring for herself by reason of old age, infirmity, and her inability to withstand undue and inappropriate pressures exerted upon her by certain of her children, jointly and severally." Martha appealed her case to the Court of Appeals of Indiana and lost. Why did the court rule against her?

*On the Court's Ruling.* The appellate court supported the finding of the lower court. Even though Martha's personal physician and daughter argued that she was capable of managing her own affairs, her sons' testimony held sway. "Advanced age" (she was seventy-seven) and its attendant "infirmity of confusion," according to the court, made Martha an excellent candidate for forfeiture of personal and financial decision-making. As the following passage taken from appellate records show, however, the Indiana court had difficulty with its decision:

> Through these cases [that we have just discussed] we perceive a general commitment to the principle that the appointment of a guardian over one's estate must be grounded on a finding that the person was unable to reasonably deal with his business affairs because of an impairment in his mental judgment, albeit with the recognition that mental attributes can be affected by physical disabilities. Thus no matter how incapacitated a person may be physically, he still has the option of managing his property through an agent, if the function of his mind is unimpaired. To exclude an evaluation of a person's mental awareness, under the rubrics "old age, infirmity or other incapacity" would make the possibility for a finding of incompetency too broad. Instead the evaluation of whether a person is incompetent should concern his total physiology both physical and mental.

In the case at bar almost no testimony suggested that Martha Wurm was mentally incapable of handling her affairs. Unfortunately for Martha, though, her seven children all disagreed about their mother's decision-making capacity. Because the trial court witnessed the hostile demeanor and attitude of her adult children, the Court of Appeals concluded that Martha was incompetent because she could not withstand the undue influence exerted upon her by certain of her children. In a strongly worded dissenting opinion, Judge Staton focused on what he believed to be a major weakness in the case against Martha Wurm, namely, insufficient evidence.

The evidence is insufficient to establish a guardianship. The evidence did establish that Mrs. Wurm was an intelligent seventy-seven-year-old lady who had cared for her sick husband before his death and taken care of the family business during his illness. She had seven grown children. She was good about writing letters to her children and letting them know what she was doing. Her letters are well written and very rational. The one hundred sixty acre farm is rented . . . at twenty dollars an acre. Mr. Wurm, before his death, had someone in Auburn do the family taxes. There is no evidence which would show that Mrs. Wurm could not follow the same procedure with the family tax return. Mrs. Wurm knew the balances in her bank account and prepared the necessary checks to pay bills. She knew the amount and location of her property. She was mentally competent by any rational standard. She was competent under the statutory standard.

Mrs. Wurm walked a flight of stairs to visit her doctor regularly. She took her medicine as directed and paid her bills promptly. She had back trouble and could not drive an automobile, but a daughter . . . furnished the needed transportation. She was living with her daughter, Marilyn, who looked after any needs that Mrs. Wurm could not satisfy for physical reasons.

The evidence does show that some of Mrs. Wurm's children were worried that she might make a bad judgment in the future when dealing with her property, but none of them could specifically point to any judgment or exercise of will which had harmed their mother or her property. They merely expressed anxieties because she was so good and easy-going. She was seventy-seven years old. She had agreed to sign a consent and waiver to a guardianship right after her husband's death which had been urged upon her by most of her children. Upon reflection, she changed her mind, but most of the children didn't change their minds to insist on a guardianship. Now, Mrs. Wurm finds herself and her property shackled with a guardianship. Her liberty is lost.

The case of *In the Matter of Wurm* reflects a catch-22 situation driven by the vague and ill-defined concept of "undue influence." It is disturbing in its irony since three of the adult children responsible for pressuring their mother into signing financial documents then filed a petition claiming that seventy-seven-year-old Martha Wurm was "incompetent and accordingly incapable of either managing her property or caring for herself by reason of old age, infirmity, and her inability to withstand undue and inappropriate pressures exerted upon her by certain of her children."

# "PROGRESSIVE" CODES CONTAIN VALUE JUDGMENTS

*The case of* Epperson v. Epperson *illustrates the flawed statutory assumption that there are universal and nonageist standards concerning what constitutes the "responsible" or "reasonable" decision required to establish capacity or competence in many state codes. There are no neutral criteria used by the court to determine when a decision or behavior is responsible, effective, or proper. As noted by Professor Jan Ellen Rein, the emphasis should be, instead, on "the reasoning process rather than the information available to the decisionmaker."*[15]

## Case 4.12. Epperson v. Epperson

According to son Robert and reported in case documents, Verner Lee Epperson had become difficult to manage following the second of two strokes. Because Verner's wife believed she could no longer care for her husband, who had driven a car contrary to doctor's orders and was "heavily on sleeping pills" (as quoted in court records), she placed Verner in a nursing home. Mr. Epperson wanted to return to his home, and the institution's officials told Verner's son that they did not have the legal right to keep him there if he did not want to stay. Robert filed for and won a temporary guardianship over the person and property of his father. Verner's appeal to the Superior Court for a reversal of the order was unsuccessful, and the now-seventy-nine-year-old man approached the Court of Appeals of Georgia for help.

The director of nursing at Verner Epperson's nursing home facility confirmed that he needed complete care when he first arrived, but that "he had been classified as a 'minimal assist' for a year or longer, . . . needing 'supervision and some assistance at times.' " He was, she reported, both oriented and lucid. According to court documents, she testified that "he can ambulate, he can walk, he can feed himself, he can dress himself, if he falls he can get up, if his shoe comes off he can put it back on, you know, he can do all of those things, but I think he would need some supervision. . . ." He was, she concluded, ready to return home with assistance.

The charge nurse at the convalescent home agreed. Mr. Epperson should be allowed to go home once home assistance could be arranged for him. A court-appointed psychologist concurred with the opinion that Verner Epperson could be managed at home in a less restrictive environment, despite, as court documents state, "family concerns of potential abusiveness towards Mrs. Epperson if he returned home."

Court records show that Mr. Epperson also testified on his own behalf. He affirmed that he had lived at the same address since 1937 and loved his home. In hopes of securing his freedom, Verner agreed that "if his wife stayed with him after he went home, he would 'let her be boss,' and 'do what she says.' " Nonetheless, the Court of Appeals affirmed the lower courts' rulings against Verner. Why?

*On the Court's Ruling.* The court found by clear and convincing evidence that, "because of advanced age and physical disability, and Mr. Epperson's apparent lack of understanding of the 'significant responsible decisions' he would otherwise need to make himself *prior* to leaving [the nursing home] in order to ensure his very survival, a guardian should be appointed over his person and property." Verner's unfortunate personality condemned him to a lifetime in the nursing home as the legally incapacitated ward of his son.

As officials at the nursing home had previously agreed, the court noted that Mr. Epperson needed assistance and was "headstrong." He had disregarded the doctor in the past (driving a car and abusing sleeping pills), and both his son and his wife had testified that they could not control him prior to the time they placed him in the nursing home. Should Verner be allowed to return home, son Robert swore under oath, his mother would have to move away "due to the stress and potential for verbal abuse." Clearly the petitioners had compelling reasons to oppose Verner's return to the family residence, and Verner had equally compelling reasons for wanting to live out his years in his beloved home.

What is black and white in this case is separated by many shades of gray. Mr. Epperson, who was seventy-nine at the time the trial court heard his case, may not have understood the "significant responsible decisions" needed to arrange his at-home care, and he definitely could not "survive independently without any type of assistance." Nevertheless, should the control of an aging, verbally abusive, physically vulnerable man automatically call for the sledgehammer of legal guardianship when less restrictive alternatives are available?

# ROLES OF COURT-APPOINTED OFFICIALS SHIFT

*Typically, an elderly person who is targeted by an involuntary conservatorship or guardianship petition has never been party to any serious court proceeding. In the following case, described in Bayles and McCartney's Pulitzer Prize-winning 1987 series for the Associated Press, the proposed ward was assigned an attorney to vigorously defend her right to live an independent life. In a proceeding that took only a few minutes to complete, Billie's attorney helped secure an unwanted guardianship over her.*

## Case 4.13. Guardianship of Billie

Billie, a fiercely independent seventy-four-year-old Fort Lauderdale woman, felt confident of her ability to counter a petition brought by social workers for a conservatorship of her person and estate. Two attorneys, two social workers, and a probate master (an attorney deputized to serve as a judge) held the hearing to determine Billie's competency. "The hearing came about only because one psychiatrist on the three-person examining committee found her competent."[16] Billie was represented by an attorney and mindful of her right to be heard. At the hearing, Billie

> sat at the table, trying to joke with the social workers and lawyers sitting around her. "Are you talking about me?" she asked the strangers who said they were there to help.
> The man beside her, her lawyer she was told, softly explained that she needed a guardian, someone who would handle the everyday worries.
> "Does this mean I won't be able to go back to where I live?" the seventy-four-year-old woman asked. "I still want to get out and take care of my house and do shopping. I feel well enough to be on my own."[17]

The attorney who was charged with Billie's defense had initially waived the hearing, telling the court that Billie was arrogant and "in my lay opinion she appeared to be in the beginning-to-middle stages of Alzheimer's disease." He concluded that "she can fool you at the beginning, but after a while you can tell she's incompetent." No court-appointed mental health professional interviewed Billie. Why did the court rule against her?

*On the Court's Ruling.* Although "bright and quick-witted in conversation," Billie was found to be incompetent because she hesitated when asked by the gathered strangers if she owned her home, could not remember the name of her bank, and could not recall the names of the last several presidents. The entire proceeding took only a few minutes. Shortly after the appointment of a guardian was made, Billie was moved from her beloved small apartment and placed in a boarding home. The court had no further contact with her beyond required paper work. Her request to return to her apartment was not granted, and Billie's guardian, a retired man with several other wards, said a return is not likely in the future:

> "In talking with the social workers, they don't think she is on the way to recovery," [he] said. "Right now, she's being well taken care of and that's the most important thing."

## DUE PROCESS RIGHTS AND CONSTITUTIONAL PROTECTIONS COMPROMISED IN HEARINGS

*As noted previously, criminals in America have greater due process rights (i.e., the right to be heard in court) than do the elderly in involuntary conservatorship/guardianship proceedings.* In re Guardianship of Bockmuller *focuses on a woman whose right to hire an attorney and try to overturn her unwanted guardianship is stripped from her by the court's adjudication of incapacity. The proposed ward in* Matter of Guardianship of Larson *tries to overturn his unwanted permanent guardian and conservator by testifying that his Fourth Amendment rights against unlawful search and seizure had been violated. The third and most controversial case of* Smith v. Smith *deals with the imposition of a guardianship over an adult who found meaning in an unpopular political organization. The case is argued—unsuccessfully—that fundamental First Amendment rights contained in our Constitution cannot be sacrificed in a protective proceeding because*

> the Constitution protects expression and association without regard to the race, creed, or political or religious affiliation of the members of the group which invokes its shield, or to the truth, popularity, or social utility of the ideas and beliefs which are offered.[18]

### Case 4.14. In re Guardianship of Bockmuller

On November 9, 1989, Mary B. Bockmuller was adjudicated incapacitated and found to require a guardian both of the person and of the estate. Judith A. Bockmuller was appointed guardian of the person and Joann Salmon guardian of Mary's property. Mary remained in her home, cared for by Judith and Judith's husband, Raymond, until being placed in a congregate living facility on the advice of Mary's family physician. While in the facility, Mary engaged the services of an attorney recommended by a friend to assist her in her determination to go home. Court records do not indicate Judith and Raymond's reaction as Mary's new lawyer, William E. Reischmann Sr., petitioned for restoration of Mary's capacity, but the new petition was denied.

*On the Court's Ruling.* The trial court found "as a matter of law there was no conflict or adverse interest or any other basis for removal of the guardians." That Mary wanted to leave her "retirement home" and go to her own home did not sway the court. Mary's attorney continued to bring proceedings before the court throughout 1990, but to no avail. Mary Bockmuller died on February 6, 1991. When the Circuit Court of Pinellas County authorized payment of attorney fees to attorney William Reischmann Sr., who had represented Mary's efforts to remove her two guardians, Judith A. Bockmuller and Joann Salmon joined forces and brought suit to appeal the order. It is this ruling, issued in the summer of 1992, that added a paradoxical flavor to the proceedings:

> 1. Section 744.3215(1)(l) does give Mary the right to counsel. However, Mary's right to contract was removed by the order determining her incapacity. Although Mary has a right to counsel, that counsel must be contracted for by one of the guardians or appointed by the court.... Because Mary's right to contract was removed, she had no power to contract with Mr. Reischmann to represent her in any proceedings.
> 2. By the time the trial court "approved" Mr. Reischmann as Mary's attorney [which it had], the court had already ruled that there was no conflict or adverse interest or other basis for the removal of the guardians. The attorney's fees charged by Mr. Reischmann for time spent for his continued attempts to accomplish a result the trial court had previously ruled against, only served to deplete Mary's estate and served no benefit whatsoever to Mary or her estate.

When ruled an incapacitated person in the eyes of the State of Florida, Mary Bockmuller was stripped of the power to use her money to fight her unwanted institutionalization. The right to an attorney can never be denied a defendant in a criminal case, but it is often denied in these comparatively benign protective proceedings. Ironically, the only people who retained the legal right to use Mary's estate to hire a new attorney and sue to remove her guardians were her own guardians.

## Case 4.15. Matter of Guardianship of Larson

On November 28, 1993, eighty-three-year-old Harold Oliver Larson, a man with no living parent, spouse, or children, suffered an apparent stroke in his Mandan home and was taken to St. Alexius Hospital in Bismarck, North Dakota. Within two weeks, he was sent to a nursing home in Mandan. Shortly after having been transferred to the convalescent facility, Harold wrote a $4,000 check payable to "cash" and gave it to a friend, Lillian Ruff. His estate at the time was approximately $190,000.

Disturbed by his brother's behavior, Warren Larson petitioned the county court to appoint a permanent guardian of the person and conservator of the estate for Harold Larson, and to appoint himself as his brother's temporary guardian and conservator on an emergency basis. At the *ex parte* hearing, held with no notice of the hearing to Harold or to his attorney, Warren introduced evidence that Harold had written the check without getting an accounting of the money, had no recollection of having authorized Lillian Ruff and attorney John Gosbee to change the locks on his home, and had been diagnosed as "suffering from dementia."

The court granted Warren Larson's request. According to court records, the court specifically found that Harold Larson "is susceptible to influence from third parties which may be detrimental to him and to his estate." After conducting a full evidentiary hearing, the lower court also entered an order appointing a public administrator as permanent guardian and conservator for Harold. Harold asserted that his rights had been violated when the court appointed a temporary guardian and conservator over him without giving him or his attorney an opportunity to be heard. He also claimed that a videotape and photographs of his cluttered home—used in court as evidence of his need for a guardian and conservator—were made without his consent and without a warrant, thus violating his Fourth Amendment rights against unlawful search and seizure under the federal constitution (rights made applicable to the states by the Fourteenth Amendment). He appealed these actions to the Supreme Court of North Dakota. On April 13, 1995, the Supreme Court ruled against him. Why?

*On the Court's Ruling.* The court's response to the issue of a possible violation of Harold's Fourth Amendment rights underscores the heavy burden carried by a proposed ward who attempts to fight the body of these ever-changing laws. From the court's written opinion:

> In support of his argument that the exclusionary rule should be applied to these proceedings, Harold Larson cites *Conservatorship and Estate of Tedesco*, 17 Cal.App4th 758, 22 Cal.App.4th 662, 27 Cal.App.4th 1274, 21 Cal.Rptr.2d 763 (1 Dist. 1993), review granted and opinion

superseded by *Conservatorship of Tedesco*, 860 P.2d 1181, 24 Cal.Rptr.2d 235 (1993), and judgment affirmed by *Conservatorship of Susan T.*, 8 Ca.4th 1005, 36 Ca.Rptr.2d 40, 884 P.2d 988 (1994). In *Tedesco*, the California Court of Appeals for the First District ruled that the exclusionary rule applies to involuntary conservatorship proceedings. The court specifically held that photographic evidence obtained by a social worker who entered a conservatee's house in violation of the Fourth Amendment must be excluded as evidence in the proceedings to appoint a conservator. However, in December 1994, subsequent to the hearing in this case for appointment of a permanent guardian and conservator for Harold Larson, the California Supreme Court reversed the lower court, and held that the exclusionary rule was not applicable to conservatorship proceedings.

What was *impermissible* as a violation of the Fourth Amendment of the Constitution of the United States when it was done in early 1994 (namely, the gathering of videographic/photographic evidence without consent and without a warrant) became *permissible* by the time Harold's appeal was heard in April of 1995.

Harold's fury that the court imposed an emergency temporary guardianship and conservatorship over him with no notice at all—thus giving him no opportunity to be heard and to speak in his own defense—was also neutralized by North Dakota's Supreme Court. Brother Warren had alleged to the court that an emergency existed. Therefore, according to the codes of North Dakota,

Under Subsection 30.1-28-10(1)(a), N.D.C.C., the court has authority to appoint a temporary guardian "without notice" if "an emergency exists." Under Subsection 30.1-29-08(2), N.D.C.C., the court, "after preliminary hearing and without notice to others," can use a conservator to preserve the property of the person to be protected while a petition for appointment of a conservator or other protective order is pending.

The court refused to address Harold Larson's "other issues which we [the Court] consider devoid of merit and not warranting explanation or discussion."

## Case 4.16. Smith v. Smith

Shortly after attending a series of lectures sponsored by Lyndon LaRouche, Lewis Dupont Smith became deeply involved in the LaRouche organization. A man of substantial wealth, Lewis made large, unsecured loans totaling $212,000 to the political group. His attempt to wire transfer an additional $75,000 to a LaRouche affiliate on April 10,

1985, was voided the next day when his parents and siblings filed a petition for the appointment of a guardian to control his considerable estate. Prior to the initial hearing on his competency, Lewis informed the trial court that he planned to move to Leesburg in order to work for the LaRouche parent organization.

During the arduous sixteen-month guardianship proceeding in Chester County's Court of Common Pleas, Lewis's relatives brought in expert witnesses (a psychiatrist and a psychologist) who testified that he suffered from a "mixed personality disorder with inadequate and immature features." The trial court was convinced that Lewis Dupont Smith could not deal with his financial matters "in even a minimal way, due to the disorganized and unrealistic way he views finances and world events." Furthermore, the court concluded, "he is a target for designing persons and is liable to dissipate his assets, and requires protection of the Court." After all, Lewis had made a bad business investment in 1981, had lost money in the stock market in 1984, and was now giving his money away to a controversial political organization.

Two expert witnesses who testified for Lewis stated their shared opinion that Lewis did not suffer from any mental illness that would impair his ability to manage his own financial affairs. Indeed, as the trial court itself recognized, "a man may do what he pleases with his personal estate during his life. He may beggar himself and his family if he chooses to commit such an act of folly." If this is so, why did the Superior Court of Pennsylvania rule against Lewis Dupont Smith, as it did?

*On the Court's Ruling.* The court ruled that Lewis Dupont Smith should not be permitted to beggar himself because he lacked the capacity to choose "in a voluntary or knowledgeable manner, and in the event he dissipated his assets, he would not be doing so freely or voluntarily." As stated in the court's rulings, Lewis suffered from an "obvious" mental condition that had made him "a victim of the LaRouche organization." What clear and convincing evidence established his incompetency? According to the records of the appellate court which later confirmed the trial court's decision, "the donations or loans he made to the LaRouche organization were manifestations of that incompetency."

The court supported its decision by quoting from President Judge Baldridge's 1947 Pennsylvania Superior Court ruling:

> Whether an alleged incompetent is found to be mentally "confused," "defective," "feeble," or "weak" is not vitally important. If, as here, it appears that one's mind is so affected that as a consequence thereof he is liable to dissipate or lose his property and become the victim of designing persons, the court, if other requirements are met, may appoint [or refuse to remove] a guardian.

Lewis had decided to lavish his time and money on an unpopular organization that "espouses a political ideology that is outside the mainstream." Had he donated his funds to a major political party or to a charity favored by his influential parents, would he have been declared incompetent by any court in America? It is an interesting question. This case is unusual in that it seems to demonstrate the use of guardianship litigation to control those whose political philosophy deviates from the cultural norm. It is, at best, an ominous precedent, for it abridges the individual's First Amendment rights. In *Clients with Destructive and Socially Harmful Choices*, legal scholar Jan Ellen Rein commented:

> The court's own assessment was that "he has a disorganized mind and compensates by setting up an oversimplified view of the world in which he is one of the good guys and 'they' are conspirators bent on mischief. As such he would be and has been an easy target for anyone who pretends to support him in his efforts to combat the bad guys."
> This evaluation could describe many ordinary citizens! Nevertheless, the court adjudged him incompetent to manage his affairs.[19]

# LACK OF AUTOMATIC PROVISION FOR TERMINATION

*Most conservatorships and guardianships end only when the elderly ward dies; a smaller number end when the guardian depletes his or her ward's asset base. This unsettling fact was demonstrated yet again in a 1997 study following sixty-one cases of guardianships that were terminated over a six-year period: "Fifty-two ended due to death of the ward, eight due to depletion of the wards' assets, and one due to the ward moving out of the court's jurisdiction."[20] Lacking the safety net of any automatic provision for termination, adult wards must petition the court and somehow prove they can make "responsible, informed decisions" and because they have, in fact, returned to competency. It is an extremely difficult task for any elderly man or woman who has not been permitted to make such decisions under the aegis of the conservatorship/guardianship, as the case of* Guardianship of Lander *demonstrates.*

## Case 4.17. Guardianship of Lander

In June of 1990, an uncontested guardianship had been placed over Charles H. Lander naming the state's Department of Human Services (DHS) as public guardian over his personal and financial affairs. In June of 1995, Mr. Lander successfully petitioned the Probate Court, Penobscot

County, for termination of the guardianship. Six months later, the Department of Human Services filed a second petition against Charles Lander and was appointed temporary guardian. Following a hearing, "a judgment was entered in February 1996, granting the petition and again appointing DHS as the public guardian."

Determined to have his unwanted guardianship terminated in court, Charles filed a petition in May of 1996, alleging that he was no longer incapacitated. The DHS claimed his petition for termination was insufficient because "it fails to allege any change in circumstances." An attorney and court visitor were appointed to represent Mr. Lander's best interests, but the court ruled that he, as petitioner, bore the burden of proof. When Charles declined to offer specific evidence of his "return to competency," the court entered a judgment denying his petition. A determined Charles Lander brought his case before the Supreme Judicial Court of Maine in May of 1997, appealing the lower court's rulings. Why did the appellate court affirm the trial court's decision?

*On the Court's Ruling.* In arguing his appeal, Charles had relied upon the following language in Maine's Probate Codes:

> Before removing a guardian, accepting the resignation of a guardian, or ordering that a ward's incapacity has terminated, the court, *following the same procedures to safeguard the rights of the ward as apply to a petition for appointment of a guardian*, may send a visitor to the residence of the present guardian and to the place where the ward resides or is detained, to observe conditions and report in writing to the court. (Court's emphasis.)

Charles argued that the statute served to allocate the burden of proof of his continuing incompetence or incapacity to the person who had petitioned for appointment of a guardian—the Department of Human Services. The court agreed that the statute's language was somewhat ambiguous. However, the court also stated that because the legislature had not specifically allocated the burden of proof even in initial guardianship proceedings, the moving party—namely, Mr. Lander as petitioner—must carry the burden of proving the alleged facts in a termination hearing.

Reminding the court of the statutory requirement that "in all review proceedings the welfare of the ward is paramount," Mr. Lander argued that

> because the welfare of the ward is paramount, and because guardianship is a substantial restriction of liberty, the ability to seek its removal should be encouraged. The State point[ed] out, however, that such an unwarranted extrapolation from the comment would subject guardians to the time and expense of defending repeated petitions for termination by wards who have no burden beyond an allegation in the petition.

Thus using its judicial discretion, Maine's highest court ruled that Mr. Lander as petitioner rather than the DHS as guardian would be required to carry the burden of proof. The court then ruled that a preponderance of the evidence proved to its satisfaction that Charles was incapacitated. Having participated in a complex legal battle for his freedom, Charles H. Lander was not able to have the burdensome guardianship terminated.

# JUDICIAL OPINIONS ARE HARD TO APPEAL

*Each involuntary conservatorship/guardianship adjudication in this section reflects more than one of the many problems characteristic of state probate codes in general. The complex case of* In re Conservatorship of Lundgaard *is no exception. At first glance, a conservatorship of person and estate over convalescing eighty-year-old Martha Lundgaard might seem appropriate. Sadly, however, her case demonstrates how conservatorship/guardianship actions can and do develop a life of their own as various participants react to the system of law rather than to the needs of the proposed ward of advanced years. Even after Martha Lundgaard demonstrated, during a hard-fought and difficult appeal, that the probate court had not met the statutory requirement by describing specific evidence of her "incapacity," her effort to overturn her unwanted conservatorship was unsuccessful.*

## Case 4.18. In re Conservatorship of Lundgaard

While seventy-nine-year-old Martha Lundgaard was convalescing first in a hospital and subsequently in a rehabilitation facility from injuries she sustained in a fall at her home, her good friend Marvin Attleson helped her handle her financial affairs. Martha had revoked the power of attorney she had previously assigned to her sister for reasons that are not discussed, although the court wondered if "Attleson may have influenced her" to take this action. Concerned about Attleson's attention to Martha, a social worker at the rehabilitation center referred the case to Adult Protective Services in August and November of 1988. Protective Services recommended pursing a conservatorship for Martha Lundgaard but nothing more was done.

On March 20, 1989, Marvin Attleson filed a conservatorship petition in the District Court, Hennepin County, Minnesota—signed by a consenting Martha—requesting that he be appointed as conservator of her person and estate. At a hearing one month later (and for reasons not included in appellate court records) the petition was dismissed. On May

24, 1989, a social worker filed a petition requesting the appointment of Thomas J. Lee (a professional conservator) as conservator of Martha Lundgaard's person and estate. A mandated report filed by a court-appointed visitor to Martha "reached no conclusion as to the necessity for appointment of a conservator," but her physician supported the conservatorship arrangement. The hearing was attended by two attorneys representing Martha Lundgaard, two of her sisters, three friends, a niece, Marvin Attleson, and three witnesses for the petitioner. None of Martha's relatives testified—it is not clear whether this was by choice or as a result of decisions made by attorneys and court officials.

According to court records, Martha's adversaries testified that she had

> short-term memory loss; she is suffering from depression and possible senile dementia; she denies her physical incapacities; she asks for help with her finances and does not understand them; and she is inconsistent and "confusing" when making decisions. She has failed to pay her [rehabilitation center's] bill, which exceeded $10,000 at the time of the hearing.

Both Marvin Attleson and a former student of Martha's testified for her in opposition to the petition. Her former student stated that

> during weekly phone conversations and monthly visits, Lundgaard did not seem confused, talked about her therapy and about trying to walk, recognized her limitations and did not discuss financial matters or ask for help in paying bills.

Mr. Attleson testified that Martha Lundgaard could manage her own affairs. Since Martha's voluntary petition for a conservatorship naming Attleson as her conservator had been dismissed by the court, he had stopped helping Martha with her finances "for fear he will be sued."

The probate court ruled that Martha Lundgaard was an incapacitated person and appointed a conservator of her person and estate. In reaching this conclusion, the court made the following findings (which are a restatement of the statutory definition of incapacitation found in Minnesota's statutes) and simply inserted "her" for "his" on a reprinted order:

> 2. The conservatee lacks sufficient understanding or capacity to make or communicate responsible decisions concerning her person and her estate or financial decisions.
> 3. The conservatee has demonstrated behavior deficits evidencing inability to meet her needs for medical care, nutrition, clothing, safety, or shelter, and to manage her estate.

Martha appealed the district court's ruling to the Court of Appeals of Minnesota, which affirmed the lower court's conservatorship orders. Why?

*On the Court's Ruling.* The appellate court prefaced its review of Martha Lundgaard's conservatorship by stating that the "probate court has broad powers in appointing [a] conservator; [the] Court of Appeals may interfere with this discretion only in case of clear abuse." Martha had contended that the lower court "did not give due consideration to the evidence in making its findings," an omission she claimed amounted to reversible error. In weighing its decision, the Court of Appeals quoted the following section from a 1984 Minnesota case:

> As a result of the 1980 legislation [making it harder to create a conservatorship] and a subsequent amendment raising the burden of persuasion, the legislature provided that in a proceeding for the involuntary appointment of a conservator, there is a legal presumption of capacity and the burden of proof is on the petitioner to prove, by clear and convincing evidence, that the proposed conservatee is incapacitated. . . . In addition, the legislature has mandated that "[i]n all cases the court *shall make specific written findings of fact*, state separately its conclusions of law, and direct the entry of an appropriate judgment or order." (Court's emphasis.)

"It is not clear," the court admitted, "which evidence the probate court considered in support of its [preprinted] findings, a process which seems to fall short of the specificity mandated by statute." Furthermore, they stated:

> There is nothing in the record to indicate her present incapacity to make or communicate responsible decisions regarding nutritional needs, clothing, and social and recreational requirements.

In reviewing the probate court's records, however, the appellate court found, in the testimony of two social workers at the rehabilitation center and of Martha's physician, "evidence indicating that Ludgaard lacks the capacity to make and communicate decisions concerning medical needs, shelter and safety." They also agreed with the lower court that Martha was "unable to manage her estate and that she has property which would be dissipated without proper management." In response to Martha's request that a less restrictive alternative to conservatorship of her person and estate should have been considered, the court stated that no less-restrictive appropriate alternatives to the conservatorship existed for Martha Lundgaard:

Her claim that she can receive sufficient help from Attleson and her relatives is contrary to the evidence: no relative has come forward to offer services in such a capacity, she alternates between trusting and not trusting those who help her, she rejected her sister's holding of her power of attorney, and the court dismissed Attleson's petition to become her conservator. Attleson now refuses to help her with her finances for fear he will be sued.

The last paragraph in a syllabus prepared by the Court of Appeals of Minnesota in *In re Conservatorship of Lundgaard* raises the question of why the court did not agree with Martha Lundgaard's assertion that the trial court committed reversible error in failing to specify the exact evidence it used in determining her incapacity. The paragraph states:

> 3. Probate court preprinted findings are not specific to the case presented and do not meet the particularity required by statute; we will be forced *in the future* to remand for specific findings. . . .
>
> We regard findings such as those present here to be *general*. Findings which do not specifically address the necessary statutory factors, such as incapacitation, how the conservator appointed is the most suitable for the specific individual at issue, etc., do not comply with the statutory requisites for creation of conservatorships and appointment of conservators. *Future use of such "general," conclusory findings will force this court to remand for findings consistent with the legislative mandate of specificity.* (Emphasis added.)

Minnesota's legislative safeguards would provide an umbrella for *future* respondents who appeal protective proceedings, but not for Martha. Because it was "reluctant to remand and dissipate an estate," the court refused to extend this legal protection to Martha Lundgaard, Incapacitated. It is a troubling and complex case, indeed.

# PAYMENTS FOR INVOLUNTARY PROCEEDINGS ARE TAKEN FROM THE WARD'S ASSETS

*Adding insult to injury, the court demands that new wards and conservatees pay for all aspects of their unwanted conservatorships and guardianships. The case of* Smeed v. Brechtel *reflects the paradox that lurks at the heart of the system of involuntary protective proceedings and forces the elderly to pay—usually for the rest of their lives—for rulings that oftentimes have no clear beneficial outcomes for them.*

## Case 4.19. Smeed v. Brechtel

Mary Smeed and the sister with whom she lived, Emily Chamberlain, appealed a Lane County Circuit Court order appointing a bank as conservator of Mary's estate—a $40,000 savings account. Relatives testified in court on Mary's behalf in an attempt to reverse the conservatorship.

The only nonrelative to speak during the hearing was a psychiatrist who testified that Mary was schizophrenic and "often out of touch with reality and 'at her worse she has delusions which affect her behavior.' " Only one example of deficient or incompetent behavior was offered: namely, that "'a profound indecisiveness' ... makes her susceptible to other people's influence." The psychiatrist expressed the following opinion:

> Q. How would you feel about her ... ability to manage a savings account of $40,000?
> A. I think that would be impossible.

No testimony was offered concerning any financial mismanagement on Mary Smeed's part. Why did the court rule against her?

*On the Court's Ruling.* Mary's unwanted guardianship was ultimately confirmed on the basis of the one psychiatrist's opinion because, explained the Chief Judge of the Court of Appeals, the testimony of Mary's relatives was "largely conflicting, confusing and unpersuasive" in his eyes. In spite of the fact that no one had demonstrated Mary's alleged incompetence by introducing even one single example of imprudent financial behavior, the court ruled that Mary Smeed should not be permitted to control her $40,000 savings account.

The bank's expenses as conservator and the fees of all lawyers who had participated in the case would be paid from Mary Smeed's small estate. Only if Mary Smeed were to become impoverished by these court-mandated withdrawals from her savings account to the point that her funds fell below a statutorily required minimum balance (now generally ranging from $3,000 to $10,000) would Mary's unwanted conservatorship be terminated before her death.

# PACE IN PROBATE COURTS, THE "COURTS OF THE DEAD"— TOO SLOW TO HANDLE LEGAL AFFAIRS OF THE ELDERLY

*The elderly who are targeted by involuntary conservatorship or guardianship proceedings rarely have the energy and money to sustain years of tedious and stressful litigation as their pleadings creep through court. The case of* Harvey v. Meador *is an example of the price—the ultimate price—paid by the men and women who are most vulnerable to such life-consuming proceedings.*

## Case 4.20. Harvey v. Meador

Guy and Joseph Harvey petitioned the Chancery Court of Wayne County, Mississippi, for their appointment as co-conservators of the estates of their four unmarried elderly uncles. At the time of the initial hearing, Joe Meador was ninety-three years of age, Alec Meador was eighty-nine, Louis Meador was eighty-two, and William Meador was eighty. All four of the elderly brothers suffered from health problems. Each of the brothers owned hundreds of acres of land in Mississippi and each had recently been convinced to sell forty acres of farm and timber land in Kentucky to three purchasers—at $135 per acre rather than its $800 to $1,000 per acre market value. The attorney who helped the three businessmen purchase the Kentucky property from the Meador brothers also represented the four elderly men in opposing their nephews' conservatorship petitions.

When the Chancery Court ruled that the nephews' evidence was insufficient to establish the need for a conservator for any of the four uncles and dismissed their petition, the nephews appealed the case to the Supreme Court of Mississippi. Why did this court reverse and remand the lower court's ruling?

*On the Court's Ruling.* By the time the appellate process was finished, the three oldest brothers had died. The court ruled that the surviving brother, Louis, "suffered from advanced age and mental weakness which led to an improvident disposition of property." It decided to "adopt a management competency test as the standard to be applied under the conservatorship statute."

A test of management competency can be answered by considering the factors of: ability to manage, or improvident disposition, or dissipation of property, or susceptibility to influence or deception by others, or other similar factors.

Applying this test to the current situation, the Supreme Court of Mississippi declared that the evidence supported the establishment of a conservatorship over Louis Meador's worldly goods.

The case of *Harvey* v. *Meador* begs the question: At what point does an involuntary "protective proceeding brought in the best interests of the proposed ward" become an *abusive* proceeding simply because the ensuing contest takes such a long time to litigate?

State courts that are notorious both for their cost and for their slow pace in probating the estates of the dead are an inappropriate setting for determinations of the personal and financial futures of living, breathing, aging men and women. Furthermore, ongoing appeals lodged against elderly men and women who have been victorious in probate court— appeals that cannot be stopped by anyone but the petitioning or moving party—invariably strip aging individuals of too many of their precious years.

ã€€ã€€ã€€ã€€ã€€ðŸ¥ã€€ã€€ðŸ¥ã€€ã€€ðŸ¥

The twenty cases we have just reviewed demonstrate many of the problems inherent in state codes and statutes controlling involuntary conservatorship/guardianship proceedings in America. These twenty cases also reflect some of the varying qualities that pervade these involuntary protective proceedings: fear, disbelief, anger, and a dangerous ignorance of how differently such statutes are actually being applied from jurisdiction to jurisdiction. Fortunately, not all of the elderly lose these court battles for personal and financial autonomy, as we are about to see. Sadly, though, even in "victory" the losses—of family, of money, of time, and of trust—are far too great.

## CASE REFERENCES

Case 4.1. *Cummings* v. *Stanford*, 388 S.E.2d 729, 193 Ga. App. 695 (1989).

Case 4.2. *Rice* v. *Floyd*, 768 S.W.2d 57 (Ky. 1989).

Case 4.3. *Roberts* v. *Powers*, 841 S.W.2d 626 (1992).

Case 4.4. *In re Tyrell*, No. 20467, P. Ct., Preble County, Ohio; No. 42, Ct. App., Preble County, Ohio, Oct. 31, 1962, appeal dismissed, 174 Ohio St. 554 (1963). Described in "The Disguised Oppression of Involuntary Guardianship: Have the Elderly Freedom to Spend?" *Yale Law Review* 73 (1964): 676–92.

Case 4.5. *Cornia* v. *Cornia*, 546 P.2d 890 (1976).

Case 4.6. *Conservatorship of Earl B.*, No. 79197, Probate Court, San Mateo County, California; January 11, 1985; Court Investigator's Report, Observations, and Statements. Described in L. Friedman and M. Savage, "Taking Care: The law of Conservatorship in California," *Southern California Law Review* 61 (1988): 273.

Case 4.7. *In re Estate of Liebling*, 254 N.E.2d 531 (1970).

Case 4.8. Guardianship of Mr. S. Described in K. Bulcroft, M. R. Kielkopf, and K. Tripp, "Elderly Wards and Their Legal Guardians: Analysis of County Probate Records in Ohio and Washington," *Gerontological Society of America* 31, no. 2 (1991): 156–64.

Case 4.9. *Stangier* v. *Stangier*, 421 P.2d 693 (1966).

Case 4.10. *Matter of Nelson*, 891 S.W.2d 181 (Mo.App.W.D. 1995).

Case 4.11. *In the Matter of Wurm*, 360 N.E.2d 12 (1977).

Case 4.12. *Epperson* v. *Epperson*, 442 S.E.2d 12, 212 Ga.App. 420 (1994).

Case 4.13.Guardianship of Billie. Described in F. Bayles and S. McCartney, "If You're Old, You Can't Be Foolish," *Los Angeles Times*, 27 September 1987, p. A2.

Case 4.14. *In re Guardianship of Bockmuller*, 602 So.2d 608 (Fla.App. 2 Dist. 1992).

Case 4.15. *Matter of Guardianship of Larson*, 530 N.W.2d 348 (N.D. 1995).

Case 4.16. *Smith* v. *Smith*, 529 A.2d 466 (Pa.Super. 1987).

Case 4.17. *Guardianship of Lander*, 697 A.2d 1298 (Me. 1997).

Case 4.18. *In re Conservatorship of Lundgaard*, 453 N.W.2d 58 (Minn.App. 1990).

Case 4.19. *Smeed* v. *Brechtel*, 567 P.2d 588 (Or.App. 1977).

Case 4.20. *Harvey* v. *Meador*, 459 So.2d 288 (Miss. 1984).

# NOTES

1. G. Atkinson, "Towards a Due Process Perspective in Conservatorship Proceedings for the Aged," *Journal of Family Law* 18, no. 4 (1980): 819–20.

2. A. M. Mitchell, "The Objects of Our Wisdom and Our Coercion: Involuntary Guardianship for Incompetents," *Southern California Law Review* 52 (1979): 1407.

3. Steven H. Giftis, *Law Dictionary* (Hauppage, N.Y.: Baron's Education Series, Inc., 1999), p. 113.

4. Ibid.

5. J. Brock, "Judicial Decisions in Guardianship Cases," in G. H. Zimny and G. T. Grossberg, eds., *Guardianship of the Elderly: Psychiatric and Judicial Aspects* (New York: Springer Publishing Company, 1998), pp. 86–101.

6. J. E. Rein, "Preserving Dignity and Self-Determination of the Elderly in the Face of Competing Interests and Grim Alternatives: A Proposal for Statutory Refocus and Reform," *George Washington Law Review* 60, no. 6 (1992): 1828 (footnote).

7. M. B. Kapp, "Legal Basis of Guardianship," in Zimny and Grossberg, *Guardianship of the Elderly,* p. 17.

8. "The Disguised Oppression of Involuntary Guardianship: Have the Elderly Freedom to Spend?" *Yale Law Journal* 3 (1964): 677.

9. Ibid., pp. 677–78.

10. L. Friedman and M. Savage, "Taking Care: The Law of Conservatorship in California," *Southern California Law Review* 61 (1988): 289.

11. Ibid., p. 289 (footnote).

12. *Connally* v. *General Const. Co.* (1926). 269 U.S. 385, 46 S.Ct. 126, 70 L.Ed. 322.

13. K. Bulcroft, M. Kielkopf, and K. Tripp, "Elderly Wards and Their Legal Guardians: Analysis of County Probate Records in Ohio and Washington," *The Gerontologist* 31, no. 2 (1991): 160.

14. Brock, op. cit., p. 87.

15. Rein, op. cit., p. 1874 (footnote).

16. Ibid.

17. F. Bayles and S. McCartney, "If You're Old, You Can't Be Foolish," *Los Angeles Times*, 27 September 1987, p. A2

18. *NAACP* v. *Button* (1963), 371 U.S. 415, 444–445, 83 S.Ct. 328, 9 L.Ed.2d 405.

19. J. E. Rein, "Clients with Destructive and Socially Harmful Choices— What's an Attorney to Do?: Within and Beyond the Competency Construct." *Fordham Law Review* 62 (1994): 1173.

20. J. N. Kirkendall, "Judicial Process in Guardianship Proceedings," in Zimny and Grossberg, *Guardianship of the Elderly,* pp. 71–72.

# CHAPTER FIVE

# INDIVIDUAL COURT STRUGGLES FOR FREEDOM

## *Victories*

*Victory at all costs, victory in spite of all terror, victory however long and hard the road may be; for without victory there is no survival.*
—Sir Winston Churchill, House of Commons, May 13, 1940

**W**e now continue with the stories of twenty men and women who managed to have their involuntary conservatorship/guardianship rulings reversed. As suggested earlier, such victories are rare. Approximately 94 percent of all initial involuntary conservatorship/guardianship litigation in America are lost by the vulnerable elderly and almost none of these losing cases are ever appealed.[1] Sadly, even when appealed, decisions made by lower courts in contested protective proceedings are rarely overturned by higher courts. In victory as in defeat, the elderly pay a substantial price for their involvement in these so-called protective proceedings in terms of monetary cost, peace of mind, and precious years lost to litigation.

The successful reversals were granted by judges in appellate, supreme, and federal courts who affirmed the right of the elderly to live as they please in spite of opposition from altruistic or heir-expectant petitioners. In reading the courts' reasons for reversing lower court rulings, one cannot help but wonder why the vulnerable elderly must go through so many years of nightmarish litigation to find a judge willing to calm the winds of involuntary conservatorship/guardianship storms before they become lethal.

The twenty cases have been organized under six main subject areas that were in most instances identified in court records as reversible errors made during the initial protective proceedings. It should be noted, of course, that most rulings do address overlapping issues, and that every successful appeal touches on several of these problematic legal topics. In brief, the judicial reasons for reversals and rulings favoring the elderly that will be discussed are:

- Petitioners' competing motives are not considered—and should be

- Due process and constitutional rights should be protected in court

- States must not misuse their *parens patriae* power

- Insufficient or incorrect proof of incompetency should not be accepted in any court

- Court procedures in contested conservatorships/guardianships should be streamlined

- Vague concepts in codes lead to subjective rulings by judges and should be carefully defined

The cases should be viewed as twenty *unique* victories rather than as a body of evidence suggesting that state conservatorship/guardianship codes themselves have changed in consistent and significant ways. There is no judicial consistency in such rulings from court to court, much less from county to county or from state to state. As Judge James Brock of Georgia warned, "the same evidence presented to two different judges may produce two different results because the judges' perception of what constitutes 'clear and convincing evidence' differs."[2] Vague statutory definitions contained in individual state laws that are then interpreted on an *ad hoc* and subjective basis by each judge in every county—such is the complex legal context in which the following court nightmares have unfolded.

# PETITIONERS' MOTIVES OR COMPETING INTERESTS CONSIDERED BY THE COURT

*Unlike the judicial determinations cited in cases 4.1 through 4.20, the court in* In re Estate of Wagner *focuses on the petitioners' motives in bringing suit against their newly widowed wealthy mother. In this case, the court emphasizes that a conservator may not be appointed over an estate "merely because potential heirs believe that there will be more left for them if [the] owner of the property is not free to deal with the property as he or she chooses."*

## Case 5.1. In re Estate of Wagner

During the three months following the death of her husband, seventy-nine-year-old Delphine Wagner leased some of her land to Scribner Alfalfa, Inc. The land had previously been farmed by her son and son-in-law, but the new lease with Scribner Alfalfa produced 160 percent greater income than had the leases to her son and son-in-law. Citing this decision as proof that Delphine Wagner was incapable of properly managing her own affairs, four of Delphine's six children petitioned the District Court for Dodge County, Nebraska, for the appointment of a conservatorship over their mother.

Using logic that was described by a later court in its written summary as "difficult to grasp," one of the petitioners stated that the transaction was evidence of mismanagement of his mother's affairs because "by receiving more income for the land, Mrs. Wagner would be required to pay more income tax." Transcripts from the County Court in Nebraska reveal that one of Delphine's petitioning sons testified as follows:

Q. You don't know whether she is mismanaging it or not?
A. Oh, I can see she's mismanaging it. I can see that. I don't have to go over.
Q. How can you see that?
A. Well, she rented it to the alfalfa mill. That's not very good business. She's only one person, that's money she's going to have to give to Uncle Sam. If my dad would have wanted more money, he'd have asked for it.
Q. She rented it to the alfalfa mill for 160 percent of what you were paying and that was a bad business decision?
A. She ain't going to gain nothing.
Q. Because of the taxes?
A. That's right. . . .

Delphine's personal physician, Dr. Roger Dilley, testified that his patient was in good health, demonstrated good comprehension, showed no problems with her memory, was well oriented, and answered questions appropriately. Tests conducted by court-appointed clinical psychologist Dr. Philip G. McLeod and two of his associates disclosed no evidence that she was unable to handle her affairs. Their report concluded that "her judgment has been good in the past and there was no evidence of poor decisions after her husband died."

In its ruling against Delphine Wagner, the County Court determined that Mrs. Wagner was unable to manage her property due to "advanced age, a continuing grief caused by the death of her husband, Roy Wagner, and the subtle direct undue influence of her daughter, Clarinda Foote, as well as the indirect influence of [a second daughter] Clara Mae and [son-in-law] Charles Lange." The petitioners had offered no proof of the nature of the undue influence other than the fact that one daughter had helped her mother with funeral arrangements.

The court appointed a conservator over Delphine, set aside the lease of the land Delphine had made to Scribner Alfalfa, Inc., and directed that she receive an allowance of $1,200 per month to "handle her day-to-day affairs and expenses." Delphine refused to accept the court's humiliating ruling and filed an immediate appeal. When the appellate court dismissed the conservatorship and returned control of her land and business affairs to Delphine, the four adult children then brought their case before the Supreme Court of Nebraska. The Supreme Court ruled with the district appellate court in Delphine Wagner's favor. Why?

*On the Court's Ruling.* The Supreme Court agreed that the evidence failed to support the need for a conservator. "One may not have his or her property taken away and placed in [the] hands of [a] conservator," the court warned, "merely because potential heirs believe that there will be more left for them if [the] owner of the property is not free to deal with the property as he or she chooses." They found the county court to be in error in determining that Mrs. Wagner was unable to manage her property yet *could* handle her day-to-day affairs:

Notwithstanding the fact that the county court determined that Mrs. Wagner was unable to manage her affairs, the court, nevertheless, found and directed that she be paid the sum of $1,200 per month in order that she many "handle her day to day affairs and expenses." The reason for concluding that she was unable to manage her property due to those matters set out in the order but, nevertheless, was able to handle her day-to-day affairs and still to subject her to the appointment of a con-servator under the language of [statue section] §30-2630 is difficult to understand. Perhaps the county court was concerned with the manner in which Mrs. Wagner would choose to deal with her assets rather than whether she would be able to effectively manage them. If that was the case, the county court was in error.

The Chief Justice continued:

> The evidence in this case establishes beyond any question that Mrs. Wagner possessed sufficient mentality to understand in a reasonable manner the business she was transacting and to know the nature and effect of her acts with reference to business affairs. As a matter of fact, it was her knowledge which apparently disturbed four of the children and caused them to seek the appointment of a conservator.

Addressing the petition's claim that Mrs. Wagner was unable to withstand the "direct and indirect undue influence" of two daughters in dealing with her business affairs, the Supreme Court reviewed earlier testimony. Attention was focused on relevant material provided by the clinical psychologist who had interviewed the proposed ward at the court's request:

> Q. Were you able to tell from the test and from the interview you did of Delphine Wagner, anything regarding her personality, whether she had a mind of her own, whether she would be influenced by others?
> A. Yes. She looked like quite a strong-willed gal; has her own opinion. I don't know her past situation. May be somewhat opinionated; feisty. Those kind of descriptive terms come to mind.

Even the children, who had stated in their petition that their mother was subject to undue influence, testified to the contrary:

> Q. Your mother is too bullheaded. She makes up her own mind?
> A. She's stubborn. You can't talk to her.
> Q. And she sticks to it when she's made it up?
> A. Whether it's right or wrong.

In language rarely found in conservatorship/guardianship filings, the court also responded to a claim that Delphine Wagner appeared to be depressed. "One might conclude," they began, "that such reaction was quite normal in view of the fact that four of her six children were attempting to have a conservator appointed for her and she was being examined by strangers in order to try and retain control over her own property. Any normal, healthy individual would undoubtedly have some sense of depression about that event."

The Supreme Court supported the district appellate court's conclusions in all regards. Unlike the rulings of many of the courts in cases we have already reviewed, this judgment swept aside the legal verbiage that had threatened Delphine Wagner's freedom after her husband had died. "It is apparent that what we are confronted with in the instant case," the court stated,

> is a situation in which Mrs. Wagner's husband, for many years, for whatever reasons, permitted several of his children to use land belonging to the Wagners at less than market rental and that upon his death Mrs. Wagner determined to become a better business person. This caused a change in the arrangements which several of her children had previously enjoyed and, for that reason, caused dissension in the family. *An effort, however, to relieve dissension is not grounds for the appointment of a conservator.* (Emphasis added.)

It is important to remember that Delphine had to overcome having been taken to court by four of her six adult children, adjudicated incapable of managing her affairs, and then move through two more court battles to secure her victory. She is one of the few who have succeeded in wresting victory from an initial legal defeat.

## HEARINGS MUST NOT COMPROMISE DUE PROCESS RIGHTS AND CONSTITUTIONAL PROTECTIONS

*The five cases that follow are joined by a common thread: the reversing judges found that the lower court rulings infringed upon various individual rights that are protected by state and federal constitutional law. The first of the five,* Katz v. Superior Court, Etc., *is a particularly interesting contrast to case 4.16,* Smith v. Smith, *which centered around the LaRouche organization rather than the Unification Church. The second case,* Goldman v. Krane, *reveals countywide practices that violated the constitutional rights of its elderly citizens. In* Matter of Conservatorship of Goodman, *the court agrees with the elderly Mr. Logan that "citizens are not to be thus lightly deprived of their constitutional rights to 'the enjoyment of the gains of their own industry."* West Virginia ex rel. Shamblin v. Collier, *is overturned because the lower court violated an individual's constitutional and due process rights in relying on insufficient evidence to support a finding of incompetence. The last of the five cases in this section,* Grant v. Johnson, *differs from all others in this book because it involves a young, competent woman of thirty-six. However, the case is included because it demonstrates how guardianship statutes have been used against a person who is mentally and physically competent—and young. Oregon's codes permitted the initial action. As a consequence of federal intervention in this particular case, Oregon's guardianship codes have since been revised.*

## Case 5.2. *Katz* v. *Superior Court, Etc.*

The Superior Court, San Francisco County, granted temporary conservators for five adult members of the Unification Church headed by Rev. Sun Myung Moon. According to testimony provided by a psychiatrist and psychologist and included in court records, the five young adults were "victims of artful and designing persons . . . [and] are victims of psychological kidnapping" by the Church's leadership. The court entered orders appointing one or both parents of each of the five young adults as temporary conservators to permit "deprogramming" from ideas allegedly instilled by the religious organization. The trial court's orders contained "no findings of fact which would disclose the ground or grounds on which the [conservatorship] orders were based." Rather than specifying facts that he considered to have been established by the evidence, the judge stated:

> "It's not a simple case. As I said, we're talking about the very essence of life here, mother, father and children. There's nothing closer in our civilization. This is the essence of civilization. The family unit is a micro-civilization. That's what it is. A great civilization is made of many, many great families, and that's what's before this Court. it's not the regular run-of-the-mill case that involves some money, or some kind of damage. It is the very essence of life."
>
> In ruling on the petitioners' requests for restrictions on the order, [the court] added: "One of the reasons that I made this Decision, I could see the love here of a parent for his child, and I don't even have to go beyond that. Even our laws of this State, the Probate laws have all been set up—the laws of succession, children succeed to the estate of their parents if the parents die intestate. So the law looks at that binding thing between a parent and a child. It is never-ending. No matter how old we are, it's there. And that was one of the things that influenced this Court."

The five conservatees brought a petition for relief from the conservatorship before the California Court of Appeal, First District. They sought either to prohibit the continuation of the orders in force or to prohibit the various temporary conservators from subjecting them to deprogramming. The appellate court granted their appeal. Why?

*On the Court's Ruling.* The Court of Appeal ruled that the section of California's Probate Code which permitted the appointment of conservators of the person and property of adults who "are likely to be deceived or imposed upon by artful or designing persons" was unconstitutionally vague.

> Although the words "likely to be deceived or imposed upon by artful or designing persons" may have some meaning when applied to the loss of property which can be measured, they are too vague to be applied in the world of ideas. In an age of subliminal advertising, television exposure, and psychological salesmanship, everyone is exposed to artful and designing persons at every turn. It is impossible to measure the degree of likelihood that some will succumb. In the field of beliefs, and particularly religious tenets, it is difficult, if not impossible, to establish a universal truth against which deceit and imposition can be measured.

The court also found that the allegations of incompetency were unsupported by evidence presented in the lower court, and that the conservatorships violated the petitioners' rights of freedom of religion and association under the federal and state constitutions. As the justices explained,

> we note that even if the organization be deemed political, and not religious, there is also freedom of association involved. In upholding the right of the NAACP and its members and lawyers to associate for the purpose of assisting persons who seek legal redress for infringements of their constitutionally guaranteed and other rights, the Supreme Court of the United States concluded by stating, "The course of our decisions in the First Amendment area makes plain that its protections would apply as fully to those who would arouse our society against the objectives of the petitioner. For the Constitution protects expression and association without regard to the race, creed, or political or religious affiliation of the members of the group which invokes its shield, or to the truth, popularity, or social utility of the ideas and beliefs which are offered."

The Court of Appeals vacated the superior court's orders appointing temporary conservators and granted the petitioners their freedom. In conclusion, the court cited a passage from *United States* v. *Ballard* (1944), quoting the words of Justice Jackson:

> "The wrong of these things, as I see it, is not in the money the victims part with half so much as in the mental and spiritual poison they get. But that is precisely the thing the Constitution put beyond the reach of the prosecutor, for the price of freedom of religion or of speech or of the

press is that we must put up with, and even pay for, a good deal of rubbish."

## Case 5.3. *Goldman* v. *Krane*

Anna Barshop, a ninety-year-old widow, lived alone in a subsidized senior citizen's housing complex. She was visited almost daily by her niece, who happened to be a physician. The director of the housing complex became concerned about Anna's ability to live independently and asked the Denver Department of Social Services to investigate. The investigating departmental social worker stated that the niece's involvement precluded the need for intervention, and closed the investigation.

The housing director responded by warning the department that the complex would "de-admit" Anna if authorities did not agree to place her in a nursing home. Without any further contact to assess Anna's physical and mental condition, without investigating the housing complex's threat of de-admission, and without notifying either Anna or her niece, the social worker secured an *ex parte* temporary guardianship for the department over Anna. The department had her transported to a hospital where, according to court records, Anna was "held incommunicado and where she was subjected to extensive examination." Anna was then placed in a nursing home. During this period, neither her physician-niece nor Anna was consulted or even advised about the existence of the involuntary guardianship.

When Anna's niece learned what had happened, she was able to have the court substitute herself as guardian in place of the department. Anna, represented by her guardian *ad litem* and her niece, brought suit against Denver's Department of Social Services and the housing complex on multiple claims. Three years after the ordeal began, the District Court entered judgment in favor of Anna Barshop and awarded her damages for unconstitutional deprivation of liberty and property rights in connection with the involuntary temporary guardianship. The Colorado Court of Appeals sustained that ruling on appeal.

*On the Court's Ruling.* This complex case exposed unconstitutional practices within the Denver Department of Social Services. Court records revealed that it was the policy or custom of the department's director to presign blank guardianship petitions, to make them available to caseworkers, and not to review petitions after they had been completed in order to verify their appropriateness. The appellate court agreed with the lower court's jury decision that the department had "acted with deliberate indifference or reckless disregard toward senior citizen's constitutional rights in petitioning for temporary guardianship." The jury's award to

Anna Barshop of $135,000 in damages was thus affirmed by the Colorado Court of Appeals.

The case in question should serve as a weapon in future conservatorship/guardianship proceedings when any public authority disregards statutory guidelines in order to "streamline" its protective powers. Although state codes are flawed in different ways (as discussed in greater detail in chapter 8), they do contain procedural safeguards that should be followed by *all* authorities.

## Case 5.4. Matter of Conservatorship of Goodman

Edgar Ray Goodman, an eighty-four-year-old widower, lived in a trailer home near one of his sons, Gene. Following the death of his wife in 1986, Edgar Goodman had given Gene a power of attorney for the purpose of handling his affairs, and deeded Gene his land and mineral rights. As stated in court records, "this obviously irritated the rest of his children, and his son Paul, Appellee, filed this action" with the Oklahoma District Court, Carter County, to appoint him conservator of his father's estate. At the time he filed the conservatorship petition, Paul "elected not to file for guardianship and allege that his father was mentally incompetent."

The trial court listened to the family squabble but was given no evidence as to the nature and extent of Edgar Goodman's property. Nonetheless, the court imposed a conservatorship over Edgar, stating that "due to his advanced age, [he] was unable to manage his property." When asked for clarification by Edgar Goodman's attorney, the trial court stated that "it was not his finding that Mr. Goodman was incompetent." Mr. Goodman claimed that the imposition of an involuntary conservatorship absent a finding that he was mentally incompetent was unconstitutional and brought his case before the Court of Appeals of Oklahoma to have the involuntary conservatorship removed. The higher court ruled in Edgar Ray Goodman's favor. Why?

*On the Court's Ruling.* In its written opinion, the Court of Appeals focused on the constitutionally protected right of eighty-six-year-old Mr. Goodman to enjoy the fruit of his own labor:

> If the only purpose of the statute is to allow a person who is, by reason of advanced age or physical incapacity, unable to manage his own property, to voluntarily apply to the court to have a conservator appointed, it is constitutional. If a purpose of the statute is to allow involuntary intervention in the property affairs of citizens, absent a finding of mental incompetence, it is unconstitutional as it is a clear violation of the State and Federal Constitutional provisions which guarantee every citizen the right to life, liberty and property.

"We find no compelling state interest," the appellate court stated, "which justifies the appointment of a conservator over the property of a mentally competent citizen, against his will." In dismissing the involuntary conservatorship against Edgar Ray Goodman, the court concluded:

> In our state Constitution, the utmost pains have been taken to preserve all the securities of individual liberty, and the courts cannot refuse obedience to its mandates. The Legislature cannot alter, annul, or avoid the constitutional safeguards of person and property set forth in the Bill of Rights. It is the duty of courts to be watchful for the constitutional rights of the citizens, and against any stealthy encroachments thereon. When the courts are confronted with a clear and explicit provision of the Constitution, and when it is proposed to avoid or modify or alter the same by a legislative act, it is their plain duty to enforce the constitutional provision, unless it is clear that such legislative act does not infringe it in letter or spirit. Citizens are not to be thus lightly deprived of their constitutional rights to "the enjoyment of the gains of their own industry."

## Case 5.5. *West Virginia ex rel. Shamblin* v. *Collier*

Emily Collier filed a petition to have her father, Tom Shamblin, declared incompetent. The only reasons cited in her petition as grounds for the incompetency determination were: "Mr. Shamblin is eighty-four years of age. His health has deteriorated with age. He has breathing problems and is very susceptible to pneumonia." Mr. Shamblin was served with a copy of the petition but, since he could not read, was not aware that an incompetency proceeding was imminent. The only family member who attended the hearing was the petitioner, Emily Collier. The hearing itself was limited in both duration and scope, according to a note made by the transcriber just prior to the court's ruling: "The statement of findings, from here on, is spoken rapidly and *sounds* as if it were being *read*" (court's emphasis). Evidence was provided at the hearing by a court-appointed guardian *ad litem* who had visited Tom once.

Based on this one visit, the *ad litem* reported that Tom Shamblin knew his age, his children's names, the year, and the name of the president of the United States. He focused on the fact that Tom Shamblin's visible "scratching problem" (later diagnosed as a treatable dry-skin disorder) was indicative of either a nervous disorder or obsessive-compulsive behavior. Additionally, the guardian *ad litem* concluded that Mr. Shamblin was "necessarily unable to manage his affairs" based on "his advanced age, his inability to read and write, and his weight of ninety-four pounds."

Testifying in court, Tom's daughter offered no testimony at all about her father's current physical condition. Her "primary concern which surfaced from her testimony, however, was the perceived escalating costs of providing care for her father." Emily Collier did submit one piece of evidence to prove that her father was incapable of managing his financial affairs, namely, that he enjoyed giving his grandchildren (her children) larger amounts of money than he could comfortably afford. After all, he had given her children $50 or $100 when he lived on a fixed income of only $980 a month. She also submitted an affidavit signed by her father's physician, who was not present at the hearing. It stated that Tom Shamblin "was unable to manage his business affairs, unable to care for his own physical well-being, and unable to attend the hearing." The signed affidavit consisted of three checked boxes on a form.

On the basis of this body of evidence, Tom Shamblin was declared to be incompetent and his daughter was appointed guardian for him. Tom was placed in an elder care facility against his will. In an attempt to void the involuntary guardianship, Tom turned to the Supreme Court of Appeals of West Virginia, and the court granted Mr. Shamblin's appeal. On what basis?

*On the Court's Ruling.* The Supreme Court granted Tom's writ of habeas corpus to permit the case to be remanded to the Jackson County Circuit Court "for further proceedings to determine whether Mr. Shamblin was properly determined to be incompetent." In commenting on the simple form document that had been submitted by the treating physician as evidence of his incompetence, the court stated that "the intention of the Legislature was to require more than a form with three checked boxes to support a determination of an individual's incompetency."

The Supreme Court acknowledged that an injustice may have occurred when the lower court issued a finding of incompetence since "in fact the individual is neither physically nor mentally incompetent." After the county commission found Tom to be competent, he proceeded to petition the court to dissolve the committee (guardianship) appointment of his daughter, Emily Collier.

Mr. Shamblin declared that terminating his rights and restricting his freedom violated his right to liberty under the state's constitution. He argued successfully that the involuntary protective proceedings also violated the intent of West Virginia's codes and ignored his due process rights by relying on insufficient evidence to support a finding of incompetence. Finally, the court responded to Sarah's concern that her father was fiscally imprudent by concluding that

at best, Shamblin merely exercised poor judgment in giving away more money than he could afford, which did not meet the requirements of

being found incompetent under West Virginia Code §27-11-1(d). . . .
Simply showing that a person is old and has had physical problems is
insufficient for finding this person incompetent.

## Case 5.6. Grant v. Johnson

Kevin Grant, the former husband of Virginia Grant, a thirty-six-year-old
mother of two, petitioned the Multnomah County Circuit Court, Judge
Eric Carpenter presiding, to appoint a temporary guardian and permanent
guardian over his ex-wife. He sought an order appointing Frances Sherrill, the mother of Virginia Grant, as "temporary guardian, without notice,
for a period not to exceed six (6) months or until such time as this court
grants petitioner's petition for establishment of a permanent guardianship
for Virginia Grant." Kevin Grant was joined in this action by his former
mother-in-law, who asked to be appointed her daughter's guardian.

Court documents included a handwritten statement by Dr. Robert H.
Gray, who had once treated Virginia Grant for gall bladder problems. Dr.
Gray stated his belief that Virginia had "a severe emotional problem over
which she has little control" and "will need long-term psychiatric assistance." An affidavit submitted by the mother-in-law declared that her
daughter needed immediate psychiatric treatment "which she undoubtedly will refuse if given an opportunity." According to Frances Sherrill's
affidavit, she had placed her daughter in a state hospital "with a diagnosis
of borderline schizophrenia" when the daughter was thirteen or fourteen.
Her affidavit provided the following:

> I believe that it is in the best interest that a guardian be appointed for
> Virginia Grant because she is unable to control her own life, let alone
> make decisions for herself or her family. . . . I believe that she is . . . in
> need of immediate psychiatric treatment which she undoubtedly will
> refuse if given an opportunity.

Virginia Grant received no notice of the petition and was not provided an opportunity to appear before Judge Carpenter or to retain
counsel. The judge granted the petition. In his order, the judge waived an
investigation and a report by a visitor as required by O.R.S. 126.103 prior
to the appointment of a temporary guardianship.

Virginia Grant's mother was named temporary guardian of her unsuspecting daughter. Pursuant to Judge Carpenter's order, Virginia was immediately placed by her mother in the locked psychiatric ward at Providence
Medical Center from November 28, 1989 until December 12, 1989. As
summarized by the court, "during portions of this time, Virginia Grant was
denied visitors, denied the use of the telephone, and denied any opportunity

to contact legal counsel. At times, [she] was placed in a ward which was locked, and her movements were monitored by video camera." On December 2, 1989, five days after she had been involuntarily hospitalized, Virginia Grant was finally served with copies of her ex-husband's "Petition for Appointment of Guardian and Temporary Guardian" and "Notice of Petition for Appointment of Guardian and Temporary Guardian."

Nine days after she had been involuntarily hospitalized, Virginia Grant was permitted to place a call to her lawyer. She was released five days later. Virginia subsequently filed an action against Judge Carpenter in the United States District Court, "seeking a declaration that the Oregon statute relating to temporary guardians, O.R.S. 126.133, is unconstitutional, and seeking an injunction that will prevent the further application of that statute to her and to others." The federal court ruled in Virginia Grant's favor, overturning the guardianship. What was the court's reasoning?

*On the Court's Ruling.* In a decision that changed Oregon's laws, the United States District Court ruled that any state statute permitting the appointment of a guardian without notice for an indefinite period and without medical evidence of the proposed ward's condition was unconstitutional. As the federal court urged, Oregon's statutes needed correction.

> The need for procedural protections in the context of the appointment of temporary guardianships is at least as critical, if not more so, than in the civil commitment proceedings which are initiated by a state. The guardianship which arises from the statute providing for the appointment of temporary guardianships entrusts the life of a person to a private party whose motives may be more questionable than the motives of a disinterested state. Additional or substitute procedures would bring before a judicial officer in a timely and meaningful manner the views of the alleged incapacitated person, and therefore would provide a significant protection for the alleged incapacitated person from an erroneous deprivation of his or her liberty. . . .
>
> Additional or substitute procedures which would provide a meaningful opportunity for an alleged incapacitated person to present his or her case to a judicial officer in an exigent manner would not place an unreasonable burden on the State of Oregon. In such a private proceeding, the State of Oregon may require a petitioner to bear the fiscal or administrative burden for services necessary to protect the rights of the alleged incapacitated person, such as attorney fees, medical fees, or fees of other third parties deemed necessary.

The United States District Court thus ruled that Virginia Grant was entitled to a declaration that O.R.S. 126.133 was unconstitutional.

# STATES' ABUSE OF THEIR POWER AS *PARENS PATRIAE*, "PARENT OF THE COUNTRY"

*In each of the following three cases, higher courts argue that the lower courts had abused their* parens patriae *power in stripping individuals of their personhood and/or property in order to protect citizens whose decisions were viewed as unreasonable or imprudent.* In re McDonnell *succeeds on appeal because, as the court declares, "no one, no matter how astute, is immune from bad investments," and the state must not use paternalistic attitudes to deprive anyone who makes imprudent choices of precious individual rights. A Department of Social Services in New York is told, in* Matter of Grinker, *that it may not use its power to "substitute themselves for [Ms. Rose's] muse and order her art sold against her wishes" simply because the state believes it can make better decisions than can the proposed ward.* McCallie v. McCallie *reveals Alabama's insistence—through two trials—that a durable power of attorney cannot be overturned by the state in its desire to appoint a guardian over an elderly woman. This case stands in striking contrast to Kentucky's earlier invalidation of a durable power of attorney in case 4.2,* Rice v. Floyd.

## Case 5.7. In re McDonnell

Seventy-three-year-old Helen McDonnell's two married daughters petitioned the County Judge's Court in Martin County, Florida, to have their mother declared incompetent and to be named guardians of her person and estate. Helen, described by court documents as "a lady of considerable wealth," acknowledged that she had made a bad investment of $10,000 and an uncollectable loan of $6,000. She was diagnosed by several physicians as suffering from "arterio-sclerotic vascular disease, congestive heart failure, early cirrhosis, gastritis and excessive use of alcohol."

Overlooked in the testimony of her daughters was the fact that much of Helen McDonnell's wealth was attributable to a successful but risky investment she had made against the advice of her husband and investment counselor. In spite of this evidence, Helen was judged mentally incompetent. The court appointed Helen's daughters as guardians over their mother's person and appointed separate guardians of her property. Two years after this guardianship action was initiated, Helen's sister petitioned the District Court of Appeal of Florida, Fourth District, for restoration of her sister's autonomy and competency. Another two years after the appeal was filed, the District Court reversed the trial court's ruling and dismissed both guardianships. Why?

*On the Court's Ruling.* The Court of Appeals determined Helen McDonnell to be "of sound mind and capable of managing her own affairs." In its findings, the court warned that

> no one, no matter how astute, is immune from bad investments. It is little more than pure speculation to conclude from these isolated examples that she cannot manage her own property or is likely to dissipate it or become the victim of designing persons. In our present day paternalistic society we must take care that in our zeal for protecting those who cannot protect themselves we do not unnecessarily deprive them of some rather precious individual rights.

However, the court also made sure that this astute septuagenarian was aware of the Sword of Damocles dangling over her head. "[Our order to restore Helen McDonnell to full competence in the eyes of the law] does not preclude an inquiry into competency at a subsequent date upon a showing of a change of condition." Helen could thus begin to anticipate a second competency lawsuit should she one day—at age eighty-five or ninety?—show "a change of condition" that attracted a renewed guardianship petition.

## Case 5.8. Matter of Grinker

Seena Rose, a fifty-nine-year-old artist, managed her life on a limited income. Saying it would be "like parting with a limb of her body," Seena refused to augment her income by selling her art work and fell into arrears in the payment of utilities and rent for the Manhattan apartment she had lived in for twenty-five years. On the basis of this financial failure, William J. Grinker, Commissioner of Social Services of the City of New York, petitioned the Supreme Court of New York County to have a conservator appointed over Seena Rose's estate. He sought permission through the conservatorship process to "negotiate the appraisal and sale of her artwork and manage her finances for their protection and best use."

According to court records, the psychiatrist who interviewed the proposed ward twice at the request of the Department of Social Services concluded that Seena Rose was "entirely unable to manage the 'system' and is unable to find housing on her own, unable to handle court proceedings, unable to apply for entitlements or any activity requiring long range planning"—even though Seena had rented her little apartment for twenty-five years. A court-appointed guardian *ad litem* recommended the appointment of a conservator because Seena Rose seemed "incapable of making any decision of what to do with [her] art work," is "unable to do anything to generate any income for herself, or to attempt to do it, that is, to sell her art work," and "is not self-supporting."

Seena was present at the conservatorship hearing but was not represented by an attorney. She testified that her promised Section 8 Federal
rent subsidy had not yet come through and, had she been told of the likelihood of such a delay, she would have rented a room in her apartment to
supplement her income. In spite of Seena's efforts at self-defense, a conservator was appointed and authorized to manage her assets and "to
commit her to an appropriate nursing care facility when medically indicated." The Supreme Court, Appellate Division, affirmed the ruling.
Seena's case was then heard "on appeal by permission" by the Court of
Appeals of New York, which reversed the two lower courts' decisions.
Why did this court rule in Seena's favor in reversing and in dismissing the
commissioner's petition?

*On the Court's Ruling.* The Court of Appeals based its reversal of the
lower court's ruling on two points of law: (1) the courts erred in empow-
ering the conservator to commit Seena Rose to a nursing home in such a
manner; and (2) the evidence failed to support the court's finding that Seena
was substantially unable to manage her property. The court stated that

> it was not established by clear and convincing evidence that artist's
> alleged mental illness caused substantial impairment of her ability to
> manage her property; although the artist failed to timely pay rent and
> utility bills, such circumstance was more likely due to her meager means,
> rather than to mental incapacity of the level required by statute; moreover,
> the artist's failure to attempt to market her artwork to remedy her periodic
> financial deficiencies did not warrant subjugation to a conservator.

The court agreed that alternatives short of appointing a conservator
were available, including the Section 8 Federal rent subsidy program the
proposed ward was already seeking.

This case is an important one in that it focuses on a fifty-nine-year-
old independent woman who was brought into the reach of conservatorship law by a well-meaning government official who believed Seena's
unwillingness to sell her paintings to raise money for her rent-controlled
apartment and pay utility bills made her a candidate for protections
afforded by New York law. Fortunately for Seena, the Supreme Court
believed the Department of Social Services "may not substitute themselves for [Ms. Rose's] muse and order her art sold against her wishes.
While personal and artistic rights are not absolute, they may not be lightly
trumped in this fashion."

Rather than find her failure to promptly pay rent as evidence of
mental incapacity, the court found that a more likely explanation for her
action was, quite simply, an insufficiency of funds. As the court added,

Appointment of a conservator, with its consequent affront to the integrity and independence of the individual, even where warranted, ought to be among the last alternatives in these dire circumstances and cases. . . . The vocation of individuals should neither immunize them from nor make them preferred candidates for protections afforded by the mental Hygiene Law [of New York].

## Case 5.9. McCallie v. McCallie

Jackie McCallie filed a petition in Probate Court of Etowah County, seeking to be appointed conservator of the estate of his mother, Ruth C. McCallie. Jackie's brother, David McCallie, who acted under the authority of the durable power of attorney his mother had executed, had the petition dismissed on the ground that he was both qualified and competent to manage his mother's affairs and a conservatorship was unnecessary.

Jackie as petitioner appealed to the Supreme Court of Alabama. He argued that although both brothers had stipulated to their mother's lack of capacity, his mother had not been examined by a physician or other qualified expert designated by the court, that a guardian *ad litem* had not been appointed to represent his mother, and that his mother had not been present at the Probate Court hearing. He claimed further that the stipulation of incapacity he entered into with David required the court to appoint him (i.e., Jackie) as a conservator. On what did the Supreme Court base its denial of Jackie McCallie's petition?

*On the Court's Ruling.* In denying Jackie's pleading, the Supreme Court cited a previous court ruling: "The finding of the probate court, based on the examination of witnesses, is presumed to be correct and will not be disturbed on appeal unless palpably erroneous." The court ruled that Martha McCallie's interests were represented by an attorney hired by David pursuant to the authority vested in him under the durable power of attorney, and the proposed ward's attorney had stipulated to her incapacity. Furthermore, Alabama constitutional statutes required the appointment of a guardian *ad litem* only if the person to be protected had no attorney. The Supreme Court continued:

Martha McCallie's personal freedoms were not in any way restricted by the probate court; to the contrary, the probate court maintained the status quo by allowing the person of her choice to continue to manage her personal affairs. Based on the circumstances here presented, it would elevate form over substance . . . for us to reverse the order of the probate court [denying a conservatorship over Mrs. McCallie] on this ground.

It is interesting to note that Jackie had filed another conservatorship proceeding against his mother just eighteen months before he filed the present petition. In response to that legal proceeding, Martha McCallie had sent the following letter (included by the Supreme Court of Alabama in its records) to Jackie and his wife:

Dear Jackie and Sonja,

I am writing you this letter today to let you know I am well in mind and body. This letter is to let you know that I love you, and that you are welcome in my home anytime, as long as it is to show me love and respect. The things that have happened in the past will not happen again if you respect me. Never again are you to try to make me change anything that I have decided is in my best interest, such as my power of attorney, my bank account, my CD, or my annuities. All of these things are as I wish them to be, and I expect you to abide by my wishes.

If my wishes are not carried out by you then I will see that my last will and testament will be rewritten to read, to Jackie T. McCallie, I leave one dollar and love and affection. This will stand up in any court of law in Ala. [*sic*] A copy of this letter is also being mailed to my attorney and the Probate Judge.

My door is always open for you, but you will respect me at all times.

With love and respect,

Your Mother

The court's ruling is of particular importance because it confirmed that a valid durable power of attorney obviates the need for a conservatorship or surrogate decision-maker—at least in the State of Alabama.

# INSUFFICIENT OR INCORRECT PROOF OF INCOMPETENCY SHOULD NOT PREVAIL IN COURT

*Cases 5.10 through 5.17 illustrate unusual examples of judges refusing to accept insufficient evidence (such as the use of property mismanagement or "inevitable and irreversible age-related decline") as proof of incapacity requiring surrogate decision-making appointments.* Matter of Estate of McPeak *and* Interdiction of Dobbins *are reversed by adjudication's that age-related infirmities alone are "insufficient to support the determination of incompetency." According to the court in* In re

Guardianship of Gallagher, *saying that an elderly person suffers from incompetence due to physical disability is not equivalent to stating that the person suffers from mental incompetence. Cases 5.13 and 5.14 survived challenges to an initial victory—challenges based on property mismanagement* (In re Lecht) *and physical frailty* (Estate of Galvin v. Galvin). *In* In re Estate of Porter, *the court overturns a decades-old decision that a person suffering from epileptic seizures is "feeble-minded" and inherently incapable of managing a substantial estate.* Conservatorship of Sanderson *spotlights California's unwillingness to*

> *allow many of the rights and privileges of everyday life to be stripped from an individual "under the same standard of proof applicable to run-of-the-mill automobile negligence actions."*

*Finally, the unusual Louisiana case of* Interdiction of Haggerty *reverses a lower court ruling—over a ninety-two-year-old woman—because it did not "indicate that she is incapable of caring for herself or her estate."*

## Case 5.10. Matter of Estate of McPeak

Physically fragile, eighty-one-year-old Della McPeak voluntarily entered a continuing care facility where she could be assisted, to the extent required, in her day-to-day care. Prior to entering the nursing home, Della had given one of her two sons power of attorney over her estate. The second son filed a petition in the Circuit Court, Hamilton County, Illinois, for the appointment of a conservator, alleging that his mother was "incompetent and incapable of managing her person and estate because of old age and deterioration of mentality."

The son brought nonexpert witnesses to court who agreed that Della McPeak was at times "forgetful, confused and repetitive, . . . [and] that her mind was deteriorating and that she was not capable of taking care of herself or her affairs." Della's supporters described her as "mentally alert despite her physical disabilities." They stated for the record that her room in the nursing home was in a wing "designated for those not requiring extensive assistance." No evidence was presented showing any mishandling of her business affairs. Nonetheless, the Circuit Court entered a judgment of incompetency and ordered that conservatorships be placed over Della McPeak's person and estate. The case was brought before the Appellate Court of Illinois, Fifth District, for reconsideration, and the lower court's ruling was overturned. Why?

*On the Court's Ruling.* The court argued that Della McPeak had intelligently and competently directed that all of her needs—both physical and financial—would be met through the devices available to her under her unique circumstances (i.e., through purposefully entering a nursing home and executing power of attorney in her son). The court continued:

> In the case at bar, the petitioner's evidence merely established the respondent's weakening of vigor, skill and acuity which is a normal concomitant to advanced years. . . . However, to simply establish certain disabilities is alone insufficient to support the determination of incompetency, the evidence must also show the respondent's incapability of managing her person or estate. The record is barren of any such evidence. In this regard, the unsubstantiated opinions of petitioner's witnesses, that respondent was not capable of taking care of herself or her affairs, without any reasons given for such conclusions, will not support an adjudication of incompetency.

Although she had lost her initial struggle to defend herself against her son's involuntary guardianship petition, Della McPeak was able to pay an attorney to protect and defend her rights and thus succeed on appeal.

## Case 5.11. Interdiction of Dobbins

In early 1984, eighty-nine-year-old Charlie Dobbins was brought to court by his nephew, Willie McKeever, who sought to have an interdiction (conservatorship or guardianship) appointed over the uncle with whom he lived. The court-appointed medical expert who examined Charlie reported that the elderly man showed good recent memory and no mental confusion at all, but he was "hard of hearing, impatient, and had difficulty understanding some of the things the doctor wanted to do during the examination." Nonetheless, continued the doctor, he declared that "even though Dobbins was 'with it' during his examination, that did not necessarily mean he was that way all the time."

The doctor concluded that Charlie Dobbins suffered from cerebral vascular disease and from "advancing senility which he did not expect to improve." He believed that Mr. Dobbins has "lost most of his ability to make good judgments," and questioned the elderly man's ability to administer his affairs. The nephew's petition was granted in August of 1984, and Mr. Dobbins was interdicted. Willie McKeever was appointed curator (a guardian or conservator) over his uncle's person and estate.

In April of 1987, thirty months later, Charlie Dobbins successfully petitioned the Third Judicial District Court, Parish of Lincoln, to revoke his interdiction. Nephew Willie McKeever sought to reinstate the interdiction through the Court of Appeal of Louisiana. Among the testimony

Mr. McKeever offered during the appellate hearing in October of 1988 was a statement that his now-ninety-two-year-old uncle "was not in good physical condition because he complained and would lay around."

Charlie Dobbins testified on his own behalf, as captured in the court records. He concluded that "the reason why he was in court was because he and Willie had fallen out and he wanted to get his clothes and money from him." He also told the court that he had no money, since his nephew was collecting his social security checks. Charlie submitted the testimony of several friends and one physician. His doctor found Charlie to be competent, stating that he had "minimal senility with mild memory impairment, normal for his age." He believed that Charlie Dobbins would be capable of making good decisions in regard to his personal and financial matters if such matters were first explained to him. The Court of Appeal of Louisiana, Second Circuit, agreed and affirmed the removal of the interdiction. Why?

*On the Court's Ruling.* The court held that Charlie Dobbins was capable—both mentally and physically—of caring for his person and administering his estate. Witnesses had testified to the now-ninety-three-year-old man's undiminished capacity as an "expert gardener" who still worked on a friend's plantation "to the best of his ability."

> We find that the trial court did not err in revoking Dobbins' interdiction. Dobbins may have some limitations due to his age, but he is well aware of them. He grooms himself and works on the Smith's plantation to the best of his ability. While Dobbins may not be able to make the best decisions concerning finances, appellant has pointed out only one occasion where Dobbins may have made a bad deal trying to buy a shed over seven years earlier. While he may need some supervision to help balance a checkbook, if he so chooses to use one, the supervision necessary for his subsistence is not of the level requiring a curator.

Charlie Dobbins was finally granted his freedom from an initial court determination that he was incapable of caring for his person and estate, but the legal system had consumed five of his precious golden years.

## Case 5.12. In re Guardianship of Gallagher

In January of 1979, an evidentiary hearing was held at the Court of Common Pleas, Probate Division, Madison County, to determine whether or not a guardianship should be appointed over the person and estate of Lucy M. Gallagher. Lucy, an elderly woman whose age is not referenced in the appellate court record, was alleged to be "an incompetent person by reason of advanced age and physical infirmity." The only individual who testified at the guardianship hearing concerning Lucy's mental alertness and competency was Paul Gallagher, a relative of her deceased husband. Paul Gallagher stated his opinion simply: "Most of the time she forgets." The court found Lucy to be incompetent and appointed Robert A. Kaveney guardian of her person and estate.

Thirteen months later, Mr. Kaveney resigned as Lucy's guardian and James W. Rolfes Sr. was appointed as successor guardian. Within two weeks of the new appointment, Lucy Gallagher filed an application for a change of guardian. According to court records, Lucy alleged

> that she does not need a guardian of the person as she is mentally competent to take care of herself; and that since she is mentally competent, she should be permitted to select her own guardian.

When her application was denied because it did not satisfy the Court's Rules of Civil Procedure, Lucy filed a motion to terminate the guardianship. Her motion was overruled. Undaunted, Lucy Gallagher took her case to the Court of Appeals of Ohio, Madison County. The appellate court reversed the lower court's ruling and terminated the guardianship. Why?

*On the Court's Ruling.* According to the Court of Appeals, the lower court had made several incorrect decisions in Lucy's case. The appellate court's greatest concern was with the fundamental adjudication of incompetency. The court argued that saying an elderly person suffers from incompetence due to physical disability is not equivalent to stating that the person suffers from mental incompetence. Ohio's guardianship statutes require that if a person is judged to be incompetent due to physical disability, his or her consent must be obtained in writing or in open court before any appointment of a guardian can be made. The original court documents show that an error was clearly made (one of several errors cited) when Lucy Gallagher's consent was not obtained prior to the appointment.

An examination of the transcript of the proceedings also revealed that the evidence before the court did not meet the required degree of proof of mental incompetency, namely, clear and convincing evidence. In reversing the lower court's finding, the Court of Appeals stated that

> regardless of the actual mental condition of Lucy Gallagher at that time, the trial court did not have before it sufficient evidence to permit that court to conclude that Lucy Gallagher was mentally incompetent; and under those circumstances a guardian could not be appointed without the consent of the appellant.

Two-and-a-half years following the initial involuntary guardianship hearing, Lucy M. Gallagher was restored to full control of her person and estate. Had Lucy succumbed to the stress of unwelcome litigation at any time during this grueling thirty-month process, she would have been unable to defend her right to personal autonomy. It is ironic that one must be especially strong—unusually competent—to overturn a lower court's decision to label an aging man or woman an incompetent. Unfortunately, the ruling by the Court of Appeals does not mean that the particular problems addressed in Ohio are solved. Elderly men and women will continue to suffer the imposition of unwarranted guardianships. It can be hoped that cases such as *In re Guardianship of Gallagher* will provide the legal precedents the elderly will need in order to overturn oppressive and unwanted involuntary conservatorships and guardianships.

## Case 5.13. In re Lecht

Audrey Paula Heller petitioned an Ohio Superior Court to have herself appointed guardian of her eighty-seven-year-old mother, Edna Siegel Lecht. She alleged that her mother was incompetent. According to the records, her evidence showed that "in the two years [Audrey Paula Heller's] brother, Stewart, held power of attorney, Mrs. Lecht's estate dwindled from $600,000 to less than $70,000." During that period of time, Audrey Heller stated, Mrs. Lecht had written Stewart two checks for approximately $100,000 and had also deeded him her former home. Mrs. Lecht argued that she was fully competent and brought expert witnesses to support her claim. The testimony of Audrey Paula Heller's expert witnesses supported the need for a guardianship over the elderly woman. When the Superior Court ruled in favor of Mrs. Lecht, Audrey appealed the decision to Ohio's Court of Appeals. Why did they agree with the lower court?

*On the Court's Ruling.* According to the appellate court, it was not an abuse of the lower court's discretion to rule that Mrs. Lecht was competent in spite of the large gifts she had made to her son. "She stated she did not want the court to adjudicate her incompetent, she only wanted the court's assistance in helping her account for her assets." In refusing to impose a proxy decision-maker for Edna Siegel Lecht, the Ohio court echoed the growing unwillingness of some state courts to label elderly people incompetent in order to control their spending habits during their golden years. *In re Lecht* stands in striking contrast to case 4.1, *Cummings v. Stanford*, in which sixty-five-year-old newly widowed Mary Cummings is found disabled "due to advanced age, and perhaps mental disability," and thus deemed incapable of managing her financial resources.

## Case 5.14. *Estate of Galvin* v. *Galvin*

According to court records, Harold Galvin was clearly experiencing difficulties following a series of "small strokes and congestive heart failure,"
"advanced multiple arthritis," and the onset of "organic brain syndrome
[that] is irreversible and progressive." Because a stroke had left him with
a weak right side, even shopping had become a daunting task for Harold,
who as he pulled a shopping cart behind his walker to accomplish that
chore. Two years after his first of several hospitalizations, Mildred Tobias
petitioned the Circuit Court, Cook County, to be appointed guardian of
Harold's estate and person.

In court, Harold's behaviors were used as evidence to support Mrs.
Tobias's allegation that Mr. Galvin was no longer competent. Under
adverse examination by the petitioner's attorney, Harold testified that he
"never had a checking account, he invented the snowmobile, at one time
he had a pet black widow spider, and he could produce fire by pointing
his finger." He also stated that he could take care of himself and did not
want a guardian.

An examining psychiatrist stated that Harold Galvin suffered from
"'some delusions' and 'hallucinations,'" had a "behavioral disorder due
to some degeneration or atrophy of the brain cells," and was therefore disabled and unable to manage his financial affairs. The expert witness did
comment on cross-examination, however, that Harold "had made some
recent improvement" and was "more oriented and more realistic." Two
male friends were ready to testify that Harold believed he had once
worked with the Shah of Iran.

During this testimony, according to court records, the trial judge
interrupted the proceedings and stated,

> There is no way in God's world that I am going to adjudicate him a dis-
> abled person. He is physically suffering from some disability. * * * He
> is eccentric * * * but there is no way I am going to adjudicate him in
> need of a guardian. * * He lives a bizarre, strange life. I might not want
> to do it, but unless you can make an offer of proof that is going to show
> me that he does not understand the things he's doing—. He understands.
> * * *. (Punctuation in original.)

The Circuit Court judge refused to hear further proof and denied the
petition. Mildred Tobias sought a reversal of his decision from the Appellate Court of Illinois, First District, First Division, claiming that the decision of the trial court was against the manifest weight of the evidence and
that the trial judge "abused his discretion and did not allow her a full

opportunity to present her case." The Appellate Court disagreed with Mrs. Tobias and affirmed the lower court's refusal to grant a guardianship over Harold Galvin. Why?

*On the Court's Ruling.* The Appellate Court's opinion reflected its interest in protecting vulnerable individuals from the imposition of unnecessary involuntary guardianships. In discussing their ruling, the court borrowed from an earlier 1980 Illinois ruling:

> Under the new sections, the legislature has made it clear that although a person may be a disabled person, in the statutory sense of not being fully able to manage his person, a guardian is not therefore permissible or appropriate, if that person is capable of making and communicating responsible decisions concerning the care of his person. Thus, a person who was physically unable to care for himself, but who could direct others in such activity, would not necessarily need a guardian over his person. Similarly, a person might be a "disabled person" but nevertheless not be in need of a guardian over his estate, because with help from others he is able to direct and manage his affairs and estate.

Mrs. Tobias's relationship to Mr. Galvin was not made clear in the appellate court records. The case itself demonstrates that eccentricity or living a "bizarre strange life" should not make an elderly man or woman a candidate for an automatic guardianship.

## Case 5.15. In re Estate of Porter

Seventy-eight-year-old William Porter petitioned the Court of Common Pleas of Alleghany County, Orphans' Court Division, to reverse the guardianship of his estate that had been put in place by his sister when he was thirty years of age. At that time, according to court records, "testimony indicated that [because William Porter] suffered from epileptic seizures, he was adjudicated a feeble-minded person and a guardian was appointed to manage his estate, which was then valued at about $60,000." The Orphans' Court denied his petition and William appealed his case to the Supreme Court of Pennsylvania.

During the subsequent hearing before the Supreme Court, a psychologist, a psychiatrist, and a physician specializing in the field of geriatrics all testified that William Porter was fully competent. The niece and nephew who opposed their uncle's petition did not present any witnesses. They argued in their opposition that William had, throughout his life, handled only small sums of money and would not be able to manage his $250,000 estate. The Supreme Court of Pennsylvania ruled in William Porter's favor. Why?

*On the Court's Ruling.* The court concluded that "the orphans' court abused its discretion by rejecting the uncontradicted testimony of appellant's experts that he is competent." The court quoted from case law established in 1905 in ruling on William's case:

> A man may do what he pleases with his personal estate during his life. He may even beggar himself and his family if he chooses to commit such an act of folly. When he dies, and then only, do the rights of his heirs attach to his estate.

Moreover, the court argued,

> the decision of the orphans' court appears to rest primarily upon the conclusion that the appellant, who is now seventy-nine years old and throughout his life has handled only small sums of money, could not successfully manage about $250,000 in cash and securities. However, regardless of how well-intentioned or how accurate that conclusion is, it is not a legally justifiable basis for continuing to deprive appellant of the full control of his property.

It took an appeal to a higher court to discover existing case law—dating back to 1905—that would grant Mr. Porter his financial autonomy. After almost fifty years as a legal incompetent, William Porter was finally restored to full competence in the eyes of the law.

## Case 5.16. *Conservatorship of Sanderson*

Mary Carter Meyer filed a petition in the Superior Court of Santa Clara County for appointment of a conservator of the person and estate of her seventy-six-year-old mother, Mary Edith Sanderson. The court petition alleged that Mary Sanderson suffered from "an organic brain disease which renders her incoherent and disoriented at certain times." Now hospitalized after having broken her hip, the petitioner continued, Mrs. Sanderson was unable to care for herself or to manage her financial resources.

The petition was supported by testimony from Mary Sanderson's family physician, Dr. J. Sewall Brown, who had recently hospitalized Mrs. Sanderson for pernicious anemia. An uncooperative patient, Mrs. Sanderson required a sitter service "at the bedside so that she would not damage herself or the other patients in the room." Within a month of being sent home, Mary was rehospitalized when her hip was broken again, this time during a brutal burglary at her house. Within three weeks, Mary was discharged to a convalescent hospital and, "two months after the hip operation, [she] was able to walk without assistance."

In his testimony in support of Mary Carter Meyer's conservatorship petition, Dr. Brown characterized Mary Sanderson as "a strong-willed, stubborn, tough person." However,

> in Dr. Brown's opinion, appellant is not competent to take care of her financial affairs. Dr. Brown testified he would be "apprehensive about her future" if appellant [Mary Edith Sanderson] were to live alone. Dr. Brown felt appellant should live in a place where she could have her own room or apartment but where meals could be provided.

Mary Sanderson's daughter testified that she had gone through her mother's house while her mother was hospitalized and had found many uncashed checks and a few unpaid bills. The petitioner expressed the opinion that her mother was "not able mentally to take care of her own affairs." According to appellate court records, Mary Carter Meyer acknowledged that Mary Sanderson had always believed her daughter was trying to take her money. She also admitted that her mother "had been consistent in this regard and had felt the same way when her physical and mental condition had been better."

When asked to testify, Mrs. Sanderson stated that she had never had a checking account and had always paid her bills by money orders or cash. When asked why she had not paid the bills her daughter had found in her home, she replied, "No, I have no reason. I just didn't get around to it." She told the court that she wanted to rent a small apartment in Palo Alto to be near friends. "I want to be on my own, come and go as I please and live by myself." Mary stated emphatically that she could manage on her own and did not want her son or daughter—or anyone else—to take care of her affairs.

The trial court found that the petition for a conservatorship over Mary Sanderson was supported by a preponderance of the evidence. Mary Carter Meyer was appointed conservator of her mother's person and estate. As described in the court records, Mrs. Sanderson, "had lived much of her life in Palo Alto and wished to obtain an apartment in Palo Alto. However, she was placed in a rest home in San Jose." Unwilling to accept the Superior Court's ruling, Mary Sanderson appealed the order to the Court of Appeal and managed to get the judgment reversed.

*On the Court's Ruling.* The Court of Appeal stated that it was reversible error for the trial court to base its ruling on the preponderance of the evidence standard rather than employing a clear and convincing standard (see glossary for definitions).

> To allow many of the rights and privileges of everyday life to be stripped from an individual "under the same standard of proof applic-

able to run-of-the-mill automobile negligence actions" cannot be tolerated.

In its written opinion, the court held that because conservatorship proceedings "deprive an individual of freedom and place a lasting stigma on the individual's reputation," the proper standard in such a case is clear and convincing evidence:

> Since the conservatee is significantly deprived of freedom by Prob[ate] Code, §1851, under which the conservator has the care, custody and control of the conservatee and may fix his or her residence and domicile at any place within the state without court permission, and since there can be little doubt that a "stigma" attaches to a person who has been determined, pursuant to Prob. Code, §1751, to be unable to feed, clothe, house himself or take care of his financial resources.

"The evidence presented at the hearing," the appellate court justices concluded, "is susceptible to the interpretation that appellant Mary Edith Sanderson is a strong-willed, tough person rather than a person who is unable to feed, clothe and house herself." Mrs. Sanderson's daughter's subsequent petition for a rehearing by the California Supreme Court was denied. *Conservatorship of Sanderson* is particularly significant because the California Court of Appeal used the case as a vehicle to establish the proper standard of proof for conservatorship matters (i.e., the standard of clear and convincing evidence) — an important development in the history of California's Probate Codes.

## Case 5.17. Interdiction of Haggerty

Ninety-two-year-old Verna Judlin Haggerty resided in a Harvey, Louisiana, nursing home. In April of 1984, a neighbor filed a petition for interdiction (as guardianships or conservatorships are called in Louisiana), alleging that due to Verna's "advanced age, physical and mental condition, Mrs. Haggerty is incapable to caring for herself and her estate." Shortly after the petition was filed, however, Verna Haggerty moved to Galveston, Texas, to live with her niece. Within half a year of Verna's move to Texas, the neighbor's petition was dismissed by the court. The former neighbor lady appealed. Deciding that the court must appoint an expert to examine Verna Haggerty prior to acting to dismiss a petition for interdiction, the trial judge signed an order of examination "requiring that Mrs. Haggerty be examined by a physician in New Orleans." Verna Haggerty's motion to vacate the order was denied.

In her motion for summary judgment, Mrs. Haggerty had asserted three legal grounds: (1) the trial court lacked jurisdiction because she now resided in Texas, (2) the protections afforded by the Louisiana interdiction had been served since Mrs. Haggerty's person and estate were being cared for by her niece, and (3) the suit should be dismissed in the interest of judicial economy. In late 1986, the Louisiana court ordered Verna to return to New Orleans to be examined by a doctor of its choosing. Verna Haggerty advised the court that she was not prepared to travel from Galveston to New Orleans for an examination.

Without the examination, the Louisiana court rule ruled against the elderly woman and entered an order of interdiction. It based its determination on the fact that Verna Haggerty was "either unable or unwilling to travel to New Orleans for the ordered examination." Verna sought a reversal upon appeal to the Louisiana court and succeeded in having the order vacated. What guided the appellate court's final ruling?

*On the Court's Ruling.* The Court of Appeal of Louisiana held that (1) the order of interdiction based on Verna Haggerty's failure to complete an examination was erroneous, and (2) the trial court's requirement that ninety-two-year-old Verna travel from Texas to New Orleans for examination constituted undue hardship. A neighbor's petition for interdiction coupled with the fact that Mrs. Haggerty did not travel to New Orleans for the court-scheduled examination "does not lead to the conclusion that she is a candidate for interdiction." In the court's words:

> Interdiction is a harsh remedy. A judgment of interdiction [or conservatorship or guardianship] amounts to civil death, it is a declaration that the interdict [or ward] is incapable of caring for herself or her estate. . . . To allow a judgment of interdiction to stand on the basis of a petition and a failed examination would be erroneous since neither of these indicate that she is incapable of caring for herself or her estate. To afford the proposed interdict a fair and measured determination the petitioner must show that Mrs. Haggerty is incapable of administering her estate and unable to care for herself. Additionally, it must be shown that there is a necessity for interdiction.

Nonetheless, Verna Judlin Haggerty did not escape Louisiana's reach entirely. The judge stipulated that the court "arrange for an expert to examine Mrs. [Haggerty] in Galveston, Texas to determine whether she is incapable of administering her estate or caring for herself." The court would then weigh whether or not she would need interdiction —especially in light of the care she was receiving from her niece. One hopes Verna Judlin Haggerty fared better under Texas skies.

# COURT PROCEDURES IN CONTESTED CONSERVATORSHIPS/GUARDIANSHIPS SHOULD BE CHANGED

*The cases of* In re Bolander *and* In re Serafin *reflect two different complexities inherent in court hearings concerning conservatorship/ guardianship proceedings. The former illustrates the time-consuming, elaborate steps through which an elderly person must go to contest an unwanted guardianship, while the latter case reveals the absurdity of requiring a proposed ward to pay for the costs of an unwanted temporary guardianship—even when the case was dismissed with prejudice for want of prosecution. In* In re Serafin, *litigation over court fees continued for almost two years following the expiration of Mrs. Serafin's unnecessary temporary guardianship.*

## Case 5.18. In re Bolander

In May of 1991, Esther Weber Bolander's niece filed a petition in the Lake County Court of Common Pleas to become guardian of her aunt's person and estate. Following a hearing on the guardianship application and against the elderly woman's wishes, a court-appointed official was named guardian over Esther's estate. According to court records, the appointment was predicated solely upon the court's finding that Esther "was incompetent as a result of being legally blind." Although the trial court did not state that it found Esther to be mentally impaired due to her blindness, it made the assumption that her blindness left her incompetent to manage her financial affairs.

Esther Bolander immediately appealed the involuntary guardianship but her appeal was denied because she had "failed to provide a proper transcript of the hearing" on the application. While a second appeal was pending, Esther had completed two clinical interviews with a court-appointed psychiatrist. In March of 1992, the psychiatrist submitted a report finding Esther Bolander to be fully capable of handling her day-to-day affairs.

> Esther Bolander is lonely, is desirous of attention and affection, and has a propensity, by her own admission, to be attracted to younger men. This, coupled with her past behavior of giving away a large sum of money, indicates that she is vulnerable and could be easily swayed. Hopefully, some protections, short of guardianship, can be implemented so that Mrs. Bolander's funds are not mishandled. Her funds need to be protected so that they can be utilized in her best interests. *In my opinion,*

*however, she possesses sufficient mental capabilities to handle her day-to-day affairs."* (Court's emphasis.)

Esther's second motion for reconsideration was also denied in May of 1992. She had based her effort to dismiss the guardianship on two legal arguments: (1) since the guardianship had been imposed as a result of a physical disability, it had been void from the beginning because she had never consented to its imposition, and (2) even if the guardianship had been proper at its inception, the fact that a psychiatrist had found her to be mentally competent meant that her consent was required in order for the guardianship to continue. Without the benefit of an oral hearing on this matter, the probate court denied Esther Bolander's motion because "it had not been filed in a timely manner." Not until July of 1993 did Esther get a final ruling from the Court of Appeals of Ohio about her unwanted guardianship. The appellate court reversed the lower court's rulings and terminated Esther's onerous guardianship.

*On the Court's Ruling.* In its ruling, the Court of Appeals affirmed that the psychiatrist's 1992 report contained sufficient evidence "to rebut the presumption of continuing incompetence." According to the court,

> [under Ohio's] old definition, a person could be found incompetent solely upon the ground that a physical disability had rendered her incapable of taking proper care of herself or her property; i.e., it was not necessary to also show that the physical disability had rendered the person mentally impaired. Under the new definition [as of January, 1990], though, a trial court must find that the person is mentally impaired before it can ultimately conclude that she is incompetent. While the person's mental impairment can be the result of a physical disability, the physical disability itself cannot form the basis of a finding of incompetency. In other words, a guardianship can no longer be imposed under R.C. 2111.02 simply because a person has a physical ailment.

In its final comments on the matter, the Court of Appeals of Ohio, Lake County, said of this independent elderly woman: "As long as she is determined to be competent, she may spend her money as she pleases."

Esther Bolander had to move through two courts that had found her "incompetent as a result of being legally blind" before reaching a panel of judges who knew that Ohio's guardianship codes had changed. This case serves as a reminder that finding an attorney who is up-to-the-minute with a state's unique conservatorship/guardianship codes is crucially important for the elderly person who has been ordered to appear in court for a hearing on his or her competence or incapacity. The statutory revision that finally led to the dismissal of Esther Bolander's involuntary guardianship had been in place since January of 1990 — sixteen full months before the initial guardianship action was filed.

## Case 5.19. In re Serafin

In March of 1993, Joseph and John Krolopp filed a petition in the Circuit Court of McHenry County, Illinois, for both a temporary and permanent guardian of the estate of their mother, Rita Mary Serafin. According to court records, they brought their petition "to preserve the financial and personal well being of Rita Serafin, who was believed to suffer from a chronic mental disturbance or personality disorder and was unable to make responsible decisions with respect to the care of her estate valued at over $500,000." The brothers alleged that their mother's property (then the subject of a forfeiture proceeding in a separate case) would be lost to forfeiture unless appropriate steps were taken.

The court immediately appointed John E. Ridgway as guardian *ad litem*, appointed James E. Berner as Rita's counsel, and ordered a medical examination of the proposed ward. In April, Rita's attorney filed to dismiss the petition, arguing that it was not well-founded in fact or law. Nonetheless, the court ordered a temporary guardianship of Rita Serafin's estate and appointed Joseph and John Krolopp as limited coguardians of their mother's estate. In June, the guardian *ad litem* moved for an order for payment of his fees in the amount of $1,168.75.

In January of 1994, nine months after the appointment of the temporary limited guardianship over her estate, Rita Serafin approached the court to impound the records and dismiss her case with prejudice (for want of prosecution), stating that "the temporary sixty-day guardianship had expired and that there had been no further proceedings." Her sons filed in May of 1994 to resist the assessment of the guardian ad litem's fees against them, arguing that they should be assessed against Mrs. Serafin. Two months later, after finally hearing testimony on the fee issue, the court ordered Rita to pay the fees, "an amount which it found to be reasonable." Rita responded by filing a notice of appeal to the Appellate Court of Illinois, Second District. Her action forced the court to stay the order for the payment of fees.

> [Rita Mary Serafin] argues that she is not liable for the fees of the GAL [guardian *ad litem*] because there was never a finding that she was disabled, petitioners never sought a hearing on the petition for the appointment of a permanent guardian and the case was dismissed for want of prosecution. [She] asserts that she should not be held liable for the GAL's fees where it appears she was not adjudicated a "disabled person" and there was no "administration" of her estate.

Mrs. Serafin stated that the initial litigation was "unnecessary and perhaps frivolous." She argued that she should not be held liable for the GAL's fees because she had not been adjudicated a disabled person and there had been no administration of her estate. On this issue, Rita was unsuccessful.

> The appeals court found no abuse of discretion in taxing the ward for fees because the guardian undertook proper duties at the court's behest—including a review of respondent's medical evaluation—that were necessary to protect the ward's best interests. A guardian ad litem may provide extensive and valuable services in representing the interests of a ward without ever administering any property on the ward's behalf.

## VAGUE CONCEPTS IN CODES LEAD TO SUBJECTIVE RULINGS BY JUDGES

*The last case,* LeWinter v. Guardianship of LeWinter *illustrates a point made in the introduction to this section, namely, that vague definitions in the conservatorship/guardianship statutes of each state permit individual judges to supply* ad hoc *subjective interpretations on a case by case basis.*

### Case 5.20. LeWinter v. Guardianship of LeWinter

In September of 1991, Norman LeWinter, described in court records as the "financially dissatisfied adopted son" of ninety-four-year-old Louis LeWinter, petitioned the Circuit Court of Dade County, Florida, to determine whether his father was mentally and physically incapacitated and to secure an emergency temporary guardian for the elderly man. The court appointed a committee of two doctors and one lay person to examine Louis. At the hearing, Louis LeWinter agreed to a temporary guardian for a period of sixty days to "arrange for his care and to preserve, protect, assemble, and inventory his property." He stated clearly for the record that he did not want his son involved in the management of his affairs. The court arranged to transfer Louis LeWinter from The Jewish Home and Hospital where he was staying, back to his apartment on Miami Beach as he had requested.

At the end of the sixty-day period, a second hearing was conducted to determine the issue of incapacity and the need for a permanent guardianship. The committee's earlier report was received in evidence at that time. According to that report, Louis was not able " 'to make informed decisions regarding his right to contract' or 'his right to consent to medical treatment,' but that in all other respects he was able to make informed decisions in his life." One point of evidence contained in the report was that Louis LeWinter "acknowledged signing papers presented by his son and an unknown female attorney without understanding the content of the papers."

The circuit court ruled that this established by clear and convincing evidence that Mr. LeWinter was mentally incapacitated and incapable of exercising the right to contract, to make large gifts, to determine medical treatment, and to determine daily care. The court subsequently appointed a limited guardian to exercise such rights for him. Louis LeWinter appealed the Circuit Court's decision to the District Court of Appeal of Florida, Third District. The battle for his autonomy had already consumed one year of this ninety-four-year-old man's life. The Court of Appeal reversed the lower court's ruling. Why?

*On the Court's Ruling.* The court ruled that the order appointing a guardianship over Mr. LeWinter was not supported by competent evidence. It is true, the court agreed, that the report of the original examining committee did contain findings that Louis LeWinter then lacked the capacity to perform the functions listed in the order. However, the report had been completed over six weeks before the hearing and was rendered "entirely valueless by the admitted fact that Mr. LeWinter's condition had markedly improved in the meantime." The appellate court also commented on the fact that the trial judge had contributed his nonexpert opinion as though it were evidence.

> The trial judge's own opinion that the ward was incapacitated by mere lapses of attention and memory is a mere nonexpert conclusion entitled to no evidentiary weight. . . . While the trial court may, indeed must, determine the credibility and weight of the evidence, it is not empowered to create that evidence from whole cloth. . . .

For example, the record contains the following:

> THE COURT: "You see, Counsel, we are going from one thing to another, and I am convinced that, I want the record, so the Third District knows it, that Mr. LeWinter, in my opinion, cannot follow what is going on." (In footnote.)

Because the lower court's order was not supported by clear and convincing evidence yet would have a "profound effect upon [Mr. LeWinter's] privacy and dignity," the guardianship petition was dismissed.

≈  ≈  ≈

We shall now move on to review the cases of fifteen elderly men and women who have had guardians or conservators appointed as their substitute decision-makers and either could not or did not successfully appeal the trial courts' rulings. What has happened to them? Who is monitoring their court-appointed guardians to ensure that the interests of these vulnerable individuals are being served? How well is this system working? The answers to these questions will become all too clear in the next chapter.

## CASE REFERENCES

Case 5.1. *In re Estate of Wagner*, 367 N.W.2d 736 (Neb. 1985).
Case 5.2. *Katz v. Superior Court, Etc.*, 141 Cal.Rptr.234 (Cal.App. 1977).
Case 5.3. *Goldman v. Krane*, 786 P.2d 437 (Colo.App. 1989).
Case 5.4. *Matter of Conservatorship of Goodman*, 766 P.2d 1010 (Okl.App. 1988).
Case 5.5. *West Virginia ex rel. Shamblin v. Collier*, 445 S.E.2d 736 (W.Va. 1994).
Case 5.6. *Grant v. Johnson*, 757 F.Supp. 1127 (D.Or. 1991).
Case 5.7. *In re McDonnell*, 266 So.2d 87 (Fla. 1972).
Case 5.8. *Matter of Grinker*, 573 N.E.2d 536 (N.Y. 1991).
Case 5.9. *McCallie v. McCallie*, 660 So.2d 584 (Ala. 1995).
Case 5.10. *Matter of Estate of McPeak*, 368 N.E.2d 957 (Ill.App. 1977).
Case 5.11. *Interdiction of Dobbins*, 535 So.2d 1079 (La.App. 2 Cir. 1988).
Case 5.12. *In re Guardianship of Gallagher*, 441 N.E.2d 593 (Ohio App. 1981).
Case 5.13. *In re Lecht*, (Ohio Ct.App. Feb. 15, 1996, unpublished opinion; Ohio Sup.Ct. rules apply). Described in *Mental and Physical Disability Law Reporter*, May-June 1996, p. 349.
Case 5.14. *Estate of Galvin v. Galvin*, 445 N.E.2d 1223 (Ill.App. 1 Dist. 1983).
Case 5.15. *In re Estate of Porter*, 345 A.2d 171 (Pa. 1975).
Case 5.16. *Conservatorship of Sanderson*, 106 Cal.App.3d 611; 165 Cal.Rptr. 217 (Cal. 1980).
Case 5.17. *Interdiction of Haggerty*, 519 So.2d 868 (La.App. 4 Cir. 1988).
Case 5.18. *In re Bolander*, 624 N.E.2d 322 (Ohio App. 11 Dist. 1993).
Case 5.19. *In re Serafin*, 649 N.E.2d 972 (Ill.App. 2 Dist. 1995).
Case 5.20. *LeWinter v. Guardianship of LeWinter*, 606 So.2d 387 (Fla.App. 3 Dist. 1992).

## NOTES

1. J. E. Rein, "Preserving Dignity and Self-Determination of the Elderly in the Face of Competing Interests and Grim Alternatives: A Proposal for Statutory Refocus and Reform," *George Washington Law Review* 60 (1992): 1880.

2. J. Brock, "Judicial Decisions in Guardianship Cases," in G. H. Zimny and G. T. Grossberg, eds., *Guardianship of the Elderly: Psychiatric and Judicial Aspects* (New York: Springer Publishing Company, 1998), p. 87.

# CHAPTER SIX

# WHO IS GUARDING
# THE GUARDIANS?

*The misery of a child is interesting to a mother, the misery of a young man is interesting to a young woman, the misery of an old man is interesting to nobody.*

— Victor Hugo, *Les Misérables* (1862)

Once an adult is placed under the benevolent dictatorship of a guardian or conservator, how does he or she fare? The following fifteen cases have been chosen with care. Each speaks of a system of laws run amok, capable of victimizing the elderly men and women it was designed to protect. States have had little success in their attempts to legislate standards for conservators and guardians. "We have tried to get legislation starting back in 1984," said Judith Chinello, a conservator in Southern California and President of the Professional Fiduciary Association of California. "We believe there is a real need because it is such an unusual industry, such a vulnerable class of client."[1] As quoted previously, Don Green, former chairman of the State Bar of California's probate section, spoke of his organization's unsuccessful attempt to regulate conservators and guardians: "It's crazy to put people's welfare and their estates in the hands of private conservators [and guardians] who the state has screened less than it screens barbers."[2]

We shall now examine the uneven outcomes of fifteen unique conservatorships and guardianships. With four exceptions, the citations for the cases differ from most of those we have already reviewed in chapters 4 and 5. Why? The cases used in this chapter result not from readily accessible court records but rather from major newspaper and journal accounts filed by investigative reporters and outraged attorneys who respond when conservatorship/guardianship abuses spill over into the public arena.

These are the stories of fifteen elderly men and women who, having been judged incapable of looking after their personal and financial affairs, are left to the mercy of relatives or to the integrity of strangers. In reading the following accounts of people whose legal status has been reduced by the courts to that of powerless and dependent children, ask yourself the question: Who is guarding the guardians? All too often the answer is no one.

## Case 6.1. Guardianship of Florence Peters

Unable to cope with his eighty-five-year-old wife's ongoing health problems, Florence Peters' husband had his wife declared incompetent in court. As described in the *George Washington Law Review* in 1992, she was promptly institutionalized and received no subsequent visitation from her husband. During her convalescence, Florence Peters managed to win back her civil rights. She won the battle—but soon lost the war. Neither her husband nor her court-appointed female guardian moved to release Florence from her convalescent center and permit her to return home. Was Florence aided by the court?

*Result.* No. Florence remained institutionalized until her death. Neither her husband nor her guardian attended her funeral. They were honeymooning together in upstate New York.

## Case 6.2. Guardianship of Minnie Monoff

A guardian was appointed to protect the affairs of Minnie Monoff while she recovered from a stroke in a Kansas hospital. Home at last, Minnie looked forward to visits from friends and neighbors, to assistance from Meals on Wheels, and to raising her chickens. How did the guardianship function for Minnie?

*Result.* As reported by Fred Bayles and Scott McCartney in their Pulitzer Prize winning article in the *Los Angeles Times*, when the friend who had been named her guardian came calling, Minnie, angry and offended by the guardianship, locked herself in her house and refused to come out. The guardian secured an emergency court order, had Minnie sedated by a nurse, had the county sheriff remove her from her home, and had her placed in a nursing home. The court order had been signed by the judge only hours before he received a letter from Minnie's sister opposing the guardianship. Minnie's court-appointed lawyer had waived a hearing on the order without talking to his client, "in part out of concern for the eighty-two-year-old woman's health in the summer heat."

The court, charged with overseeing guardianship cases, turned a deaf ear to Minnie's pleas from the nursing home. "You don't know what a sick feeling I had, to leave my home, where I was happy and taking care of myself. . . . It's rotten. It's no good," she cried. Minnie persevered and, following five weeks of effort, succeeded in having her guardianship overturned.

Home at last, eighty-two-year-old Minnie Monoff reflected about her experience of being locked in by a system that refused to listen to her. "There's not many able to fight like me. A lot of people would just take it and say, 'Well, I can't do anything about it.' I wouldn't want anybody to go through what I went through." Frightened by the ease with which the system forced her into a nursing home, she sent a warning to her peers: "Like a criminal—that's the way they treated me, and that's the way I felt. I don't trust these courts. . . . How can one person help yourself when you get a gang like that against you?"

The court-appointed attorney who had not spoken with Minnie Monoff prior to her extraction from her home and placement in a nursing home offered a different opinion: "I tried to represent her the best that I could, and I still think I did her a hell of a job."

## Case 6.3. Conservatorship of Nelta Bradner

At the age of seventy, Nelta Bradner had preselected a friend to serve as her conservator should she ever lose the capacity to care for herself. Within two years, Nelta's Alzheimer's had progressed to the point that help was needed. This was provided not by Nelta Bradner's nominated friend but by a professional Riverside County conservator, Bonnie Cambalik. Cambalik had gotten Nelta to change her nomination to Cambalik's firm, West Coast Conservatorship, Inc. Although a stranger to Nelta, Cambalik also arranged for West Coast's attorney to change Nelta's will without consulting or informing Nelta's attorney. How did Nelta fare under the protection of her new, court-appointed professional conservator?

*Result.* As described in the January 2000 issue of *California Lawyer*, while Nelta was confined to a nursing home and bedridden in a fetal position, Bonnie Cambalik reported expenses averaging at least $1,000 for her client's personal needs. In May of 1993 alone, Cambalik's bill for Nelta's groceries totaled $1,250—"an inordinate sum given Bradner's condition."

When authorities were called in to investigate West Coast Conservatorships, Inc., Nelta's case was exposed. Missing jewelry, including a medallion that was inscribed with Nelta Bradner's name, was recovered from West Coast's office safe. Cambalik had told investigators that the missing items had been stolen by caregivers in Nelta's nursing home. On November 9, 1999, Cambalik was arrested and charged with theft, embezzlement, perjury, and conspiracy (*People* v. *Cambalik*, Cr No. 88557).

Barbara Jagiello, the San Francisco "Guardian Angel" who helped unearth the county-wide scandal, stated: "If she had just taken the money and given them good care, I guess I wouldn't be so upset. But she didn't. She stole their money and abused them."

## Case 6.4. Bryan v. Holzer

In March of 1979, Beatrice Irene Bryan, a retired psychologist, was declared incompetent and in need of a conservator to manage her financial affairs. According to court records, the court appointed her nephew James A. Bryan as conservator of his elderly maiden aunt's considerable estate. James filed an initial estate inventory with the court at the beginning of 1980. His second accounting, filed in June of 1983, was approved by the court "with reservations" concerning $28,000 listed as a "joint business investment" between Mr. Bryan and his ward.

By June of 1987, some four years later, the estate's attorneys requested a hearing on the status of Beatrice Bryan's conservatorship. "Approximately six months later the conservator [Mr. Bryan] was removed by court order because of delays in filing accountings and inventories." Frank Holzer was named by the court as Beatrice Irene Bryan's new conservator. Was Beatrice's new court-appointed conservator able to restore the funds missing from her estate?

*Result.* Yes. Frank Holzer filed a complaint in chancery court against James Bryan and his wife, Elizabeth, claiming they had breached their fiduciary duty as conservator. A public accountant and retired IRS criminal investigator in the intelligence division was appointed by the court to provide a detailed report of the conservatorship estate's status. After a careful examination, he delivered his opinion that "many discrepancies and questionable transactions existed in the conservatorship account."

> After the hearings the chancery court found that the Bryans had, "acted in collusion in converting to their own use a sum exceeding $100,000 belonging to the ward." The court concluded they had misappropriated $177,159.44 from the ward's account, even though a small portion of these funds might arguably have been used indirectly for the ward's benefit.

According to court documents, "the overwhelming remainder of the misappropriated expended funds was not used for the benefit of the ward and, in fact, appear to have been embezzled."

James and Elizabeth Bryan appealed the chancery court's judgment of $177,159.44 to the Supreme Court of Mississippi. The Supreme Court affirmed the lower court's judgment "as to all aspects concerning James and Elizabeth Bryan." The Bryans had "breached a sacred and honored fiduciary duty," the court stated in its final ruling.

## Case 6.5. Conservatorship of John Nagle

As described in the *Los Angeles Times*, the public guardian's office of Santa Clara County was appointed conservator of seventy-seven-year-old John Nagle and his small estate in 1983. How did John do under the watchful eye of his court-appointed guardian?

*Result.* Mr. Nagle was not visited by his conservator even once during the following two years. He died of starvation. Santa Clara County's grand jury blamed the public guardian's office for his 1985 death. "The grand jury's report helped establish new guidelines for the office."

## Case 6.6. Guardianship of Maverick

By the time she was eighty-one years old, Maverick—so nicknamed for her feisty independence— had buried or divorced five husbands and lived frugally off of her monthly income of $1,200. As reported by the *Seattle Times* in 1995, only after her daughter began signing her name to her mother's checks and pocketing the funds did anyone realize the extent of Maverick's diminished capacity to manage her affairs. Maverick's bank asked the state to intervene. A professional guardianship service was appointed to clean her apartment, to shop for her groceries, and to safeguard Maverick's person, income, and $26,000 nest egg. "In the eyes of the law, Maverick became 'the ward,' a name that could squeeze the life out of someone just by the way it's printed on the page." How did Maverick do under the compassionate eye of the State of Washington?

*Result.* In court records filed only because Maverick's apartment manager and state caseworker "decided that wasn't the way things should be," it is shown that during the first four months of her guardianship, two guardianship-related bills alone consumed more than a third of Maverick's $26,000 nest egg. The court-appointed Bellevue attorney who had visited Maverick and had recommended the appointment of a professional guardianship service submitted a bill for $3,281 for his work. The guardianship services billed her small estate over $7,000 in fees. Sixty-five dollars an hour for making grocery lists and $50 per hour for doing the shopping were defended by the company as "accepted rates that guardianships charge." Maverick continued to live in her small apartment, eating the cookies and T.V. dinners provided by her new guardians. The cookies were delivered in 10-pound packages because they were Maverick's favorite food.

According to a state social worker who investigated, Maverick's guardian had neither taken her to see a doctor to attend to her seriously swollen ankles nor cleaned her filthy apartment. The codirector of the professional guardianship service asserts that "he and his partner have made good decisions under difficult circumstances."

> "It's our most painful case," [he] says. "We have a really complicated woman with complicated needs who is very independent and resistant to people helping her."

Under "guardianship protection," Maverick's expenses totaled more than $4,000 a month. As summarized by Tacoma lawyer Doug Schafer, "There is no effective oversight, licensing or supervision of this growing profession, this guardianship industry. It's a time bomb."

> Frank Hibbard, legal-services developer for the state's Adult Services Administration, agrees. "We need some industry self-regulation or state regulation, because there is no way to keep a dishonest guardian out of the business," he says. Furthermore, there are no industry standards, no way to force innovation or use of lower-cost arrangements such as bill-paying services. Hibbard, among others, says the courts are too crowded, understaffed and underfunded to provide the line-by-line scrutiny guardianship accounts need. "Go down and sit there in a court," he says. "Tell me how you can get reasoned justice out of a court that is like a zoo."

## Case 6.7. Guardianship of Marguerite Van Etten

In a Washington Post story titled "Subcommittee Hears Story of Abuse," Molly Sinclair tells the story of sixty-year-old Marguerite Van Etten who was involved in an automobile accident that left her in a coma for two months. During that time, Mrs. Van Etten's daughter secured a guardianship over her mother to pay her bills legally and to handle her affairs. Marguerite was moved from her home in Broward County, Florida, to her daughter's home in Maryland.

After recovering, Mrs. Van Etten returned to Florida against her daughter's wishes—returned no longer as an independent adult but as

"'83-0449; Van Etten, Mentally Incompetent" in the eyes of the law. Her driver's license had been revoked as had been her voting privileges, and her house was bare. Her furniture had been shipped to Maryland before she was declared incompetent. According to Mrs. Van Etten, the loss of her right to vote was the proverbial last straw. "I decided to do everything possible to learn about guardianships and existing laws" to reverse the guardianship, she said. How did Marguerite do?

*Result.* Marguerite Van Etten conducted her research in libraries and courts, paid for a psychiatric evaluation that affirmed her good health, and hired a good lawyer. Within seven months, she was "restored to competency" when her guardianship was terminated. The experience cost her an estimated $40,000.

> "I learned that common criminals had more rights than a person under a guardianship. . . ." [Marguerite] Van Etten warned that what happened to her could happen to anyone else. "All you have to do is have a stroke or be in a coma and they can take away all your rights."

## Case 6.8. In re Interdiction of Ronstrom

A Louisiana court determined that George Nelson Ronstrom needed curators (as guardians are called in Louisiana) to protect his person and estate. His wife, who cared for him in their home, became curator of his person. A bank was appointed curator of George's estate—an estate that consisted of hundreds of art objects and pieces of antique furniture valued by a court-appointed appraiser at $157,837. What steps did the bank take to preserve Mr. Ronstrom's estate?

*Result.* Billing the cost to their client's estate, the bank hired a twenty-four-hour guard service for ten months to "protect" George's art works and furniture. Mr. Ronstrom's wife protested to Louisiana's Court of Appeal. The court ruled that the assets could have been auctioned off or placed in a warehouse at much less expense. According to court records:

> The present case presents a picture of even greater mismanagement. The moveable property in question was valued by court appointed appraisers, paid for by the estate, at $157,837.00. . . . To date the curator [bank] has expended approximately $80,000.00 on twenty-four hour guard service.
>
> This expense alone amounts to approximately half of the appraised value of the movable property of the estate. . . . Given these values, the only ones which appear on the record, such an expenditure represents gross mismanagement and waste of the estate.

The court ordered that the bank be removed as curator, effective immediately. Unfortunately, as summarized by Linda Weeks of the Florida's Bar Association disability committee in her discussion of contemporary guardianship practices, "There's the way it should be, and there's the way it is—the way you can get away with."[3]

## Case 6.9. Guardianship of Sarah

Shortly before she reached the age of ninety, Sarah, who according to the *Los Angeles Times* had no relatives or friends, came under the care of a court-appointed guardian in Dade County, Florida. The guardian moved Sarah into an adult congregate living facility. How did she do under Florida's care?

*Result.* Sarah came to the attention of a special grand jury in Miami when her congregate care facility was closed by the state. Now ninety-two, Sarah was found living in squalor and in "intolerable living conditions" even though her bank account contained $150,000. Her guardian, who had not filed a court-mandated report in two years, was the owner of the adult home—"a conflict that violated Florida law." Said Frank Repensek, executive director of the nonprofit Guardianship Program of Dade County: "The thing that scares the hell out of me is that people are acting as guardian without any kind of supervision."

## Case 6.10. Matter of Guardianship of Renz

Mary Lou Renz became the ward of a court-appointed guardian when, in late 1991, the Burleigh County Public Administrator petitioned the trial court for guardianship. According to court records, Mary had had a long history of alcohol abuse and had undergone numerous inpatient treatments for alcoholism both at the North Dakota State Hospital and at a neighboring addiction facility. After a "particularly serious incident of alcohol abuse," a hearing was held at County Court, Burleigh County, South Central Judicial District. The trial court found Mary Renz "unable to provide for her personal care or perform necessary daily activities due to chronic alcoholism" and appointed a limited guardianship over her legal and financial affairs and a full guardianship over Mary's living arrangements.

By March of 1992, Mary had been moved into a structured care facility and eventually attained sobriety in that setting. In September of that year, her guardian petitioned the court for authority to sell Mary Renz's home and automobile to pay for ongoing care. Mary petitioned the court to terminate her guardianship and stop the sale of her home and car, basing her defense on her recent sobriety. She argued that "although she is an alcoholic with a long history of unsuccessful treatment for alcoholism, she presently is sober and thus, no longer is an incapacitated person." She cited in her defense a 1982 case in California, *Estate of Murphy* (134 Cal.App.3d 15, 184 Cal.Rptr. 363) in which

> the court held that a trial court may not find an alcoholic residing in a care facility and currently able to manage his own affairs "gravely disabled" based only on the likelihood that, were the court to terminate the conservatorship, he would begin drinking again.

*Result.* The County Court denied Mary's petition, whereupon she appealed to the Supreme Court of North Dakota. Her appeal was unsuccessful. Mary's court-appointed guardian was given permission against his now-sober ward's pleas not to sell her home and her automobile. According to court records,

> since she has lived . . . [in] a structured care facility, Renz has remained sober and regularly attends Alcoholics Anonymous meetings. . . . Renz's argument makes an unfounded leap from the fact that she may be sober while she is in a structured facility and under a guardian's care to the assertion that she is capable of maintaining her sobriety without the structure and support furnished under a guardianship. . . .
> Accordingly, we pay no heed to the California precedents because they pay no heed to either historical or prognostic evidence.

One cannot help but wonder how Mary Renz—who "began drinking following the death of her husband"—will deal with the subsequent double blows of losing her car and her home.

## Case 6.11. Guardianship of Violet

Eighty-one-year-old Violet could no longer manage alone. Her daughter was nominated and confirmed as her mother's official guardian by the Chicago court. Did Violet enjoy life with her daughter and grandchildren?

*Result.* A visiting social worker found Violet lying in a urine-soaked bed, dehydrated, and suffering from severe malnutrition. She had been left in the care of her grandchildren who allegedly called her "Fido" and fed her only once a day. The grandchildren allegedly spent Violet's Social Security payments. Although her daughter and grandchildren denied any wrong-doing, the judge placed Violet under the protection of the public guardian.

## Case 6.12. Conservatorship of Helen Conrad

As reported by Tom Gorman in the April 25, 1999, *Los Angeles Times*, Riverside County's sole probate court judge had decided that mentally frail Helen Conrad, a childless widow in her nineties, could no longer manage her personal and financial affairs. He appointed a private conservator to protect Helen. Helen Conrad's new conservator fired the two in-home caregivers who had helped her for six years, and replaced them at Helen's Sun City retirement home with employees from her own private home healthcare company. How did Helen Conrad fare under the protection of her court-appointed conservator? Helen's case was later described in the January 2000 issue to *California Lawyer* to illustrate "the biggest elder-care scandal to ever hit the state" (see also case 6.3, "Conservatorship of Nelta Bradner" in chapter 6).

*Result.* According to probate court records, Helen Conrad's conservator spent over $264,000 of Helen's $300,000 estate in less than two years. Almost $170,000 of that amount went to the conservator's home healthcare company to provide Helen's care—at a cost of more than twice the $3,000 monthly fee Helen had previously paid for her own home care. About the time the judge ordered the conservator to "refund" some of these healthcare payments by forfeiting future conservatorship fees, the private conservator moved Helen Conrad from her familiar Sun City retirement home into a cheaper facility. Her estate had dwindled to $13,000.

"It's worse than grave robbery," said Jay Orr, who supervises special investigations for the Riverside County district attorney's office. "It's not so much the dollar loss, but it speaks to an institutional breakdown . . . where the checks and balances of the system failed and the victims are people who were at the end of their lives and are the most vulnerable."

## Case 6.13. Guardianship of Jessie Linthicum

Writing in the *Washington Post*, Sandra Evans reported the case of seventy-six-year-old Jessie Linthicum of Virginia who became her daughter's ward after a doctor testified that her elderly mother had become incompetent. According to court documents, the doctor deferred to the daughter's opinion and, in turn, the court-appointed guardian *ad litem* deferred to the doctor's opinion. Did Jessie need the help of a surrogate decision-maker, and did her daughter provide the assistance her mother was said to require?

*Result.* One month after becoming the ward of her daughter, who had moved into her mother's house "to keep up repairs," Jessie Linthicum was placed in a nursing home and involuntarily confined to a ward with the facility's severely mentally ill patients. Jessie remained a virtual prisoner in the nursing home for nearly a year until friends successfully helped her petition the court for a transfer back to her beloved home. She legally regained her competency by having her unnecessary guardianship terminated. The daughter stated that she had placed her mother in the nursing home only because the strain of "caring for her at home had become too great."

## Case 6.14. U.S. v. Young

In 1970, a probate court in Massachusetts appointed Howard Young, an attorney and former judge, as guardian for a disabled veteran who received benefits from the Veterans' Administration. By 1985, the veteran's assets totaled more than $250,000. According to court records, Howard Young filed for personal bankruptcy in August of that year.

When officials of the Veterans' Administration noticed that Mr. Young had not filed any guardianship accounting information for the year 1986, they made a request for the missing documentation. Only following many delays and the issuance of a court order did Howard Young submit an accounting of his ward's money. He left blank the sections where his ward's brokerage securities had been listed in all previous records.

In April of 1988, Mr. Young eventually supplemented his accountings for 1986 and 1987, stating for the record that he had "decided to transfer the long-range certificates of deposit to a two-year program of real estate and bloodstock investment [in a company that] . . . has among its owners certain members of my family who have expertise in these areas." As described in court records, the "real estate and bloodstock" referred to a Kentucky horse breeding farm he had invested in for his daughter and a racehorse he had purchased for the farm. Both investments had soured. What did the Probate Court do to protect the veteran's dwindling funds?

*Result.* A new guardian was appointed. Upon failing to replenish his former ward's estate, Mr. Young was "convicted of embezzlement and mail fraud by the United States District Court for the District of Massachusetts." His appeal to the United States Court of Appeals, First Circuit, was unsuccessful: Howard Young was sentenced to twelve months in prison. As summarized by the final court,

> [the] guardian's conviction for embezzlement was sufficiently supported by evidence that, at time when he was in financial trouble, he sold safe securities in which he had invested ward's money and reinvested money in risky business venture owned by his daughter, while declining to provide guardianship accounting information.

## Case 6.15. Guardianship of Beulah Holt

In his 1976 petition to have his sixty-six-year-old mother declared incompetent, Beulah Esther Holt's son John E. Holt submitted a two-sentence statement from a doctor: "It is my medical opinion that Mrs. Beulah Holt is unable to take care of her affairs. Therefore I recommend a power of attorney [*sic*]." As described in the *Washington Post*, the petition stated that Beulah Holt, recently retired from Arlington government, was incapacitated "by reason of advanced age and impaired health." A guardian *ad litem* appointed by the Virginia court reported that the proposed ward had refused to answer his questions. Neither Beulah nor her son were present at the hearing.

Nonetheless, the court stripped Beulah Holt of her rights (including the right to vote) and granted Beulah's son control over her personal and financial affairs. Beulah was moved out of her apartment and into her son's home against her will. How well did the guardianship serve this presumably intelligent sixty-six-year-old woman?

*Result.* For eleven years, she was known in Arlington Circuit Court Records as "Beulah Esther Holt, Incompetent." "It was like a bad marriage," Beulah said in describing why she waited so long before challenging the guardianship. "I kept thinking things would get better." When things did not improve and with the help of Legal Aid attorneys she had contacted through adult protective services, Beulah managed to have the guardianship overturned. She charged in court that her son had improperly managed her estate, had taken excessive amounts of money for room and board for her involuntary confinement in his home, and had paid for full-time housemaids out of her funds. "We did the best we could for her," John Holt said in an interview, adding that his mother, Beulah, had "an amazing transformation" at the end of 1986.

Freed at last, seventy-seven-year-old Beulah Holt moved into an apartment of her own and began enjoying trips to Florida and Cape Cod. Commenting about her guardianship experience, she expressed dismay at the ease with which her life was handed over to her son.

> "It's like planting you someplace," she said. "I keep wondering how [the judge] could do this without examining me. They could do it to anybody. . . . I would hate for what happened to me to happen to anyone else."

Discussing Beulah Holt's case in 1988, Joy Duke spoke as adult protective services' manager in Virginia's Department of Social Services. "Family members [appointed as guardians] have such awesome power to do or not do. The incapacitated person is at the mercy of the family member. There is no way ot know about or rectify that situation."

                                   ❧ ❧ ❧

We live in a time when the growing number of court-appointed conservators and guardians is increasing so rapidly that state probate courts cannot keep track of them all. It is impossible to estimate the number of people in the "guardianship business" because "there's no regulation, no licensing, no testing."[4] As summarized by Jan Ellen Rein:

> An often overlooked issue in the ethics debate is whether—even if the client's condition theoretically warrants guardianship—the treatment of wards under guardianship or conservatorship in practice is decent enough to make guardianship a morally permissible option.[5]

Clearly, there are much less abusive ways to help friends and neighbors as they age. We shall now review currently available local, state, and federally sponsored alternatives to unwanted proxy decision-making arrangements.

# CASE REFERENCES

Case 6.1. Guardianship of Florence Peters. Described in J. E. Rein, "Preserving Dignity and Self-Determination of the Elderly in the Face of Competing Interests and Grim Alternatives: A Proposal for Statutory Refocus and Reform," *George Washington Law Review* 60 (1992): 1871 (footnote).
Case 6.2. Guardianship of Minnie Monoff. Described in F. Bayles and S. McCartney, "Minnie Monoff Didn't Want Protection; She Wanted Freedom," *Los Angeles Times*, 27 September 1987, p. A2.
Case 6.3. Conservatorship of Nelta Bradner. Described in Christopher Manes, "Guardian Angels," *California Lawyer* (January 2000): 34–40.
Case 6.4. *Bryan v. Holzer*, 589 So.2d 648 (Miss. 1991)
Case 6.5. Conservatorship of John Nagle. Described in F. Bayles and S. McCartney "California's Public Guardians: Stewards of Elderly beset With Cases," *Los Angeles Times*, 27 September 1987, pp. 28–29.
Case 6.6. Guardianship of Maverick. Described in C. M. Ostrom, "Who Guards People from the Guardians Watching over Them?" *Seattle Times*, 25 September 1995, pp. A1, A7.
Case 6.7. Guardianship of Marguerite Van Etten. Described in M. Sinclair, "Subcommittee Hears Stories of Abuse," *Washington Post*, 26 September 1987, p. A3.
Case 6.8. *In re Interdiction of Ronstrom*, 436 So.2d 588 (La.App. 4 Cir. 1983)

Case 6.9. Guardianship of Sarah. Described by F. Bayles and S. McCartney, "Minnie Monoff Didn't Want Protection; She Wanted Freedom," *Los Angeles Times*, 27 September 1987, p. A27. I have added the pseudonym "Sarah"; no name is given in original.

Case 6.10. *Matter of Guardianship of Renz*, 507 N.W.2d 76 (N.D. 1993)

Case 6.11. Guardianship of Violet. Described in F. Bayles and S. McCartney, "Minnie Monoff Didn't Want Protection; She Wanted Freedom," *Los Angeles Times*, 27 September 1987, p. A2. I have added the pseudonym "Violet"; no name is given in original.

Case 6.12. Conservatorship of Helen Conrad. Described in Tom Gorman, "Conservator Suspected of Bilking the Frail," *Los Angeles Times*, 25 April 1999, pp. A1, A29, A31, A32.

Case 6.13. Guardianship of Jessie Linthicum. Described in S. Evans, "Lax Guardianship Rules Frighten Va. Elderly," *Washington Post*, 18 July 1988, p. A1.

Case 6.14. *U.S. v. Young*, 955 F.2d 99 (1st Cir. 1992)

Case 6.15. Guardianship of Beulah Holt. Described in S. Evans, "Lax Guardianship Rules Frighten Va. Elderly," *Washington Post*, July 18, 1988, p. A1.

# NOTES

1. S. Emmons, "Conservators' Reach Can Be a Surprise," *Los Angeles Times*, 23 November 1997, p. A29.

2. Ibid.

3. F. Bayles and S. McCartney, "Minnie Monoff Didn't Want Protection; She Wanted Freedom," *Los Angeles Times*, 27 September 1987, p. 27.

4. D. Starkman, "Guardians May Need Someone to Watch Over Them," *Wall Street Journal*, 8 May 1998, p. B1.

5. J. E. Rein, "Clients With Destructive and Socially Harmful Choices— What's an Attorney To Do? Within and Beyond the Competency Construct," *Fordham Law Review* 62 (1994): 1157.

# CHAPTER SEVEN

# ALTERNATIVES TO "PROTECTIVE PROCEEDINGS"

*When a man carries out the principals of conscientiousness and reciprocity he is not far from the universal law. What you do not wish others should do unto you, do not do unto them.*
—Confucius (551–479 B.C.E.), *The Golden Mean of Tsesze XIII*

According to a recent survey published in *Newsweek*, almost twenty-five million men and women are caring for aging relatives.[1] More than eight million of them are handling that responsibility long distance. Wendy Lustbader and Nancy R. Hooyman, eldercare experts and authors of *Taking Care of Aging Family Members*, list even more surprising statistics: nearly 80 percent of those twenty-five million caregivers are women, and one-third of them are age sixty-five and older.[2] It is estimated that women in the "sandwich generation" can expect to spend seventeen years of their lives taking care of their children—and eighteen years helping an aging parent.[3]

We have reviewed fifty-five cases involving the use of adversarial involuntary conservatorship/guardianship pleadings to subdue the elderly, to control the disposition of their assets, and to protect them from their own "unreasonable choices" (and "unreasonable" means, of course, whatever the sitting judge decides it means, no more, no less). It is a brutal way to treat aging relatives. As legal scholar Jan Ellen Rein so

167

aptly described adjudications of incompetence in protective proceedings to help the elderly, "using an incompetency finding to avoid a bad result is like, if the reader will excuse the hyperbole, using a small nuclear device to destroy a dangerous building."[4]

How, then, can we help support the independence of our aged friends and relatives whose decision-making powers are intact? There are respectful alternatives in almost all communities that provide the personal care and day-to-day financial assistance needed by dependent but autonomous elderly people. All of these options keep the seniors out of conservatorship/guardianship courts and avoid incompetence or incapacity determinations for their implementation. In most instances, eldercare alternatives focus on the solution overwhelmingly favored by elderly care recipients: home care rather than nursing homes. Where do older people live in our country now? Wendy Lustbader and Nancy R. Hooyman have gathered the following figures:

- 43 percent have lived in their present home for over twenty years

- 5 percent live in retirement communities

- Almost 30 percent live alone (32 percent of women, 22 percent of men)

- 33 percent of men and 50 percent of women over age sixty-five who are widowed, separated, or divorced live with adult children or other family members.[5]

Although only a small percentage of the elderly are placed in nursing homes, the specter of institutionalization looms large in the population group aged sixty-five and above. In a recent survey conducted by the American Association of Retired Persons (AARP),

> when cost considerations were eliminated, eighty-seven and one-half percent of the respondents age sixty-five or older said they would prefer home care to nursing-home care. They do not view the nursing home as a place to get better; they view it as a harbinger of death —a dismal way station from which there is no escape but death.[6]

Even though today's seniors can choose from a variety of living arrangements including assisted living and continuous-care facilities, the greatest number prefer to stay in their own homes. This has led to a vast array of home-healthcare services and a doubling of certified homecare agencies since 1989.[7] With the profusion of services has also come confusion. How can we sort through the options and help our elderly relatives age in place? For adult children who live far from their parents, how is this done? For those who can afford it, the rapidly growing profession of geriatric care management provides the answer.

# GERIATRIC CARE MANAGEMENT

Geriatric care managers are private social workers, geriatric nurses, and elder law and daily money management experts who specialize in the problems of the older persons. Suzanne McNeely, president of Santa Barbara's oldest private geriatric care company, described the care manager as "the hub of the wheel" who "helps older people and their families evaluate their needs, identify potential solutions, seek out services, and put a plan in place to provide for current and future care needs."[8]

> They develop a long-term supportive relationship with the older person and with his or her family throughout the aging process. They do whatever it takes to help run a person's life with the goal of helping him or her "age in place."
>
> They conduct assessments, provide information about resources, and make referrals. They identify issues and problems in regard to the social, legal, financial, and functional areas of life. They coordinate and monitor delivery of care, assist with the identification of alternative living arrangements, and facilitate moves into long-term care facilities.
>
> Care managers know the strengths of each long-term care facility and will recommend specific places depending on what is best for their clients' needs.[9]

There are many advantages to the use of private geriatric care managers.[10] Most importantly, they are experts on the resources that are available to seniors in their community. Care managers are available in emergencies twenty-four hours a day, seven days a week, not just during the typical working hours of a social service agency. Family members develop a long-term relationship with "their" care manager, who can then focus on finding the most appropriate services for the elderly rather than matching the client to an available program. Geriatric care managers are free of the budgetary constraints of a public agency and can thus take a broader or more flexible approach to arranging appropriate care. Let's look at two examples of this flexibility:

> One example is helping an aged woman, who uses a cane and needs help walking, attend a funeral of a friend. One simple solution, hiring a

car and chauffeur for two hours to transport the elder and an escort, is impossible for most nonprofit or public-sector agencies.

In another case, . . . one aged California couple wanted to have someone cook them a hot noon meal daily. [The] challenge was that both were Russian-born and wanted ethnic food. Their case manager finally found an instructor on cooking Russian food who was available at midday.[11]

What do experts in the public social services arena say about these private geriatric care managers? A typical response came from Louise Currey of Santa Barbara County's Geriatric Assessment, who supports the hiring of a care manager—particularly for adult children who live far from their parents. "I recommend care managers all the time to people who can afford them," Currey said. "It's usually cheaper than hiring n attorney. Care managers provide complex care with an individualized approach. They're wonderful for family members who need someone else to be the 'bad guy' and put things together for them."[12]

A good geriatric care management organization provides a host of services to support the independence and well-being of elderly men and women. "At best," wrote Sue Shellenbarger in the *Wall Street Journal*, geriatric care managers do perform much like family."[13]

In southern Florida, care managers at Rona Bartelstone Associates, Fort Lauderdale, took aged clients into their own homes during Hurricane Andrew. In Falls Church, Va., a care manager with the Ann E. O'Neil agency cheered up an aged client during a dreaded move into an assisted-living facility by bringing her baby along; the child's presence was "wonderful therapy," Ms. O'Neil says.[14]

At worst, the problems that arise with unethical or inept care managers can be daunting—and expensive. The following cases demonstrate the problems that can arise when care managers go beyond their fields of expertise or are not adequately supervised by the clients who have hired them.

Arabella Dorth, a word processor for a San Francisco law firm, relied briefly on a San Diego care manager to oversee her Alzheimer's-afflicted mother. Ms. Dorth needed to secure the legal right to manage her mother's affairs. But the care manager, instead of helping her take the relatively simple step of getting power of attorney, filed a legal petition for a highly restrictive type of conservatorship designed to lock up criminally insane people. Dismayed, Ms. Dorth fired her. . . .

At $50 to $100 an hour, care managers' fees can mount fast. A New York social worker was socked with $10,000 in vaguely worded bills by a care-management agency for overseeing home-health services for her aunt in Connecticut for about a year. "I didn't monitor them well enough," the social worker says. "It was an expensive lesson."[15]

Such problems can be avoided with prior planning. If you intend to hire a geriatric care manager, first call the National Association of Professional Geriatric Care Managers to make sure the person you select is certified.*

Members of the National Association of Professional Geriatric Care Managers abide by a Pledge of Ethics covering ten issues: provision of service, self-determination, loyalty, termination of service, substitute judgment, confidentiality, referrals/disclosure, cooperation, qualifications, and discrimination. A certified geriatric care management organization will also state its objectives clearly and in writing. One such licensed and bonded organization in California provides the following formal description of its range of services for individualized eldercare:

- *Assessment.* A home or facility visit is made and all appropriate parties consulted in order to make an initial assessment of the medical, psychosocial, financial and/or legal issues. A written report of the identified needs, problems and recommendations is provided.

- *Care Management.* Acting as a liaison between the older adult, their family and service providers, we plan for care, make arrangements for and coordinate services, then monitor the ongoing situation and changing needs.

- *Conservatorship.* Serving as a court-appointed legal representative for an incapacitated older adult, we will arrange for their care and protection and/or manage their assets.

- *Daily Money Management.* We will pay bills, reconcile checkbooks, file medical claims, evaluate insurance coverage and plan for current and future budget needs.

- *Administration/Assistant Care Management.* Whenever possible, all administrative assistance and support will be provided by our support staff to our care managers, daily money managers and caregiver coordinator in order to keep our fees to a minimum.

- *Entitlement Applications.* We will apply for entitlement programs, such as MediCal, SSI, Social Security Disability, etc., meant to preserve or supplement resources.

---

*The association is headquartered in Tucson, Arizona, and can be reached at (520) 881-8008 (see appendix C under "Major National Organizations" for the Association's mailing address).

- *Managed Home Care.* We screen and identify caregivers whose skills and personalities match the job requirements, orient them to the specific duties and establish a system of accountability. Monitoring and support by a professional care manager is required during the initial ninety day period when caregivers are placed by Senior Planning Services.

- All time spent with clients, their families or other persons involved; travel, telephone contacts, care planning and documentation is charged at the stated fee rate. Clerical support, facsimiles and copies are included in the base rate with the exception of long distance phone calls which will be billed at Senior Planning Services cost.[16]

An initial consultation is conducted free of charge to determine if the organization's services will meet a family's needs. As indicated, care management services are then based on an hourly rate.

# AREA AGENCIES ON AGING: SENIOR CONNECTION AND ELDERCARE LOCATOR

If the use of private professional geriatric care management is simply too costly for your budget, there is a second excellent road to follow for help with eldercare needs. It is one that had been built by our federal government with little fanfare, yet reaches into every community in America. This path begins in the business or residential white pages of your local telephone directory under the entry "Area Agency on Aging." The Area Agency on Aging is a nonprofit organization funded by the Older Americans Act to allocate federal and state dollars to local agencies. In turn, these local agencies insure that supportive, health-promotion, and nutrition-enhancing services are available to older adults in every part of the United States. Services funded from the Older Americans Act that established this system of Area Agencies on Aging include:

- Senior Information and Assistance

- In-Home Supportive Services

- Respite Care

- Home Delivered Meals

- Congregate Lunch Programs

- Senior Citizens Centers

- Adult Day Center Services

- Long Term Care Ombudsman

- Legal Services

- Home Repair

- Transportation Services

- Health Promotion[17]

It is not even necessary for you to determine which services your elderly relative may need before calling for help. Simply telephone your local Area Agency on Aging and request a copy of their current Senior Resource Directory. The directory is available at no cost and will provide you with a listing of nonprofit and governmental agencies in your community that offer services to senior citizens. The directory includes display ads for for-profit eldercare organizations in your area as well.

Armed with a copy of your local Senior Resource Directory, you will be ready to continue your eldercare reconnaissance mission with a call to the "Senior Connection." It is available to anyone toll-free at (800) 350-6065. The Senior Connection is a specialized senior information and assistance service of the Area Agency on Aging and will help you with information, referral services, follow-up, and education. In most cases, the Senior Connection will begin by helping you identify the specific problems you are trying to resolve for your aging relative or friend. You will be given referrals to community resources, and assisted repeatedly if the nonprofit agencies you then contact cannot be of help due to long waiting lists or because you do not meet eligibility requirements such as age and income.

If you are one of the many men and women who are attempting to arrange eldercare long distance, your task will be more complex. Fortunately, the United States Administration on Aging, the National Association of Area Agencies on Aging and the National Association of State Units on Aging have collaborated to provide assistance for individuals who are trying to arrange supportive care for elderly men and women who do not live in their communities.[18] This toll-free telephone service, known as the "Eldercare Locator," makes it possible to locate specific resources for elders living far away.*

---

*The Eldercare Locator's number is (800) 677-1116 and is available weekdays from 9 AM until 9 PM, Eastern Standard Time. The Eldercare Locator can refer callers to an extensive network of organizations providing services for the elderly.

Whether your eldercare budget suggests the use of a professional geriatric care manager or necessitates the use of services available through nonprofit and governmental agencies, you must plan ahead. A trip to a local bookstore is a good place to find a roadmap to begin the planning and preparation that are such crucial components of effective caretaking. In sections variously labeled as "Issues of Aging," "Family," or "Aging in America," bookstores offer a wealth of new resource guides for eldercare. Two excellent examples (among many) are Wendy Lustbader and Nancy R. Hooyman's *Taking Care of Aging Family Members*,[19] and Joy Loverde's *The Complete Eldercare Planner: Where to Start, Questions to Ask, and How to Find Help*.[20]

"Most of us are inadequately prepared, emotionally and otherwise, to face the complex issues associated with caring for aging family members," Joy Loverde states in her *Complete Eldercare Planner*.[21] She continues: "This is because each eldercare problem can be made up of a combination of issues. How one family addresses an eldercare issue is not necessarily how another family approaches the same problem. What works one day could change drastically, overnight. . . . The answer lies in planning ahead."

> Planning . . . takes on a whole new level of meaning when it comes to caring for an aging relative: We family caregivers can plan on this time in our lives to be uncertain and unpredictable. Existing family decision-making patterns will no longer apply. We soon realize that we will not be returning to what we experienced as family life in our past. What we *can* plan on is a constant change in circumstances that involves the entire family—sometimes suddenly, sometimes so gradually that we may not even realize that change has occurred. No matter how carefully we make eldercare preparations, the only thing we can plan on is changing our plans.[22]

As part of her work with the National Council on the Aging's recent study, Donna Wagner authored the Councils' study on *Caring Across the Miles*.[23] She joins other experts in warning against delays in mapping out plans for care. "The worst time to do the planning is when there's a crisis," says Donna Wagner, "but that's what typically happens." There is an impressive array of resources available to seniors, but prior planning is essential.

Appendix C in this volume provides lists of additional resources for the elderly. This information is presented in six categories: major national organizations, national legal organizations for the elderly, congressional committees on issues of aging, state offices of aging, state long-term-care ombudsman programs, and related websites. Wherever you turn for assistance, you will be told that the demand for supportive services for the elderly has exceeded the supply. Local, state, and federal funding cannot keep up with our country's growing need for alternate arrangements that support the independence of an aging population. The following advice, listed in one Area Agency on Aging's *Senior Resource Directory*, should be remembered as your eldercare plans develop:

> If you determine that you are eligible for a particular service and it is the service that will best meet your needs, then the next question is when can the service begin.
>
> Recently, the demand for service has exceeded the supply. Home Health Agencies, as an example, are having an increasingly difficult time finding trained personnel; this limits the availability of services. . . . The consequence is many agencies have waiting lists.
>
> Our best advice is, if there is a waiting list, get on it. You may have to settle for another service that either may cost more than you can afford or does not quite meet your needs. If you don't need the service when your name comes up on the list, they will go to the next person. Don't think that you can wait until the agency no longer has a waiting list. It may not happen.[24]

## ADULT PROTECTIVE SERVICES

Earlier in chapter 6 we followed the case of eighty-one-year-old Violet (case 6.11) who was placed under the guardianship of her daughter. Violet's grandchildren called her "Fido" and fed her dogfood while they spent her Social Security payments. Violet's abuse was discovered by a visiting social worker who quickly moved to protect the vulnerable, elderly woman. Our review of current alternatives to involuntary conservatorships and guardianships to protect elderly men and women must include a brief discussion of the agency Violet's social worker used to safeguard her client: Adult Protective Services, as it is most often (but not always) called. Remember that your State Office of Aging (see appendix C) will help if you are unable to locate the proper adult protective authorities in your community.

The House Select Committee on Aging is attempting to focus attention on the growing problem of elder abuse in our country. It is not a new problem, but it is increasing as the graying of America expands the numbers of seniors who are being cared for by overburdened adult children and frustrated spouses. How do legal agencies now define "elder abuse"? It has several key components.

- *Passive Neglect*: Unintentional failure to fulfill a caretaking obligation; infliction of distress without conscious or willful intent, etc.

- *Psychological Abuse*: Infliction of mental anguish by demanding, name-calling, insulting, ignoring, humiliating, frightening, threatening, isolating, etc.

- *Material/Financial Abuse*: Illegally or unethically exploiting by using funds, property, or other assets of an older person for personal gain, etc.

- *Active Neglect*: Intentional failure to fulfill caregiving obligations; infliction of physical or emotional stress or injury; abandonment; denial of food, medication, personal hygiene, etc.

- *Physical Abuse*: Infliction of physical pain or injury; physical coercion; confinement; slapping, bruising, sexually molesting, cutting, lacerating, burning, restraining, pushing, shoving, etc.[25]

Abuse of the elderly may be intentional, but it may also be caused by a caregiver's growing inability to meet the older person's needs. However, as underscored by the Area Agency on Aging, elder abuse "can be reflective of a stressed family or long-standing difficult parent-child relationship."[26] Sadly, it is endemic throughout our nation: in private homes, in retirement communities, in continuing-care facilities, and in nursing homes.

When you suspect an elderly man or woman is being abused or neglected in any of the manners listed above, it is important to call the department of social service's Adult Protective Services (APS). You may discuss your concerns anonymously with staff members of APS, or choose to initiate a report that will become the focus of an immediate investigation. Referrals for any case of suspected abuse, neglect or exploitation of an adult can be obtained through Adult Protective Services' toll-free intake line at (800) 624-8404. Contact your State Long-Term-Care Ombudsman (listed in appendix C) to report suspected abuse or neglect in residential and nursing home caretaking facilities. In an emergency, pick up your phone and simply dial 911.

As they age, the elderly become increasingly dependent upon the kindness of friends and relatives in their immediate world. We help protect infants and children from abuse because they are powerless to protect themselves. We can do no less for the people who have, in a very real sense, made our lives possible.

# NOTES

1. C. Kalb, "Focus on Your Health: Caring From Afar," *Newsweek*, 22 September 1997, pp. 87–88.

2. W. Lustbader and N. R. Hooyman, *Taking Care of Aging Family Members* (New York: The Free Press, 1994).

3. Ibid.

4. J. E. Rein, "Beyond the Competency Construct," *Fordham Law Review* 62 (1994): 1168–69.

5. Lustbader and Hooyman, *Taking Care of Aging Family Members*, p. 14.

6. J. E. Rein, "Preserving Dignity and Self-Determination of the Elderly in the Face of Competing Interests and Grim Alternatives: A Proposal for Statutory Refocus and Reform," *George Washington Law Review* 60 (1992): 1860–61.

7. Kalb, "Focus on Your Health."

8. T. Reece, "Private Geriatric Care Managers Fill a Real Need," *Santa Barbara News-Press*, 3 February 1997, p. B1.

9. Ibid.

10. "Advice for Family Caregivers," in *Families of the Aged* (Silver Spring, Md.: CD Publications, 1988).

11. Ibid., p. 2.

12. Reece, "Private Geriatric Care Managers Fill a Real Need."

13. S. Shellenbarger, "Taking Steps to Ensure Your Care Manager Meets Elder's Needs," *The Wall Street Journal*, 25 October 1995, p. B1.

14. Ibid.

15. Ibid.

16. *Senior Planning Services Fee Schedule, 1997* (Santa Barbara, California).

17. *Santa Barbara County Senior Resource Directory, 97–98 Edition*, Area Agency on Aging for San Luis Obispo and Santa Barbara Counties, p. 4.

18. Ibid.

19. Lustbader and Hooyman, *Taking Care of Aging Family Members*.

20. J. Loverde, *The Complete Eldercare Planner: Where to Start, Questions to Ask, and How to Find Help* (New York: Hyperion, 1997).

21. Ibid., p. 5.

22. Ibid.

23. Kalb, "Focus on Your Health."

24. *Santa Barbara County Senior Resource Directory, 97–98 Edition*, p. 6.

25. Ibid., p. 21.

26. Ibid.

# CHAPTER EIGHT

# HOW SHOULD OUR LAWS BE CHANGED?

*It usually takes a hundred years to make a law, and then, after it has done its work, it usually takes a hundred years to get rid of it.*
—Henry Ward Beecher (1887), *Proverbs from Plymouth Pulpit*

**W**hat is wrong with our current conservatorship and guardianship codes and what might be done to correct them? In general, there are fourteen problem areas common to involuntary conservatorship/ guardianship proceedings throughout America that are most in need of statutory reform. They are:

1. State misuse of *parens patriae* negates our right to personal autonomy (i.e., our right to make decisions and mistakes)
2. The motives or competing interests of those who petition for the proceedings are not investigated—and should be
3. Language in "progressive" codes and statutes contains value judgments
4. Court tests of property mismanagement are biased against the elderly
5. Words used in involuntary proceedings are poorly defined—or not defined at all
6. Notice given to the proposed conservatee or ward is insufficient

7. Roles of court-appointed officials are ambiguous and/or can change abruptly
8. The burden of proof shifts to the person allegedly in need of oversight
9. Hearing inequities compromise due process protections
10. Probate courts are the slow courts of the dead
11. Payment for these involuntary proceedings is taken from the proposed ward's or conservatee's assets
12. No one is guarding the guardians
13. Codes lack any automatic provision for termination
14. Judicial decisions are hard to appeal

Let's begin our assessment of how these codes should be changed by discussing the states' use of the legal theory that gives them the right to intrude into the lives of elderly citizens: *parens patriae.*

# 1. STATE MISUSE OF *PARENS PATRIAE* NEGATES OUR RIGHT TO PERSONAL AUTONOMY

As we learned previously, the rationale used by state legislative bodies to strip aging men and women of their personhood and property flows from the doctrine of *parens patriae*, literally "parent of the country." *Parens patriae* refers to the benevolent role of the state as guardian of persons under legal disability (originally limited to infants and lunatics). By means of the doctrine of *parens patriae*, however, states now claim an inherent power *and* duty to protect those citizens who are deemed unable to care for themselves simply because they are old.

Condemned to an almost total loss of decision-making power by these involuntary proceedings, older Americans are being pushed from a state of competence into a state of incompetence by the very interventions that were supposedly designed to protect them. State legislators who craft our codes must remember that every American, regardless of age or physical capacity, has an inherent, inalienable right to be *different*. Each of us, again regardless of age, should feel free to deviate from current societal or cultural norms and values and not fear being punished for such deviations.

The single most important change our state governments might make would be to cease using their *parens patriae* power to interfere in the lives of aging people and *guarantee that the elderly who possess intact decision-making powers would never be subjected to involuntary conservatorship/guardianship proceedings*. Anything less, including the codes and statutes as they exist today, represents an indefensible manifestation of an ageist, paternalistic bias on the part of one group (legislators who make our codes and court officials who enforce them) against another (the chronologically old).

There should be no de facto presumption that elders are incompetent and in need of surrogate management. There should be no statutory diminution of an elderly person's right to be left alone. If people choose not to care "properly" for themselves or for their property yet have the capacity to do so (that is, individuals who choose to be "deviant" or different from the norm), they should not be declared incapacitated. As one thoughtful justice observed in *In re Fisher* in 1989,

> the fact that someone else might, or could make better choices is not the point. In a constitutional system such as ours which prizes and protects individual liberties to make decisions, even bad ones, the right to make those decisions must be preserved. . . . The integrity of the elderly, no less than any other group of our citizens, should not be invaded, nor their freedom of choice taken from them by the state simply because we believe that decisions could be "better" made by someone else.[1]

It is ironic in the extreme that the sole modern justification of the state's *parens patriae* power to appoint a guardian or conservator is the proposed ward's well-being.

## 2. THE MOTIVES OR COMPETING INTERESTS OF THOSE WHO PETITION FOR THE PROCEEDINGS ARE NOT INVESTIGATED— AND SHOULD BE

In defining its interest purely in terms of the elderly person, the state fails to acknowledge the difference between its interest and anyone else's and thus characterizes the proceeding as nonadversarial. This is patently untrue. Legal scholar Gregory Atkinson presented the problem in his thoughtful essay "Towards a Due Process Perspective in Conservatorship Proceedings for the Aged":

> In cases where the state or aged person is not petitioning, the proposed conservatee's [or ward's] children or close relatives usually are. When the petitioner has an expectancy or vested interest in the proposed conservatee's estate, there is a conflict between the best interests of the petitioner and the aged. Because the proceeding is traditionally defined as

not being adversary, the hearing is completed without recognizing the petitioner's motivation. Children or close relatives are among the first to be appointed [guardians or] conservators.[2]

The courts invite abuse at the hands of openly self-interested people who seek conservatorships or guardianships of their "unproductive elderly." When an involuntary guardianship or conservatorship is imposed in spite of an aging individual's vigorous objections, the court serves the financial interests of family members or other third parties. This is an action that leaps far beyond the confines of the *parens patriae* concept and denies the proposed ward's most fundamental rights of life, liberty, and the pursuit of happiness.

Because involuntary conservatorship/guardianship hearings are now mischaracterized as nonadversarial proceedings, the competing interests of petitioners are not investigated by the court. What should be done to correct this inequity, short of unwinding the entire complex ball of egregious legislation? Jan Ellen Rein of the McGeorge School of Law proposed a solution.

> Our legal system should recognize frankly that whenever a court imposes guardianship or conservatorship over a proposed ward's objection or reluctance for the convenience, mental well-being, or financial interests of family members or other third parties, the court is going beyond the confines of the *parens patriae* concept to interfere with fundamental liberty interests, potentially including freedom from involuntary physical confinement. Before a court interferes with such fundamental interests over the proposed ward's objections, the petitioner should be required by statute to prove by clear and convincing evidence that such a drastic step is absolutely necessary to protect third-party or societal interests of the highest magnitude—i.e., the life and physical safety (not just the convenience, emotional reassurance, or financial hopes) of others—from an imminent threat of serious harm posed by the proposed ward's behavior.[3]

Many involuntary petitions are driven by expedience and the competing economic interests of third parties. Hospitals, nursing homes, continuing care facilities and other third parties often require conservatorships or guardianships over their patients to insure collection of outstanding bills and/or to evict the elderly from their premises. In all too many cases, convalescent centers will refuse admittance to adults who are not represented by court-appointed surrogate decision-makers. This practice, while not legally required, has become the price of admission in the face of an increasing demand for the limited space available in convalescent and nursing homes.

Unfortunately, although convenience is hardly a justification for the imposition of unnecessary incompetency adjudications over aging adults, the practice is wide spread. As these proceedings become part of the placement process in nursing facilities, guardianships and conservatorships are often used for elderly individuals whose *only* disabilities are physical. In whatever guise, withdrawing decision-making powers from elderly individuals simply because they are physically incapable of personally executing their decisions is wrong.

At least one state has made an attempt to address this inequity. Colorado's *Revised Statutes* now require that an evidentiary (evidence gathering) hearing be held to consider factual circumstances and determine whether the *petitioner* is a person interested in the welfare of the allegedly incapacitated individual. This is not perfect, but it is a move in the right direction.

# 3. LANGUAGE IN "PROGRESSIVE" CODES AND STATUTES CONTAINS VALUE JUDGMENTS

Value-laden terms contained in state statutes do not serve the elderly well. As you read the following codes quoted from some of our more "progressive" states, pay special attention to the terms that have been italicized for emphasis. The passages contain one tacit yet false assumption: namely, that there are universal and nonageist standards concerning how one "properly" provides for personal needs or "properly" manages affairs or makes "responsible" decisions.

> *California Probate Code* § 1801(a) . . . A conservator of the person may be appointed for a person who is unable *properly* to provide for his or her personal needs. . . .

> *Minnesota State* § 525.54.3 . . . Appointment of a guardian or conservator may be made in relation to the estate and financial affairs of an adult person: . . . (b) involuntarily, upon the court's determination that (1) the person is unable to manage the person's property and affairs *effectively* because the person is an incapacitated person, and (2) the person has property which will be dissipated unless *proper* management is provided. . . . "Incapacitated person" means, in the case of guardianship or conservatorship . . . , any adult person who is impaired to the extent that the person lacks sufficient understanding or capacity to make or communicate *responsible* decisions concerning the person's estate or financial affairs, and who has demonstrated *deficits in behavior* which evidence an inability to manage the estate. . . .

*Uniform Probate Code* § 5-103(7) . . . "Incapacitated person" means any person who is impaired . . . to the extent of lacking sufficient understanding or capacity to make or communicate *responsible* decisions.[4]

It is important to ask *who* determines whether or not a decision is "responsible," "effective" or "proper." For instance, a seventy-five-year-old woman with a large estate who has comparatively few years left in which to enjoy her wealth might make financial decisions that are responsible, effective, and proper for her, yet her decisions would be viewed as imprudent if made by a single, middle-aged parent who is putting her children through college.

You might ask: What *is* a "responsible decision"? There are no neutral criteria determining if and when a decision or behavior is responsible, effective or proper. These are terms of comparative value only, requiring a normative standard for their meaning. In a culture that values youth, being old is laden with negatives. Unwittingly, the courts become enforcers of ageist biases and punish the elderly by imposing our society's values—sifted through the judges' personal values—on proposed wards.

In order to improve the language in our state codes, every passage in every sentence must be screened for the value-laden modifiers that subtly cloak the elderly in a presumption of incompetence or incapacity. Such terms should be removed. No court in the land should expect the aged to make decisions that are "responsible" (whatever that means) in the eyes of a judge if all other citizens are allowed to make mistakes and to make irresponsible decisions that are socially unacceptable or unwise. Statutes should focus on an individual's *ability* to make a decision rather than the outcome of the decision itself. As Professor Rein[5] noted, this " 'deliberate decisions' formulation . . . emphasizes the reasoning process rather than the information available to the decisionmaker."[6]

# 4. COURT TESTS OF PROPERTY MISMANAGEMENT ARE BIASED AGAINST THE ELDERLY

Although only a small percentage of our aging population in America will develop dementia, time will bring some degree of mental or physical incapacity to most of us. Granted, the severity and rate of decline will vary for each individual. Unfortunately, probate and surrogate courts require a very minimal standard of evidence of incapacity in involuntary conservatorship/guardianship hearings which, when combined with any suggestion of property mismanagement, will oftentimes serve to convince courts of incompetence or incapacity. Using property management as the "test" of mental incapacity is particularly problematic.

Ironically, the very changes in financial decision-making made possible by the autonomy that age brings may be used by petitioners as signs of "fiscal mismanagement" in a conservatorship forum. Often widowed and lacking any legal dependents, the elder may approach his or her golden years with the decision to save less and consume at a higher rate in his or her remaining life span. Prudent tax management encourages *inter vivos* gifts for the transfer of wealth prior to the inevitable imposition of punitive death or inheritance taxes. Perhaps the individual has even planned for retirement and set aside a private " 'spendthrift fund' for carefree years."[7] Yet judges and/or juries in conservatorship/guardianship courts most often measure the aged person's fiscal behavior against the norms created by the necessarily more conservative consumption patterns of middle-aged adults.

Compounding this inequity, evidence of supposed incompetent property management almost always involves gift transactions rather than improvident contracting or imprudent business mismanagement. A standard of "dissipation" has been cited by the courts in the very subjective area of gifts, and the concept of dissipation is determined only by the worthiness and identification of the recipient and his or her relationship to the proposed conservatee or ward.

> *In re Wingert.* . . . On superficial observation, the court found Mrs. Wingert to be charming and intelligent; it commented on her mental alertness at the hearing. Nevertheless, on evidence showing gifts of over $32,000 to a couple who moved in and promised to take care of her, the court appointed a guardian. It was left with "no doubt . . . of senility." The court compared her generous gifts to her earlier stingy nature. Whether she is " 'confused,' 'defective,' 'feeble' or 'weak' is not vitally important. If . . . [her] mind is so affected that as a consequence thereof [she] is liable to dissipate or lose property and become the victim of designing persons, the court . . . may appoint a guardian."[8]

The proposed conservatee's or ward's decisions vis-à-vis property management should be eliminated as a criterion for adjudications of incompetence and incapacity. After all, states are supposed to intervene to limit an individual's personal or financial autonomy only when vital societal interests are at stake. Many competency determinations have even been decided against elderly people who were cheated out of their assets by unscrupulous con-artists.

An excellent suggestion has been made to remedy this situation, namely, regulation of the predator. Proceed against the victimizer rather than the victim. As law professor Jan Ellen Rein commented in "Clients with Destructive and Socially Harmful Choices—What's an Attorney to Do? Within and Beyond the Competency Construct," "interference with the predator is morally preferable because the predator is the one who, with premeditation, used unscrupulous, sometimes vicious, tactics to prey on competent but trusting and vulnerable individuals."[9] The courts should enjoin predators and prevent them from harming the elderly without questioning their victims' competency—even if the aging individual's personality leads him or her to make the same mistake a second or third time.

The suggested solution of punishing the predator rather than his or her victim is not a perfect one. Yes, there are truly gullible older people who may be repeatedly victimized by scam artists; but there are equally gullible younger people, too. Should anyone suffer the indignity of an involuntary conservatorship or guardianship merely as a consequence of his or her gullibility? The answer is no.

# 5. WORDS USED IN INVOLUNTARY PROCEEDINGS ARE POORLY DEFINED —OR NOT DEFINED AT ALL

By now, the reader should be keenly aware that an adjudication of legal incompetence or incapacity in most states restricts an individual in profound ways. The finding reduces the elderly person to the status of an infant, eliminating his or her rights to

> make contracts; sell, purchase, mortgage, or lease property; make gifts; travel, or decide where to live; vote, or hold elected office; initiate or defend against suits [including a suit to challenge the imposition of the conservatorship or guardianship]; make a will, or revoke one; engage in certain professions; lend or borrow money; appoint agents; divorce, or marry; refuse medical treatment; keep and care for children; serve on a jury; be a witness to any legal document; drive a car; pay or collect debts; manage or run a business.[10]

Unfortunately, as we also have seen, the key words driving conservatorship/guardianship determinations are so vague as to provide little or no protection for the autonomy interests of the proposed wards and conservatees. Lacking quantifiable legal definitions, how does one use valid or reliable instruments to assess whether or not a targeted elder is "incapacitated," "incompetent," or incapable of resisting "undue influence"? It cannot be done.

Because the definitions of incompetence and incapacity that are used in involuntary conservatorship/guardianship proceedings are overbroad and vague, a judge now has almost total discretion to decide whether or not a targeted elder meets his or her *personal* conceptualization of these crucial terms. Judicial determinations based on imprecise statutory standards render the entire involuntary proceeding inherently unfair.

Remember the case of eighty-five-year-old Walter Tyrell (case 4.4) who had planned so carefully for his final years? His future life as a powerless ward of the court was decided by demeanor evidence during the trial. The sitting judge agreed with a physician's report that Mr. Tyrell's "smile is at times not normal; his eyes do not focus properly at all times; his gait and reflexes are not normal; and . . . he is not laying his cane aside but dropping it."[11] To that judge on that day in that court in that district and in that state, incompetence could be found in mere gestures.

## a. Functional Definitions of Capacity and Competence

What is being attempted in various jurisdictions is a movement away from a focus on an individual's mental status and toward an assessment of an individual's ability to function and make decisions. Nonetheless, states are continuing to insert value-laden terms (such as "properly" and "responsible") even in their functional definitions of capacity and competence. This is problematic. Can a bad choice made by a competent mind ever be distinguished from a bad choice made by an incompetent mind? It is egregious that so-called bad or irresponsible choices are being used as *proof* of incompetence against the elderly in far too many involuntary conservatorship/guardianship hearings.

Statutory definitions of incompetence and incapacity should focus on the ability of an individual to make deliberate decisions and not on whether their decisions are "responsible" in the eyes of a particular judge on a particular day. There must be objective standards for legal incapacity. Subjective judicial beliefs concerning such matters do not belong in our courts, and subjective analyses of an individual's life decisions should not be part of state law. In a culture enchanted with youth, the eccentricities of adults who happen to be old are judged as signs of incapacity or incompetence. Yet are they any different from the eccentricities displayed by younger adults?

Writing in the *Emory Law Journal,* Alison P. Barnes proposed a unified court of proxies to supervise the appointment and oversight of all surrogate decision-makers. Her model contained the following descriptions of people who would be subject to the court — and why.

A person subject to the court should be one who, because of mental illness, developmental disability, addiction to drugs or alcohol, or other mental disorder, is incapable of understanding and evaluating information essential to making or communicating decisions necessary in order independently to secure food, clothing, shelter, or medical care, or to manage property or financial affairs.

Evidence of incapacity should include a physical examination, a mental status examination, and a functional assessment. Incapacity should be shown by recurring acts or occurrences within the preceding six month period, and not by isolated instances of negligence or bad judgment, or by refusal of medical care alone. Disability should include mental disorders and should be of sufficient severity to cause significant deterioration in the person's health or circumstances, or to present a likelihood that significant harm will occur.

Emergency intervention should be justified only if it is likely that significant harm to the individual or others is imminent. If the person has been maintained by voluntary assistance, the petitioner must show why that assistance is no longer available or sufficient to meet the person's needs. Long term intervention based on functional status should be justified only when the individual is dangerous to self or to others.[12]

This conceptualization of competent decision-making focuses on "making or communicating decisions necessary in order independently to secure food, clothing, shelter, or medical care, or to manage property or financial affairs." It does not require that such decisions be "reasonable" or "responsible," thus avoiding the damage such value-laden modifiers leave in their wake in the conservatorship/guardianship arena. This is a good step in the right direction. Age, eccentricity, medical diagnosis and undue influence should no longer be deemed sufficient to trigger a presumptive need for a surrogate decision-maker.

## b. On the Concept of "Undue Influence"

My mother's case (described in the introduction) was driven by a single, ill-defined concept called "undue influence." Her experience can be used to illustrate the extent to which a paid expert witness can and will go to support vague claims against an elderly respondent in court. In this case, the petitioners used allegations that undue influence had somehow robbed my capable mother of the capacity to make independent decisions.

A court-appointed psychiatrist supervised my mother's ten-hour-long mental and physical health evaluation at a geriatric hospital of the court's choosing. Subsequently, the psychiatrist testified that his court-appointed patient had "problems in judgment [which were never specified] rendering her susceptible to undue influence" (which was not defined). "Unfortunately," the court's psychiatrist continued in his formal written report,

> there is no precise test with which to measure this. While [she] may be free from a definite mental disorder and individually seems capable of managing her person and estate, there are definite psychological problems in the family system which does suggest undue influence. Dynamically it seems very similar to situations in which a person may be involved in a cult.[13]

For the trier of facts, undue influence refers to persuasion, pressure, or influence short of actual force—but stronger than mere advice—that so overpowers the dominated party's free will or judgment that he or she cannot act intelligently and voluntarily.[14] The person being unduly influenced acts, instead, subject to the will of the dominating party.

The psychiatrist had no choice but to agree that our mother did not meet California's criteria for the imposition of a conservatorship since she was clearly competent to handle her personal and financial matters. Even though neither he nor any other geriatric psychiatrist had found any evidence of alleged incapacity, the court-appointed psychiatrist made a remarkable assertion. He concluded that our close-knit family was actually a *cult* run by the three adult daughters who were helping their mother fight off the unwanted involuntary conservatorship action. According to his testimony, although she was "capable of managing her person and [complex] estate," our mother was the hapless victim of the cult's undue influence. It seemed an audacious leap of reasoning, yet it almost succeeded.

What is clearly needed is an elimination of such propositions as "a person can lack capacity or competence due to the undue influence of others." This change might be facilitated by the inclusion of a broader definition of *autonomy* in any evaluation of the undue influence offense. During the thirty months prior to the beginning of her court battles, only three of my mother's adult children had been helping her deal with the emotional and physical stress inherent in caring for her institutionalized husband. Did their attention constitute loving support? Or was it "undue influence"? Should the petitioners who distanced themselves from their parents for two years be praised by the courts for cleverly resisting the temptation to participate in a cult of undue influence, or should they be viewed as hypocritical, uncaring, or insensitive?

Unwrapped and naked, the concept of "undue influence" in family relationships is absurd. People bonded by complex chronic-care needs develop unique relationships that beg a new definition of healthy autonomy. These are not "cults." As consulting policy analyst Alison Barnes stated, the definition must take into account "the critical significance of a trusting relationship to successful long-term care."[15] My mother turned to three daughters for help in her hour of need and trusted them. Had she also fallen ill, she knew her three daughters would not abandon her.

As they exist now, our codes describe a very narrow type of autonomy. It is based on an elderly individual's capacity to function totally alone, free from any and all "interference." Anything short of this artificial standard raises the specter of undue influence in conservatorship/guardianship proceedings. This is unacceptable. The law should not require elderly people to manage alone, left in splendid isolation. Rather, the vague criteria driving the facile misuse of undue influence allegations must be clarified. Decision-making is not always (*nor should it be*) a solitary affair when an elderly person asks for help from family members he or she has come to trust. As summarized by the court in *Wilson* v. *Wehunt* in 1994,

> evidence of concern and care on the part of a child and the acceptance
> of that care by the parent should not be equated with subservience on
> the part of the parent or dominance on the part of the child.[16]

Our courts do not use standardized psychological instruments in assessing competence, capacity, undue influence, or mental disability in the aging population. Why is this? It is really quite simple: none exist. The very words used in conservatorship/guardianship protective proceedings lack operational or functional legal definitions. Lacking a legal definition of what it is you hope to assess, the use of standardized testing is just pomp and circumstance. It feels good to do so and looks nice on paper, but it signifies almost nothing other than the individual evaluator's bias.

## 6. NOTICE GIVEN TO THE PROPOSED CONSERVATEE OR WARD IS INSUFFICIENT

By the time my mother received the two-inch-thick bundle of conservatorship petitions that marked the beginning of her nightmare in Probate Court, the petitioners had been preparing their complex case for five months. Because they suggested—but were never asked to prove— the existence of an "emergency" situation, they effectively limited the time she had available to respond to the petitions to four working days. Due process rights were seriously abridged.

In states throughout America, the time frame is equally grim. In the best of cases, most contemporary statutes permit an insufficient period of time between the delivery of the notice of the hearing to the proposed ward and the date on which the incapacity/incompetency hearing will be held. This makes it very difficult for the elderly to prepare a defense. In the worst of cases, petitioners will use allegations in *ex parte* proceedings to strip the targeted elderly of any notice at all, thus depriving them of their due process rights entirely. This is an outrageous aspect of involuntary conservatorship/guardianship litigation involving people who merely want to be left alone. If these proceedings are to continue, the notice requirements must be substantial—and guaranteed. No exceptions given. The court must not be permitted under any circumstances to eliminate or restrict the warning period that is granted any proposed conservatee or ward about an upcoming involuntary competency/capacity hearing. The notice should also include any and all information that might help respondents mount their defense should they choose to contest the petition.

Notice should also specify both the legal rights extended to the proposed conservatee or ward during the protective proceedings and the consequences of being declared incompetent or incapacitated. Those rights should include (as are characteristic in the eighteen states following some or all of the Uniform Probate Code): the right to be present in person at the hearing, to be represented by an attorney, to present evidence, to cross-examine and subpoena witnesses, and to a trial by jury. Statutory reform should also grant the respondent the right to delay the date of the hearing for good cause. After all, the right to adequate notice is guaranteed in our Constitution by the Fourteenth Amendment, which establishes at the state level that no person shall be deprived of life, liberty, or property without due process of law.

## 7. ROLES OF COURT-APPOINTED OFFICIALS ARE AMBIGUOUS AND/OR CAN CHANGE ABRUPTLY

As we know, most aging people who are targeted by these involuntary conservatorship/guardianship petitions have never been involved in court proceedings. The documents they are required to translate from formal legalese into informal English contain words and descriptions that are ill-defined, poorly understood, and presented in small type. Titles assigned to court-appointed officials—court investigator, guardian *ad litem*, and probate volunteer panel attorney for the respondent, to name three—are confusing. What is more, the roles played by these court-appointed officials can actually change in midstream with the court's blessing. Any and all court-generated complexity will work against the best interests of the elderly men and women for whose benefit these involuntary petitions are supposedly filed.

## a. Role Ambiguity

In many states, courts will appoint a guardian *ad litem* in conservatorship/guardianship cases to perform duties not normally associated with the role of guardians *ad litem* in traditional litigation. The guardian *ad litem* or "guardian for the purposes of the lawsuit," who may or may not be an attorney, is sent by the court to evaluate the facts of a case and give the judge a recommendation concerning a particular desired outcome. Because this is threatening in unacceptable ways to the proposed ward or conservatee's rights to due process, procedural safeguards are needed. Clinical Professor James M. Peden of the Thomas M. Cooley Law School at the University of Detroit discussed this problem in his study, "The Guardian Ad Litem Under the Guardianship Reform Act: A Profusion of Duties, a Confusion of Roles." His observations are striking:

> If the recommendation in any way addresses the ultimate issue of whether the respondent can make informed decisions, then the guardian ad litem has effectively made a finding of fact and conclusion of law, without the benefit of sworn testimony or allowance for cross-examination of witnesses. Such a decision is a unilateral determination on the part of the guardian ad litem and is easily based on intuition rather than competent, relevant evidence. All too often, the guardian ad litem renders the recommendation based on a half-hour interview of the respondent. This does not comport with established concepts of due process, nor is there a parallel practice in other areas of litigation.[17]

When the roles to be played by court appointees are not made clear, some functions may be overlooked or performed by unqualified individuals. How can this be condoned?

## b. The Confusion of Changing Roles

The proposed ward can be harmed beyond repair not only by a confusion of roles, but also by a changing of the roles assigned to court officials. When my mother's legal team of private lawyers had her court-appointed attorney dismissed prior to the second court hearing, the judge immediately gave his Probate Volunteer Panel attorney a new role in the litigation as "amicus" or "friend of the court." Information that had been gathered from a new client under what that client had assumed to be the cloak of attorney-client privilege was suddenly being used by the PVP-attorney-now-amicus against her in court. Adding insult to injury, my mother was eventually required to pay this attorney cum amicus the sum of $18,000 for this work.

In this manner, special rules seem to apply during involuntary conservatorship/guardianship proceedings, and these special rules deprive the victimized elder of his or her due process and constitutional rights. At best, the proposed ward or conservatee may be confused by the lack of clarity concerning the roles these unfamiliar officials will play in his or her competency/incapacity determinations. At worst, the uninformed elder can be sabotaged by the changeable nature of the roles court officials are permitted to assume.

Notice to the proposed ward or conservatee should contain language preventing this unnecessary cross-contamination of roles. The targeted elder should understand precisely what every court-appointed official can and will do; the roles of these officials should be limited in scope and not subject to any unexpected or spontaneous changes. As Professor Peden concludes,

> To remove any doubt about who the guardian ad litem is and what his duties are, the statute should redefine the guardian ad litem as a court officer responsible to the court, whose function is to insure adequate notice to the respondent and ascertain whether legal counsel, either retained or court-appointed, will be appearing on behalf of the respondent. In addition to the duties contained in the present statute, the respondent should be informed that the guardian ad litem is a court officer, and in no way represents him, and that anything the respondent relates to the officer may and probably will be repeated in court, either in testimony or in written form.[18]

## 8. THE BURDEN OF PROOF SHIFTS TO THE PERSON ALLEGEDLY IN NEED OF OVERSIGHT

In today's involuntary conservatorship/guardianship proceedings, the evidence weighed by the trier of fact consists almost exclusively of the petitioners' allegations and the court-mandated reports submitted by examiners. Once such material is presented, however, the burden of proof unintentionally but inevitably shifts to the potential conservatee or ward. The proposed conservatee or ward must then try to demonstrate his or her competence or capacity—a task that is difficult, if not impossible.

Hearsay evidence submitted by a petitioner is hard to neutralize. Grappling with hearsay feels much like entering a hall of mirrors. One wanders through mazes of confusing, often insulting or humiliating statements having no basis in truth. Unfortunately, placing hearsay on the plane more normally reserved for fact serves to dignify the material and give it a semblance of truth.

Additionally, as researchers have noted, because incompetency and incapacity are such legally vague concepts in conservatorship and guardianship matters, the courts often act as though the proposed ward or conservatee is presumed incompetent before the hearing begins. How does one battle gossipy allegations while attempting to reverse the court's tacit presumption of incompetence? How does one overcome the fact that age alone in many states is admitted as evidence of presumptive incompetence or mental illness? The proposed conservatee or ward will have an uphill battle even in the best of circumstances.

One answer to part of this dilemma would be to require all judges ruling on all conservatorship/guardianship matters to reject statutorily insufficient evidence—beginning with hearsay. Hearsay refers to testimony given by a witness who relates not what he or she knows personally but what others have told him or her. Hearsay is legal gossip and has no place in proceedings that are intended to strip vulnerable elderly men and women of their decision-making powers for the rest of their lives. Such evidence is routinely excluded from civil commitment proceedings. It should be excluded when an elderly person's fundamental liberties are at stake. The elderly respondent deserves nothing less than a label of competent-until-proven-incompetent.

In our country's criminal justice system, a grand jury hearing is convened to determine the merit of any charges before an individual can be indicted. What is needed in conservatorship/guardianship proceedings is an analogous step during which all petitioners' cases are reviewed and all initial claims of incapacity or incompetence are carefully weighed. A panel of geriatric experts could be seated to evaluate proposed wards for *functional deficits only*. Functional deficits are clearly identified problematic behaviors that have causal links to mental illness. They are not mere manifestations of an individual's unique or eccentric ways of going through the world. If such an evaluation were done prior to the conservatorship/guardianship hearings, information concerning the proposed ward's competence (or lack thereof) might be made available to the court that tries the facts. As the system exists now, an accusation is made by a petitioner and filed with the court, and the targeted elder must then wage an expensive defense—even if the allegation is totally without merit.

# 9. HEARING INEQUITIES COMPROMISE DUE PROCESS PROTECTIONS

Once ensnared in the judicial process, the elderly's rights to a fair hearing are severely compromised. As we have already noted, fewer than 14 percent of all proposed wards or conservatees attend the hearings that will determine their future. The picture in many states is even more bleak, as we shall now see.

## a. Attendance at the Hearing

In some states, officials believe these so-called protective proceedings are so "nonadversarial" in nature that the proposed wards should never even be allowed to attend the hearings. Determinations would then rise and fall on the merits of the petitioner's allegations and any documentation that may have been submitted on the respondent's behalf. This should not happen in America.

## b. Legal Representation

Even though almost all petitioners are represented by attorneys in court, in too many states the elderly individual is not assigned an attorney if he or she cannot afford independent counsel. Without counsel, an allegedly incompetent or incapacitated person will remain unaware of his or her available rights and options. He or she will have no fierce advocate to organize a strong case in an attempt to resist the imposition of an unwanted and unnecessary conservator or guardian. The unrepresented individual will lose, and the so-called hearing will be a meaningless formality. Sad but true, a national study revealed that of the few proposed wards who attended their hearings, over 44 percent were not represented by an attorney.[19]

## c. Medical Evaluations

We have seen that medical evaluations are used as evidence in competency/capacity determinations even though there are no clear standards in our codes concerning: (1) what should be in these medical reports, and (2) how or if a given medical condition actually affects mental capacity. Although they are rife with problems, these evaluations must be required in all cases if they are considered to be helpful to the trier of fact. Imagine how insubstantial an elderly respondent would seem to a judge if he/she were neither present in court, were not represented by counsel, and had not been brought to life by the precise words of a medical or psychiatric report. Would any of the judges in the cases we reviewed have tried terribly hard to create an image of a functioning, competent flesh-and-blood elderly person had he or she only the damning words of the petitioners to read?

Inequities occurring during the hearing should be modified by specific statutory reform. Older people who are forced into involuntary conservatorship/guardianship proceedings should be guaranteed representation by independent counsel. Every proposed ward or conservatee should be in court in person for his or her hearing unless he or she is absolutely incapable of attending, in which case the proceedings should be conducted wherever the individual resides. Systematic gerontological and medical assessments should be used in every jurisdiction for all proposed wards and conservatees, and at least one of the persons who prepared the report should appear in court. After all, when a doctor's written opinion alone is submitted with the petition, hearsay evidence again enters the proceeding.

### d. The Court Setting

A final suggestion for procedural change of the hearing itself concerns whether or not these involuntary actions should be conducted in our modern courtrooms. Is it time to abandon the formal court setting and permit all fact finding to take place in the environment most familiar to the elderly person? Taking the hearing to the respondent, rather than the reverse, might enhance the fundamental fairness of the intrusive, stressful proceeding and focus on the reality of the respondent's circumstances rather than on a petitioner's interpretation of those circumstances.[20]

## 10. PROBATE COURTS ARE THE SLOW COURTS OF THE DEAD

One of the more peculiar factors working against the elderly in conservatorship/guardianship proceedings across America concerns the nature of the courts in which these actions take place. The probate or chancery or surrogate's courts are notorious for their slowness and cost. Why? Because they are, in essence, the courts of the dead. They are accustomed to processing or probating the estates of people who have died. As policy analyst Alison Barnes observed in her study of guardianship reform, "Whether due to superstitious dislike by the public and the bar . . . , probate courts tend to be a low priority when funds and bench assignments are distributed."[21] These courts are held in low esteem by members of the legal community.

Do aging individuals whose remaining life spans are short deserve to have to spend years of that precious allotment in a court that moves at a snail's pace? My mother's case was postponed again and again by judges who failed to consider how poorly their delays served the vulnerable woman. Three of the four elderly uncles targeted by their nephews' petitions in case 4.20 were victims of these egregiously slow courts. They died before the final appellate process was even completed. Does the anachronistic placement of conservatorship/guardianship cases in courts of the dead serve the interests of the elderly? Not at all.

An interesting proposal to move these protective proceedings out of probate courts and into a new jurisdiction has been suggested by Alison Barnes.[22] In the course of her discussion concerning issues relating to proxy decision-making, Ms. Barnes recommends a new tribunal that could be placed within an existing branch of the judiciary. This new jurisdiction would benefit from a relaxing of tediously slow procedural rules. Such a tribunal could examine social and interpersonal issues in a manner more akin to our current juvenile courts than to our ponderously slow probate courts. The revised system could make use of a reasonable "flat fee per case," allowing physicians, psychiatrists, psychologists, and private attorneys to contribute without excess cost. Panel members of a conservatorship/guardianship tribunal would become accustomed to the unique needs of the elderly who appear before them. Unlike judges in more traditional legal settings, they would receive training in issues of aging to avoid the powerful "-isms" that color current proceedings: ageism, sexism, and paternalism.

# 11. PAYMENT FOR THESE INVOLUNTARY PROCEEDINGS IS TAKEN FROM THE PROPOSED WARD'S OR CONSERVATEE'S ASSETS

If an involuntary conservatorship/guardianship petition is successful in any regard, every bill generated by every participant in the proceedings will eventually be paid out of the remaining assets of the new ward or conservatee. The courts thus use the legal system as an instrument of harassment and force the elderly to pay for an unwanted, unpleasant, and expensive experience that has no beneficial outcome for them.

Suggestions have been made that every state should be required to pay for specific aspects of proceedings that they require, such as any and all mandatory competency or capacity examinations, psychiatric evaluations, and interviews conducted by court investigators. Because self-interested petitioners have little to lose in initiating conservatorship/guardianship actions and proposed conservatees and wards have nothing to gain, "allocating the costs to the government may be justified as good public policy. . . . Proposed wards are [thus] protected from expending their assets to challenge an otherwise biased preparation of facts."[23]

Better yet, perhaps these hostile proceedings should come with the danger of a different sort of financial penalty. We should require that if anyone petitions the court for an involuntary conservatorship/guardianship over an elderly individual and does not succeed, the losing party must pay all costs for all participants—including those of the targeted elder and of the court, as well their own attorney's costs. It is an idea whose time has come.

# 12. NO ONE IS GUARDING THE GUARDIANS

As though the process of being adjudicated incompetent or incapacitated were not sufficiently horrific, the elderly man or woman who becomes a ward or conservatee is all too often victimized by the guardian or conservator who has been appointed by the court as a surrogate decision-maker for personal and/or financial affairs. We have seen fifteen examples of this painful reality. Who now regulates the burgeoning conservatorship/guardianship industry that has been created by our codes? Are overburdened courts checking to see that the vulnerable elderly who have been processed, labeled, and summarily dismissed by them as nonpersons are receiving proper care? And are guardians and conservators required to have *any* qualifications or special training in order to care for their wards and conservatees? The answers to these questions are: no one, no, and no. The entire system is rife with abuse because no one is guarding the guardians.

John Hartman, a thirty-four-year-old convict serving a five-year prison term for abusing his position as public guardian, spoke of this very real problem before the House Subcommittee on Health and Long-Term Care. Mr. Hartman had been working as a janitor in a local tavern when he was hired to work in the public guardian's office. During his eight-year tenure there, he was put in charge of the well-being of 210 wards—210 men and women—and a combined $1.5 million in income and assets. After admitting to embezzling the accounts for a total of $129,506, John Harman described the guardianship system as "completely unregulated."[24]

In a landmark study of over 400 guardianships, researchers George J.

Alexander and Travis H. D. Lewin concluded that wards ended up worse in every case following the imposition of guardians: "The authors reported that they could find no benefit that could not have been achieved without a finding of incompetency and that in almost every case examined the aged incompetent was in a worse position after he or she was adjudicated incompetent than before."[25]

## a. The Use of Limited Guardianships

During the years since the Alexander and Lewin report was released, improvements have been encouraged. In August of 1980, the American Bar Association endorsed the use of limited guardianships:

> The American Bar Association calls upon all states to assist persons of diminished mental capacity to live with maximum self-sufficiency in the general community, by enacting laws allowing court appointment of limited or partial guardians, where persons of diminished capacity need some, but not total, assistance in making decisions concerning their personal affairs or estate.[26]

A majority of states now permit courts to create limited conservatorships and guardianships that address the ward's unique deficits rather than the more traditional plenary arrangements. Unfortunately, as John W. Parry and Sally Balch Hurme reported for the American Bar Association Commission on the Mentally Disabled, "not very many jurisdictions explicitly mandate that courts consider limited guardianships . . . and, without an explicit mandate, judges too often never bother to tailor the guardianship orders to the ward's individual needs."[27] Such legislation is almost meaningless if the states fail to require its implementation.

## b. Court-Ordered Financial and Personal Status Reports

All state codes contain either statutory financial and personal status reporting requirements for conservators and guardians or make such accountings discretionary.[28] In most states, guardians or conservators of the person are required to file annual personal status reports on their wards. These reports vary widely in content, as do the periodic financial accountings most courts require of guardians and conservators of the estate. How is this system working throughout the United States? Not very well at all, as Parry and Hurme agree.

> Although the better statutes require the filing of financial accountings and personal status reports, a survey by the ABA Commissions on the

Mentally Disabled and Legal Problems of the Elderly for the guardianship monitoring report revealed a very different situation when it comes
to local practices.

Every jurisdiction except for West Virginia, for example, has a
statute that at least refers to the guardian's duty to provide financial
accountings. Yet the survey of practices indicated that in eighteen jurisdictions, the court took no action if an accounting was not filed, and in
six jurisdictions, no one looked at the accounting even when it was
filed.

Of the forty-three jurisdictions that require personal status reports,
the survey revealed that the statutory requirements were uniformly
enforced in only eighteen of them. Based on the survey responses
received from nineteen other jurisdictions, it appears that in some counties, the reports are filed routinely, while in other counties, in the same
state, they are not. Moreover, in eleven jurisdictions, all the respondents
indicated that guardians are not routinely required to file status reports.[29]

Obviously, there is a major enforcement/compliance problem with
these status reports even in the best of circumstances. In its 1987 report on
*Guardians of the Elderly—An Ailing System*, the Associated Press found
that nearly half of the accountings in the forty-four states that required
them were either missing or incomplete.[30] There are not enough laws in the
world to protect the newly created ward if the laws on conservator-
ship/guardianship monitoring that already exist are not being enforced.

What is more, there are only a few jurisdictions (including Alaska,
California, the District of Columbia, Florida, and Washington) where conservators and guardians are required to file prospective rather than retro-
spective reports.[31] A report describing what happened to the ward during
the previous year is only slightly more valuable than no report at all. One
that gives an outline of how the ward will be helped during the coming
year is infinitely better—if it is filed, and if it is read by the court. Unfortunately, according to John Parry and Sally Balch Hurme, "only a few
jurisdictions require the courts to review reports once they are filed."[32]

## c. Court-Appointed Visitors

In some jurisdictions, states have established a system of court-appointed
visitors who meet periodically with the ward to evaluate his or her well-
being. This monitoring approach creates a new layer of expenses that are
assessed against the wards' estates. In California's Los Angeles County,
for example, the court-appointed visitor will bill a conservatee's estate
over $300 for his or her annual visits—even if the incapacitated conser-
vatee is unaware of his or her presence and is incapable of making any

response to the visitor's questions. Well-intentioned ideas are not always good ones.

In general, state and district courts are not doing a good job of overseeing the actions of guardians and conservators. It is hard to imagine that this will change.

> Much of the legislation needed for courts to carry out adequate monitoring and enforcement is on the books, or courts possess the equitable powers necessary to make an effective contribution. Most states, however, lack comprehensive monitoring and enforcement schemes, relying instead on piecemeal legislation and sometimes uncertain equitable discretion.
>
> Considerably more needs to be done in this area of the law nationwide.... Too many courts, however, are just beginning to confront these issues and either their commitment to guardianship monitoring and enforcement is uncertain or, worse, it is clear they have no intention of using additional, scarce, judicial resources on guardianship matters.[33]

# 13. CODES LACK ANY AUTOMATIC PROVISION FOR TERMINATION

Most conservatorships and guardianships of the person and of the estate continue uninterrupted until the ward or conservatee dies. There is a rare exception to this grim statistic, however. Some are terminated when a ward returns to court and convinces a judge that he or she has "returned to competence/capacity" (whatever that might represent). This successful—and rare—procedure is called a *restoration hearing.*

In all too many states, the ward or conservatee is not permitted to file an application for a restoration hearing because he or she has been adjudicated incompetent or incapacitated and thus cannot contract to hire an attorney. In most states, though, any adult who is an "interested party" may file the request for a restoration hearing. At the hearing, the ward must present evidence of his or her capacity to manage his/her personal and/or financial affairs. Note that evidence demonstrating only "improper care by a guardian or conservator or evidence that he or she is antagonistic to the ward's best interest will not be enough to restore competence."[34]

An aged ward or conservatee whose financial decisions have been wrested from his or her control may try to terminate the conservatorship or guardianship by showing that the necessity for a surrogate decision-maker no longer exists. But how does the elderly person demonstrate competence in the area of property management if, as a result of the court's imposition of a conservatorship over his or her estate, he or she

has not been permitted to make a single independent property management decision? It is almost impossible.

The reality is that a conservatorship/guardianship of the person
and/or estate, once put in place, can rarely be removed. It should never be
treated as an interim custody intended to conserve property for the aged
until such time as he or she can do with it as he or she pleases. The
rigidity and permanence of the process smacks of generational injustice
as the elderly person's freedom to dispose of property is curtailed in favor
of the protection of family interests (read "inheritances").

Statutory reform must include automatic provisions for review or termination to give elderly wards and conservatees hope that their unwanted
and onerous conservatorships and guardianships can be ended. Prisoners
who have committed heinous crimes are guaranteed regular hearings with
parole boards in an attempt to secure their freedom. Aging wards and conservatees, who have never compromised the life, health, or safety of another
human being, deserve no less of a chance to be released from their prisons.

# 14. JUDICIAL DECISIONS ARE
# HARD TO APPEAL

The right to appeal a conservatorship or guardianship ruling is limited in
most states and openly denied in some. In states permitting appeal of
these involuntary proceedings, the right to appeal is limited procedurally.
In essence, the appellate court will accept as true all facts determined by
the lower court. The appellate court does not hear new facts or reweigh
old evidence. Experts in this field emphasize how important it is that the
elderly who are targeted by these involuntary proceedings be represented
by attorneys, since attorneys may succeed in excluding much adverse evidence from the hearings themselves.

What does an appellate court do? Let me quote from an expert,
Robert N. Brown, Professor of Law at the University of Detroit School of
Law and Director of its Health Law Center:

> The appellate court will hear arguments concerning the constitutionality
> of the state's guardianship or conservatorship statutes; whether certain
> evidence that was objected to at the hearing was properly excluded or
> admitted; whether there is some basis in the evidence for the lower
> court's determinations; and whether certain procedural aspects of the
> hearing, such as notice, were sufficient to protect one's rights.[35]

It takes a great deal of tenacity, determination and money for men and
women who have been ruled incompetent to go back into the legal fray.

They must display remarkable courage in the face of great adversity. We already know that conservatorship and guardianship adjudications are almost never appealed.[36] Is there something that could be done to make a successful appeal more attainable? Yes.

Judges who currently preside over these lower circuit court cases rarely write or publish opinions explaining their rulings and reciting their reasons for granting or denying these petitions. The mere fact that little is written about these mercurial determinations leads to a lack of accountability. It is this lack of judicial accountability that harms the ward or conservatee. Jan Ellen Rein proposed an excellent solution to the problem.

> Perhaps a statutory requirement that probate judges publish short reports or opinions briefly summarizing the evidence of incapacity presented, the reasons for imposition of the guardianship, the nature and extent of the ward's decisionmaking deficiency, and the interests sought to be protected or incidentally served by the court's order would promote accountability and provide some concrete basis for appealing perfunctory or inappropriate decisions.
>
> Some commentators may object that this would severely burden our already overburdened courts, but fundamental rights should not be sacrificed for administrative convenience.[37]

You might be surprised to learn that one of the judges in my mother's case announced in court that he thought he might appoint a temporary conservator of her estate because, after all, "it won't hurt anyone."[38] Only those with access to the court reporter's transcript of the hearing would know this is the actual standard of evidence—evidence by whim and whimsy—being used in some conservatorship/guardianship courts today. Judges must be held accountable for their quixotic and highly personal interpretations of state statutes. By requiring them to explain and publish their judicial determinations, legislators would give the vulnerable elderly in America a much-needed window of opportunity to have unfair decisions reversed in a court of appeal.

ðŠ    ðŠ    ðŠ

As we have just seen, even though they are described solely in terms of benefit to the elderly our country's involuntary conservatorship and guardianship proceedings are based upon dangerously flawed codes and governed by potentially harmful procedural guidelines. Will some or all of the fourteen problems discussed in this section be corrected in meaningful ways before these conservatorship/guardianship laws are used against you or against  someone you love? Probably not. However, there are five important steps you can take now to protect your future self and safeguard your retirement years. These steps are the heart of our final chapter.

# NOTES

1. *In re Fisher*, 552 N.Y.S.2d 807 (Sup. Ct. 1989).
2. G. Atkinson, "Towards a Due Process Perspective in Conservatorship Proceedings for the Aged," *Journal of Family Law* 18, no. 4 (1980): 833.
3. J. E. Rein, "Preserving Dignity and Self-Determination of the Elderly in the Face of Competing Interests and Grim Alternatives: A Proposal for Statutory Refocus and Reform," *George Washington Law Review* 60, no. 6 (1992): 1870.
4. Ibid., p. 1873.
5. Ibid.
6. Ibid., p. 1874 (footnote).
7. "The Disguised Oppression of Involuntary Guardianship: Have the Elderly Freedom to Spend?" *Yale Law Journal* 73 (1964): 682.
8. Ibid.
9. J. E. Rein, "Clients with Destructive and Socially Harmful Choices—What's an Attorney to Do? Within and Beyond the Competency Construct," *Fordham Law Review* 62 (1994): 1172.
10. W. C. Schmidt, "Guardianship of the Elderly in Florida," *Florida Bar Journal* 55 (1981): 189.
11. "The Disguised Oppression," p. 677.
12. A. P. Barnes, "Beyond Guardianship Reform: A Reevaluation of Autonomy and Beneficence for a System of Principled Decision-Making in Long Term Care," *Emory Law Journal* 41 (1992): 755.
13. Taken from court transcript.
14. J. E. Spar and A. S. Garb, "Assessing Competency to Make a Will," *American Journal of Psychiatry* 149, no. 2 (1992): 169–74.
15. Barnes, "Beyond Guardianship Reform," p. 687.
16. *Wilson v. Wehunt*, 631 So.2d 991, 995 (Ala. 1994), quoted in Ray D. Madoff, "Unmasking Undue Influence," *Minnesota Law Review* 81 (1997): 577.
17. J. M. Peden, "The Guardian Ad Litem Under the Guardianship Reform Act: A Profusion of Duties, a Confusion of Roles," *University of Detroit Law Review* 68 (1990): 29.
18. Ibid., p. 32.
19. P. M. Keith and R. R. Wacker, "Implementation of Recommended Guardianship Practices and Outcomes of Hearings for Older Persons," *The Gerontologist* 33, no. 1 (1993): 84.
20. Barnes, "Beyond Guardianship Reform," p. 701.
21. Ibid., p. 689.
22. Ibid., p. 698.
23. P. Tor, "Finding Incompetency in Guardianship: Standardizing the Process," *Arizona Law Review* 35 (1993): 763.

24. M. Sinclair, "Subcommittee Hears Stories of Abuse," *Washington Post*, 26 September 1987, p. A3.

25. Quoted in J. E. Rein, "Preserving Dignity and Self-Determination of the Elderly," p. 1834 (footnote).

26. Quoted in J. W. Parry and Sally Balch Hurme, "Guardianship Monitoring and Enforcement Nationwide," *Mental and Physical Disability Law Reporter* 15, no. 3 (1991): 304.

27. Ibid., p. 305.

28. Ibid.

29. Ibid.

30. Associated Press, *Guardians of the Elderly—An Ailing System* 1 (Special Report, 1987).

31. Parry and Hurme, "Guardianship Monitoring and Enforcement Nationwide."

32. Ibid., p. 307.

33. Ibid., p. 308.

34. R. N. Brown, *The Rights of Older Persons: A Basic Guide to the Legal Rights of Older Persons Under Current Law*, 2d ed. (Washington, D.C.: ACLU, 1989), p. 346..

35. Ibid.

36. Rein, "Preserving Dignity and Self-Determination of the Elderly," p. 1880.

37. Ibid.

38. Taken from court transcript.

# CHAPTER NINE

# SAVING YOURSELF FROM YOUR HEIRS AND PROTECTORS

*If a man take no thought about what is distant, he will find sorrow near at hand.*

— Confucius (551–479 B.C.E.)

s a group, Americans over fifty are becoming increasingly adept at managing investments, minimizing taxes, and even planning inheritance strategies for future beneficiaries. However, it is what they are *not* doing that puts these men and women at risk of hostile involuntary conservatorship/guardianship proceedings as they age. Whether through benign complacency or blissful ignorance, they are not planning for physical and/or mental incapacity during their lifetime. If you do not make such plans before you need them, you can be sure of one thing and one thing only: if you ever become the target of a so-called protective proceeding, someone else will be making all of your final personal and financial decisions for you — and, as we have seen in fifty-five actual examples, *that* person might not have your best interests at heart.

It is clear by now that the use of involuntary conservatorship/ guardianship litigation to seize control of the personal and financial decision-making powers of recalcitrant elders is a growing but secretive problem in America. It is a very real nightmare that is rarely discussed beyond the confines of county probate courtrooms, yet wreaks havoc upon the targeted elderly who lose these legal battles 94 percent of the time. Lest you succumb to the temptation to minimize the catastrophic nature of such unwanted "protective proceedings," let's review the rights an elderly man or woman surrenders in these actions. The following section is taken from Virginia's guardianship codes and summarizes the possible consequences of the hearing for the allegedly incompetent adult:

> At the hearing you may lose many of your rights. A guardian may be appointed to make personal decisions for you. A conservator may be appointed to make decisions concerning your property and finances. The appointment may affect control of how you spend your money, how your property is managed and controlled, who makes your medical decisions, where you live, whether you are allowed to vote, and other important rights. (§37.1-134.10[D])

It is a perilous problem, indeed. How easy to avert one's gaze from the issue and repeat, "This could never happen to me." This is an unwise assumption, usually based on the belief that being part of a supportive and loving family will protect you from the nightmare of involuntary conservatorship/guardianship litigation as you age. Scan all forty cases numbered from 4.1 through 5.20 and note: almost 25 percent of these petitions were filed by social workers, social welfare agencies, and neighbors.

Mary Cummings, Glen Hawkins, and the men and women whose cases we have reviewed never guessed that such devastating litigation existed in America. After all, ours is a country in which individual rights to life, liberty, property, and the pursuit of happiness are guaranteed. Unfortunately, each state has extended its *parens patriae* power to interfere in the lives of aging people in surprising ways. Rather than hide from this painful reality, we can confront and disarm this legal time bomb by making adequate self-protective arrangements well in advance of our potential mental or physical frailty. As we have seen, not doing so is a risk with painful consequences that are almost beyond imagination.

How to proceed? There are five steps that will help protect you from the indignity of involuntary "protective proceedings" and serve to safeguard your retirement years. The steps are not complex, yet they will require thoughtful preliminary consideration of how you may want to discuss such matters with the "significant others" in your life. Life partners, adult children, close friends, trusted associates—members of your "convoy of social support," as John W. Rowe, M.D., and Robert L. Kahn, Ph.D.[1] (authors of the MacArthur Foundation Study's *Successful Aging*) described the supportive relationships with which each of us moves through life—will be slotted into the lists you will prepare in planning for possible incapacity during your lifetime. Is there one best way to discuss your future financial and healthcare wishes with those you love and respect? Is there an optimal approach to sharing and evaluating with a spouse or relative the manner in which you want to assign durable powers, allocate assets in revocable trusts, make your wishes known in living wills, and nominate a guardian or conservator for your future self? No. But there will be a way that works best for you.

Some choose to begin the planning process with an initial visit to an attorney. The visit can serve two major purposes. First, the experienced professional will help you identify the individuals in your particular "convoy of support" who might best protect your person and/or estate during times of future incapacity. Second, an attorney can assist in creating a framework for your actual discussion with the individuals you will ask to serve as your guardian or conservator (should the need arise) or to hold your durable powers of attorney. Such powers cannot be lightly given or received, and an attorney can and should clarify for all parties the risks and responsibilities involved.

Other men and women prefer to discuss their initial planning first with the individuals they hope will serve in their fiscal and/or personal stead should the need arise, and then formalize their choices with appropriate attorneys. A third approach is easier but far less felicitous, namely, simply filling out the necessary paperwork with the names of current friends or relatives and hoping that each chosen individual will be able and willing to serve you when the time comes. It is important to realize that members of your immediate support network will change over your lifetime, with losses from death, estrangement, divorce, and distance, and with subsequent replacements you cannot yet imagine. A casual list of people who may or may not be willing to guide your final years of life as you would wish exposes your retirement years to unnecessary peril— perils highlighted by the Virginia State code quoted above. Discuss your thoughts about planning for future incapacity with those you most trust; finalize your decisions with an appropriate attorney; review and update your various legal choices of conservator, guardian, and holder of your durable powers of attorney every three to five years for "goodness of fit"—and then relax. Until these laws are changed, you will have done everything you can do to protect yourself from their destructive powers.

In these final pages, you will learn about the five steps you can take *now* to ensure that your choices will be honored during your lifetime. Your planning will begin with selecting the right attorney and continue with two major steps involving two types of advance directives: directives for *property management* (financial durable powers, revocable trusts, and convenience joint tenancies), and directives for your *personal care* (durable powers for health care, and living wills). Steps four and five (see outline below) can be used to put extra protections in place that will help you if you become the target of unwanted surrogate decision-making litigation. Once you have completed these steps, your safety net will be in place to safeguard you and your assets throughout your remaining years.

In essence, then, your crucial self-protective planning measures are:

1. Working with the right attorney
    a. How do I find a good attorney?
    b. What should I ask him or her?

2. For property management
    a. Durable powers of attorney
    b. Revocable trusts
    c. Durable power of attorney in conjunction with revocable living trusts
    d. "Convenience" joint tenancies (accounts)

3. For healthcare decisions
    a. Durable power of attorney for healthcare decisions
    b. Living wills

4. Preselecting a conservator or guardian

5. Preventing future challenges to your legal directives

You must begin by selecting an appropriate attorney. It can be a daunting task. When asked what advice she would give to anyone who needed help in finding a good lawyer, my mother's advice was succinct: *"Do not go to a corporate attorney unless you are a Big Business!"*[2] The costs incurred in her case—well over one million dollars and counting— were partly a function of a legal system run amok and partly the result of a remarkable growth of billings that occurred when a major legal firm focused its expensive attention on one individual as client. *Almost half a ton of legal paperwork* was generated by her case. This veritable Devil's Tower of documentation represented a massive duplication of originals that was needed to feed the filing cabinets of her litigators, trust attorneys, junior attorneys, probate specialists, paralegals, conservators' attorneys, the court—and my mother herself. The importance of finding the right attorney for the right job cannot be overemphasized.

# 1. WORKING WITH THE RIGHT ATTORNEY

If you have reason to believe you might be getting close to the dangerous flames of a possible involuntary conservatorship or guardianship proceeding, you should consult an Elder Law or Probate Law attorney who *specializes* in this unique area of law. Remember: if you select an attorney who must research these obscure codes before filing a single motion in your behalf, you will be paying for that attorney's *practice* in the purest sense of that term. You do not want an attorney who must *practice* before he or she can help you!

If your need is for an attorney who can help you prepare property management and healthcare devices to guard your future freedom from unwanted surrogate decision-making as you age, you should consult a very different specialist. You will want to consult an attorney skilled in Wills, Trusts, and Estate Planning law.

## a. How do I find a good attorney?

In its February 1996 issue, *Consumer Reports* published the results of replies from approximately 30,000 readers who had returned surveys concerning their personal experiences with lawyers.[3] In their survey, the authors found that people who located an attorney through personal contacts or a business organization were generally happier than those who found one through an advertisement or phone directory. An excellent suggestion, then, is to ask a lawyer you trust—a family friend, an attorney who has helped you with unrelated matters—to give you several recommendations.

Start compiling a list of candidates for the job. If you have access to a law library or large public or private library, do a bit of research on your list of candidates in the *Martindale-Hubbell* legal directory.[4] The directory will give you helpful information: where each lawyer went to law school, when each was admitted to the state bar, and (sometimes but not always) his or her area of expertise. You might call your local bar association or state disciplinary agency to ask about licensure, complaints, and possible past disciplinary actions. Check your telephone directory's list of state court offices; state disciplinary agencies are often part of the State Supreme Court or State Bar Association. Feel free to call the American Bar Association in Chicago at (312) 988-5000. If you are one of the eighty-eight million Americans who have joined a legal-services plan, your choice of lawyer and extent of coverage are often limited. Nevertheless, the answers to our next question will be crucial in helping *everyone* find the right attorney for the job at hand.

## b. What should I ask a lawyer?

Because the use of temporary or "emergency" petitions left her with only four working days in which to mount her entire defense, my mother turned to her Trust Attorney for help with her involuntary conservatorship litigation. You, however, will have the time not only to locate exactly the kind of specialist you need, but also to prepare a list of questions to ask each lawyer during a first (and possibly last) interview.

The following list from *Consumer Reports* will put you firmly in the driver's seat in your all-important initial discussion. You will note that some of the questions are relevant only to adversarial litigation (such as an involuntary conservatorship/guardianship case), while others are more clearly intended as general questions regarding non-adversarial legal tasks (such as the crafting of wills, trusts, and estate planning instruments). Do not be timid when asking these questions. Do not be embarrassed. If you feel you cannot communicate openly and comfortably with the first attorney on your list, move on to the second.

### What to Ask a Lawyer

- What's your experience in this field? How have you handled matters like mine?

- What are the possible outcomes?

- How long do you expect this matter to take?

- How will you keep me informed as the case progresses?

- Will anyone else be working on my case?

- How do you charge? If you charge by the hour, what is your hourly rate? Will junior attorneys or paralegals in your office be able to handle some of the administrative work at a lower rate? If you charge a fixed fee, what is it—and what happens if something unforeseen occurs? . . .

- Beyond fees, what kinds of expenses will there be, and how do you calculate them?

- What's a ballpark figure for my total bill?

- Will you put your estimates in writing?

- How often will I be billed? If we have a disagreement over billing, will I be charged for the time spentdisputing the bill? Will you agree to mandatory arbitration if we can't settle a dispute?

- How can I help you help me? Can I do some of the work? What other information do you need from me?

- What are my alternatives? Do you recommend arbitration of mediation? Do you know good arbitrators or mediators?

P.S. Ask for an explanation when an answer isn't clear. If the lawyer can't explain or treats a request for clarification in an condescending manner, cross his or her name off the list.[5]

It is an unfortunate reality that finding legal representation in America can be difficult for those who are wealthy—and almost impossible for those who are not. Legal Services Corp., which sponsors legal aid for people near or below the federal poverty level, calculates that it can now provide only one lawyer for every 10,000 clients who are eligible and need an attorney.[6] Ironically, however, their very poverty often shields the poor from involuntary conservatorship/guardianship litigation since the impetus pushing many elderly persons into court actions today is money—*their* money. Remember, heir-petitioners often use these mischaracterized "protective proceedings" to secure anticipated inheritances, not just to annoy an aging relative. When money drops out of the equation, the financially motivated will have little interest in taking their fiercely independent relatives to court.

If paying for an attorney to generate the property and healthcare directives you will need is a problem, there are two avenues worth exploring. First, ask the attorney you have selected if he or she will accept monthly payments from you for services rendered. Second, ask if he or she will do your legal tasks *pro bono*, for no fee. Attorneys in every state are encouraged to donate a percentage of their time to individuals who otherwise could not afford legal representation. It does not hurt to ask. After all, *you* must be the defender of your own future and autonomy. If the worst thing an attorney can say is no, then the momentary disappointment you might experience will be a very small price to pay in your search to find the help you need.

Having selected your attorney, you can begin the process of directing the future course of your property management decisions in the event you lose the capacity to control your own financial affairs.

# 2. FOR PROPERTY MANAGEMENT

Estate and elder law attorneys generally recommend the use of two types of financial planning devices to ensure that the financial affairs of an individual who becomes incapacitated will be handled by a legal fiduciary.[7] You must double the stitches in your safety net and use both. The two mechanisms authorize a chosen proxy to assume management of your estate automatically should you become incapacitated. They are *durable powers of attorney* and *living trusts*. The third financial device that you will want to consider is the *joint deposit* or *convenience account*.

## a. Durable Powers of Attorney

A *power of attorney* is a written authorization in which you (the principal) grant decision-making power to another person (the agent or attorney-in-fact) to act in your place. The traditional power of attorney remains valid only as long as you remain capable or legally competent to terminate it. It will have no power to protect you if you become incompetent! According to Robert N. Brown in *The Rights of Older Persons*, it is this limiting feature that makes the nondurable power of attorney "useless as a device to plan for possible future mental incapacity or disability."[8]

In contrast, a *durable power of attorney* continues in effect, or becomes effective, after the principal's physical or mental incapacity.[9] In order to be a durable power, the written instrument must state specifically that it is unaffected by the principal's future incapacity or incompetence. A durable power of attorney may grant general power to the chosen agent (to act for you generally in all matters), special power (carrying rights with respect to a specialized activity), or limited power (a general power with stated limitations). In all cases, the agent's authority cannot exceed the powers you as principal have specified. The durable power of attorney is permitted in all states and the District of Columbia. How will a durable power of attorney help you?

Durable powers often are used to authorize financial transactions and property management. By arranging property management through a trusted agent, the principal (you) may avoid one of the most common grounds for appointment of a conservator or guardian of your estate. Several courts have stated that judicially imposed property management through surrogate decision-making proceedings is unnecessary if an incapacitated person has already made his or her own arrangements.[10]

Thus, an *immediately effective durable general power of attorney* is an excellent approach to planning for your potential physical or mental incapacity.[11] Name one or more trusted individuals to function on your behalf as attorney-in-fact in all matters. Once this durable power is in place, all people involved will agree that the durable power of attorney will only be used if a court determines that you have you become incapacitated and unable to manage your own affairs. Many states also allow a "standby" or *springing durable power of attorney* that comes into effect only upon a finding of the principal's incapacity and is suspended when the principal regains his or her capacity. A clear and functional definition of incapacity or disability must be defined in the document itself.

Unfortunately, ominous judicial pronouncements and practical complications have shaken the once-solid belief that these durable powers of attorney would always protect the principal from future involuntary conservatorships and guardianships. An example of the first was highlighted in case 4.2, *Rice* v. *Floyd*. This case contained a 1989 decision by the Supreme Court of Kentucky in which the justices ruled that "the existence of a durable power of attorney cannot prevent the institution of guardianship proceedings."[12] Two lower courts had ruled that an elderly defendant's durable power of attorney made a guardianship unnecessary because it fulfilled all of the purposes for which a guardian was being sought by the petitioner. The Supreme Court disagreed. Even though the state of Kentucky had, in creating the durable power of attorney, provided the means by which its competent citizens could arrange for the handling of their affairs should they decline into incompetence, the Supreme Court neutralized the "durable" aspect of the durable power of attorney.

A second difficulty with durable powers of attorney involves practical considerations. There is a widespread reluctance on the part of third parties (such as banks and brokerage firms) to recognize the chosen agent's authority. Indeed, banks will often refuse to accept durable powers unless they are executed on the banks' own forms. New York and Washington are among the few states that require third-party acceptance of a durable power of attorney executed in conformity with models crafted by state law.[13]

You can enhance the likelihood that your durable powers of attorney will be accepted by having them witnessed and notarized. An inducement clause can be included that holds all third parties harmless for acts undertaken by the agent after the power has been revoked. A third mechanism often used to encourage acceptance of powers that authorize health-care decisions involves distributing copies to physicians in advance. Finally, as recommended by Professor Brown, "to protect confidentiality, a principal might want to execute a durable power for healthcare decisions in a separate document from a [durable] power for financial matters."[14] This will be discussed later under section 3, "For Healthcare Decisions."

Are there any major flaws with the use of durable powers of attorney as "least restrictive alternatives" to conservatorship or guardianship? If so, what should you guard against? It is wise to question any legal instrument that gives another human being the right to control your money. The durable powers of attorney are vulnerable in one key area: the person you chose as your agent may turn out to be a scoundrel. He or she will be authorized to do anything and everything with your property—including squandering it all—and this fiduciary abuse often goes totally unnoticed, as we have seen.

What can you do? You must review your choices of agent or attorney-in-fact with your attorney every three to five years, just to make sure they are still appropriate choices. The person you select will be your surrogate in exercising the powers you grant him or her. Remember that *you* rather than an unknown judge will also be choosing the specific powers you wish to delegate to this surrogate. These warnings apply equally to our next property management planning device, the revocable living trust. Let's look at the role such a trust can play in your future well-being.

## b. Revocable Trusts

A *revocable living trust* is a trust that can be changed or terminated by its creator as he or she wishes during the creator's lifetime.[15] This *inter vivos* (during lifetime) method of estate planning permits you as estate owner to place some or all of your property into a revocable trust, administer and invest the trust property, and distribute trust income as you, the creator, wish. Because it is a revocable trust, you may take trust assets back (and out of the trust) at any given time.

The revocable living trust becomes irrevocable upon your death. Where permitted by law, property can be "poured over" from the creator's will into the trust. Revocable trusts can thus be used as will substitutes. How can this financial device be incorporated into a plan to protect you against the future imposition of an unwanted conservator or guardian over your estate? If you should become physically or mentally incapacitated or unable to manage your own affairs, a successor trustee (named by you in the trust document) will continue to manage all trust property for your benefit without interruption. Furthermore, as we shall now see, the revocable living trust can be combined with a durable power of attorney to provide added protection from unwanted interference in your financial affairs as you age.

## c. Durable Powers of Attorney in Conjunction with Revocable Living Trusts

A solid approach to planning for your own potential physical or mental incompetence is to have an existing (or springing) durable power of attorney which grants the person you have chosen as your trusted attorney-in-fact or agent the power to transfer some or all of your assets into a previously established revocable living trust.[16] Thus, should you become incapacitated in a defined way, your chosen attorney-in-fact can use the durable power of attorney to manage your fund's assets for your benefit during your time of incapacity. The formerly revocable trust becomes irrevocable and unchangeable upon the event of your physical or mental incapacity and inability to manage your own affairs.

### d. "Convenience" Joint Tenancies (Accounts)

Another financial device you can arrange proactively as a part of a sub-stituted plan of property management is the *joint deposit* or *convenience account*. Establish joint bank accounts, certificates of deposit, or similar deposits with another trusted person with the expectation that that indi-vidual will use the money in those accounts to take care of you in your time of need. There is an obvious flaw in this plan, however. Since each party to the account is legally entitled to withdraw the funds as he or she sees fit, you will have no guarantee that the joint account will be used as you intended once you have become incapacitated. As financial consul-tants C. Victor Hallman and Jerry S. Rosenbloom warn in *Personal Financial Planning*, "as a practical and legal matter, these convenience joint accounts are a questionable solution to the incapacity problem in most cases."[17] Be sure to discuss the uses and abuses of joint tenancy accounts with the attorney who is helping you safeguard your future.

## 3. FOR HEALTHCARE DECISIONS

There are two legal directives used in most states that permit us to con-trol our personal healthcare decisions as we age. One is the *durable power of attorney for healthcare decisions*, and the second is the *living will*. Needless to say, neither device is foolproof. Because they are func-tioning in a hostile litigious environment, physicians are often reluctant— or not permitted by state law—to accept a durable power's authorization for life-and-death decisions. Many physicians simply ignore or override the choices delineated in a living will.

Nonetheless, all of us must work diligently to strengthen the safety nets that will protect us as we age. It is important to ask the same attorney who is helping you with property management advance directives to dis-cuss which healthcare directives you should put in place now to control the kinds of medical interventions you will receive in the future. Because medical science is greatly expanding our chance to almost outlive our bodies—to exist as strong-minded individuals in increasingly fragile con-tainers—we owe this thoughtful deliberation to our future selves.

### a. Durable Power of Attorney for Healthcare Decisions

The first such device, one of the durable powers we discussed previously, is the *durable power of attorney for healthcare decisions*. This must be executed when you are competent to do so. It is used to appoint an attorney-in-fact who will make medical decisions for you should you become incapacitated. Such decisions may be limited by state law and will be limited by the guidelines you establish when you create the durable powers. The healthcare power of attorney can be a separate legal document, or it can be a portion of a larger durable power that also covers property management. Again, it is important to specify the people in whom you would entrust your very survival, and it is equally important to review your choices on a regular basis.

A durable power of attorney for health care decisions can be effective in avoiding guardianship or conservatorship of the person. How so? As Professor Brown noted, because these durable powers can include most aspects of personal decisionmaking (such as arrangements for residential placement, access to records, and even for some healthcare decisions), the courts tend not to interfere in these areas since the proposed ward has already made his or her arrangements.[18] State statutes authorizing an agent to make healthcare decisions through a durable power of attorney generally require that the documents be witnessed and notarized.

Most commentators believe durable powers of attorney can be used for healthcare decisions without specific statutory authorization. Several courts have stated that the existence of a durable power addressing health-care decisions is evidence of the principal's intentions which should be followed. For example, a principal could make her wishes concerning treatment by artificial life-support systems, such as feeding tubes or respirators, known in the power of attorney and could designate an agent to make any relevant necessary decisions.[19] Unfortunately, the law guiding the creation and use of durable powers of attorney for healthcare decisions is too new to be universal in its use or acceptance across America. Please remember that it is important that you seek legal counsel concerning the use of these health care devices *in your state*. If you move, you will need to have your durable powers reviewed by an attorney in your new state.

It may be helpful at this point to look at an advance directive pulled directly from current codes. This particular example is contained in the Oregon Revised Statutes, section 127.531, 1995 edition. In this fairly representative advance directive, the individual must specify the health care he or she would wish to receive—or to avoid—should the circumstance arise. The format appears precisely as shown in chapter 127 under "Form of Advance Directive."

127.531 Form of advance directive. (1) The form of an advance directive executed by an Oregon resident must be the same as the form set forth in this section to be valid. In any place in the form that requires the initials of the principal, any mark by the principal is effective to indicate the principal's intent. (2) An advance directive shall be in the following form:

---

ADVANCE DIRECTIVE
YOU DO NOT HAVE TO FILL OUT AND SIGN THIS FORM

PART A: IMPORTANT INFORMATION ABOUT THIS ADVANCE DIRECTIVE

This is an important legal document. It can control critical decisions about your health care. Before signing, consider these important facts:

Facts About Part B
(Appointing a Health Care Representative)

You have the right to name a person to direct your health care when you cannot do so. This person is called your "health care representative." You can do this by using Part B of this form. Your representative must accept on Part E of this form.

You can write in this document any restrictions you want on how your representative will make decisions for you. Your representative must follow your desires as stated in this document or otherwise made known. If your desires are unknown, your representative must try to act in your best interest. Your representative can resign at any time.

Facts About Part C
(Giving Health Care Instructions)

You also have the right to give instructions for health care providers to follow if you become unable to direct your care. You can do this by using Part C of this form.

Facts About Completing This Form

This form is valid only if you sign it voluntarily and when you are of sound mind. If you do not want an advance directive, you do not have to sign this form.
Unless you have limited the duration of this advance directive, it will not expire. If you have set an expiration date, and you become unable to direct your health care before that date, this advance directive will not

expire until you are able to make those decisions again.

You may revoke this document at any time. To do so, notify your representative and your health care provider of the revocation. Despite this document, you have the right to decide your own health care as long as you are able to do so. If there is anything in this document that you do not understand, ask a lawyer to explain it to you.

You may sign PART B, PART C, or both parts. You may cross out words that don't express your wishes or add words that better express your wishes. Witnesses must sign PART D.

Print your NAME, BIRTHDATE AND ADDRESS here:

_____

(Name)


_____

(Birthdate)


_____
_____

(Address)

Unless revoked or suspended, this advance directive will continue for:
INITIAL ONE:

\_\_ My entire life
\_\_ Other period (\_\_ Years)

## PART B: APPOINTMENT OF HEALTH CARE REPRESENTATIVE

I appoint _____ as my health care representative. My representative's address is _____ and telephone number is

_____.

I appoint _____ as my alternate health care representative. My alternate's address is _____ and telephone number is _____.

I authorize my representative (or alternate) to direct my health care when I can't do so.

NOTE: You may not appoint your doctor, an employee of your doctor, or an owner, operator or employee of your health care facility, unless that person is related to you by blood, marriage or adoption or that person was appointed before your admission into the health care facility.

1. Limits.
Special Conditions or Instructions:

_____

_____

INITIAL IF THIS APPLIES:

__ I have executed a Health Care Instruction or Directive to Physicians. My representative is to honor it.
2. Life Support.
"Life support" refers to any medical means for maintaining life, including procedures, devices and medications. If you refuse life support, you will still get routine measures to keep you clean and comfortable.
INITIAL IF THIS APPLIES:

__ My representative MAY decide about life support for me. (If you don't initial this space, then your representative MAY NOT decide about life support.)
3. Tube Feeding.

One sort of life support is food and water supplied artificially by medical device, known as tube feeding.
INITIAL IF THIS APPLIES:

__ My representative MAY decide about tube feeding for me. (If you don't initial this space, then your representative MAY NOT decide about tube feeding.)

_____
(Date)

SIGN HERE TO APPOINT A HEALTH CARE REPRESENTATIVE

_____
(Signature of person making appointment)

PART C: HEALTH CARE INSTRUCTIONS

NOTE: In filling out these instructions, keep the following in mind: - The term "as my physician recommends" means that you want your physician to try life support if your physician believes it could be helpful and then discontinue it if it is not helping your health condition or symptoms.

- "Life support" and "tube feeding" are defined in Part B above.
- If you refuse tube feeding, you should understand that malnutrition, dehydration and death will probably result.
- You will get care for your comfort and cleanliness, no matter what choices you make.
- You may either give specific instructions by filling out Items 1 to 4 below, or you may use the general instruction provided by Item 5.

Here are my desires about my health care if my doctor and another knowledgeable doctor confirm that I am in a medical condition described below:

1. Close to Death. If I am close to death and life support would only postpone the moment of my death:
A. INITIAL ONE:
__ I want to receive tube feeding.
__ I want tube feeding only as my physician recommends.
__ I DO NOT WANT tube feeding.
B. INITIAL ONE:
__ I want any other life support that may apply.
__ I want life support only as my physician recommends.
__ I want NO life support.

2. Permanently Unconscious. If I am unconscious and it is very unlikely that I will ever become conscious again:
A. INITIAL ONE:
__ I want to receive tube feeding.
__ I want tube feeding only as my physician recommends.
__ I DO NOT WANT tube feeding.
B. INITIAL ONE:
__ I want any other life support that may apply.
__ I want life support only as my physician recommends.
__ I want NO life support.

3. Advanced Progressive Illness. If I have a progressive illness that will be fatal and is in an advanced stage, and I am consistently and permanently unable to communicate by any means, swallow food and water safely, care for myself and recognize my family and other people, and it is very unlikely that my condition will substantially improve:
A. INITIAL ONE:
__ I want to receive tube feeding.
__ I want tube feeding only as my physician recommends.

__ I DO NOT WANT tube feeding.
B. INITIAL ONE:
__ I want any other life support that may apply.
__ I want life support only as my physician recommends.
__ I want NO life support.

4. Extraordinary Suffering. If life support would not help my medical condition and would make me suffer permanent and severe pain:
A. INITIAL ONE:
__ I want to receive tube feeding.
__ I want tube feeding only as my physician recommends.
__ I DO NOT WANT tube feeding.
B. INITIAL ONE:
__ I want any other life support that may apply.
__ I want life support only as my physician recommends.
__ I want NO life support.

5. General Instruction.
INITIAL IF THIS APPLIES:
__ I do not want my life to be prolonged by life support. I also do not want tube feeding as life support. I want my doctors to allow me to die naturally if my doctor and another knowledgeable doctor confirm I am in any of the medical conditions listed in Items 1 to 4 above.

6. Additional Conditions or Instructions.

_____
_____
_____
_____

(Insert description of what you want done.)

7. Other Documents. A "health care power of attorney" is any document you may have signed to appoint a representative to make health care decisions for you.
INITIAL ONE:
__ I have previously signed a health care power of attorney. I want it to remain in effect unless I appointed a health care representative after signing the health care power of attorney.
__ I have a health care power of attorney, and I REVOKE IT.
__ I DO NOT have a health care power of attorney.

_____
(Date)

SIGN HERE TO GIVE INSTRUCTIONS

_____

(Signature)

## PART D: DECLARATION OF WITNESSES

We declare that the person signing this advance directive:
(a) Is personally known to us or has provided proof of identity;
(b) Signed or acknowledged that person's signature on this advance directive in our presence;
(c) Appears to be of sound mind and not under duress, fraud or undue influence;
(d) Has not appointed either of us as health care representative or alternative representative; and
(e) Is not a patient for whom either of us is attending physician.
Witnessed By:

_____  _____

(Signature of    (Printed Name
Witness/Date)    of Witness)

_____  _____

(Signature of    (Printed Name of
Witness/Date     of Witness)

NOTE: One witness must not be a relative (by blood, marriage or adoption) of the person signing this advance directive. That witness must also not be entitled to any portion of the person's estate upon death. That witness must also not own, operate or be employed at a health care facility where the person is a patient or resident.

## PART E: ACCEPTANCE BY HEALTH CARE REPRESENTATIVE

I accept this appointment and agree to serve as health care representative. I understand I must act consistently with the desires of the person I represent, as expressed in this advance directive or otherwise made known to me. If I do not know the desires of the person I represent, I have a duty to act in what I believe in good faith to be that person's best interest. I understand that this document allows me to decide about that person's health care only while that person cannot do so. I understand that the person who appointed me may revoke this appointment. If I learn that this document has been suspended or revoked, I will inform the person's current health care provider if known to me.

_____

(Signature of Health Care Representative/Date)

_____

(Printed name)

_____

(Signature of Alternate Health Care Representative/Date)

_____

(Printed name)

_____

<1993 c.767 s8 (enacted in lieu of 127.530)>

A comment on healthcare proxies in general must be added at this point. There have been several recent and disquieting empirical studies about healthcare decisions made by proxies. We use these directives to consign our future physical and mental well-being to surrogates, assuming that they will make healthcare decisions (when we lack the capacity to do so) that will perfectly and faithfully reflect our own. This is not always so. Research now suggests that surrogate decisions made even by family members about an elder's critical care are *not* necessarily the same as those the elder would have made for himself or herself.[20] The more specific your healthcare advance directive, the more likely your wishes will be honored.

## b. Living Wills

Most states do permit competent adults to create *living wills* that can also serve to direct their health care in very specific ways and under equally specific circumstances. When executed in accordance with statutory mandates, living wills give directives to healthcare providers to initiate or withhold life-sustaining procedures.[21] These documents state the precise medical conditions under which terminally ill patients would not want to be kept alive.

What might those directives entail? A glance at some of the provisions in Florida's living will statute quickly reveals the gravity of the issues that can be decided by trusted others (or unknown others) at this perilous time in your life.

Florida's living will statute applies only to life-prolonging procedures for persons who have been diagnosed as terminally ill. In 1990, the definition of life-prolonging procedures was expanded to include sustenance necessary to survival. Artificial nutrition and hydration may be withheld or withdrawn, according to the patient's directive, if the attending physician and one other physician, neither of whom have a financial interest in the health care facility in which the patient is receiving care, certify that sustenance is a life-prolonging procedure and that death is imminent. The patient's next of kin can prevent the withdrawal of artificial nutrition and hydration for a reasonable period or time. . . .

The Florida statute further provides that any person who withholds life-sustaining treatment in accordance with a declaration is immune from criminal prosecution and civil liability unless it can be shown that treatment was not performed in good faith compliance with the declaration's terms. A person who provides life-sustaining procedures, despite knowledge of a declaration to refuse them, is guilty of a third degree felony. One who withholds life-prolonging procedures, despite knowledge that a declaration has been revoked, is guilty of a second degree felony.[22]

Although living wills and durable powers of attorney for healthcare decisions are similar in purpose, they do differ in at least four significant ways, as noted by Hallman and Rosenbloom.[23] First, living wills apply only to end-of-life, terminal situations. Second, under the living will statutes of different states, not all types of care can be refused. Third, durable powers permit you (the principal of the instrument) to specify or limit the terms and conditions of the power exactly as you wish. And fourth, of the two, only a durable power permits you to name a specific individual (your attorney-in-fact) to make all healthcare decisions if and when you become incompetent to do so.

With just a living will, can you rest assured the medical care you receive at the end of your life is guided strictly by your wishes? Unfortunately, no. A recently completed ten-year study of almost 9,105 terminally ill patients shed light on the major problem with the use of living wills, namely, there is a consistent failure of communication among physicians, patients, and their families.[24] In the study, 2,534 patients were assigned trained nurse-advocates to help make dying a more humane experience. The patients' written instructions to doctors and family members detailed pain-control measures and "do not resuscitate" orders.

Despite these intense efforts, "these patients continued to spend their final days in a coma or attached to an artificial breathing machine. Complaints of pain actually increased, and the staggering costs of intensive care in a hospital were not reduced."[25] The $28 million study, financed by the Robert Wood Johnson Foundation of Princeton, New Jersey, disturbed medical ethicists and revealed flaws in America's healthcare system in general—and with living wills in particular.

George Annas, director of the Law, Medicine and Ethics Program at Boston University, said it proves doctors pay little attention to the wishes and feelings of patients. "Physicians simply have never taken the rights of hospitalized patients seriously," Annas said. "There is no excuse to this indifference to human suffering, which amounts to systematic patient abuse."[26]

Even when patients specifically ordered physicians not to use any aggressive treatments to prolong their lives, their wishes were either ignored or misunderstood. Dr. William Knaus, a critical-care specialist who directed the study, said "the results shocked me. The tools that experts thought would work didn't make a bit of difference."[27]

Because a living will is not legally binding, you must protect your well-being by executing a living will *and* durable powers of attorney for healthcare decisions. Information about both is available through the American Association of Retired Persons' Legal Counsel for the Elderly (LCE). The LCE has prepared a state-specific guide containing living will and healthcare power-of-attorney forms that comply with each state's specific laws and practices. The guide, *Planning for Incapacity: A Self-Help Guide to Advance Directives*, comes both with instructions on preparing and individualizing the forms and with a "sensitive discussion of common concerns about advance directives."[28] Although no publication will obviate the need for a competent attorney to finalize the legal documentation of your wishes, AARP's material will provide an important foundation for your understanding of how these directives work in your particular state. You can obtain copies of the planning guide for your state by writing or calling AARP's Legal Counsel for the Elderly.*

Choice in Dying, the national nonprofit organization that was instrumental in the development of our country's first living will over thirty years ago, is working on implementing changes to its basic will to answer questions raised about the cold, medical-technical quality of the document. They are hoping to incorporate ideas from a new living will that is now available from cocreators Jim Towey, founder and president of Aging with Dignity, and Miami nurse Kate Callahan. Towey lived as a volunteer in Mother Teresa's Washington AIDS hospice for a year after working with the dying in Mother Teresa's Calcutta hospice. He spoke of the lonely people he visited in American hospitals, attached to machines: "The overmedicalization of the dying process is degrading people."[29] Towey and Callahan, guided by a hospital chaplain, created the new type of living will in response to their "deep, heartfelt belief that living wills that only look at ventilators and feeding tubes just aren't enough."[30] They called their eight-page document "Five Wishes."

---

*For the address and telephone number of the Legal Counsel for the Elderly, see appendix C, under the heading, "National Legal Organizations for the Elderly."

The name Five Wishes comes from the five sections of the will. Two deal with traditional choices about medical treatment and picking someone to make health care decisions when a person is no longer able to. The other three parts are new. One is titled "How Comfortable You Want To Be." Another is "How You Want People To Treat You." The third is "What You Want Your Loved Ones To Know."

Choices range from having people around to being treated with kindness to requesting and granting forgiveness for past hurts. "It deals with things of the heart, and that's why I think people are responding," Towey said. . . .

Vicki Weisfeld, with the Robert Wood Johnson Foundation, called Five Wishes "revolutionarily different" from the typical living will, which is often legalistic and "a little intimidating." She praised Five Wishes for being easy to understand and touching issues that people care most about."What I think it will do really is force other states and other people promoting living wills to re-examine what they're doing," she said.[31]

The new Five Wishes living will thus addresses more than the use of high-tech medical support; it deals with basic care and family feuds. With over 40,000 copies of the document being shipped by Aging with Dignity every month, it has obviously struck a chord throughout America even though we as a group dislike talking about dying—or planning for our incapacity. Three out of four people currently do not have living wills to speak for them when they are incapable of doing so themselves. Perhaps Five Wishes will improve these numbers.*

# 4. PRESELECTING A CONSERVATOR OR GUARDIAN

The fourth protective step you can take is ironic, to be sure, but it could one day save your life. It is the preselection of a conservator or guardian. Why, if your unwavering goal in making advance directives is to avoid becoming the ward of a conservator or guardian, would you ever consider doing this? The preselection or preappointment of a conservator or guardian is needed to deal with two "worst-case scenarios." In the first, you *haven't* put advance directives in place and an angry adult child petitions the court to have you declared incompetent. In the second scenario, you *have* signed your advance directives, but in a future nightmare of involuntary conservatorship/guardianship litigation a judge simply

---

*For the address and telephone number of Aging with Dignity, see appendix C under the heading, "Major National Organizations."

decides that a conservator or guardian is just what you need—in spite of all of the planning you have done (see case 4.2 for an example of this particular judicial response).

If you were to be confronted at a vulnerable time by one of these outrageous but real possibilities, you would want to know that no one but you would select the person who would serve as your surrogate or proxy decision-maker. You have the right of preselection if your choices are witnessed and documented by an attorney. It is a difficult task, but it is better than trusting your fate to judicial whimsy.

Be mindful that an important component in the preselection of a conservator or guardian concerns the list of candidates you must prepare. Your list should contain, in order of preference, the names and addresses of those individuals you would want to function in this capacity should a conservator or guardian be mandated by a court that has overridden your basic durable powers of attorney. Since the purpose of preselection would be negated if none of the people you had chosen were available when needed (through death, relocation or alienation), your list should contain *at least* three names. There is definitely safety in numbers in these proceedings. Your preselection document should also contain language that nullifies your selection of a spouse as guardian/conservator if you are divorced from that spouse before a guardian or conservator is appointed.

An equally powerful aspect in the preselection process concerns your right to disqualify specific individuals from ever serving as guardian or conservator of your person or estate. This exclusion clause will protect you from the ultimate indignity of surrendering your autonomy to people you have reason to fear or dislike. Use it!

The state of Texas has devised an especially well-balanced document concerning this preselection process. It is contained in Section 679 of the Texas Probate Codes under the heading, "Designation of Guardians Before Need Arises." Note that in Texas, the process is referred to as a "designation of guardian," while several states use the word "nomination" to describe the same preselection procedure. The following document is an excellent guide to your task, but you must confer with an attorney to complete a legal preselection in your state.

[PROBATE CODE, Texas] Sec. 679. Designation of Guardian Before Need Arises.

(a) A person other than an incapacitated person may designate by a written declaration persons to serve as guardian of the person of the declarant or the estate of the declarant if the declarant becomes incapacitated. The declaration must be attested to by at least two credible witnesses 14 years of age or older who are not named as guardian or alternate guardian in the declaration.

(b) A declarant may, in the declaration, disqualify named persons from serving as guardian of the declarant's person or estate, and the persons named may not be appointed guardian under any circumstances.

(c) The declaration must have attached a self-proving affidavit signed by the declarant and the witnesses attesting to the competence of the declarant and the execution of the declaration. A properly executed and witnessed declaration and affidavit are prima facie evidence that the declarant was competent at the time the declarant executed the declaration and that the guardian named in the declaration would serve the best interests of the ward.

(d) The declaration and affidavit may be filed with the court at any time after the application for appointment of a guardian is filed and before a guardian is appointed. Unless the court finds that the person designated in the declaration to serve as guardian is disqualified or would not serve the best interests of the ward, the court shall appoint the person as guardian in preference to those otherwise entitled to serve as guardian under this code. If the designated guardian does not qualify, is dead, refuses to serve, resigns, or dies after being appointed guardian, or is otherwise unavailable to serve as guardian, the court shall appoint the next eligible designated alternate guardian named in the declaration. If the guardian and all alternate guardians do not qualify, are dead, refuse to serve, or later die or resign, the court shall appoint another person to serve as otherwise provided by this code.

(e) The declarant may revoke a declaration in any manner provided for the revocation of a will under Section 63 of this code, including the subsequent reexecution of the declaration in the manner required for the original declaration.

(f) If a declarant designates the declarant's spouse to serve as guardian under this section, and the declarant is subsequently divorced from that spouse before a guardian is appointed, the provision of the declaration designating the spouse has no effect.

(g) A declaration and affidavit may be in any form adequate to clearly indicate the declarant's intention to designate a guardian. The following forms may, but need not, be used:

DECLARATION OF GUARDIAN IN THE EVENT OF LATER INCAPACITY OR NEED OF GUARDIAN

I, _____, make this Declaration of Guardian, to operate if the need for a guardian for me later arises.

1. I designate _____ to serve as guardian of my person,

_____ as first alternate guardian of my person, _____ as second alternate guardian of my person, and _____ as third alternate guardian of my person.

2. I designate _____ to serve as guardian of my estate, _____ as first alternate guardian of my estate, _____ as second alternate guardian of my estate, and _____ as third alternate guardian of my estate.

3. If any guardian or alternate guardian dies, does not qualify, or resigns, the next named alternate guardian becomes my guardian.

4. I expressly disqualify the following persons from serving as guardian of my person: _____, _____, and _____.

5. I expressly disqualify the following persons from serving as guardian of my estate: _____, _____, and _____.

Signed this ___ day of _____, 20___.


Declarant


Witness


Witness


## SELF-PROVING AFFIDAVIT

Before me, the undersigned authority, on this date personally appeared the declarant, and _____ and _____ as witnesses, and all being duly sworn, the declarant said that the above instrument was his or her Declaration of Guardian and that the declarant had made and executed it for the purposes expressed in the declaration. The witnesses declared to me that they are each 14 years of age or older, that they saw the declarant sign the declaration, that they signed the declaration as witnesses, and that the declarant appeared to them to be of sound mind.

Declarant


Affiant


Affiant

Subscribed and sworn to before me by the above named declarant and affiants on this _____ day of _____, 20__.


Notary Public in and for the State of Texas
My Commission expires:


Added by Acts 1993, 73rd Leg., ch. 957, Sec. 1, eff. Sept. 1, 1993.


# 5. PREVENTING FUTURE CHALLENGES TO YOUR LEGAL DIRECTIVES

We have seen that a majority of the involuntary conservatorship/guardianship proceedings in our country are thinly disguised predeath or antemortem will contests during which angry heir-petitioners, aided and abetted by the courts, secure their inheritances from vulnerable elderly relatives. Is there anything that can be done now, while you are competent, to increase your chances of success in a hypothetical future court battle waged by people who will try to prove you were incompetent or lacked capacity at the time you signed your advance directives? It is a logical question. After all, durable powers, revocable trusts, living wills, and preselection instruments all derive their power from the fact that you are believed to be competent at the moment you sign them. Thus, financially motivated petitioners will try to neutralize these directives by alleging or proving in court to a specific judge's satisfaction that you were not. What can be done to establish your capacity at the time you sign your durable powers, your revocable trust, your living will, and your list of preselected conservators and/or guardians?

In an attempt to address this problem, many prudent men and women have begun adding one last step to their defensive legal arrangements. They are videotaping their final decision-making sessions with their attorneys in the presence of forensic or geriatric psychiatrists. These Mental Health professionals serve as witnesses to competence and testamentary capacity at the moment each document is discussed and signed. Once this last step is taken, your planning for your incapacity is well and truly done.

A question is often asked: Is this step necessary—or even advisable— for most people? There is an interesting flow of debate in the legal community concerning the wisdom of videotaping final advance directive and testamentary sessions. Lawyers on one side of the debate emphasize that expert witnesses from the field of Mental Health already testify in conservatorship/guardianship proceedings on issues concerning an individual's competence, testamentary capacity and ability to withstand undue influence. We have reviewed these aspects in chapter 3. According to Dr. James Spar of UCLA's Department of Psychiatry and Biobehavioral Sciences and attorney Andrew Garb of Loeb and Loeb of Los Angeles, this psychiatric or psychological testimony covers the individual's global mental status, germane aspects of mental functioning (such as reasoning, judgment, and memory), intact elements with respect to testamentary capacity (i.e., understanding the nature of the testamentary act, the nature of his/her assets, and the objects of his/her affection), and a diagnostic impression.[32] Such experts can even structure an evaluation of the ambiguous "undue influence" allegation in terms of a human being's enduring personality traits. These issues are discussed in court, and they can be discussed by an expert on videotape in the presence of the person whose wishes are being memorialized by his or her attorney. This can be done, no doubt about it. Why, then, are some attorneys reluctant to recommend this procedure to their aging clients?

Imagine yourself on videotape, explaining your reasons for wanting a certain relative to participate in your health care or property matters should you become incapacitated in an automobile accident. You ramble a bit, wanting to be thorough. Perhaps you twist anxiously in your chair and focus now on the camera, now on your attorney or psychiatrist, now on the hands you clasp tightly in your lap. Your words slow to a stop, your thoughts hard to put into precise language. You cannot recall the name of your old neighbor, or the name of your broker's firm. The video camera catches it all.

Fast-forward to a time when your health and your body have been compromised by age. The uncritical eye of the camera captures that, too. It is clear that you cannot hear everything very well and thus look as though you cannot understand the legal decisions being discussed. You *still* cannot recall the name of your old neighbor, and you *still* cannot remember the firm your broker works for. These memory lapses now look suspicious because you are visibly old ("and forgetful," as the unspoken modifier would suggest). Worn and wrinkled, your hands shake gently but noticeably. Your smile has been replaced by an intense frown in the stress of the moment. Medication you are taking has dried your mouth, altering the fluency of your sentences. You search for words to defend your competent choices for future incapacity, but your subdued voice, your weary face, your aged body, and your difficulties in seeing, hearing or speaking are shouting to the judge: "I am *old*." The judge, who has been educated in a system rife with paternalistic and ageist bias, watches your video and unwittingly adds, "—and not very competent."

Until all court officials are forced to confront their stereotypes and ignorance about the aging process, the wisdom of using videos of fragile elderly men and women discussing financial and healthcare advance directives continues to be debated. Once again it is important to take advantage of your knowledge about abusive involuntary conservatorship/ guardianship laws and act while your verbal fluency, mental acuity, and physical functioning are intact.

If you suffer from any condition or reaction to any medication that would affect your behavior on tape, explain that condition or medication effect as clearly as possible and then move on to describe your surrogate decision-making choices. You have a right to be old, and you have a right to be affected by time. You must seize *every* legal opportunity to safeguard your personal and financial care before you become incapacitated, and you must weave all of these strong devices into your own safety net.

## FINAL THOUGHTS

Jan Ellen Rein has puzzled over the paradox of a culture that esteems individualism yet harbors a deep prejudice against the elderly. As she explains,

> That the oldest of the old are valued, honored, and revered for their wisdom by Asian societies testifies to the fact that there is nothing inherent in the aging process to make "old" the equivalent of "incompetent," "useless," or "valueless to the community." A comparison of Eastern and Western cultures on this subject must await other research and writing. One cannot, however, resist observing how odd it is that our culture founded on individualism should treat its elders with so little respect while a culture that does not even understand individualism should treat its elders with the utmost respect and reverence.[33]

In a culture that values youthfulness such as ours, the elderly are often stereotypically viewed as inferior. After all, as many have noted, it is easier to be unkind to those we do not revere than to those we cherish. As Rein says in her research on self-determination for the elderly: "This attitude has allowed us to develop the belief that older people, as a group, are different from the rest of us; next we consider them not equal; and finally we think of them merely as objects to be passed over or stored away."[34]

We have come full circle, having witnessed the presumption that "incompetence is an elder's natural state"[35] firsthand, in involuntary conservatorship/guardianship proceedings throughout America. Our current probate codes and statutes seem almost fatally flawed. Even though it is not difficult to pinpoint statutory reforms that would improve our codes' more egregious shortcomings (as we have done in the preceding chapter), it would be a triumph of almost foolish optimism over reality to believe that these mischaracterized "protective proceedings" will be changed in the near future. Legal reform moves at a glacial pace.

The fifty-five cases we studied revealed the elder abuse that is sanctioned in our courts as aging men and women fall victim to laws designed to "help" them. As they exist now, our state codes can be used against us as we age. Thus, until they are changed, we must be vigilant in our own defense. We do have five powerful legal weapons to use in our battle for life-long personal and financial autonomy. It is now up to you to be your own best ally and save yourself from your heirs and protectors—for as long as you live.

# NOTES

1. J. W. Rowe and R. L. Kahn, *Successful Aging* (New York: Pantheon Books, 1998).

2. Personal communication, February 18, 1996.

3. "When You Need A Lawyer," *Consumer Reports* (February 1996): 34–39.

4. Ibid.

5. Ibid., p. 35.

6. Ibid.

7. J. E. Rein, "Preserving Dignity and Self-Determination of the Elderly in the Face of Competing Interests and Grim Alternatives: A Proposal for Statutory Refocus and Reform," *George Washington Law Review* 60, no. 6 (1992): 1842.

8. R. N. Brown, *The Rights of Older Persons* (Washington, D.C.: ACLU, 1989), p. 350.

9. G. V. Hallman and J. S. Rosenbloom, *Personal Financial Planning* (New York: McGraw-Hill, Inc., 1993).

10. Ibid., p. 351.

11. Brown, op. cit., p. 478.

12. *Wagner* v. *Morgan* (Kentucky, 1989).

13. Brown, op. cit., p. 351.

14. Ibid., p. 352.

15. Hallman and Rosenbloom, op. cit., p. 475.

16. Ibid.

17. Ibid., p. 479.

18. Brown, op. cit.

19. Ibid., p. 351.

20. Uhlmann et al., "Physicians' and Spouses' Predictions of Elderly Patients' Resuscitation Preferences," *Journal of Gerontology* 43, M1115, reported in J. E. Rein, "Preserving Dignity," op. cit., p. 1826.

21. A. P. Barnes, "Beyond Guardianship Reform: A Reevaluation of Autonomy and Beneficence for a System of Principled Decision-Making in Long Term Care," *Emory Law Journal* 41 (1992): 665.

22. Ibid., pp. 665–66.

23. Hallman and Rosenbloom, op. cit., p. 480.

24. R. S. Boyd, "Death with Dignigty Still Eludes the Nation's Dying," *Santa Barbara News-Press*, 22 November 1995, p. A2.

25. Ibid.

26. Ibid.

27. Ibid.

28. "Resource Guide: Serving Your Needs," *Modern Maturity* (March-April 1996): 89.

29. Ibid.

30. J. Hallifax, "New 5-Part Living Will Sparks Big Response," *Santa Barbara News-Press*, (8 September 1997), p. D4.

31. Ibid.

32. J. E. Spar and A. S. Garb, "Assessing Competency to Make a Will," *American Journal of Psychiatry* 149, no. 2 (1992): 169–74.

33. Ibid., p. 1842.

34. Brickner, quoted in Rein, op. cit., p. 1843.

35. Rein, op. cit., 1843.

# APPENDIX A

# STATE CODES AND STATUTES

J ust as conservatorship/guardianship codes and statutes differ from state to state, so, too, do the actual proceedings as they unfold in each county's or parish's courts. The summaries in this section contain legal guidelines for involuntary hearings involving normal adults—that is, adults who are not mentally ill or developmentally disabled and who have not asked to have a guardianship or conservatorship established over their person or estate. Each state's relevant legal citations (code/statute numbers where the laws can be found) are provided. It is my hope that this section will provide enough information to permit the reader to begin the process of legal self-education that may prove to be essential to his or her future well-being.

Individual state codes and statutes are available at no charge in public law libraries throughout America. Law librarians are particularly helpful if you have not searched for material in a law library before. Many university law libraries also permit limited public access. Because the law is a living, changing entity and the codes may alter in any given year, be sure to read the "Supplement" (contained in a pocket in the back of the relevant volume) and check for any and all recent changes in your state's conservatorship/guardianship codes. The Internet also provides useful tools for locating state statutes. I found the Cornell Law Library website to be particularly thorough and easy to use. It can be located at: http://www.cornell.edu/statutes.html.

We now move to summaries of each state's conservatorship and guardianship codes. Try to find the answers to the following questions in your state's statutes:

- What legal terms are used in your state's current protective proceedings? Does your state's code speak of "conservatorship" or "guardianship" petitions of the person and/or of the estate? Would you be described as an "incompetent," "incapacitated," or "disabled" adult in court? What are the legal meanings of these terms?

- In which courts are conservatorship/guardianship cases heard in your state?

- What criteria exist in your state for the court-ordered appointment of a guardian or conservator? What is the nature of the supporting evidence that would be used against you in court?

- How much time are you given — via court order — before you must appear in court and attempt to prove your right to personal and/or financial autonomy? Can your right to proper notice be taken away by the court? Under what circumstances?

- What is your right to be heard in court, to have legal representation (even if you can't afford a lawyer), and to have a jury trial before the issue of your alleged incapacity or incompetence is determined by a judge?

- Where can you locate your state's guardianship or conservatorship codes and statutes?

In reading the material relating to your state's codes, remember that in most jurisdictions a judge may appoint a conservator or guardian in an *ex parte* proceeding *and give no notice at all* to the elderly person targeted by the petition *if* the petitioner claims an "emergency" exists. Oftentimes no proof is required beyond an initial allegation. Look for the relevant "temporary guardianship/conservatorship laws" cited in your state's codes and read the section carefully. Finally, remember that when all is said and done, your right to an independent, autonomous life as you age can be voided by the opinion of one single judge.

*Alabama.* Probate courts have jurisdiction over conservatorship and guardianship proceedings, although their administration may be removed to circuit court. Guardians may be appointed for any incapacitated adult and conservators for the incapacitated person's estate. An "incapacitated person" is any adult (that is, nineteen years of age or older) "who is impaired by reason of mental illness, mental deficiency, physical illness or disability, *physical or mental infirmities accompanying advanced age*, chronic use of drugs, chronic intoxication, or other cause (except minority) to the extent of lacking sufficient understanding or capacity to make or communicate responsible decisions" (Alabama Code §26-2A-20[8], emphasis added). The court may appoint a conservator to handle a person's estate and affairs if the court determines that:

> (i) the person is unable to manage property and business affairs effectively for such reasons as mental illness, mental deficiency, physical illness or disability, *physical or mental infirmities accompanying advanced age*, chronic use of drugs, chronic intoxication, confinement, detention by a foreign power, or disappearance; and that (ii) (aa) the person has property that will be wasted or dissipated unless property management is provided, or that (bb) funds are needed for the health, support, education, or maintenance of the person or of those entitled to the person's support and that protection is necessary or desirable to obtain or provide the funds. (§26-2A-130, emphasis added)

Any interested person may file a petition for a conservatorship or guardianship. The proposed ward must be given fourteen days notice to prepare for his or her hearing on issues of his/her incapacity in the conservatorship or guardianship petition, although "the court for good cause shown may provide for a different . . . time of giving notice for any hearing" (§26-2A-50[c]). No notice is required if the petitioner claims good cause exists for an emergency or temporary guardianship or conservatorship, although the temporary orders may not extend beyond fifteen days.

If the allegedly incapacitated person is not represented by counsel, the court will appoint an attorney—granted the powers and duties of a guardian ad litem—to represent him or her in the proceeding. The proposed ward must be examined by a physician or other qualified person appointed by the court, who shall then submit a written report to the court. A court representative will also be appointed to interview the person alleged to be incapacitated and to interview the individual who filed the petition.

The proposed ward is entitled to be present at the hearing (unless his or her presence in court would be harmful), to present evidence, to cross-examine witnesses (including the court-appointed physician or other qualified person and court representative), to demand a trial by jury, and to request that the hearing be closed. Any "qualified person" may be appointed guardian/conservator, although the court may also appoint a corporation as conservator of the estate of a protected person.

Among the powers the court may exercise directly or through a conservator in respect to the business affairs and estate of a "protected person" are:

> [The] power to make gifts; to convey or release contingent and expectant interests in property, including marital property rights and any right of survivorship incident to joint tenancy or tenancy by the entirety; to exercise or release powers held by the protected person as trustee, personal representative, custodian for minors, conservator, or donee of a power of appointment; to enter into contracts; to create revocable or irrevocable trusts of property of the estate which may extend beyond the disability or life of the protected person; to exercise options of the protected person to purchase securities or other property; to exercise rights to elect options and change beneficiaries under insurance and annuity policies and to surrender the policies for their cash value; to exercise any right to an elective share in the estate of the person's deceased spouse and to renounce or disclaim any interest by testate or intestate succession or by inter vivos transfer. (§26-2A-136[3])

Reasonable compensation will be paid from the new ward's estate for any attorney, court representative, physician, guardian, conservator or special conservator appointed in a protective proceeding "whose services resulted in a protective order [or guardianship order] that was beneficial to a protected person's estate [or was beneficial to a ward]" (§26-2A-142). Unless required more frequently by the court, the conservator must make an accounting to the court at lease once in three years. (See Alabama Uniform Guardianship and Protective Proceedings Act, Alabama Code §26-2A-1 et seq. for conservatorship and guardianship laws; Alabama Code §26-2A-107 for emergency temporary conservatorship/guardianship codes.)

*Alaska.* Alaska follows the Uniform Probate Code, including all 1975 Official Amendments. Superior courts have jurisdiction to appoint guardians over the person of incapacitated adults and conservators over the estates of adults who are unable to manage their property. An "incapacitated person" is "a person whose ability to receive and evaluate information or to communicate decisions is impaired for reasons other than minority to the extent that the person lacks the ability to provide the essential requirements for the person's physical health or safety without court-ordered assistance" (Alaska Statutes §13.26.005 [4]). A guardianship is used "only as is necessary to promote and protect the well-being of the person, shall be designed to encourage the development of maximum self-reliance and independence of the person, and shall be ordered only to the extent necessitated by the person's actual mental and physical limitations" (§13.26.090). There is no presumption that the incapacitated person for whom a guardian has been appointed is incompetent.

Protective proceedings can be held to evaluate the capacity of an adult to effectively manage his or her estate. A conservator will be appointed to administer his/her estate if the court determines that "(A) the person is unable to manage the person's property and affairs effectively for reasons such as mental illness, mental deficiency, *physical illness or disability, advanced age*, chronic use of drugs, chronic intoxication, confinement, detention by a foreign power, or disappearance" (§13.26.165[2], emphasis added); that the adult has property that will be wasted or dissipated; or that funds needed to support the individual or others must be protected.

Any interested person may petition the court for a finding of incapacity and the appointment of a guardian and/or conservator. The guardianship hearing commences within 120 days from the filing of the petitioner's request for a hearing on the issue of incapacity. The court will appoint a visitor to arrange for evaluations of the proposed ward and for written reports that will be filed with the court within ninety days. "The court shall also appoint an expert who has expertise in regard to the alleged or admitted incapacity to investigate the issue of incapacity" (§13.26.106[c]).

Both the petitioner and the respondent are permitted to file responses to the final evaluation within ten days of receiving it. During the evaluation, the proposed ward or respondent does have the right to remain silent or to refuse to answer questions if the answers may incriminate him or her, but he or she "may be required to submit to interviews for the purpose of ascertaining whether the ward or respondent lacks the capacity to make informed decisions about care and treatment services" (§13.26. 209[a]).

At the hearing, the respondent has the right to (1) present evidence on his/her own behalf, (2) cross-examine adverse witnesses, (3) remain silent, (4) close the hearing to the public, (5) be present "unless the court determines that the respondent's conduct in the courtroom is so disruptive that the proceedings cannot reasonably continue with the respondent present" (§13.26.113[a][5]), and (6) be tried by a jury on the issue of incapacity. The burden of proof—by clear and convincing evidence—is upon the petitioner. "If the respondent is found to be incapacitated, the court shall determine the extent of the incapacity and the feasibility of alternatives to guardianship to meet the needs of the respondent"

(§13.26.113[c]). The court may appoint a partial guardian if the proposed ward is found capable of performing some, but not all, of the functions necessary to care for him- or herself. If a guardian must be appointed, the court is expected to consider the ward's preference.

A temporary or emergency guardianship may be granted upon the filing of the petition with no notice to the allegedly incapacitated adult, although a special hearing must be held within seventy-two hours of the appointment. (Note: the court may also authorize an immediate temporary guardianship even if no guardianship petition is pending if the court has reason to believe an apparently incapacitated person would suffer the risk of harm in delay [§13.26.140][f]). Under Alaska's emergency powers, the temporary guardian has the right to hospitalize the ward without advance court approval.

The court also has powers over the estate and affairs of protected people which it may exercise directly or through a conservator:

> 3. After hearing and upon determining that a basis for an appointment or other protective order exists with respect to a person for reasons other than minority, the court has, for the benefit of the person and members of the person's household, all the powers over the person's estate and affairs which the person could exercise if present and not under disability, except the power to make a will; these powers include, but are not limited to the power to make gifts, to convey or release contingent and expectant interests in property including marital property rights and any right of survivorship incident to joint tenancy or tenancy by the entirety, to exercise or release powers as trustee, personal representative, custodian for minors, conservator, or donee of a power of appointment, to enter into contracts, to create revocable or irrevocable trusts of property of the estate which may extend beyond the person's disability or life, to exercise options of the disabled person to purchase securities or other property, to exercise rights to elect options and change beneficiaries under insurance and annuity policies and to surrender the policies for their cash value, to exercise the right to an elective share in the estate of a deceased spouse and to renounce any interest by testate or intestate succession or by inter vivos transfer. . . . (§13.26.200[3])

The conservator is permitted to employ attorneys, auditors, investment advisors, and others to advise or assist him/her in the performance of administrative duties, even though they are persons associated with the conservator. (See Alaska Statutes, Title 13: Decedents' Estates, Guardianships, Transfers, and Trusts, Chapter 13: Protection of Persons Under Disability and Their Property, §13.26.090 et seq. for guardianship/conservatorship laws; Alaska Statutes §13.26.140 et seq. for emergency temporary guardianship laws.)

*Arizona.* Arizona has adopted the Uniform Probate Code, although not the 1977 or later amendments. Superior courts have jurisdiction over guardianships and protective proceedings (conservatorships). Permanent and/or temporary guardians may be appointed for incapacitated persons; permanent and/or temporary conservators may be appointed for the estates and affairs of persons under other disabilities. A disabled or "incapacitated person" is "any person who is impaired by reason of mental illness, mental deficiency, mental disorder, physical illness or disability, chronic use of drugs, chronic intoxication or other cause, except minority, to the extent that he lacks sufficient understanding or capacity to make or communicate responsible decisions concerning his person" (Arizona Revised Statutes §14-5101[1]).

A conservator of the estate may be appointed if the proposed ward (1) is unable to manage his or her estate and affairs effectively "for reasons such as mental illness, mental deficiency, mental disorder, physical illness or disability, chronic use of drugs, chronic intoxication, confinement, detention by a foreign power or disappearance" (§14-5401[2][a]), and (2) the individual has property which "will be wasted or dissipated unless proper management is provided, or that funds are needed for the support, care and welfare of the person or those entitled to be supported by the person and that protection is necessary or desirable to obtain or provide funds" (§14-5401[2][b]).

Guardianships/conservatorships are permitted when they are deemed desirable to protect the interests of the incompetent. Any interested adult may file for a temporary or permanent guardianship or conservatorship, and a hearing date on the issues of incapacity will be set by the court. After reading the petition the court may, under certain circumstances, enter a finding of interim incapacity and may appoint a temporary guardian and/or conservator without notice to the proposed ward or to his/her attorney (§14-5310[B] and §14-5401.01[B]). A conservatorship may be established for the estate of a nonresident in the county in which he or she has property, regardless of the appointment of a guardian elsewhere.

If the proposed ward lacks an attorney, the court will appoint legal representation. The proposed ward is entitled to be present at the hearing, to present evidence, to cross-examine witnesses (including the court-appointed examiner and investigator), and to a trial by jury. The hearing may be closed to the public at the proposed ward's request. A functional assessment by a court-appointed physician, psychologist, or registered nurse must be submitted in writing as medical evidence. A court investigator will also interview the proposed ward and submit a written report to the court. "An order adjudicating incapacity may specify a minimum period, not exceeding one year, during which no petition for an adjudication that the ward is no longer incapacitated may be filed without special leave" (§14-5307[B]).

Once appointed, a guardian of an incapacitated person has the same powers, rights and duties towards the ward as that of a parent towards a child. Furthermore, "to the extent that it is consistent with the terms of any order by a court of competent jurisdiction . . . , the guardian is entitled to custody of the person of the ward and may establish the ward's place of abode within or without this state" (§14-5312[A][1]). The conservator may invest and reinvest funds of the estate as would a trustee, without court authorization or confirmation. The conservator of the ward's estate must file an inventory with the court of the estate owned by the protected person within ninety days of his or her appointment as conservator, and must file an annual accounting of the subsequent administration of the estate.

> Whenever a principal designates another his attorney-in-fact or agent by a power of attorney in writing and the writing contains the words "this power of attorney shall not be affected by disability of the principal," or "this power of attorney shall become effective upon the disability of the principal," or similar words showing the intent of the principal that the authority conferred shall be exercisable notwithstanding his disability, the authority of the attorney-in-fact or agent is exercisable by him as provided in the power on behalf of the principal notwithstanding later disability or incapacity of the principal at law or later uncertainty as to whether the principal is dead or alive. . . . The conservator has the same power the principal would have had if he were not disabled or incompetent, to revoke, suspend or terminate all or any part of the power of attorney or agency. (§14-5501)

If the conservator is not an authorized fiduciary such as a national banking association or savings and loan association, the conservator of the estate must post bond in the amount of the estate's value plus one year's expected income—unless the court reduces or eliminates the bond "for good cause shown" (§14-5411[A]). All "reasonable compensation" for services rendered by any investigator, accountant, lawyer, physician, conservator or special court-appointed conservator will be paid by the ward's estate. (See Arizona Revised Statutes, Title 14: Decedents' Estates, Guardianships, Protective Proceedings, and Trusts, Chapter 5: Protection of Persons Under Disability and Their Property, §14-5101 et seq. for guardianship and conservatorship codes; Arizona Revised Statutes, §14-5310/§14-5401.01 for emergency temporary guardianship/conservatorship laws.)

*Arkansas.* Guardianships can be appointed through probate courts over both the person and estate of an adult (eighteen years of age or older) who is judged to be incapacitated. In Arkansas, an "incapacitated person" is "a person who is impaired by reason of a disability such as mental illness, mental deficiency, physical illness, chronic use of drugs, or chronic intoxication, to the extent of lacking sufficient understanding or capacity to make or communicate decisions to meet the essential requirements for his health or safety or to manage his estate. Nothing in this chapter shall be construed to mean a person is incapacitated for the sole reasons he relies consistently on treatment by spiritual means through prayer alone for healing in accordance with his religious tradition and is being furnished with such treatment" (Arkansas Code §28-65-101). Guardianships are to be used to promote and protect the incapacitated individual's person and property, while encouraging the development of independence and maximum self-reliance. In Arkansas, a man or woman for whom a guardian has been appointed "is not presumed to be incompetent" (§28-65-106).

Notice of the hearing of the petition for the appointment of a permanent guardian must be served at least twenty days before the hearing is to be held. If a temporary or emergency guardianship is requested, the court may appoint a guardian of the person or of the estate or both with or without notice. "Within three (3) working days of the entry of the temporary guardianship order, a full hearing on the merits shall be held" (§28-65-218[f]).

Evidence of incapacity required by the court shall include the sworn written or oral testimony of one or more qualified professionals (physicians, licensed psychologists, or licensed certified social workers with a background in the particular alleged disability of the proposed ward). An "evaluation," which must be conducted prior to the court hearing, means "a professional assessment of the abilities of the respondent and the impact of any impairments on the individual's capability to meet the essential requirements for his health or safety or to manage his estate" (§28-65-101[5]).

The proposed ward has the right to be present at the hearing, to be represented by an attorney, to present evidence on his/her own behalf, to require the presence of one or more of the evaluating professionals, to cross-examine adverse witnesses, and to remain silent. The petitioner has the burden of proving incapacity by clear and convincing evidence. If, during the proceedings on the issues of incapacity, the court finds that alternatives to guardianship are sufficient to meet the needs of the respondent, the court may dismiss the action.

Consistent with and out of the resources of the ward's estate, it is the duty of the guardian of the person to care for and maintain the ward.

He/she may be required to submit reports on the condition of his/her ward to the court at regular intervals. "It shall be the duty of the guardian of the estate to exercise due care to protect and preserve it, to invest it and apply it as provided in this chapter" (§28-65-301[b]). With express court approval, a guardian may consent on behalf of the incapacitated ward to many decisions: withholding life-saving treatment, authorizing experimental medical procedures, authorizing termination of parental rights, and prohibiting the ward from voting or obtaining a driver's license. The guardian of the estate may be authorized to continue the ward's business affairs, although:

> It is specifically recognized that the operation of any business undertaking involves hazards, chance, and danger of loss. In recognition of this fact, it is declared to be the legislative intent that no guardian shall be held personally liable for loss resulting from mere lack of familiarity with the business operations, mistakes of judgment made in good faith, or like causes. (§28-65-307[c])

All guardians are required to file annual reports with the court. The report must contain information concerning the ward's mental, physical, and social conditions, his/her living arrangements, and the need for continued guardianship services. The guardian of an estate will be required to file an annual accounting of the ward's estate "if the guardian has been delegated that responsibility by the court order" (§28-65-322[4]). (See Arkansas Code, Title 28: Wills, Estates, and Fiduciary Relationships, Subtitle 5: Fiduciary Relationships, Chapter 65: Guardians Generally, §28-65-101 et seq. for guardianship laws; Arkansas Code §28-65-218 for emergency temporary guardianship laws.)

*California.* County superior courts in California have jurisdiction over conservatorship matters in their probate court divisions. A conservator of the person can be established over the person of an adult (eighteen or older) who is incapable or "unable to provide properly for his or her personal needs for physical health, food, clothing, or shelter . . ." (California Probate Code §1801[a]). A conservator of the estate may be appointed for a person who is "substantially unable to manage his or her own financial resources or resist fraud" or, in the eyes of the court, is susceptible to the undue influence of designing persons in managing his/her financial affairs (§1801[b]).

> A limited conservator of the person or of the estate, or both, may be appointed for a developmentally disabled adult. A limited conservatorship may be utilized only as necessary to promote and protect the well-

being of the individual, shall be designed to encourage the development of maximum self-reliance and independence of the individual, and shall be ordered only to the extent necessitated by the individual's proven mental and adaptive limitations. The conservatee of the limited conservator shall not be presumed to be incompetent. (§1801[d])

Any interested person or "interested public entity or officer" may file for the conservatorship. Notice is given to the alleged incompetent, spouses, relatives, and interested people. The respondent is entitled to fifteen days to prepare a defense and appear in court for a hearing on the issues of incapacity raised in the petition. However, this mandatory hearing notice may be cut to five days if the petitioner claims "good cause" exists for the appointment of an immediate temporary conservator. If the petition is filed by anyone other than the proposed conservatee (i.e., if it is an involuntary conservatorship petition), the court clerk must issue a citation to the proposed conservatee warning that:

1. The proposed conservatee may be adjudged unable to provide for personal needs or to manage financial resources and, by reason thereof, a conservator may be appointed for the person or estate or both.

2. Such adjudication may affect or transfer to the conservator the proposed conservatee's right to contract, in whole or in part, to manage and control property, to give informed consent for medical treatment, and to fix a residence.

3. The proposed conservatee may be disqualified from voting if not capable of completing an affidavit of voter registration. (§1823[b])

Legal counsel will be appointed by the court for the proposed conservatee if the individual is not otherwise represented. Appearance in court is mandatory except when his/her presence would be harmful to the respondent's physical or emotional well-being, when the proposed conservatee is out of the state when notice is served, or when the proposed ward has told the court investigator that he/she will not contest the action. If the respondent is unwilling or unable to attend the hearing, medical evidence may be submitted concerning his or her incapacity.

Psychiatric or psychological evaluations are required by the court, and a court investigator must interview the proposed conservatee personally and file a written report with the court five days prior to the initial hearing. The report is confidential in theory, but is made available "to parties, persons given notice of the petition who have requested this report or who have appeared in the proceedings, their attorneys, and the court. The court has discretion at any other time to release the report, if it would serve the interests of the conservatee" (§1826[n]). The proposed conservatee has the right to oppose the proceeding and the right to request a jury trial. The standard of proof for the appointment of a conservator is clear and convincing evidence.

Any competent person, including a nonresident, may be appointed conservator of the estate or person (§2100 et seq.), but "the selection of a conservator of the person or estate, or both, is solely in the discretion of the court" (§1812[a]). In California, the appointment of a conservator of the estate is an adjudication that the conservatee lacks the legal capacity to enter into transactions that obligate the conservatorship estate. A conservator may determine the residence of the conservatee at either of the following: "(1) Any place within this state without the permission of the court" (§2352[a][1]), or "(2) A place not within this state if permission of the court is first obtained" (§2352[a][2]). California's conservatorship law is subject to valid and effective health care directives of the conservatee and a power of attorney for health care, whether or not it is a durable power. The court may, in its discretion, grant the conservator the following powers:

b. The power to operate at the risk of the estate a business, farm, or enterprise constituting an asset of the estate . . .

d. The power to sell at public or private sale real or personal property of the estate . . .

f. The power to borrow money and give security for the repayment thereof.

g. The power to purchase real or personal property . . .

q. The power to employ attorneys, accountants, investment counsel, agents, depositories, and employees and to pay the expense. (§2591)

The court may choose to increase or decrease the amount of the bond that is required of the conservator. "A conservatorship continues until terminated by the death of the conservatee or by order of the court" (§1860[a]). (See California Probate Code, Division 4: Guardianship, Conservatorship, and Other Protective Proceedings, Part 3: Conservatorship, §1800 et seq. for conservatorship laws; California Probate Code §§2250-2258 for emergency temporary conservatorship laws.)

*Colorado.* Colorado adopted the Uniform Probate Code with substantial variations from the official text; the 1975 Amendments were not adopted. Jurisdiction over guardianship and conservatorship proceedings is in probate court in Denver and in district courts elsewhere. Guardianships are awarded over incapacitated adults (age twenty-one or older); conservatorships are granted in protective proceedings over the estates of persons with other disabilities. "The court may appoint a guardian as requested if it is satisfied that the person for whom care is sought is incapacitated and that the appointment is necessary or desirable as a means of providing continuing care and supervision of the incapacitated person" (Colorado Revised Statutes §15-14-304). An "incapacitated person" is "any person who is impaired by reason of mental illness, mental deficiency, physical illness or disability, chronic use of drugs, chronic intoxication, or other cause (except minority) to the extent that he lacks sufficient understanding or capacity to make or communicate responsible decisions concerning his person" (§15-14-101). Also the court may appoint a conservator over the estate and affairs of a person

> if the court determines that the person is unable to manage his property and affairs effectively for reasons such as mental illness, mental deficiency, physical illness or disability, chronic use of drugs, chronic intoxication, confinement, detention by a foreign power, or disappearance; and that the person has property which will be wasted or dissipated unless proper management is provided, or that funds are needed for the support, care, and welfare of the person or those entitled to be supported by him and that protection is necessary or desirable to obtain or provide funds. (§15-14-401[3])

Any interested person may file the petition, and upon the filing of the petition the court will set a date for a hearing on the issues of incapacity. Unless the allegedly incapacitated person has counsel of his/her own, the court will appoint a visitor to meet with the proposed ward, explain the nature of the petition and its consequences, interview the petitioner(s), interview "any physician or other person who is known to have evaluated or rendered care, counsel, treatment, or service to the person in the recent past" (§15-14-303[2][d]), and submit a written report to the court. The visitor is "a person who has such training as the court deems appropriate and is an officer, employee, or special appointee of the court with no personal interest in the proceedings" (§15-14-308). The court visitor may also be appointed as a guardian ad litem.

> The court may appoint a physician to examine the person alleged to be incapacitated, who shall submit to the court a written report which shall include: A description of the nature and degree of any current incapacity or disability, including the medical history if reasonably available; a medical prognosis specifying the estimated severity and duration of any current incapacity or disability; a statement as to how or in what manner the person's ability to make or communicate responsible decisions con-

cerning his person has been affected by the underlying condition of his physical or mental health; a statement as to whether any current medication affects the demeanor of the person or his ability to participate fully in any court proceeding; and any other matter required by the court or by court rule. (§15-14-303[3])

An evidentiary hearing will also be held to consider the factual circumstances to determine whether the petitioner is a person interested in the welfare of the allegedly incapacitated individual. Notice of the hearing for an emergency or temporary guardianship petition is not required. The court may exercise the power of guardian or appoint a temporary guardian if an emergency exists and the allegedly incapacitated person has no guardian.

The proposed ward has the right to retain legal counsel, and an attorney will be appointed if needed. The proposed ward also has the right to be present in court, to present evidence, to cross-examine witnesses, to a trial by jury, and to a closed hearing. The standard of proof in such proceedings is clear and convincing evidence. Once appointed, a guardian's powers include: establishing the abode of the ward within or without the State of Colorado; obtaining hospital or institutional care and treatment for mental illness or alcoholism; providing the care, comfort, and maintenance of the ward; and, to the extent authorized by the court, giving consents or approvals for medical or other professional care, counsel, treatment or service. "A guardian . . . , by a properly executed power of attorney, may delegate to another person, for a period not exceeding nine months, any of his powers regarding care, custody, or property of the [ward]" (§15-14-104).

A conservatorship hearing may be held either in the Colorado location in which the proposed conservatee resides or, if the person does not live in Colorado, in any place where he/she has property. Notice of the proceeding must be given at least ten days before the date of the hearing.

Unless the person to be protected has counsel of his own choice, the court may appoint a lawyer to represent him who then has the power and duties of a guardian ad litem. If the alleged disability is mental illness, mental deficiency, physical illness or disability, *advanced age*, chronic use of drug, or chronic intoxication, the court may direct that the person to be protected be examined by a physician designated by the court, preferable a physician who is not connected with any institution in which the person is a patient or is detained. The visitor may be a guardian ad litem or an officer or employee of the court. (§15-14-407[2], emphasis added)

The court may appoint as conservator over the estate of an individual, a trust company, or bank with general power to serve as trustee. Among the powers of the conservator are distribution of income or principal of the estate without court authorization according to provisions in §15-14-425(1), and gifting to charity if the estate is ample, in amounts not to exceed 20 percent of the yearly estate income.

> If not otherwise compensated for services rendered, any visitor, any attorney whose services in the course of representing an interested person resulted in a protective order or were beneficial to a protected person's estate, any physician, any conservator, or any special conservator appointed in a protective proceeding is entitled to reasonable compensation from the estate. (§15-14-414)

(See Colorado Revised Statutes, Volume 5, Title 15: Probate, Trusts, and Fiduciaries, Article 14: Persons Under Disability—Protection, §15-14-101 et seq. for guardianship and conservatorship laws; Colorado Revised Statutes §15-14-310 for emergency temporary guardianship laws.)

*Connecticut.* Conservatorships may be appointed in probate court over "incapables" or over their estates. " 'Incapable of caring for one's self' means a mental, emotional or physical condition resulting from mental illness, mental deficiency, physical illness or disability, chronic use of drugs or alcohol, or confinement, which results in the person's inability to provide medical care for physical and mental health needs, nutritious meals, clothing, safe and adequately heated and ventilated shelter, personal hygiene and protection from physical abuse or harm and which results in endangerment to such person's health" (General Statutes of Connecticut §45a-644[c]). Similarly:

> "Incapable of managing his or her affairs" means that a person has a mental, emotional or physical condition resulting from mental illness, mental deficiency, physical illness or disability, chronic use of drugs or alcohol, or confinement, which prevents that person from performing the functions inherent in managing his or her affairs, and the person has property which will be wasted or dissipated unless proper management is provided, or that funds are needed for the support, care or welfare of the person or those entitled to be supported by that person and that the person is unable to take the necessary steps to obtain or provide funds which are needed for the support, care or welfare of the person or those entitled to be supported by such person. (§45a-644[d])

Notice of the hearing must be given seven days before the hearing date, "which date shall not be more than thirty days after the receipt of the application by the Court of Probate unless continued for cause shown" (§45a-649(a)). No notice is required if an emergency temporary conservatorship is sought. If the court makes an *ex parte* appointment of a temporary conservator, a hearing must be held on the issue within seventy-two hours if requested.

The proposed conservatee has a right to be present at the hearing and a right to be represented by an attorney at his or her own expense. If he/she cannot pay for an attorney, the court will appoint and pay for counsel our of the Probate Court Administration Fund. "If the respondent notifies the court in any manner that he or she wants to attend the hearing on the application but is unable to do so because of physical incapacity, the court shall schedule the hearing on the application at a place which would facilitate attendance by the respondent but if not practical, then the judge shall visit the respondent, if he or she is in the state of Connecticut, before the hearing" (§45a-649).

Evidence heard by the court shall include a written report or testimony by one or more licensed physicians who have examined the allegedly incapable adult within thirty days preceding the hearing. The court may waive this requirement if the respondent is absent or refuses to be examined, or if the alleged incapacity is not medical in nature. The court may consider as evidence the "physical and social functioning level or ability of the respondent" (§45a-650). The standard used in Connecticut's courts in conservatorship hearings is clear and convincing evidence.

If no "suitable conservator" can be found for certain people with limited resources, the Commissioner of Social Services will accept appointment as conservator of the estate and/or person of any "incapable" who is sixty years of age or older. A conservatorship of an estate may be terminated if the court determines the ward has no assets. Section 45a-660(c) was amended to read that on and after July 1, 1998, "the court shall review each conservatorship at least every three years, and shall either continue, modify or terminate the order for conservatorship." (See General Statutes of Connecticut, Volume 12, Title 45a: Probate Courts and procedure, Chapter 802h: Protected Persons and Their Property, §45a-644 et seq. for conservatorship laws; General Statutes of Connecticut §45a-654 for emergency temporary conservatorship laws.)

*Delaware.* Guardianships in Delaware are appointed in the Court of Chancery over the person and/or property of any disabled person resident in the State. " 'Disabled person' means any person who:

> 2. By reason of mental or physical incapacity is unable properly to manage or care for their own person or property, or both, and, in conse-

quence thereof, is in danger of dissipating or losing such property or of becoming the victim of designing persons or, in the case where a guardian of the person is sought, such person is in danger of substantially endangering [his or her] own health, or of becoming subject to abuse by other persons or of becoming the victim of designing persons. ... (Delaware Code, Title 12, §3901[a])

Any person who, while not a resident of Delaware, owns property in the state may be subject to a guardianship of property proceeding. "The Court cannot base property guardianship only on the generous—or perverse—conduct of an old man any more than it can on that of a young man; the Court is empowered to act only when such conduct is a product of age or infirmity. *In re Conner*, Del. Ch., 226 A.2d 126 (1967)."

Upon the filing of a guardianship petition, the Court will fix a time and place for a hearing on the issues of alleged disability, and "provide for reasonable notice" (§3901[3][c]) to the proposed ward. The proposed ward is entitled to representation by counsel. When a petition for an emergency guardianship is filed, provisions for both notice and a hearing may be dropped:

If, upon the filing of a petition, the Court finds the allegedly disabled person is in danger of incurring imminent serious physical harm or substantial economic loss or expense the Court may without notice and hearing appoint an interim guardian of the person or property to serve for a period of up to thirty days; provided that a hearing shall be held within thirty days of such appointment. ... (§3901[3][d])

Once the Court has appointed a guardian of the person for a disabled adult, the guardian may "exercise the same powers, rights and duties respecting the care, maintenance and treatment of the disabled person that a parent has respecting the parent's own unemancipated minor child" (§3922[b]). The guardian may change the new ward's residence within Delaware, will take reasonable care of the ward's clothing, furniture, vehicle, and other personal effects, and may arrange medical or other professional care for his or her ward. Among the many powers granted the guardian of the property (without specific Court confirmation), unless specifically restricted by the Court, are the powers to: invest and reinvest estate property; organize and dispose of such assets; deposit estate funds in a bank, including one operated by the guardian; and sell or organize stock.

While the guardian of a ward's property must account for the money, effects and property of the disabled person at the end of one year from the date of his or her appointment and not more often than once in two years thereafter, the guardian of the person "shall have no duty to account or otherwise report to the Court, except as provided by order of the Court" (§3941[a]). The guardian may hire accountants, investment counsel, attorneys-at-law and other professional advisers and pay their "reasonable fees and expenses" (§3921[e]). (See Delaware Code, Title 12, Chapter 39: Guardianship, §3901 et seq. for guardianship laws; Delaware Code §3901(d) for emergency temporary guardianship laws.)

*District of Columbia.* The Superior Court's probate division has exclusive jurisdiction to appoint a guardian for the person and a conservator for the estate of an incapacitated adult (over eighteen). An "incapacitated individual" is "an adult whose ability to receive and evaluate information effectively or to communicate decisions is impaired to such an extent that he or she lacks the capacity to manage all or some of his or her financial resources or to meet all or some essential requirements for his or her physical health, safety, habilitation, or therapeutic needs without court-ordered assistance or the appointment of a guardian or conservator" (District of Columbia Code §21-2011[11]). The codes provide the following definition for the phrase, "meet essential requirements for physical health or safety": "[It] means those actions necessary to provide health care, food, shelter, clothing, personal hygiene, and other care without which serious physical injury or illness is more likely than not to occur" (§21-2011[16]). In the District of Columbia, a finding that an individual is incapacitated is not intended to be a finding of legal incompetence.

Notice of the guardianship and/or conservatorship proceeding must be personally delivered to the proposed ward at least fourteen days before the hearing or mailed to that individual at least seventeen days prior to the time set for the hearing; or the court, "for good cause shown," may select a different method or time for giving notice for any hearing. If an emergency is alleged to exist, the court may, with no notice, appoint a temporary guardian whose authority extends for fifteen days only. Upon the filing of the emergency petition, counsel must be appointed for the allegedly incapacitated individual. He/she may request a hearing on issues of incapacity at any time within the period of the temporary guardianship, and the hearing will be heard within forty-eight hours.

Legal counsel shall be appointed for any allegedly incapacitated individual unless he/she is represented by an attorney, and the proposed ward's presence at the hearing is mandatory unless "good cause is shown for the absence" (§21-2041[h]). An appropriately qualified examiner (e.g., a gerontologist, psychiatrist, or qualified mental retardation professional) and a visitor appointed by the court (i.e., an officer, employee, or special appointee of the court) shall interview the proposed ward and submit written reports to the court, but the court may waive these appointments. The allegedly incapacitated individual is entitled to present evidence and to cross-examine witnesses, including the court-appointed examiner or visitor. The hearing may be closed to the public at the ward's request. The standard of proof in such proceedings is clear and convincing evidence.

In appointing the person most qualified to be guardian or conservator, the court "may pass over a person having priority and appoint a person having a lower priority or no priority" (§21-2043[d] and §21-205[b]). The conservator of the estate must post bond in the amount of the estate's value plus one year's expected income, and file an annual account of the conservatorship estate with the court on the anniversary date of appointment.

> a. As approved by order of the court, any visitor, attorney, examiner, conservator, special conservator, guardian ad litem, or guardian is entitled to compensation for services rendered either in a guardianship proceeding, protective proceeding, or in connection with a guardianship or protective arrangement. . . . Compensation shall be paid from the estate of the ward or person or, if the estate of the ward or person will be depleted by payouts made under this subsection, from a fund established by the District. (§21-2060)

(See District of Columbia Code, Chapter 20: Guardianship, Protective Proceedings, and Durable Power of Attorney, §21-2001 et seq. for guardianship and conservatorship laws; District of Columbia Code §21-2046 for emergency temporary guardianship laws.)

*Florida.* The circuit court has jurisdiction of guardianship proceedings. Guardianship law in Florida is a modified version of the Uniform Veterans' Guardianship Act. Guardians or plenary guardians can be appointed by the court to act on behalf of an incapacitated individual's person or property, or both. "'Guardian' means a person who has been appointed by the court to act on behalf of a ward's person or property, or both" (Florida Statutes Annotated §744.102[8]).

> "Incapacitated person" means a person who has been judicially determined to lack the capacity to manage at least some of the property or to meet at least some of the essential health and safety requirements of such person.
>
> a. To "manage property" means to take those actions necessary to obtain, administer, and dispose of real and personal property, intangible property, business property, benefits, and income.
> b. To "meet essential requirements for health or safety" means to take those actions necessary to provide the health care, food, shelter,

clothing, personal hygiene, or other care without which serious and imminent physical injury or illness is more likely than not to occur. (§774.102[10]).

Notice of the hearing must be given to the proposed ward, his or her attorney, and to all next of kin identified in the petition. The notice of the filing of a petition to determine incapacity must also be read to the alleged incapacitated person. If the court finds that there appears to be imminent danger of harm to the person or property of the allegedly incapacitated adult, the court may appoint an emergency temporary guardian for the person, property, or both. "The authority of an emergency temporary guardian expires sixty days after the date of appointment or when a guardian is appointed, whichever occurs first. The authority of the emergency temporary guardian may be extended for an additional thirty days upon a showing that the emergency conditions still exist" (§744.3031[3]). In all cases involving an adjudication of incapacity, the court shall appoint an attorney for the allegedly incapacitated individual unless the individual has hired counsel of his or her own.

Within five days after the petition for a determination of incapacity has been filed, the court shall appoint an examining committee consisting of three members. One member must be a psychiatrist or other physician. The remaining members must be either a psychologist, gerontologist, another psychiatrist, or other physician, a registered nurse, nurse practitioner, licensed social worker, a person with an advanced degree in gerontology from an accredited institution of higher education, or other person who by knowledge, skill, experience, training, or education may, in the court's discretion, advise the court in the form of an expert opinion. One of the three members of the committee must have knowledge of the type of incapacity alleged in the petition. Unless good cause is shown, the attending or family physician may not be appointed to the committee. (Florida Statutes Annotated §744.331[3][a])

Each committee member will examine the allegedly incapacitated person to determine need for a guardianship, and the examining committee must submit a report within fifteen days after appointment. The petitioner and respondent's attorney must receive a copy of the committee's report at least five days before the hearing. If indicated, the comprehensive exam must include: a physical examination, a mental health examination, and a functional assessment. The final report must, to the extent possible, include: a diagnosis, prognosis, and recommended course of treatment; a summary of the alleged incapacitated person's ability to retain his or her rights (to marry, vote, contract, drive, determine his or her residence, consent to medical treatment, etc.); and a description of the individual's diminished capacity to exercise certain rights. "If the examining committee concludes that the alleged incapacitated person is not incapacitated in any respect, the court shall dismiss the petition" (§744.331[4]).

The adjudicatory hearing on the merits of the petition must be set no more than fourteen days after the filing of the committee's report "unless good cause is shown" (§744.331 [5][a]). Mandatory attendance in court may be waived for good cause at the discretion of the court. At the hearing, the alleged incapacitated person has the right to remain silent and refuse to testify, to agree to testify, to present evidence, to call witnesses, to confront and cross-examine all witnesses, and to have the hearing open or closed. A guardian *ad litem* may be appointed by the court to represent the interests of the ward or of the ward's estate. The partial or total incapacity of the person must be established by clear and convincing evidence. "In any order declaring a person incapacitated the court must find that alternatives to guardianship were considered and that no alternative to guardianship will sufficiently address the problems of the ward" (§744.331[6][b]).

Priority in the appointment of a guardian falls first to the ward's relatives and persons with relevant experience; people whose appointment would represent a conflict of interest are disqualified. Within sixty days after his or her letters of guardianship are signed, the guardian must file an initial guardianship report with the court consisting of a verified inventory and an initial guardianship plan. "The initial guardianship plan for an incapacitated person must be based on the recommendations of the examining committee's examination, as incorporated into the order determining incapacity" (§744.363[2]). The plan must cover the coming fiscal year and be filed on an annual basis thereafter. It is the duty of the clerk of the circuit court to review the initial and annual guardianship reports, and the court or appointed general or special masters must then review the clerk's findings.

Among the powers of the guardian upon court approval are to "borrow money, with or without security, to be repaid from the property or otherwise and advance money for the protection of the estate" (§744.441[9]), "sell, mortgage, or lease any real or personal property of the estate, including homestead property, or any interest therein for cash or credit, or for part cash and part credit, and with or without security for unpaid balances" (§744.441[12]), and "continue any unincorporated business or venture in which the ward was engaged" (§744.441[13]). The guardian of the estate must post bond equal to the value of the ward's negotiable assets. (See Florida Statutes Annotated, Title 43 (XLIII):

Domestic Relations, Chapter 744: Guardianship, §744.1012 et seq. for guardianship laws; Florida Statutes Annotated §744.3031 for emergency temporary guardianship laws.)

*Georgia.* Guardianships are appointed in county probate court over the person and/or property of incapacitated adults (eighteen or older). Specifically, "a judge of the probate court may appoint guardians over the person of adults who are incapacitated by reason of mental illness, mental retardation, mental disability, physical illness or disability, chronic use of drugs or alcohol, or other cause, to the extent that such adults lack sufficient understanding or capacity to make significant responsible decisions concerning their persons or to the extent that they are incapable of communicating them" (Georgia Code §29-5-1[a][1]). The judge is also empowered to appoint guardians of the estate or property of "adults who are incapacitated by reason of mental illness, mental retardation, mental disability, physical illness or disability, chronic use of drugs or alcohol, detention by a foreign power, disappearance, or other cause, to the extent that such adults are incapable of managing their estate and that the appointment is necessary either because the property will be wasted or dissipated unless proper management is provided or because the property is needed for the support, care, or well-being of such adults or those entitled to be supported by such adults" (§29-5-1[a][2]).

Any interested person—resident or nonresident of the state—or the Department of Human Resources may file a petition to become guardian of an allegedly incapacitated adult. In all cases "except those sworn to by two or more petitioners under oath and except those involving detention by a foreign power or disappearance" (§29-5-6[a][3]), the petition must be supported by an affidavit of a licensed physician or licensed psychologist. Notice must be served at least ten days prior to the guardianship hearing unless the petitioner claims the existence of an emergency. If the petitioner alleges that the proposed ward is gravely incapacitated and that an emergency guardianship is necessary, a hearing for a temporary must be held in no sooner than three days. However, an emergency guardianship over the person or property can be appointed immediately, prior to a hearing on the issues of incapacity. The petition for an emergency guardianship must either include an affidavit sworn by a physician or psychologist or be "supported by the oath of at least two petitioners" (§29-5-8[c]).

The proposed ward has the right to a court-appointed legal representative unless he or she has already retained an attorney. Mandatory attendance at the hearing may be waived for good cause, and the hearing may be closed to the public at the ward's request. Medical evidence of the alleged incapacity must be gathered by a court-appointed physician or psychologist once the petition is filed. Any statements made by the proposed ward during the court-ordered evaluation are privileged but "shall be competent evidence in a proceeding under this chapter only" (§29-5-6[c][3]). Within seven days of the examination, a written report must be filed with the court. During his or her appointment with the proposed ward, the physician or psychologist must determine the individual's mental and physical state and condition, overall social condition (including support, care, education, and well-being), and needs for a foreseeable period of time.

Notice of an evidentiary hearing on the issues of incapacity must be received not less than ten days before the hearing is to be held. The proposed ward has the right to legal assistance and to subpoena and cross-examine witnesses, including the evaluation psychologist or physician. If both parties agree, evidence may be presented by deposition. "The burden of proof shall be upon the petitioner and the standard used by the court in reaching its decision shall be clear and convincing evidence" (§29-5-6[e][4]).

If a guardian of the person is appointed, the ward can no longer contract marriage, make other contracts, consent to medical treatment, establish where he or she will live, and may not bring or defend a lawsuit (except an action relating to the guardianship). If a guardian of the property is appointed, the ward may no longer buy, sell, or otherwise dispose of real, personal or trust property, enter into business or commercial transactions, or make contracts. Furthermore, "the court may authorize the guardian of the property to make transfers of the ward's personal or real property, outright or in trust, on behalf of the ward, upon a finding that a competent reasonable person in the ward's circumstances would make the transfers" (§29-5-5.1[a]). The guardian of the estate must post a bond equal to double the value of the ward's estate. Georgia limits the fees paid to an evaluating physician or psychologist and to the allegedly incapacitated person's appointed attorney to seventy-five dollars and actual expenses. (See Georgia Code §29-5-1 et seq. for guardianship laws; Georgia Code §29-5-8 for emergency temporary guardianship laws.)

*Hawaii.* Hawaii has adopted the Uniform Probate Code, excluding the 1975 and 1977 Official Amendments, with major modifications. Family court has jurisdiction over guardianships of the person, and a court of competent jurisdiction presides over protective proceedings for guardianships of the estate. If protective and guardianship proceedings have been initiated over the estate and person of one individual, they may be consolidated in either the family court or the court.

"Incapacitated person" means "any person who is impaired by reason of mental illness, mental deficiency, physical illness or disability, advanced age, chronic use of drugs, chronic intoxication, or other cause (except minority) to the extent that the person lacks sufficient understanding or capacity to make or communicate responsible decisions concerning one's person" (Hawaii Uniform Probate Code §560:5-101[2]). A "guardianship proceeding" is a proceeding to appoint a guardian of the person for an incapacitated person (§560:5-101[1]). A "protective proceeding" is one held to determine that a person cannot "effectively manage or apply the person's estate to necessary ends, either because the person lacks the ability or is otherwise inconvenienced" (§560:5-101[3]).

Any adult interested in the incapacitated person's welfare or estate may file for a guardianship. Once a petition has been filed, the date for a hearing on relevant issues is set by the court/family court. "If at any time in the proceeding the court determines that the interests of the allegedly incapacitated person are or may be inadequately represented, it shall appoint a guardian ad litem" (§560:5-303[b]). The court may appoint a physician or licensed psychologist to examine the proposed ward and to submit a report in writing to the court. A family court officer also may be assigned to interview the proposed ward and submit a written report to the court.

The proposed ward is entitled to be present at the hearing in person, to hear all evidence, to be represented by an attorney, to present evidence, and to cross-examine all witnesses. If an emergency is said to exist, the family court may, with or without notice to the proposed ward, appoint a temporary guardian of the person (for a period not to exceed 90 days) pending notice and hearing. The issue of incapacity may be determined at a closed hearing (§560:5-303[6]). "The family court, for good cause, may pass over a person having priority [as guardian for the incapacitated individual] and appoint a person having less or no priority" (§560:5-311[b]).

Once appointed, the guardian of the person may determine the new ward's place of abode within or without the State of Hawaii, and may give "any consents or approvals that may be necessary to enable the ward to receive medical or other professional care, counsel, treatment or service" (§560:5-312[a][3]). Among the powers given the guardian of the property is the power to "collect, hold, and retain assets of the estate including land in another state, until, in the guardian's judgment, disposition of the assets should be made, and the assets may be retained even though they include an asset in which the guardian is personally interested" (§560:5-424[1]). Every guardian of the estate must account to the court periodically as the court may direct. (See Hawaii Uniform Probate Code, Article V: Protection of Persons Under Disability and Their Property, §560:5-301 et seq. for laws on guardianships and protective proceedings; Hawaii UPC §560:5-310 for emergency temporary guardianship laws.)

*Idaho.* The Uniform Probate Code has been adopted, including 1979 Amendments but excluding 1975 and 1977 Amendments. Guardianships are appointed in district court for incapacitated people and conservators are appointed for the estates and affairs of people under other disabilities. A disabled or "incapacitated person" is "any person who is impaired by reason or mental illness, mental deficiency, physical illness or disability, chronic use of drugs, chronic intoxication, or other cause (except minority) to the extent that he lacks sufficient understanding or capacity to make or communicate responsible decisions concerning his person, provided that the term shall not refer to a developmentally disabled person" (Idaho Uniform Probate Code §15-5-101[a]).

"Incapacity" is further defined as a legal rather than medical term that "shall be construed to mean or refer to any person who has suffered, is suffering, or is likely to suffer, substantial harm due to an inability to provide for his personal needs for food, clothing, shelter, health care, or safety, or an inability to manage his or her property or financial affairs" (§15-5-101[a][1]). A conservator may be appointed over the estate and affairs of a person if: "(1) the person is unable to manage his property and affairs effectively for reasons such as mental illness, mental deficiency, physical illness or disability, chronic use of drugs, chronic intoxication, confinement, detention by a foreign power, or disappearance; and (2) the person has property which will be wasted or dissipated unless proper management is provided, or that funds are needed for the support, care and welfare of the person or those entitled to be supported by him and that protection is necessary or desirable to obtain or provide funds" (§15-5-401[b][1]).

Any person interested in the allegedly incapacitated person's welfare may petition for a finding of incapacity and appointment of a limited or general guardian or conservator. A hearing can be held within forty-eight hours of the initial filing of the petition if an emergency is said to exist. On a petition for the appointment of a conservator, the proposed conservatee must receive notice of the proceedings at least fourteen days before the date of the hearing. If the person to be protected is not a resident of the state, the proceedings will take place wherever he or she has property in the state. The court shall set a date for the general hearing on the issues of incapacity, and will appoint an attorney for the proposed ward "who shall have the powers and duties of a guardian ad litem" (§15-5-303[b]) if the allegedly incapacitated person does not have counsel of his or her own choice. If a conservatorship is being sought, the court may—but is not required to—appoint a lawyer to represent the proposed conservatee. Written reports will be submitted to the court by a visitor sent by the court and either a physician or a court-appointed "other qualified person." The person alleged to be incapacitated is entitled to be present at the hearing, to see or hear all evidence bearing upon his or her condition, to present evidence, and to cross-examine all witnesses. The hearing may be closed to the public if the person alleged to be incapacitated or his or her counsel so requests.

Concerning the procedure for a hearing on a conservatorship petition,

> If the alleged disability is mental illness, mental deficiency, physical illness or disability, advanced age, chronic use of drugs, or chronic intoxication, the court may direct that the person to be protected be examined by a physician designated by the court, preferably a physician who is not connected with any institution in which the person or patient is detained. The court may send a visitor to interview the person to be protected. The visitor may be a guardian ad litem or an officer or employee of the court. (§15-5-407[b])

Once appointed, the guardian of the person may determine the ward's place of abode either within or without the state, care for the ward's clothing, furniture, vehicles and other personal effects, consent to medical or other professional care for the ward and—if no conservator for the estate has been appointed—"receive money and tangible property deliverable to the ward and apply the money and property for support, care and education of the ward" (§15-5-312[4][B]). Without court authorization, the conservator of the estate may control estate assets including land in another state until "in his judgment, disposition of the assets should be made, and the assets may be retained even though they include an asset in which he is personally interested" (§15-5-424[c][1]), continue or participate in the ward's business affairs, invest and reinvest estate assets, acquire or dispose of an estate asset including land in another state, and employ attorneys, auditors, investment advisors, or agents even if they are associated with the conservator to help him or her in the administration of his or her duties. Both the conservator and guardian must submit a written annual report to the court concerning the status of the ward and of the ward's estate. (See Idaho Statutes, Title 15: Uniform Probate Code, Chapter 5: Protection of Persons Under Disability and Their Property, §15-5-101 et seq. for guardianship and conservatorship laws; Idaho Uniform Probate Code §15-5-310 for emergency temporary guardianship laws.)

*Illinois.* Guardianships may be appointed in circuit courts over the person and/or estate of "disabled persons." A "disabled person" is "a person eighteen years or older who (a) because of mental deterioration or physical incapacity is not fully able to manage his person or estate, or (b) is a person with mental illness or a person with a developmental disability and who because of his mental illness or developmental disability is not fully able to manage his person or estate, or (c) because of gambling, idleness, debauchery or excessive use of intoxicants or drugs, so spends or wastes his estate as to expose himself or his family to want or suffering" (Illinois Compiled Statutes 755 ILCS 5/11a-2). The court may appoint: (1) a guardian of the estate of a disabled adult "if because of his disability he is unable to manage his estate or financial affairs" (755 ILCS 5/11a-3[a][2]); (2) a guardian of the person "if because of his disability he lacks sufficient understanding or capacity to make or communicate responsible decisions concerning the care of his person" (755 ILCS 5/11a-3[a][1]); (3) a guardian of both person and estate (a plenary guardian); or (4) a temporary guardian of the person or estate or both upon a showing that an emergency exists.

> Guardianship shall be utilized only as is necessary to promote the well-being of the disabled person, to protect him from neglect, exploitation, or abuse, and to encourage development of his maximum self-reliance and independence. (755 ILCS 5/11a-3[b])

Once filed, the petition for adjudication of disability and appointment of a guardian of the estate or of the person or both of an alleged disabled person may be dismissed or withdrawn only with the court's permission. A hearing date will be set within thirty days of the filing of the guardianship petition, and the respondent must be personally served with a copy of the petition not less that fourteen days before the hearing. The court may—but is not required in all cases to—appoint a guardian *ad litem* to discuss the guardianship proceedings with the respondent prior to the hearing. "The guardian ad litem shall also attempt to elicit the respondent's position concerning the adjudication of disability, the proposed guardian, a proposed change in residential placement, changes in care that might result from the guardianship, and other areas of inquiry deemed appropriate by the court" (755 ILCS 5/11a-10[a]).

Legal counsel will be appointed if requested or if the respondent opposes the guardian *ad litem*'s recommendations to the court, and the hearing may be closed to the public at the ward's request or the request of the guardian *ad litem* or of the respondent's counsel. The respondent is entitled to a jury trial, to present evidence, and to confront and cross-examine all witnesses. The court must enter a written order describing the factual basis for its findings and specifying the responsibilities and powers of the guardian and "the legal disabilities to which the respondent is subject" (755 ILCS 5/11a-12[c]).

The selection of a guardian will be made at the court's discretion, whether or not the disabled person had already designated a guardian while of sound mind and memory. The guardian of the person may or may not be required to file status reports concerning the disabled person with the court at intervals determined by the court. "A guardian acting as a surrogate decision maker under the Health Care Surrogate Act shall have all the rights of a surrogate under that Act without court order including the right to make medical treatment decisions such as decisions to forgo or withdraw life-sustaining treatment" (755 ILCS 5/11a-17[d]). The guardian of the estate may be authorized by the circuit court to exercise all of the powers over the estate and business affairs of the ward that the ward would exercise if present and not under disability. (See Illinois Compiled Statutes, Chapter 755: Estates, Probate Act of 1975, 755 ILCS 5/, Article XIa, Guardians for Disabled Adults, 755 ILCS 5/11a-2 et seq. for guardianship laws; Illinois Compiled Statutes 755 ILCS 5/11a-4 for emergency temporary guardianship laws.)

*Indiana.* Jurisdiction to appoint guardians (or conservators) over the person and/or property of incapacitated persons rests in probate court and the mental health division of municipal court, which has concurrent jurisdiction in matters relating to guardianship in connection with mental health proceedings. In Indiana, "the terms guardian and conservator are interchangeable" (Indiana Code 29-3-1-6). An "incapacitated person" is defined as any individual who

> 1. cannot be located upon reasonable inquiry; (2) is unable: (a) to manage in whole or in part the individual's property; (b) to provide self-care; or (c) both; because of insanity, mental illness, mental deficiency, physical illness, infirmity, habitual drunkenness, excessive use of drugs, incarceration, confinement, detention, duress, fraud, undue influence of others on the individual, or other incapacity; or (3) has a developmental disability. (IC 29-3-1-7.5)

"All findings, orders, or other proceedings under this article shall be in the discretion of the court unless otherwise provided in this article" (IC 29-3-2-4). Any person may file a petition for the appointment of him- or herself or another as guardian of the allegedly incapacitated individual. Notice must be served to the proposed ward ten days before the hearing. The proposed ward must be present at the hearing unless the court determines by evidence that his or her health or safety is threatened, the incapacitated person is unavailable due to disappearance or absence from the state, or the person has consented to the appointment.

At its discretion, the court may appoint an attorney to represent the allegedly incapacitated person. A temporary guardian may be appointed by the court without any notice and without a hearing if the court finds "immediate and irreparable harm in delay" (IC 29-3-3-4[a][4]). If a temporary guardian is appointed without notice and the alleged incapacitated person files a petition requesting the termination of the temporary guardianship, the court will hear and determine the merits of the petition "at the earliest possible time" (IC 29-3-3-4[a][4]).

If, following an adjudication of incapacity, a guardian is appointed, first priority is to be given to persons designated in durable powers of attorney. However, the court in its wisdom may pass over any person having priority and appoint an individual having a lower priority or no priority at all. The guardian of an incapacitated person is responsible for the individual's care and custody and for the preservation of his or her property as ordered by the court.

The guardian of the estate has the power to take possession of the ward's property, to continue all businesses of the ward and, with the court's permission, to sell, lease and mortgage the ward's property. The court may terminate the guardianship if "the guardianship property is reduced to three thousand five hundred dollars ($3,500)" (IC 29-3-12-1[c][1]). (See Indiana Code, Title 29: Probate, Article 3: Guardianships and Protective Proceedings, IC 29-3-1 et seq. for guardianship laws; IC 29-3-3-4 for emergency temporary guardianship laws.)

*Iowa.* District probate court has jurisdiction to appoint a guardian of the person for an incompetent individual whose decision-making capacity is so impaired that "the person is unable to care for the person's personal safety or to attend to or provide for necessities for the person such as food, shelter, clothing, or medical care, without which physical injury or illness might occur" (Iowa Code, §633.552[2][a]). A conservator of the estate may be appointed over an adult whose "decision-making capacity is so impaired that the person is unable to make, communicate, or carry out important decisions concerning the person's financial affairs" (§633.566(2)[a]).

Notice to the proposed ward in a guardianship proceeding must "advise the proposed ward . . . of the right to counsel and the potential deprivation of the proposed ward's civil rights" (§633.562). A temporary guardianship or temporary conservatorship may be appointed only after a hearing and subject to conditions to be determined by the court. The proposed ward is entitled to legal representation at a guardianship hearing and will be assigned legal representation in a conservatorship proceeding "if the court determines that it would be in the ward's best interest" (§633.575[6]).

> In a proceeding for the appointment of a conservator, the proposed ward shall be given written notice which advises the proposed ward that if a conservator is appointed, the conservator may, without court approval, manage the proposed ward's principal, income, and investments, sue and defend any claim by or against the ward, sell and transfer personal property, and vote at corporate meetings. The notice shall also advise the proposed ward that, upon the court's approval, the conservator may invest the ward's funds, execute leases, make payments to or for the benefit of the ward, support the ward's legal dependents, compromise or settle any claim, and do any other thing that the court determines is in the ward's best interests. (Iowa Code §633.576)

The determination of incompetency of the proposed ward in guardianship and conservatorship proceedings must be supported by clear and convincing evidence, and the burden of persuasion is on the petitioner. A petition nominating a person for appointment to serve as a conservator may request that the appointment be made without bond. A guardian has the same responsibilities towards his or her ward as does a parent towards an unemancipated minor. The conservator has the authority (with court approval) to sell property of the ward for any purpose deemed conducive to the ward's interest. Guardians and conservators must file reports as provided by §633.677 through §633.682. (See Iowa Code, Title XV: Judicial Branch and Judicial Procedures, Subtitle 4: Probate—Fiduciaries, 633: Probate Code, §633.551 et seq. for guardianship and conservatorship laws; Iowa Code §633.558 and §633.573 for temporary guardianship and temporary conservatorship laws.)

*Kansas.* A guardian may be appointed in district court to control an adult determined to be a "disabled person" and a conservator to control the disabled person's estate. A "disabled person" is "any adult person whose ability to receive and evaluate information effectively or to communicate decisions, or both, is impaired to such an extent that the person lacks the capacity to manage such person's financial resources or, except for reason of indigency, to meet essential requirements for such person's physical health or safety, or both" (Kansas Statutes §59-3002). A guardian may be appointed for a disabled person who lacks the capacity to meet his or her essential requirements for physical health, safety, or both. A conservator will be appointed for a disabled person who lacks the capacity to manage his or her financial resources.

Any adult may file a petition, and the petition may be accompanied by, or the court may require it be accompanied by:

a statement in writing of a physician or psychologist stating that the physician or psychologist has examined the proposed ward or proposed conservatee and the results of the examination on the issue of whether the proposed ward or proposed conservatee is a disabled person or the court may allow such petition to be accompanied by a verified statement by the petitioner that the proposed ward or proposed conservatee has refused to submit to an examination by a physician or psychologist. (§59-3009[a][9])

Notice must be given to the proposed ward at least five days before the hearing, and the hearing must take place no earlier than seven days or later than fourteen days after the date of the filing of the petition. An order of continuance may be granted either to the petitioner or to the proposed ward or proposed conservatee "for good cause shown" (§59-011[a][2]). If a petition for an emergency guardianship appointment is filed, a hearing must be held within forty-eight hours, although the court may choose to make an immediate appointment with no notice at all. The court will order a mental evaluation at the time notice is served on the proposed ward or proposed conservatee. No later than three days prior to the date of the hearing, the evaluation must be submitted to the court in writing.

An attorney will be appointed by the court if needed. Barring a finding that it would be injurious to the allegedly incapacitated person's welfare, his or her presence is required in court. People not necessary to the hearing may be excluded. If the court finds that the disabled individual should be permitted to make some decisions concerning his or her person or property, a guardian or conservator may be appointed with specified, limited powers.

The guardian's general powers and duties include taking charge of the person of the ward and providing for the ward's care, treatment, habilitation, education, support and maintenance, and to file an annual accounting. The conservator is subject to the control and direction of the court "at all times and in all things" (§59-3019). The court will conduct a review of the conservatorship or guardianship or both within three years from the date each was appointed, and hold reviews each three years thereafter. (See Kansas Statutes, Chapter 59: Probate Code, Article 30: Guardians or Conservators, §59-3001 et seq. for guardianship/conservatorship laws; Kansas Statutes §59-3036 for emergency temporary guardianship or conservatorship laws.)

*Kentucky.* The appointment of guardians over the person and conservators over the estate of "disabled persons" is under the jurisdiction of Kentucky's district courts. The word "disabled" means a legal rather than a medical disability. It is determined by functional inabilities and refers to any person age fourteen or older who is:

a. Unable to make informed decisions with respect to his personal affairs to such an extent that he lacks the capacity to provide for his physical health and safety, including but not limited to health care, food, shelter, clothing or personal hygiene; or

b. Unable to make informed choices with respect to his financial resources to such an extent that he lacks the capacity to manage his property effectively by those actions necessary to obtain, administer, and dispose of both real and personal property. (Kentucky Revised Statutes §387.510)

A functional inability will be demonstrated by acts or occurrences during the six months prior to the filing of the guardianship and/or conservatorship petition rather than by isolated instances of negligence, improvidence, or other unusual behavior.

If the petition for determination of disability contains an appropriate evaluation report when filed, the court will then establish the date and place of a hearing to be held within thirty days; but if no evaluation report is included, the hearing will be held within sixty days of the date of filing. Fourteen days prior to a hearing on the guardianship or conservatorship (or both), the allegedly disabled individual must be notified of the petition that has been filed by an "interested party or entity."

The respondent has a right to court-appointed counsel, a jury trial at the hearing, to present evidence and to confront and cross-examine all witnesses, and the option to close the hearing to the public. An interdisciplinary evaluation report prepared by a physician, psychologist, and social worker will be used as supporting evidence. If the petitioner claims an emergency exists, a hearing can be held within forty-eight hours of the delivery of notice to the person targeted by the petition for an emergency temporary appointment of a limited guardianship or limited conservatorship. The standard of proof required is clear and convincing evidence.

The court will appoint an individual or entity it deems best qualified and willing to serve. The guardian is charged with encouraging the ward to develop or regain his or her capacity to meet personal needs and to manage financial matters. He or she has the power to establish the ward's place of abode within the state, and to give necessary consent to enable the ward to receive medical or professional care, counsel and treatment. The guardian must file annual reports with the court concerning the ward's mental, physical, and social condition.

The conservator will control and protect the ward's real and personal property and income. He or she must file a verified inventory of the ward's property within sixty days of appointment and file biennial reports thereafter. (See Kentucky Revised Statutes, Title XXXIII, Chapter 387, §387.500 et seq. for guardianship and conservatorship laws; Kentucky

Revised Statutes §387.740 for emergency temporary guardianship and conservatorship laws.)

*Louisiana.* The jurisdiction for protective proceedings in Louisiana is probate court. The terminology used in such proceedings in Louisiana is relatively unique among the states. Any judge of the domicile or residence of an "insane person" or one "incapable of handling his estate through infirmity" may appoint curators in interdiction proceedings to administer the "interdict's" estate or provide for the needs of the "incapacitated person"(Louisiana Statutes Annotated, Civil Code Article 389; see Appendix B for discussion of "interdiction"). According to the code, "no person above the age of majority, who is subject to an habitual state of imbecility, insanity or madness, shall be allowed to take care of his own person and administer his estate, although such person shall, at times, appear to have the possession of his reason" (Art. 389). Thus, "when a person is declared incapable by reason of mental retardation, mental disability, or other infirmity . . . of caring for his own person or of administering his estate, a court of competent jurisdiction may appoint a limited curator to such person or his estate" (Art. 389.1).

> Not only lunatics and idiots are liable to be interdicted, but likewise all persons who, owing to any infirmity, are incapable of taking care of their persons and administering their estates. Such persons shall be placed under the care of a curator, who shall be appointed and shall administer in conformity with the rules contained in the present chapter. (Art. 422)

In a proceeding to have an individual fully interdicted, the petitioning party must prove, by clear and convincing evidence, that the person to be interdicted is mentally incapable of administering his/her estate and unable to care for his/her person. However, a provisional curator or administrator *pro tempore* may also be appointed immediately upon the filing of the petition if such an action is deemed by the court to be necessary. All costs shall be paid out of the estate of the respondent if he or she is interdicted (Art. 397).

Acts that were completed before the petition for the interdiction can be annulled as a result of "notorious insanity"; that is, if it can be proved that the party who contracted with the interdicted person "could not have been deceived as to the situation of [the interdict's] mind" at the time the acts were completed (Art. 402). The judge may order that the interdicted person be cared for in his or her own house, be placed in a "bettering house," or be confined in safe custody elsewhere. The judge will also appoint a superintendent to the interdicted person who will report to the judge at lease once every three months on the well-being of the interdict. The judge will visit the person interdicted whenever he deems it expedient to do so. The curator may obtain the court's approval to place the interdict's property in trust. (See Louisiana Statutes Annotated, Civil Code, Art. 389 et seq. for laws on interdiction proceedings; Louisiana Statutes Annotated, Art. 394 for law on emergency temporary proceedings.)

*Maine.* Maine adopted the Uniform Probate Code, including the 1975 Official Amendments and excluding the 1977 and 1979 Amendments. Jurisdiction for the appointment of a guardian over an incapacitated person and a conservator over a protected person's estate is assumed by the probate court. An "incapacitated person" is "any person who is impaired by reason of mental illness, mental deficiency, physical illness or disability, chronic use of drugs, chronic intoxication, or other cause except minority to the extent that he lacks sufficient understanding or capacity to make or communicate responsible decisions concerning his person" (Maine Revised Statutes, 18A §5-101[1]). Appointment of a conservator over the estate may be made if the court determines that

> i. the person is unable to manage his property and affairs effectively for reasons such as mental illness, mental deficiency, physical illness or disability, chronic use of drugs, chronic intoxication, confinement, detention by a foreign power, or disappearance; and
> ii. the person has property which will be wasted or dissipated unless proper management is provided, or that funds are needed for the support, care and welfare of the person or those entitled to be supported by him and that protection is necessary or desirable to obtain or provide funds. (18A §5-401[2])

Upon the filing of a petition for a finding of incapacity by any person who is interested in his or her estate, affairs or welfare, the allegedly incapacitated adult is given fourteen days to appear in court for a hearing on the issues of incapacity. An emergency temporary or ex parte guardianship or conservatorship appointment can be made by the court, but the petition must be accompanied by an affidavit setting forth facts alleging an emergency. If an emergency temporary guardian or conservator is appointed, the court must, within two working days, appoint a visitor or guardian ad litem to visit the allegedly incapacitated person, explain the meaning and consequences of the appointment, and file a report to the court within ten days (18A, §5-310-A [a, a-1]). If the individual wishes to contest any aspect of the temporary guardianship, the court will hold an expedited hearing within forty days of the entry of the ex parte order (18A, §5-310-A, [b]).

Unless the allegedly incapacitated person is already represented by an attorney, the court shall appoint one or more of the following: a visitor, a guardian ad litem or an attorney to represent the allegedly incapacitated person in the proceeding. If it comes to the court's attention that the allegedly incapacitated person wishes to contest any aspect of the proceeding or to seek any limitation of the proposed guardian's powers, the court shall appoint an attorney to represent the allegedly incapacitated person. The cost of this appointment of the visitor, guardian ad litem or attorney must be paid from the estate of the allegedly incapacitated person if the court is satisfied sufficient funds are available. (18A, §5-303[b])

The proposed ward/conservatee will be examined by a court-appointed physician or licensed psychologist "acceptable to the court" whose written report to the court must provide diagnoses, a description of the allegedly incapacitated person's mental and functional limitations, and prognoses. If appointed, the visitor or guardian *ad litem* must interview both the person alleged to be incapacitated and the person seeking appointment as guardian, evaluate the residence of the current and proposed residence of the allegedly incapacitated individual, and submit a written report to the court. A visitor in guardianship proceedings is "a person who is trained in law, nursing, social work, or has other significant qualifications that make him suitable to perform the function, and is an officer, employee or special appointee of the court with no interest in the proceedings" (18A, §5-308). All reports are to be submitted to the court and to all parties of record at least ten days prior to the hearing on the petition. The proposed ward/conservatee is entitled to be present at the hearing, to see and hear all evidence, to be represented by counsel, to present evidence and cross-examine witnesses (including the physician, the visitor, and the guardian ad litem), and to a closed hearing if desired.

The powers and duties of a guardian are those of parent to unemancipated minor child, including: custody of the person; establishment of the ward's place of abode within or without the State of Maine; placement of the ward in any hospital or institution for care; and care of the ward's clothing, furniture, vehicles, and personal effects (18A, §5-312[1, 2]). Among the guardian's powers is the right to "withhold or withdraw life-sustaining treatment . . . without court approval unless the guardian's decision is made against the advice of the ward's primary physician and in the absence of instructions from the ward made while the ward had capacity" (18A, §5-312[3]).

The conservator of a protected person may, without court authorization or confirmation, collect, hold, and retain assets of the estate until he or she believes disposition of the assets should be made; participate in the operation of the conservatee's business; invest and reinvest estate assets; deposit estate funds in a bank "including a bank operated by the conservator"; buy and sell estate assets including land in another state; borrow money to be repaid from estate assets; and hire attorneys, auditors, investment advisors, or agents—even though they are associated with the conservator—to advise and/or assist the conservator (18A, §5-424[c]). (See Maine Revised Statutes, Title 18-A: Probate Codes, Article V: Protection of Persons under Disability and Their Property, §5-101 et seq. for guardianship and conservatorship laws; Maine Revised Statutes, §5-310 and §5-408-A for emergency temporary guardianship and conservatorship statutes.)

*Maryland.* Circuit courts have exclusive jurisdiction to appoint guardians of the person and of the property of disabled people. A guardian of the person will be appointed for an adult (eighteen and older) who "lacks sufficient understanding or capacity to make or communicate responsible decisions concerning his person, including provisions for health care, food, clothing, or shelter, because of any mental disability, senility, other mental weakness, disease, habitual drunkenness, or addiction to drugs, and that no less restrictive form of intervention is available which is consistent with the person's welfare and safety" (Maryland Estate and Trusts Code, §13-705[b]). The appointment of a guardian of the person is not evidence that the disabled person is incompetent.

A guardian of the property of a disabled person will be appointed if "the person is unable to manage his property and affairs effectively because of physical or mental disability, disease, habitual drunkenness, addiction to drugs, imprisonment, compulsory hospitalization, confinement, detention by a foreign power, or disappearance" (§13-201[c][1]). This adjudication under Maryland's code is to have no bearing on the issue of the allegedly disabled person's capacity to care for his or her own person.

The court shall appoint counsel for the proposed ward if he or she has none. The person alleged to be disabled is entitled to be present at the hearing unless he or she has waived that right "or cannot be present because of physical or mental incapacity" (§13-705[e]). The respondent also has the right to present evidence and cross-examine witnesses. All hearings are "confidential and sealed unless otherwise ordered by a court of competent jurisdiction for good cause shown" (§13-705[e]). The court may grant a petitioner's request for an emergency temporary guardianship without notice for a period of seventy-two hours (which may be continued or extended until the appointment of a permanent guardian at the discretion of the court). The standard of proof in all such proceedings is that of clear and convincing evidence.

A person appointed guardian of the estate of an incapacitated adult in Maryland may sell, mortgage, exchange or lease the ward's property or borrow money without court authorization or confirmation, and has broad powers (again without court approval) to invest in any property and to deposit investment funds in checking accounts. The guardian of a person may establish the ward's place of abode within or without the State without court authorization. (See Maryland Statutes, Article: Estates and Trusts, §13-101 et seq. for guardianship laws; Maryland Statutes, §13-709 for emergency temporary guardianship laws.)

*Massachusetts*. Guardianships of the person are appointed by decree of probate court for "mentally ill persons, mentally retarded persons, persons unable to make or communicate informed decisions due to physical incapacity or illness, and spendthrifts" (General Laws of Massachusetts, Chapter 201: §1); and conservators of the property may be appointed "if a person by reason of mental weakness is unable to properly care for his property" (c. 201: §16). A "spendthrift" is

> a person who, by excessive drinking, gaming, idleness, or debauchery of any kind, so spends, wastes or lessens his estate as to expose himself or his family to want or suffering, or the department of public welfare, to charge or expense for his support or for the support of his family. . . . The department of public welfare or a relative of the alleged spendthrift, may file a petition in the probate court, stating the facts and circumstances of the case and praying that a guardian be appointed. If after notice as provided in the following section, and after hearing, the court finds that he is a spendthrift, it shall appoint a guardian of his person and estate. (c. 201: §8)

Although the proposed ward is supposed to receive notice seven days prior to the date of the hearing, a temporary guardian or temporary conservator may be appointed by the court "for cause shown" without any notice at all if the court is satisfied that an emergency exists. A temporary guardianship or temporary conservatorship will continue: until the appointment of a permanent guardian or permanent conservator, until it is ordered dismissed by the supreme judicial court, or until the trust is legally terminated.

The conservator or guardian must manage the estate of the incapacitated adult "frugally and without waste" and exercise "any or all powers over the estate and business affairs of the ward which the ward could exercise if present and not under disability" (c. 201: §38). The probate court may authorize the conservator or guardian to exercise many powers, including: the creation of revocable or irrevocable trusts which may extend beyond the ward's disability; the making of gifts; the making of contracts; and the surrendering of policies for their cash value. (See General Laws of Massachusetts, Chapter 201, Guardians and Conservators, §1 et seq. for guardianship and conservatorship laws; General Laws of Massachusetts, Chapter 201, §§14, 15 and 21 for emergency temporary guardianship and conservatorship statutes.)

*Michigan.* Probate courts have jurisdiction over proceedings for the appointment of guardians of the person and conservators of the estate of legally incapacitated adults (eighteen and above) who are residents or have any property within the state of Michigan. An "incapacitated person" is "an individual who is impaired by reason of mental illness, mental deficiency, physical illness or disability, chronic use of drugs, chronic intoxication, or other cause, not including minority, to the extent of lacking sufficient understanding or capacity to make or communicate informed decisions" (Michigan Code §700.1105[a]). A conservator of the estate may be appointed for an individual who is "unable to manage property and business affairs effectively for reasons such as mental illness, mental deficiency, physical illness or disability, chronic use of drugs, chronic intoxication, confinement, detention by a foreign power, or disappearance" (§700.5401[3][a]).

Upon the filing of a petition of the person or of the estate by any person interested in the individual's welfare, the court shall set a date for a hearing on the issue of incapacity. If the allegedly incapacitated person does not have counsel and wishes to contest the petition in any regard, the court shall appoint a guardian *ad litem* to represent him or her in the guardianship or conservatorship protective proceedings. If the individual to be protected is mentally competent but aged or physically infirm, the court will not automatically assign a guardian *ad litem* to represent the person in the proceeding.

If the court deems it necessary, an allegedly incapacitated individual will be examined by a court-appointed physician or mental health professional who will submit a written report to the court at least five days before the hearing. The proposed ward also has the right to secure an independent evaluation at his or her expense (or if indigent, at the expense of the state) (§700.5304[2]). A report submitted for this purpose must contain:

a. A detailed description of the individual's physical or psychological infirmities.
b. An explanation of how and to what extent each infirmity interferes with the individual's ability to receive or evaluate information in making decisions.

c. A listing of all medications the individual is receiving, the dosage of each medication and a description of the effects each medication has upon the individual's behavior.
d. A prognosis for improvement in the individual's condition and a recommendation for the most appropriate rehabilitation plan.
e. The signatures of all individuals who performed the evaluations upon which the report is based. (§700.5304[3])

The proposed ward is entitled to be present at the hearing, to examine all evidence bearing upon his or her condition, to present evidence, to cross-examine witnesses (including the court-appointed physician or mental health professional and the court visitor), and to a trial by jury. The hearing may be closed at the request of the alleged incapacitated individual or individual to be protected.

A guardian will be appointed if the court is "satisfied by clear and convincing evidence" that the individual is incapacitated and that a guardian is needed to provide continuing care and supervision. Clear and convincing evidence is also required during a conservatorship hearing. At the discretion of the judge, a limited guardian may be appointed to provide specific care that is beyond the capacity of the ward to organize. If a petitioner asserts that an emergency exists requiring the immediate appointment of a guardian, the court shall provide notify the allegedly incapacitated individual and hold a hearing. If a temporary guardian is appointed by the court upon a showing that the individual is incapacitated, a hearing with notice must be held within twenty-eight days.

The guardian is entitled to custody of the person of the ward and may establish the ward's residence within or without the state, giving notice to the court within fourteen days of a change in the ward's place of residence (§700.5314[a]). The court will review the guardianship not later than one year after its initiation and not later than every three years after each review. The conservator must account for his or her administration of the trust not less than annually, unless the court directs otherwise.

Among other powers and duties, a guardian is authorized to give medical consent for the ward, while a conservator holds title to all of the ward's property as trustee and may deal with his or her real estate without obtaining court authorization or confirmation. "If not otherwise compensated for services rendered, a visitor, guardian ad litem, attorney, physician, conservator, or special conservator appointed in a protective proceeding, is entitled to reasonable compensation from the estate" (§700.5413). (See Michigan Compiled Laws, Act 386 of 1998, Article V, Protection of an Individual Under Disability and His or Her Property: Part I, §700.5101 et seq. for general provisions; Part 3, §700.5301 et seq. for guardianship codes; and Part 4, §700.5401 et seq. for conservatorship codes; Michigan Compiled Laws §700.5312 and §700.5407[2][a] for emergency temporary guardianship/conservatorship laws.)

*Minnesota.* The probate court may appoint one or more persons as guardian of the person or estate or both, or as conservator of the person or estate or both, of any incapacitated person. A guardian is appointed by the court to exercise all of the designated powers and duties for the care of his or her ward, the ward's estate, or both, and a conservator exercises some, but not all, of such powers for the care of the conservatee, the conservatee's estate, or both. An "incapacitated person" in the case of guardianship or conservatorship of the person is "any adult person who is impaired to the extent of lacking sufficient understanding or capacity to make or communicate responsible decisions, and who has demonstrated deficits in behavior which evidence an inability to meet personal needs for medical care, nutrition, clothing, shelter or safety" (Minnesota Statutes §525.54, Subd. 2). An appointment of a guardianship or conservatorship of the estate may be made involuntarily if

> 1. the person is unable to manage the person's property and affairs effectively because the person is an incapacitated person, and (2) the person has property which will be dissipated unless proper management is provided, or that funds are needed for the support, care and welfare of the person or those entitled to be supported by the person, and (3) a guardian or conservator is necessary to adequately protect the person's estate or financial affairs. (§525.54, Subd. 3)

An "incapacitated person" in relationship to an estate is an adult who "lacks sufficient understanding or capacity to make or communicate responsible decisions concerning the person's estate or financial affairs, and who has demonstrated deficits in behavior which evidence an inability to manage the estate" (§525.54, Subd. 3).

Notice of the hearing must be given the proposed ward/conservatee at least fourteen days prior to the hearing. The court may waive both notice and hearing requirements, however, if there is a showing that "immediate and reasonably foreseeable and irreparable harm to the person or the person's estate will result from a forty-eight-hour delay" (§525.591, Subd. 2a).

Notice of the hearing must be easily understood and clearly state the rights that will be transferred from the allegedly incapacitated person to the guardian or conservator, including the right to manage and control property, to enter into contracts, and to determine residence. The proposed ward or conservatee has the right to attend the hearing, to present evidence to oppose the petition, and to summon and cross-examine witnesses (§525.55, Subd. 2). The court must appoint an attorney to represent the proposed ward or conservatee unless he or she has already secured counsel (or is in the Eighth Judicial District).

The appointment of a guardian is evidence of the incompetency of the ward, although the appointment of a conservator is not evidence of incompetency on the part of the conservatee (§525.54). A guardian or conservator retains the power to give "any necessary consent to enable the ward or conservatee to receive necessary medical or other professional care, counsel, treatment or service, except that no guardian or conservator may give consent for psychosurgery, electroshock, sterilization, or experimental treatment of any kind unless the procedure is first approved by order of the court" (§525.56, Subd. [4] [a]). The requirement of annual accounts (concerning both the person and estate of the ward/conservatee) may be waived by the court. Furthermore,

> if a ward or conservatee has made a financial transaction or gift or entered into a contract during the two-year period before establishment of the guardianship or conservatorship, the guardian or conservator may petition for court review of the transaction, gift, or contract. If the court finds that the ward or conservatee was incompetent or subject to duress, coercion, or undue influence when the transaction, gift, or contract was made, the court may declare the transaction, gift, or contract void except as against a bona fide transferee for value and order reimbursement or other appropriate relief. (§525.56, Subd. 5)

(See Minnesota Statutes, Chapter 525: Probate Proceedings, §525.539 et seq. for guardianship and conservatorship laws; Minnesota Statutes §525.591, Subd. 2a for emergency temporary guardianship and conservatorship laws.)

*Mississippi.* The creation of guardianships and conservatorships is within the jurisdiction of the chancery court. A guardian may be appointed for any person under an identified "legal disability" (minority, incompetence, idiocy, lunacy, unsound mind, alcoholism, addiction to drugs or felony conviction (Mississippi Code §93-13-5 et seq.). In Mississippi, the term "unsound mind" includes idiots, lunatics, and "persons non compos mentis" (§1-3-57). The application may be filed by a relative, friend, or any interested party—or upon the court's own motion.

During the chancery court's evaluation of the appointment of a guardian for an incompetent adult, "infirmities of old age shall not be considered elements of infirmities" (§93-13-121). The chancery court, if satisfied in its hearing that a person is an habitual drunkard, or an habitual user of cocaine, opium, or morphine, shall appoint a guardian to take care of him and his estate, both real and personal, and the costs will be paid out of the estate. The court or chancellor may direct the person's confinement in an asylum (§93-13-131).

The conservatorship procedure for persons incapable of managing their property is intended to encompass a broader class of people than just the incompetent. Thus, the chancery court may appoint a conservatorship over the estate of a person who "by reason of advanced age, physical incapacity or mental weakness is incapable of managing his own estate" (§93-13-251). If the court deems it advisable, the conservator may have charge and custody of the person as well as of the property "subject to the direction of the appointing court."

> If someone will not qualify as guardian of a ward who has property, it shall be the duty of the chancery court or the chancellor in vacation to appoint the clerk of said court to be the guardian of the ward, who shall discharge the duties of guardian. . . . He shall be . . . allowed not more than ten percent (10%) of the amount of the estate, if finally settled. (§93-13-21)

Upon a showing of the existence of an emergency, a temporary guardianship may be established before notice is given to the proposed ward. Notice must be given to the targeted elderly person five days before the hearing for a permanent guardianship or conservatorship. During the hearing, the judge will decide the number and character of witnesses called and the proof to be presented with the exception of the requirement that at least two physicians or one physician and one psychologist examine the proposed ward and summarize his or her results in writing for the court.

The conservator shall "have the same duties, powers and responsibilities as a guardian of a minor" (§93-13-259). A guardian of the estate of a person of unsound mind may be terminated when the funds of the ward have diminished to $2,000 or less "and there is no prospect of further receipts to come into the hands of the guardian" (§93-13-75). (See Mississippi Code, Title 93: Domestic Relations, Chapter 13: Guardians and Conservators, §93-13-5 et seq. for guardianship and conservatorship laws; Mississippi Code §93-13-111 for emergency temporary guardianship laws.)

*Missouri.* Probate court has jurisdiction over conservatorship and guardianship proceedings. Conservators may be appointed for any disabled person's estate, and guardians over any incapacitated person. An "incapacitated person" is defined as "one who is unable by reason of any physical or mental condition to receive and evaluate information or to communicate decisions to such an extent that he lacks capacity to meet essential requirements for food, clothing, shelter, safety or other care such that serious physical injury, illness, or disease is likely to occur" (Missouri Revised Statutes §475.010[9]). Thus, incapacity requires the existence of some physical or mental condition which puts the person at risk.

The concept of disability deals with the ability of an adult to manage his or her financial resources. A "disabled person" is one who is "unable by reason of any physical or mental condition to receive or evaluate information or to communicate decisions to such an extent that the person lacks the ability to manage financial resources" (§475.010[4][a]). Disability and incapacity must be proven by clear and convincing evidence. Special attention is given to those who seek spiritual healing:

> Nothing in this chapter shall be construed to constitute evidence of incapacity or partial incapacity of a person solely because such person refuses medical treatment upon the grounds that such person has consistently relied on prayer for healing in accordance with the religion of any church which teaches reliance on spiritual means for healing. (§475.011)

Notice of the guardianship or conservatorship hearing must be given to the proposed ward/conservatee a "reasonable time before the date set for the hearing" (§475.075[2]). The court shall immediately appoint an attorney to safeguard and advance the proposed ward's interests, although the court-appointed attorney may withdraw if the respondent hires private counsel to appear on his or her behalf. The court may require that the proposed ward be examined by a court-appointed physician, licensed psychologist "or other professional" who will then submit a written report to the court and to counsel for all parties. "Anything respondent says may be used at the court hearing, and in making the determination of incapacity or disability" (§475.075.4[4]).

The respondent has the right to be represented by an attorney, to have a jury trial, to present evidence in his or her behalf, to cross-examine witnesses who testify against him or her, to remain silent, to have the hearing opened or closed to the public as desired, and to be present at the hearing. The proposed ward also has "the right to a hearing conducted in accordance with the rules of evidence in civil proceedings, except as modified by this chapter" (§475.075.8[7]).

If an emergency situation is said to exist which presents a "substantial risk that serious physical harm will occur to his person or irreparable damage will occur to his property" (§475.075.11), the court may—after notifying such person's attorney and others as specified and after hearing—appoint a guardian or conservator *ad litem* for a period not to exceed thirty days. The orders may be extended from time to time, not exceeding thirty days each time. In Missouri, "a person who has been adjudicated incapacitated or disabled or both shall be presumed to be incompetent" (§475.078.3). The costs of the incapacity/disability hearings shall be paid by the individual's estate if he or she is found to be incapacitated or disabled.

The court will review the status of every ward and protectee under its jurisdiction at least once a year. The court may terminate a guardianship or conservatorship if the conservatorship estate is exhausted or "if the guardianship or conservatorship is no longer necessary for any other reason" (§475.083.2[2]). A guardian may not institutionalize his or her ward in a mental health or mental retardation facility "for more than thirty days for any purpose without court order except as otherwise provided by law" (§475.120.5).

The conservator of the estate must take possession of all of his or her ward's real and personal property and of rents, income, and all profits therefrom. "In all cases where the court deems it advantageous to continue the business of a protectee, such business may be continued by the conservator of the estate" (§475.155). (See Missouri Revised Statutes, Chapter 475: Probate Code—Guardianship, Section 475.010 et seq. for guardianship/conservatorship laws; Missouri Revised Statutes §475.075.11 for emergency temporary guardianship laws.)

*Montana.* Montana adopted the Uniform Probate Code but excluded the 1975 and 1977 Amendments. Title 72 contains the state's exceptions to the UPC. In particular, a critical provision in Montana's statutes that is *not* a part of the Uniform Probate Code states:

> Guardianship for an incapacitated person may be used only as is necessary to promote and protect the well-being of the person. The guardianship must be designed to encourage the development of maximum self-reliance and independence in the person and may be ordered only to the extent that the person's actual mental and physical limitations require it. An incapacitated person for whom a guardian has been appointed is not presumed to be incompetent and retains all legal and civil rights except those that have been expressly limited by court order or have been specifically granted to the guardian by the court (Montana Code Annotated §72-5-306)

District courts have jurisdiction to appoint guardians over the person of incapacitated persons and conservators over the estates of persons under other disability. "Incapacitated person" means "any person who is impaired by reason of mental illness, mental deficiency, physical illness or disability, chronic use of drugs, chronic intoxication, or other cause (except minority) to the extent that he lacks sufficient understanding or capacity to make or communicate responsible decisions concerning his person or which cause has so impaired the person's judgment that he is incapable of realizing and making a rational decision with respect to his need for treatment" (§72-5-101[1]). "Advanced age" is included in the descriptors permitting the appointment of a conservator in the State of Montana:

> Appointment of a conservator or other protective order may be made in relation to the estate and affairs of a person if the court determines that:
> a. the person is unable to manage his property and affairs effectively for reasons such as mental illness, mental deficiency, physical illness or disability, advanced age, chronic use of drugs, chronic intoxication, confinement, detention by a foreign power, or disappearance; and
> b. the person has property which will be wasted or dissipated unless proper management is provided or that funds are needed for the support, care, and welfare of the person or those entitled to be supported by him and that protection is necessary or desirable to obtain or provide funds. (§72-5-409[2])

The allegedly incapacitated person or any person interested in his or her welfare, including the county attorney, may file a petition seeking a finding of incapacity, and the court shall set a date for the hearing on the issue (§72-5-315). If an emergency is alleged to exist, the court may exercise the power of a guardian pending notice and hearing, or appoint a temporary guardian for the person for up to six months—with or without notice. While a petition for the appointment of a conservator is pending and "without notice to others, the court has power to preserve and apply the property of the person to be protected as may be required for his benefit or the benefit of his dependents" (§72-5-421).

Evidence to be submitted for the guardianship or conservatorship hearing must include reports from a court-appointed physician and, whenever possible, from a court visitor. The visitor will also interview the person who filed the petition, interview the person nominated to serve as guardian, and visit the current and proposed residence of the allegedly incapacitated individual.

> Whenever possible without undue delay or expense beyond the ability to pay of the alleged incapacitated person, the court, in formulating the judgment, shall utilize the services of any public or charitable agency that offers or is willing to evaluate the condition of the allegedly incapacitated person and make recommendations to the court regarding the most appropriate form of state intervention in his affairs. (§72-5-315[3])

The proposed ward may have counsel of his own choice, or the court may appoint counsel with the powers and duties of a guardian ad litem. The person alleged to be incapacitated is entitled to be present at the hearing in person, to present evidence, to cross-examine witnesses (including the court-appointed physician and the visitor), to trial by jury, and to have a closed hearing if requested. If the petition seeks a conservatorship of the estate, the court must appoint a lawyer to represent the allegedly incapacitated adult. The standard of proof is not clear and convincing; rather, it is "the court's satisfaction" (§72-5-316[1]).

The appointed guardian of an incapacitated person has the same powers, rights, and duties to his or her ward that a parent has for his or her unemancipated minor child. The guardian is entitled to the custody of the person of the ward and may establish the ward's residency either within or without the State of Montana. The conservator of the estate may, without court authorization, collect, hold, and retain assets of the estate; receive additions to the estate; continue or participate in the operation of any business or other enterprise; invest and reinvest estate assets; subdivide, develop, or dedicate land to public use; and allocate items of income or expense to either estate income or principal, as provided by law. (See Montana Code Annotated, Title 72: Estates, Trusts, and Fiduciary Relationships, Chapters 1-5: Uniform Probate Code, Part 3 [Chapter 5]: Guardians of Incapacitated Persons, §72-5-101 et seq. for guardianship/conservatorship laws; Montana Code Annotated §72-5-317 and 72-5-421 for emergency temporary guardianship and conservatorship laws.)

*Nebraska.* Nebraska adopted the Uniform Probate Code with modifications. County courts have exclusive original jurisdiction to appoint guardians for incapacitated people and conservators for people under other disability, and to process their accounts. The state's definition of an "incapacitated person" is "any person who is impaired by reason of mental illness, mental deficiency, physical illness or disability, chronic use of drugs, chronic intoxication, or other cause (except minority) to the extent that the person lacks sufficient understanding or capacity to make or communicate responsible decisions concerning himself or herself" (Nebraska Uniform Probate Code, Revised Statutes §30-2601[1]). The legislative intent supporting the State's code is as follows:

> The Legislature recognizes the need for providing mechanisms for intervening in the lives of certain persons who are impaired by reason of disability. It is the intent of the Legislature to authorize the use of guardianships and conservatorships for such intervention. It is also the intent of the Legislature to encourage the least restrictive alternative possible on the impaired person's exercise of personal and civil rights

consistent with the impaired person's need for services by encouraging judges to utilize limited guardianships if appropriate. (§30-2601.02)

A conservator of the estate and property affairs may be appointed if the court is satisfied by clear and convincing evidence that

(i) the person is unable to manage his or her property and property affairs effectively for reasons such as mental illness, mental deficiency, physical illness or disability, chronic use of drugs, chronic intoxication, confinement, or lack of discretion in managing benefits received from public funds, detention by a foreign power, or disappearance; and (ii) the person has property which will be wasted or dissipated unless proper management is provided, or that funds are needed for the support, care, and welfare of the person or those entitled to be supported by him or her and that protection is necessary or desirable to obtain or provide funds. (§30-2630[2])

Any interested person may file a petition for a guardian of the person and/or conservator of the estate. The court shall set a date for a hearing on the issues of incapacity. Notice must be served upon the proposed ward at least fourteen days prior to the hearing. Unless the proposed ward has retained counsel already, the court may appoint an attorney to represent him or her in the proceeding. If the petitioner requests the appointment of a temporary guardianship or conservatorship and the court finds reasonable cause in the petition to believe the allegations of potential harm made by the petitioner, the court may appoint a temporary guardian or conservator without notice for a period of ten days (which may be extended).

Medical evidence may be supplied to the court for the hearing by a court-appointed visitor and physician. The hearing may be closed to the public at the ward's request. The proposed ward has the right to appear at the hearing and to oppose the petition, to see and hear all evidence, to present evidence, to compel the attendance of witnesses, to cross-examine witnesses (including the court-appointed physician and visitor appointed by the court), to request that the hearing be closed, and to appeal any final orders or judgments. The standard of proof required is clear and convincing evidence. "After appointment, the ward may retain an attorney for the sole purpose of challenging the guardianship, the terms of the guardianship, or the actions of the guardian on behalf of the ward" (§30-2620[9]).

Unless waived by the court, the person appointed as guardian or conservator must successfully complete within three months of his or her appointment a training program approved by the State Court Administrator.

The guardian of an incapacitated person has the same rights, powers, and duties concerning his or her ward that a parent has toward his or her unemancipated minor child. (See Nebraska Uniform Probate Code, Revised Statutes, Chapter 30, §30-2619 et seq. for guardianship and conservatorship laws; Nebraska Uniform Probate Code §30-2626 and §30-2630.01 for emergency temporary guardianship and conservatorship laws.)

*Nevada.* Guardians are appointed for "insane or mentally incompetent persons" over both the person and estate of the allegedly incompetent individual (age eighteen or above). " 'Incompetent' includes any person who, by reason of mental illness, mental deficiency, advanced age, disease, weakness of mind or any other cause, is unable, without assistance, properly to manage and take care of himself or his property" (Nevada Revised Statutes §159.019). The jurisdiction for the appointment of a guardian is in any court having jurisdiction of the persons and/or estates of the incompetent person. Notice must be served by certified mail at least twenty days before the hearing, and the alleged incompetent must attend the hearing "unless good cause" is shown to exist.

The citation must state that the proposed ward "may be adjudged to be incompetent or of limited capacity and a guardian may be appointed for him" (§159.048[1]). Upon the filing of the petition, the court may appoint an investigator (an employee of a social service agency, family service officer of the court, or other qualified person) who will file a written report stating his opinion of the proposed ward's incapacity. The hearing will be held to "show cause why a guardian should not be appointed for the proposed ward" (§159.047[1]).

The proposed ward has the right to appear at the hearing to oppose the petition and the right to be represented by an attorney, who may be appointed for him by court if he is unable to retain one. If requesting appointment of a temporary guardian, the petitioner must present facts showing that the proposed ward faces substantial and immediate risk of financial loss or physical harm or needs immediate medical attention and that he or she lacks the capacity to respond to the risk of loss or harm. The court may appoint a temporary guardian for a limited period without notice, although a hearing must be held within ten days to determine the need to extend the temporary guardianship (§159.052). The petitioner has the burden of proving that the appointment of a guardian is necessary.

A guardian of the person is charged with the care, custody, and control of the ward, supplying him or her with food, clothing, and shelter, and authorizing medical, surgical, dental, psychiatric, psychological, hygienic, or other remedial care. A guardian of the estate may, with prior approval of the court, sell, lease, or place in trust any property of the ward, and may borrow money for the account of the ward. A guardian of the person and of the estate must file annual reports that are reviewed by the court. (See Nevada Revised Statutes, Chapter 159: Guardianships, §159.013 et seq. for guardianship laws; Nevada Revised Statutes §159.052 for emergency temporary guardianship laws.)

*New Hampshire.* Probate courts have jurisdiction to appoint guardians of the person and conservators of the estate of an incapacitated person. The term " 'incapacity' . . . shall be construed to mean or refer to any person who has suffered, is suffering or is likely to suffer substantial harm due to an inability to provide for his personal needs for food, clothing, shelter, health care or safety or an inability to manage his or her property or financial affairs. Inability to provide for personal needs or to manage property shall be evidenced by acts or occurrences, or statements which strongly indicate imminent acts or occurrences" (New Hampshire Revised Statutes §464-A:2). "Incapacity" is a legal rather than medical disability and should be measured by functional limitations.

> All evidence of inability must have occurred within six months prior to the filing of the petition and at least one incidence of such behavior must have occurred within twenty days of the filing of the petition for guardianship. Isolated instances of simple negligence or improvidence, lack of resources or any act, occurrence or statement if that act, occurrence or statement is the product of an informed judgment shall not constitute evidence of inability to provide for personal needs or to manage property. (§464-A:2[XI])

Any relative, interested person, or public official may petition the court for a finding of incapacity and the appointment of a guardian or conservator. The allegedly incapacitated individual has an absolute and unconditional right to legal counsel and to receive notice of the hearing fourteen days in advance unless, in the eyes of the petitioner and the court, an "emergency" exists. If the proposed ward opposes the appointment of a temporary guardian, the court will not make the appointment without a hearing attended by the proposed ward, his or her attorney, the petitioner and the proposed temporary guardian. The petitioner carries the burden of proof to show need for the temporary guardian. "Appointment of a temporary guardian shall not be evidence of incapacity in the petition, hearing or finding, for regular guardianship powers" (§464-A:12[V]). The guardianship hearing shall be closed unless the proposed ward or his or her counsel requests that it be open.

The proposed ward must be present at the guardianship hearing unless he or she is physically unable to attend or the court receives a physician's affidavit at least twenty-four hours prior to the hearing stating: (1) that the physical, emotional, or psychological condition of the ward is such that attending the hearing will cause the proposed ward to suffer harm; or (2) that the proposed ward lacks the ability to understand the nature and consequence of the proceedings (§464-A:8). Proof of incapacity must be established "beyond a reasonable doubt."

"Under no circumstances shall the court appoint as guardian a person excluded from consideration by name in the instrument" (§464-A:10[II]). Once appointed, a guardian may establish the ward's place of abode within or without the state of New Hampshire. He or she may admit a ward to a state institution with prior approval of the probate court or without prior approval of the court upon written certification by a licensed physician if "the placement is in the ward's best interest and is the least restrictive placement available" (§464-A:25[2]). The conservator or guardian of the estate shall have the power—without court authorization—to perform every act that "persons of prudence, discretion and intelligence and exercising judgment and care as in the management of their own affairs would perform for the purposes of the guardianship" (§464-A:26[II]). Although the guardian or conservator of the estate is required to file an annual accounting with the probate court, the court may choose to rule that an annual report is not needed.

The guardian of the person must file an annual report under oath within thirty days after the anniversary date of the initial appointment. All costs incurred by the imposition of a guardianship shall be borne by the proposed ward except in cases in which the petitioner filed the petition in bad faith. In such cases, the petitioner will bear all costs of the proceeding. The costs incurred in the petition for a conservatorship will be paid by the estate of the new conservatee. (See New Hampshire Revised Statutes, Title 44, Guardians and Conservators, Chapter 464-A, §464-A1 et seq. for guardianship and conservatorship laws; New Hampshire Revised Statutes §464-A:12 for emergency temporary guardianship/conservatorship laws.)

*New Jersey.* The Superior Court has jurisdiction over the determination and appointment of guardianships for the person and/or estate of an allegedly incapacitated person. An incapacitated person is "a person who is impaired by reason of mental illness or mental deficiency to the extent that he lacks sufficient capacity to govern himself and manage his affairs" (New Jersey Permanent Statutes, §3B:1-2). The term may also be used to designate an individual who is "impaired by reason of physical illness or disability, chronic use of drugs, chronic alcoholism or other cause (except minority) to the extent that he lacks sufficient capacity to govern himself and manage his affairs" (§3B:1-2).

In civil actions or proceedings held to determine lack of capacity or for the appointment of a guardian for an alleged incapacitated person, the trial on the issue of incapacity may be held without a jury unless it is demanded by the alleged incapacitated person or another adult on his behalf. The proposed ward must be notified of the incapacity hearing twenty days before the hearing is to be held. However, if the court decides good cause exists, it may shorten or waive this notice entirely.

The court may appoint legal counsel for the alleged incapacitated person if necessary, and will appoint a guardian *ad litem.* Medical reports from two reputable physicians must be submitted to the court as evidence to support the petition for a guardianship. Once appointed, a guardian is not personally liable for the support of the ward, but has control of the person and/or property of the ward.

The Superior Court may, at some point, rule that the incapacitated person has returned to competence:

> The Superior Court may adjudicate that the incapacitated person has returned to capacity and restore to him his estate if the court is satisfied that he has recovered his sound reason and is fit to govern himself and manage his affairs, or, in the case of an incapacitated person determined to be mentally incapacitated by reason of chronic alcoholism, that he has reformed and become habitually sober and has continued so for one year next preceding the commencement of the action, and in the case of an incapacitated person determined to be mentally incapacitated by reason of chronic use of drugs that he has reformed and has not been a chronic user of drugs for one year next preceding the commencement of the action. (3B:12-28)

New Jersey also permits the appointment of a conservator to manage the estate of a conservatee if—and only if—the proposed conservatee wants such assistance. (See New Jersey Permanent Statutes, Title 3B, Administration of Estates—Decedents and Others, §3B:12-1, §3B:12-25 et seq. for guardianship laws; New Jersey Permanent Statutes §3B:12-32 for emergency temporary guardianship laws.)

*New Mexico.* New Mexico adopted the Uniform Probate Code, with significant omissions and amendments. District courts have jurisdiction to appoint guardians over the person of incapacitated people and conservators over the estates of persons under other disability. An "incapacitated person" is one who "demonstrates over time either partial or complete functional impairment by reason of mental illness, mental deficiency, physical illness or disability, chronic use of drugs, chronic intoxication or other cause, except minority, to the extent that he is unable to manage his personal affairs or he is unable to manage his property or financial affairs or both" (New Mexico Statutes Annotated §45-5-101[F]). "Inability to manage his estate or financial affairs or both" signifies "gross mismanagement, as evidenced by recent behavior, or one's income and resources or medical inability to manage one's income and resources that has led or is likely in the near future to lead to financial vulnerability" (§45-5-101[H]). "Inability to manage his personal care" means "the inability, as evidenced by recent behavior, to meet one's needs for medical care, nutrition, clothing, shelter, hygiene or safety so that physical injury, illness or disease has occurred or is likely to occur in the near future" (§45-5-101[G]).

Any interested person may petition the district court for the appointment of a guardian of the person and/or conservator of the estate for the person who is alleged to be incapacitated, and the court will assign a hearing date for the issues of incapacity. At least fourteen days' notice must be given before the hearing takes place. If a temporary guardian or temporary conservatorship is sought, the court may make the emergency appointment without notice. The duration of the temporary powers will not exceed sixty days unless extended to ninety days by court order. Also,

> on two days' notice to the party who obtained the appointment of a temporary conservator without notice or on such shorter notice to that party as the court may prescribe, the person to be protected may appear and move for dissolution or modification of the court's order, and, in that event, the court shall proceed to hear and determine such motion as expeditiously as the ends of justice require. (§45-5-408[C])

An attorney with the duties of a guardian ad litem must represent the proposed ward/conservatee at the hearing. The court must appoint a visitor to interview the person seeking the appointment and must appoint a qualified healthcare professional to examine the proposed ward prior to the hearing. The hearing will be closed unless the alleged incapacitated person requests otherwise.

Upon the request either of the petitioner or of the alleged incapacitated person, the court will schedule a jury trial. Prior to the hearing, a guardian *ad litem* will interview the proposed ward and present his or her declared position to the court. The guardian *ad litem* will also interview the visitor, the qualified healthcare professional and the proposed guardian, and review all reports that are submitted to the court. If the court determines that the alleged incapacitated person retains the capacity to care for himself, the court will dismiss the petition.

"A guardian of an incapacitated person has the same powers, rights and duties respecting the incapacitated person that a parent has respecting his unemancipated minor child" (§45-5-312[B]). Among the powers exercised through a conservator in respect to the ward's estate are: making gifts, entering into contracts, and "creat[ing] revocable or irrevocable trusts of property of the estate which may extend beyond the disability or life of the person" (§45-5-402.1[B][3][e]). (See New Mexico Statutes Annotated, Chapter 45: Uniform Probate Code, §45-5-101 et seq. for guardianship and conservatorship laws; New Mexico Statutes Annotated §45-5-310 and §45-5-408 for temporary guardianship/conservatorship laws.)

*New York.* Both the supreme court and county courts (and New York City's Surrogate's Court) have jurisdiction over the appointment of guardians for the person and/or estate of incapacitated people. The court may appoint a guardian for the person if the court determines the appointment to be necessary to provide for personal needs of that individual, including food, clothing, shelter, health care, or safety, and/or to manage property and the financial affairs of that person, provided that person agrees to that appointment or is incapacitated as defined under Article 81 of the Mental Hygiene Law. Any guardian appointed under Article 81 will be granted only those powers necessary to provide for the personal needs and/or property management of the incapacitated person in such manner as is appropriate to the individual and which must constitute the least restrictive form of intervention (New York Mental Hygiene Law §81.02[a][2]). In New York, the determination of incapacity is based upon clear and convincing evidence that a person is likely to suffer harm because

1. the person is unable to provide for personal needs and/or property management; and
2. the person cannot adequately understand and appreciate the nature and consequences of such inability. (§81.02[b])

Once the petition is filed by an interested adult, the court will set a date no more than twenty-eight days from the date of the filing on which the order to show cause is returnable, and may set a date less than twenty-eight days from that date "for good cause shown." A copy of the petition must be delivered personally to the proposed ward not less than fourteen days prior to the return date of the order to show cause—or within a shorter time period "for good cause shown." Notice must be given to the person alleged to be incapacitated in large type, plain language, and in a language other than English if necessary. The notice specifies both the rights that will be lost by the individual should a guardian be appointed and the individual's right to fight the petition (rights including demanding a trial by jury and representation by a lawyer, which the court will appoint if necessary).

At the time the order to show cause is issued, the court will also appoint a court evaluator, drawn from a list maintained by the office of court administration, who has "knowledge of property management, personal care skills, the problems associated with disabilities, and the private and public resources available for the type of limitations the person is alleged to have, including, but not limited to, an attorney-at-law, physician, psychologist, accountant, social worker, or nurse" (§81.09[b][1]). The evaluator will meet with the person alleged to be incapacitated and explain the nature and possible consequences of the proceeding and the general powers and duties of a guardian. Upon completion of his or her interview, the evaluator will file a written report with the court. The report must contain specific conclusions, including:

> How is the person alleged to be incapacitated functioning with respect to the activities of daily living and what is the prognosis and reversibility of any physical and mental disabilities, alcoholism or substance dependence? The response to this question shall be based on the evaluator's own assessment of the person alleged to be incapacitated to the extent possible, and where necessary, on the examination of assessments by third parties, including records of medical, psychological and/or psychiatric examinations obtained pursuant to subdivision (d) of this section. As part of this review, the court evaluator shall consider the diagnostic and assessment procedures used to determine the prognosis and reversibility of any disability and the necessity, efficacy, and dose of each prescribed medication. (§81.09[5][vii])

The proposed ward must be present at the hearing unless "completely unable to participate." He or she has the right to present evidence, call witnesses, including expert witnesses, to cross examine all witnesses, and to request that the court records be sealed. It should be noted, however, that "the court may, for good cause shown, waive the rules of evidence" (§81.12[b]). At the commencement of the proceeding or at any subsequent state of the proceeding prior to the actual appointment of a guardian, the court may appoint a temporary guardian upon a showing of danger in the reasonably foreseeable future to the health and well-being of the allegedly incapacitated person, or of danger of waste, misappropriation, or loss of property of the allegedly incapacitated person (M. H. L. §81.23[a]).

Once appointed, a guardian must file initial and annual reports and "visit the incapacitated person not less than four times a year or more frequently as specified in the court order" (§81.20[4, 5]). The guardian's powers include the power to make gifts, to create revocable or irrevocable trusts of property of the estate, to change beneficiaries under insurance and annuity policies, and to apply for government and private benefits. The court may grant extensive additional powers to the guardian: control of travel, choice of the ward's place of abode, type of personal care or assistance, and consent to or refusal of routine or major medical or dental treatment. (See New York State Consolidated Laws, Mental Hygiene, Title EA81, Article 81: Proceedings for Appointment of a Guardian for Personal Needs or Property Management, §81.01 et seq. for guardianship laws; New York State Consolidated Laws §81.23 for temporary guardianship laws.)

*North Carolina.* Clerks of Superior Court have original jurisdiction in the State of North Carolina for the appointment of guardians of the person and/or estate for incompetent people. A guardianship may be established over an "incompetent adult" who "lacks sufficient capacity to manage the adult's own affairs or to make or communicate important decisions concerning the adult's person, family, or property whether such lack of capacity is due to mental illness, mental retardation, epilepsy, cerebral palsy, autism, inebriety, senility, disease, injury, or similar cause or condition" (North Carolina General Statutes, Chapter 35A, §35A-1101[7]).

Within five days after the filing of the petition, the clerk must issue a written notice of the date, time, and place for the hearing on the issues of incompetence. Notice must be given not less than ten days before the hearing to the alleged incompetent, his or her counsel or guardian *ad litem*, next of kin and such other people as are designated by the clerk. Unless the proposed ward has retained counsel, the clerk must appoint as guardian *ad litem* an attorney to represent him or her.

The alleged incompetent has the right, upon request, to a trial by jury. "The petitioner and the respondent are entitled to present testimony and documentary evidence, to subpoena witnesses and the production of documents, and to examine and cross-examine witnesses" (§35A-1112[b]). The clerk may order a multidisciplinary evaluation of the respondent and also order the respondent to attend the evaluation (§35A-111[b]). The required report must be filed with the clerk within thirty days and may be considered at the hearing for adjudication of incompetence. If "good cause" can be shown, a temporary or interim guardian can be appointed immediately. Decisions are made by the superior court clerk or the jury:

> d. If the finder of fact, whether the clerk or the jury, finds by clear, cogent, and convincing evidence that the respondent is incompetent, the clerk shall enter an order adjudicating the respondent incompetent. The clerk may include in the order findings on the nature and extent of the ward's incompetence. (§35A-1112[d])
> e. Following an adjudication of incompetence, the clerk shall either

appoint a guardian ... or, for good cause shown, transfer the proceeding for the appointment of a guardian to any county identified in G.S. 35A-1103. (§35A-1112[e])

"In every instance the clerk shall base the appointment of a guardian or guardians on the best interest of the ward" (§35A-1214). The newly appointed guardian of the person may establish the ward's place of abode within or without North Carolina, may consent to medical, legal, psychological, or other professional care, and is entitled to be reimbursed out of the ward's estate for expenditures incurred in the performance of his or her duties as guardian. The guardian of the estate has control of all of the ward's estate—"any interest in real property, ... intangible personal property, and tangible personal property, and includes any interest in joint accounts or jointly held property" (§35A-1202[5]). (See North Carolina General Statutes, Chapter 35A: Incompetency and Guardianship, Subchapter 1: Proceedings to Determine Incompetence, Article 1: Determination of Incompetence, §35A-1101 et seq. for guardianship laws; North Carolina General Statutes §35A-1114 for temporary guardianship laws.)

*North Dakota.* North Dakota follows the statutes of the Uniform Probate Code and has adopted the following Amendments: 1975, 1977, 1979, part of 1982, 1989, and 1991. District court of each county has jurisdiction in all proceedings to appoint guardians over the person of incapacitated people. An "incapacitated person" is "any adult person who is impaired by reason of mental illness, mental deficiency, physical illness or disability, or chemical dependency to the extent that the person lacks capacity to make or communicate responsible decisions concerning that person's matters of residence, education, medical treatment, legal affairs, vocation, finance, or other matters, or which incapacity endangers the person's health or safety" (North Dakota Century Code §30.1-26-01[2]).

A conservator may be appointed in a protective proceeding over an individual's estate and financial affairs if the court determines that:

a. The person is unable to manage the person's property and affairs effectively for reasons such as mental illness, mental deficiency, physical illness or disability, advanced age, chronic use of drugs, chronic intoxication, confinement, detention by a foreign power, or disappearance.
b. The person has property which will be wasted or dissipated unless proper management is provided. (§30.1-29-01[2])

Upon the filing of a petition by an interested person for the appointment of a guardian and/or conservator, the court shall set a date for a hearing. If the interested petitioner files for a temporary guardianship on the basis of an "emergency," notice to the proposed ward is not required prior to the court's ruling on the application for the temporary. The court shall appoint an attorney to act as guardian *ad litem* and appoint a visitor to interview both the proposed guardian and the proposed ward. The court may appoint an attorney to represent the person to be protected in a conservatorship or protective proceeding.

Written medical evidence must be submitted by a court-appointed physician or clinical psychologist in guardianship proceedings. The report must contain information on any current incapacity or disability, a medical prognosis or psychological evaluation, "[a] statement as to how or in what manner any underlying condition of physical or mental health affects the proposed ward's ability to provide for personal needs" (§30.1-28-03[5][c]), and information concerning the proposed ward's capacity to participate in the court proceedings.

The proposed ward must be present at the hearing unless "good cause" exists. He or she has the right to present evidence and to cross-examine all witnesses. The hearing may be closed at the proposed ward's request. "Age, eccentricity, poverty, or medical diagnosis alone is not sufficient to justify a finding of incapacity" (§30.1-28-04[2][a]). Need for a guardian or conservator must be proven by clear and convincing evidence.

The guardian is entitled to custody of the person of the ward and may establish the ward's residence within or without the state of North Dakota. "No guardian may voluntarily admit a ward to a mental health facility or state institution for a period of more than forty-five days without a mental health commitment proceeding or other court order" (§30.1-28-12[2]). The conservator must post bond equal to the value of the ward's estate plus one year's income and file a complete inventory of the protected person's estate within ninety days after appointment. Unless the court directs otherwise, the conservator must file annual accountings for his or her administration of the trust. (See North Dakota Century Code, Article V: Protection of Persons Under Disability and Their Property, Chapter 30.1-26 et seq. for guardianship and conservatorship laws; North Dakota Century Code §30.1-28-10 for emergency temporary guardianship laws.)

*Ohio.* The probate court has exclusive jurisdiction to appoint guardians over the person and/or estate of an incompetent adult. "Incompetent" is defined as "any person who is so mentally impaired as a result of a mental or physical illness or disability, or mental retardation, or as a result of chronic substance abuse, that he is incapable of taking proper care of the person's self or property or fails to provide for the person's family or other persons whom the person is charged by law to provide, or any person confined to a correctional institution within this state" (Ohio Revised Code, Title 21, Chapter 11, Section 2111.01[D]). (Note: Any *competent* adult who is physically infirm may petition the court to place his person and/or his property under a conservatorship with the court; the petitioner either may grant specific powers to his conservator or may limit the powers granted by law to the conservator or court.)

The court must give the proposed ward a seven-day notice prior to the appointment of a guardian but may, at its discretion, appoint an emergency guardian with no notice when the alleged incompetent has not yet been placed under a guardianship, an emergency exists, and immediate action is required to prevent significant injury to his or her person or estate (§2111.021). The alleged incompetent has the right to be represented by independent counsel of his choice or to have counsel at court expense if indigent, to have a friend or family member of his choice present, and to have evidence of an independent expert evaluation introduced. A court-appointed physician or other qualified person may be asked to submit medical evidence to address the issue of incompetence during the hearing (§2111.031). Upon service of notice, a probate court investigator will be appointed to investigate the alleged incompetent and report back to the court. The burden of proving incompetency at the hearing is by clear and convincing evidence.

The guardian of the incompetent is required to file a report with the court (including present address of guardian and ward "and other pertinent facts") two years after the date of appointment and biennially thereafter. Included in that report will be "a statement by a licensed physician, licensed clinical psychologist, licensed independent social worker, licensed professional clinical counselor, or mental retardation team that has evaluated or examined the ward within three months prior to the date of the report as to the need for continuing the guardianship" (§2111.49[A][1][i]). The guardian of the incompetent's estate must file a full inventory of the real and personal property of the ward within three months after appointment as guardian. The guardian may petition the court for an order to terminate the guardianship when the estate of the ward is valued at ten thousand dollars or less. (See Ohio Revised Code, Title 21, Chapter 11, §2111.01 et seq. for guardianship laws; Ohio Revised Code, §2111.02 for temporary guardianship laws.)

*Oklahoma.* District courts have jurisdiction over the appointment of guardians for the person and estate of an incapacitated person. An "incapacitated person" is a person eighteen years of age or older:

a. who is impaired by reason of:
   1. mental illness . . . ,
   2. mental retardation or developmental disability . . . ,
   3. physical illness or disability,
   4. drug or alcohol dependency . . . , or
   5. such other similar cause, and
b. whose ability to receive and evaluate information effectively or to make and to communicate responsible decisions is impaired to such an extent that said person:
   1. lacks the capacity to meet essential requirements for his physical health or safety, or
   2. is unable to manage his financial resources. (Oklahoma State Statutes §30-1-111.10)

Whenever the term "incompetent person" is used in the Oklahoma statutes to describe a man or woman who has been found to be impaired in a manner listed above, the term has the same meaning as "incapacitated person." However, a finding that an individual is *partially* incapacitated does not constitute a finding of legal incompetence (§30-1-111.19).

Oklahoma provides its citizens with ready access to information about guardianship/conservatorship matters:

The Administrative Office of the Courts shall prepare a guardianship and conservatorship handbook for distribution to the district courts. The handbook shall be written in clear, simple language and shall include information about the laws and procedures which apply to adult guardianships and conservatorships and the duties and responsibilities of such guardians and conservators. In conjunction with the guardianship handbook, the Administrative Office of the Courts shall develop a summary of the duties of guardians and conservators including, but not limited to, statutory notices, timetables, and required court approvals. The summary shall emphasize the significance of timely accountability to the court and to the ward as well as the sanctions and penalties which may be imposed for failure to comply with the requirements of the law or orders of the court. Copies of the handbook shall be made available to the public through the offices of the district court clerks. (§30-1-124)

The court will set a date for a hearing on the petition for no more than thirty days after the filing of the petition (§30-3-109). Notice of the guardianship hearing must be personally served on the proposed ward at least ten days before the time set for the hearing (§30-3-110[C][1]). A special guardian may be appointed by the court for a period of ten days without notice upon the initial filing of the petition if submitted "evidence" shows both incapacity and an imminent threat to the person or financial resources of the proposed ward (§30-3-115[A]).

The allegedly incapacitated person has the right to: be present at the hearing, compel the attendance of witnesses, present evidence, cross-examine witnesses, appeal adverse orders and judgments, representation by a court-appointed attorney upon request, and to request that the proceedings be closed to the public. "If the subject of the proceeding does not request the appointment of an attorney and the court determines that the subject of the proceeding is capable of making an informed decision regarding the appointment of an attorney, the court shall not appoint an attorney" (§30-3-107[B][2][c]). If the judge believes an examination of the proposed ward is necessary, he or she will order that an evaluation be done. Medical evidence may consist of a report completed by a physician, psychologist, social worker, or other expert; such an evaluation must be submitted to the court prior to the hearing.

A ward may lose any or all of the following rights as a result of the appointment of a guardianship of the person: to vote; to serve as a juror; to drive; to be licensed or continue to practice his or her profession; to make personal medical decisions "including but not limited to decisions to withhold or withdraw life-sustaining procedures, to donate organs, to undergo elective surgery, or to consent to routine or necessary medical or other professional care, treatment or advice" (§30-3-113[B][5]). A guardian of the person may also establish the ward's place of abode at any place within the county without permission of the court. When a guardianship of the estate is established, the ward may lose his or her right to: appoint an agent to act for him or her; enter into contracts; grant conveyances; or make gifts of property (§30-3-113[C]).

The court may, after inquiry, appoint a person as guardian "in the best interests of the ward" even if such a person is a convicted felon, is insolvent, has declared bankruptcy in the prior five years, is under a financial obligation to the new ward, or has interests that conflict with those of the ward (§30-4-105). If the inquiry determines one of these situations exists, further inquiry must determine whether the appointment of the particular individual is in the best interests of the ward. A guardian of the property may receive fees for his or her work as guardian for an amount up to seven and one-half percent of the income of the ward's estate. (See Oklahoma State Statutes, Title 30: Oklahoma Guardianship Act, §30-1-101 et seq. for guardianship laws; Oklahoma State Statutes, §30-3-115 for temporary guardianship laws.)

*Oregon.* Oregon has adopted provisions similar to the Uniform Guardianship and Protective Proceedings Act but with many modifications. Probate courts and commissioners have exclusive jurisdiction over the appointment of guardians of the ward's person and personal effects and of conservators to manage the real and personal estate of incapacitated adults. The term "incapacitated" refers to "a condition in which a person's ability to receive and evaluate information effectively or to communicate decisions is impaired to such an extent that the person presently lacks the capacity to meet the essential requirements for the person's physical health or safety. 'Meeting the essential requirements for physical health and safety' means those actions necessary to provide the health care, food, shelter, clothing, personal hygiene and other care without which serious physical injury or illness is likely to occur" (Oregon Revised Statutes §125.005[5]). Oregon's statutes contain a separate definition for a "financially incapable" condition requiring the appointment of conservators.

At least fifteen days prior to the final date for the filing of objections to the appointment of a guardian or conservator for an incapacitated person, the person alleged to be incapacitated must be personally served notice. Notice must be written in language that is "reasonably understandable by the respondent" and printed in type size no smaller than twelve-point type. It must include information concerning the right of the proposed ward/conservatee to request an attorney, to have access to personal records, to request a hearing, to present evidence and cross-examine witnesses, to request that the guardian's power (if any) be limited by the court, and to request removal or modification of the guardianship order. "The court for good cause shown may provide for a different method or time of giving notice" (§125.075[5]).

The court will appoint a visitor who has sufficient training to evaluate the "functional capacity and needs" of the respondent and to file a report to the court within fifteen days of his or her appointment, although the court may extend the time period upon showing of necessity and good cause. The visitor, who may be an officer, employee, or special appointee of the court, shall also interview the proposed fiduciary and may, subject to laws of confidentiality, interview "any physician or psychologist who has examined the respondent or protected person" (§125.150[3]).

With a finding of an emergency based on clear and convincing evidence of need, a temporary guardianship not to exceed thirty days may be appointed. Notice for the temporary must be given either two days before or within two days of the actual appointment, and a hearing must be held within two days of the appointment if requested.

The court will determine whether a guardian is needed based upon clear and convincing evidence, from information contained in the petition, the report of the court visitor, the report of a physician or psychologist who examined the respondent (if an examination was done), and evidence presented at the hearing. Among the general powers and duties of a guardian are the following: determining the abode of the incapacitated person within or without the state of Oregon; providing for the care, comfort, and maintenance of the ward; consenting to or refusing consent for health care, as defined in ORS 127.505; and applying the ward's money and property for the ward's support, care, and education (§125.315).

> Before a guardian may place an adult protected person in a mental health treatment facility, a nursing home or other residential facility, the guardian must file a statement with the court informing the court that the guardian intends to make the placement. . . . In addition to the requirements of ORS 125.070(1), the notice given to the protected person must clearly indicate the manner in which the protected person may object to the proposed placement. The guardian may thereafter place the adult protected person in a mental health treatment facility, a nursing home or other residential facility without further court order. (§125.320[3])

The guardian must file a verified written report about his or her ward with the court within thirty days after each anniversary of his or her appointment. The report must be completed on the form provided by §125.325. Bonds for the guardian and conservator may be waived by the court "for good cause shown." The conservator may, among other things, sell the protected person's principal residence "only with the prior approval of the court" (§125.430[1]) and, with court approval, create revocable or irrevocable trusts of property of the estate. Oregon's code lists twenty-eight additional acts the conservator may perform without prior court approval (see §125.445). (See Oregon Revised Statutes, Chapter 125: Protective Proceedings, §125.005 et seq. for guardianship and conservatorship laws; Oregon Revised Statutes, §125.600 et seq. for temporary guardianship/conservatorship laws.)

*Pennsylvania.* Guardianship matters are within the jurisdiction of the Orphans' Court Division of the court of common pleas. The court may appoint a guardian of the incapacitated individual's person and/or estate. An adult resident of Pennsylvania (or nonresident having property in the state) is deemed to be incapacitated if he or she is "an adult whose ability to receive and evaluate information effectively and communicate decisions in any way is impaired to such a significant extent that he is partially or totally unable to manage his financial resources or to meet essential requirements for his physical health and safety" (Pennsylvania Consolidated Statutes §5501). Any interested person may file a petition for a guardianship.

Notice of the hearing must be submitted to the proposed ward no less than twenty days in advance of the hearing in simple language and large type, stating the purpose of the proceeding and the rights that can be lost as a result of the hearing. The court may eliminate the mandated twenty-day notice and grant notice "as shall appear . . . to be feasible" for the appointment of an emergency temporary guardian of the person and/or of the estate. Unless the allegedly incapacitated person objects, the hearing will be closed to the public. The hearing may be held at the residence of the allegedly incapacitated person.

"In appropriate cases, counsel shall be appointed to represent the alleged incapacitated person in any matter for which counsel has not been retained by or on behalf of that individual" (§5511[a]). The ruling must be based upon clear and convincing evidence. To establish incapacity, the petitioner must

> present testimony, in person or by deposition from individuals qualified by training and experience in evaluating individuals with incapacities of the type alleged by the petitioner, which establishes the nature and extent of the alleged incapacities and disabilities and the person's mental, emotional and physical condition, adaptive behavior and social skills. The petition must also present evidence regarding the services being utilized to meet essential requirements for the alleged incapacitated person's physical health and safety, to manage the person's financial resources or to develop or regain the person's abilities; evidence regarding the types of assistance required by the person and as to why no less restrictive alternatives would be appropriate; and evidence regarding the probability that the extent of the person's incapacities may significantly lessen or change. (§5518)

Once a guardianship is established, the guardian must encourage the incapacitated person to "participate to the maximum extent of his abilities in all decisions which affect him, to act on his own behalf whenever he is able to do so, and to develop or regain, to the maximum extent possible, his capacity to manage his personal affairs" (§5521[a]). Unless specifically included in the court's orders, a guardian or emergency guardian may not:

> 1. Consent on behalf of the incapacitated person to an abortion, sterilization, psychosurgery, electroconvulsive therapy or removal of a healthy body organ.
> 2. Prohibit the marriage or consent to the divorce of the incapacitated person.
> 3. Consent on behalf of the incapacitated person to the performance of any experimental biomedical or behavioral medical procedure or participation in any biomedical or behavioral experiment. (§5521[d])

Guardians must file annual reports with the court concerning the well-being of the person and/or the status of the estate. (See Pennsylvania Con-

solidated Statutes, Title 20: Decedents, Estates and Fiduciaries, Chapter
55: Incapacitated Persons, §5501 et seq. for guardianship laws; Pennsylvania Consolidated Statutes §5513 for emergency temporary guardianship laws.)

*Rhode Island.* Rhode Island prefaces its chapters on limited guardianship
and guardianship of adults with the following paragraph:

> The legislature finds that adjudicating a person totally incapacitated and
> in need of a guardian deprives that person of all his or her civil and legal
> rights and that this deprivation may be unnecessary. The legislature fur-
> ther finds that it is desirable to make available, the least restrictive form
> of guardianship to assist persons who are only partially incapable of
> caring for their needs. Recognizing that every individual has unique needs
> and differing abilities, the legislature declares that it is the purpose of this
> act to promote the public welfare by establishing a system that permits
> incapacitated persons to participate as fully as possible in all decisions
> affecting them; that assists such persons in meeting the essential require-
> ments for their physical health and safety, in protecting their rights, in
> managing their financial resources, and developing or regaining their
> abilities to the maximum extent possible; and that accomplishes these
> objectives through providing, in each case, the form of assistance that
> least interferes with the legal capacity of a person to act in his or her own
> behalf. This chapter shall be liberally construed to accomplish this pur-
> pose. (Rhode Island General Laws, Title 33, §33-15-1)

Jurisdiction in guardianship/conservatorship matters is in probate
court (in the city or town where the proposed ward resides or where an
out-of-state proposed ward has property), with appeal to superior and
supreme courts. A guardian of the person and/or conservator of the estate
may be appointed for "any person who is unable to manage his or her
estate and is unable to provide for his or her personal health and safety as
a result of mental and/or physical disability as determined by the court on
the basis of oral or written evidence under oath from a qualified physician" (§33-15-8). Notice of the hearing will be given the allegedly incapacitated person fourteen days prior to the court date for the hearing; if an
emergency is said to exist, the period of required notice will be reduced
to five days or shorter, as determined by the court. The notice will be in
large type, in simple language, and will highlight both the individual's
hearing rights and the consequences of a guardianship appointment.
There is no appeal from the appointment of a temporary or emergency
guardianship.

Upon the filing of a guardianship petition, the court will appoint a guardian *ad litem* (who need not be an attorney) to visit the respondent, explain the nature of the guardianship appointment and hearing procedure, and file a report with the court three days prior to the hearing. If the respondent contests the petition, its powers, or the nominee for guardian, the court shall appoint an attorney. The allegedly incapacitated individual's treating physician must submit a decision-making assessment of the proposed ward's functional capacities, although "any professional whose training and experience aid in the assessment of functional capacity may be permitted to provide expert testimony regarding the functional assessment of the respondent" (§33-15-5[5]). At the hearing, the respondent may compel the attendance of witnesses, present evidence, and confront and cross-examine witnesses. The standard of proof used in Rhode Island is clear and convincing evidence.

Guardianship accounts containing an inventory and appraisal of all real and personal property of the new ward must be filed within thirty days of the appointment (or longer time as permitted by the probate court). He or she must file an annual account in subsequent years. Similarly, a guardian of the person must file an annual status report regarding the well-being of the ward. "Notwithstanding any provision of the general laws to the contrary, no municipality, its officers, and/or employees, individually or otherwise, shall be held civilly liable for failure to monitor guardianship estates" (§33-15-26).

The guardian may be authorized to sell the real estate of his or her ward "for the purpose of making a better investment or for any other proper purpose" (§33-15-32). A conservator may not be a person "convicted of a felony offense involving a charge of forgery, embezzlement, obtaining money under false pretenses, bribery, larceny, extortion, conspiracy to defraud, burglary, breaking and entering, or any other offense involving fraud or theft" (§33-15-44). A conservator must file inventories and bonds as is required of guardians of estates. (See Rhode Island General Laws, Title 33: Probate Practice and Procedure, Chapter 33-15: Limited Guardianship and Guardianship of Adults, §33-15-1 et seq. for guardianship and conservatorship laws; Rhode Island General Laws §33-15-8.1 for temporary guardianship/conservatorship laws.)

*South Carolina.* The Uniform Probate Code has been adopted with substantial modifications and excluding the 1975 an 1977 amendments. Guardianships over the person of incapacitated adults and conservatorships over the estate of people under other disability are in the jurisdiction of probate court. The court "may appoint a guardian as requested if it is satisfied that the person for whom a guardian is sought is incapacitated and that the appointment is necessary or desirable as a means of providing continuing care and supervision of the person of the incapacitated person" (South Carolina Code Annotated, §62-5-304). An "incapacitated person" is defined as "any person who is impaired by reason of mental illness, mental deficiency, physical illness or disability, advanced age, chronic use of drugs, chronic intoxication or other cause (except minority) to the extent that he lacks sufficient understanding or the capacity to make or communicate responsible decisions concerning his person or property" (S§62-5-101). A conservatorship can be established over an adult in a protective proceeding.

> Appointment of a conservator or other protective order may be made in relation to the estate and affairs of a person if the court determines that (i) the person is unable to manage his property and affairs effectively for reasons such as mental illness, mental deficiency, physical illness or disability, advanced age, chronic use of drugs, chronic intoxication, confinement, detention by a foreign power, or disappearance, and (ii) the person has property which will be wasted or dissipated unless proper management is provided, or that funds are needed for the support, care, and welfare of the person of those entitled to be supported by him and the protection is necessary or desirable to obtain or provide funds. (§62-5-401[2])

Upon the filing of a guardianship and/or conservatorship petition by an interested person, the court shall set a date for the hearing on the issues of incapacity. Notice must be given the proposed ward at least twenty days in advance. A court-appointed physician and second examiner will evaluate the proposed ward in a guardianship proceeding and submit written reports to the court, as will a visitor appointed by the court. One or more court-appointed physicians will examine the proposed ward in a conservatorship proceeding if the alleged disability is advanced age, physical illness or disability, mental illness or deficiency, chronic use of drugs, or chronic intoxication.

The court may make an emergency appointment of a temporary guardian for a period not to exceed six months, with or without notice. "If a temporary guardian is appointed without notice under this section, a hearing to review the appointment must be held after notice and within thirty days after the appointment of the temporary guardian" (§62-5-310[d]).

The allegedly incapacitated person is entitled to be present at the hearing, to see and hear all evidence bearing upon his or her incapacity, to present evidence (including testimony by a physician of his or her own choosing), to request a closed hearing, and to cross-examine witnesses, including the court-appointed examiners. Legal counsel having the powers of a guardian *ad litem* will be appointed if the proposed ward does not have an attorney.

If a guardian is appointed, he or she will have "the same powers, rights, and duties respecting his ward that a parent has respecting his unemancipated minor child" (§62-5-312[a]). The guardian may establish the ward's residence within or without the State of South Carolina and give consent for medical or professional care and treatment. The guardian must make an annual report to the court concerning the condition of his or her ward.

A conservator must file an annual report to the court summarizing his or her administration of the protected person's trust. Without court input, the conservator may "employ persons, including attorneys, auditors, investment advisors, or agents even though they are associated with the conservator" (§62-5-424[B][16]). With court approval, he or she may buy or sell an estate asset (including land) in another state at public or private sale, subdivide or develop land to public use, and mortgage or encumber an asset for a period of time extending within or beyond the term of the conservatorship. The conservator may petition the court to terminate the conservatorship when the protected person's estate reaches a value of less than $5,000. (See South Carolina Code Annotated, Article 5: Protection of Persons Under Disability and Their Property, §62-5-101 et seq. for guardianship and conservatorship laws; South Carolina Code Annotated §62-5-310 for emergency temporary guardianship laws.)

*South Dakota.* South Dakota has adopted the full Uniform Probate Code without significant modifications. Cases are heard by county courts. A guardian may be appointed for "an individual whose ability to respond to people, events, and environments is impaired to such an extent that the individual lacks the capacity to meet the essential requirements for his health, care, safety, habilitation or therapeutic needs without the assistance or protection of a guardian" (South Dakota Codified Laws, §29A-5-302). A conservator may be appointed over the estate of an individual "whose ability to respond to people, events and environments is impaired to such an extent that the individual lacks the capacity to manage property or financial affairs or to provide for his support or the support of legal dependents without the assistance or protection of a conservator" (§29A-5-303). The appointment of a guardian or of a conservatorship does not constitute a general finding of legal incompetence unless the court so orders.

Upon the filing of the petition and of an evaluation report, the court will issue notice fixing the date, hour and location for a hearing to take place within sixty days. The evaluation, which must summarize the condition of the person alleged to need protection, must be signed by a physician, psychiatrist or licensed psychologist; but the court, "for good cause shown, may grant leave to file the petition without an evaluation report" (§29A-5-306[9]). Notice of the hearing on the petition for the appointment of a guardian, conservator, or both, must be personally served on the adult alleged to need protection at least fourteen days prior to the hearing. If the proposed ward is absent, a copy of the notice must be published for three consecutive weeks in a newspaper of the county where the proceeding is pending, with the last publication to occur at least ten days prior to the hearing.

If there is a showing in the petition that a delay may result in "significant harm to the person or the estate" (§29A-5-315), the court may appoint a temporary guardian or conservator with no notice to the proposed ward. Within five days of such an appointment, however, the temporary guardian or conservator must mail a copy of the order of appointment to the protected person.

An attorney may be appointed if requested or needed, and a court representative will visit the proposed ward and submit a written report to the court unless the court otherwise orders. "The evaluation report, statement of financial resources, and written report of the court representative shall be sealed upon filing and may not be made a part of the public record of the proceeding" (§29A-5-311). If no attorney or court representative is appointed, the adult alleged to need protection must attend the hearing.

The hearing on the petition to appoint a guardian or conservator may be closed to the public. The proposed ward is entitled to attend the hearing, oppose the petition, be represented by an attorney of his own choice, demand a jury trial, present evidence, compel the attendance of witnesses, and to confront and cross-examine all witnesses. The standard of proof to be applied will be that of clear and convincing evidence.

A guardian must file a report with the court within sixty days of the first anniversary of his or her appointment and annually thereafter; a conservator must file an inventory of the ward's real and personal estate within ninety days following appointment and an annual report within a sixty-day period following the first anniversary of the appointment. These accounting requirements may be waived by the court. Without prior court authorization, a conservator may exercise numerous powers, among them being the right to invest and reinvest estate funds; "manage, control, convey, divide, exchange, partition and sell at public or private sale, for cash or for credit, the real and personal property of the estate" (§29A-5-411)[5]); borrow from a financial institution operated by the conservator; and to employ attorneys, accountants, investment advisors, or others and to pay them reasonable compensation. (See South Dakota Codified Laws, Chapter 29A-5: South Dakota Guardianship and Conservatorship Act,

§29A-5-101 et seq. for guardianship/conservatorship laws; South Dakota Codified Laws §29A-5-315 for temporary guardianship and conservatorship laws.)

*Tennessee.* Conservatorships over the person and/or estate of disabled persons are the province of "a court exercising probate jurisdiction or any other court of record of any county in which there is venue" (Tennessee Code §34-13-101[a]). Such courts include the chancery, circuit, law and equity and probate courts. A "disabled person" is defined as "any person eighteen (18) years of age or older determined by the court to be in need of partial or full supervision, protection and assistance by reason of mental illness, physical illness or injury, developmental disability or other mental or physical incapacity" (§34-11-101[7]). The term "fiduciary" is also used in Tennessee's code to mean "conservator."

The hearing on issues raised in the conservatorship petition must be held not less than seven days nor more than sixty days from the date of service of notice on the proposed ward or the date a guardian *ad litem* is appointed, whichever is later; and the hearing date may be extended for "good cause." If the petition contains an allegation stating that the disabled person faces a life-threatening situation, the court may hold the hearing in less than the minimum seven-day period of time. A guardian *ad litem* (who must be a lawyer licensed to practice in the state of Tennessee) will be appointed by the court to represent the allegedly disabled person unless the person is already represented by adversary counsel. The guardian *ad litem* "is not an advocate for the respondent but has a duty to determine what is best for the respondent's welfare" (§34-11-107[d][1]). The guardian *ad litem*'s written report must be submitted to the court at least three days prior to the date set for a hearing on the matter.

The rights that may be removed from the proposed ward must be stated in the conservatorship petition. They may include (but are not limited to): the right to vote, to dispose of property, to execute instruments, to make purchases, to enter into contractual relationships, to hold a valid Tennessee driver's license, to give or refuse consent to medical/mental examinations and treatment or hospitalization, and to do "any other act of legal significance the court deems necessary or advisable" (§34-13-104[8]. If the petition seeks to manage the property of the respondent, it must describe the proposed plan for the management of the respondent's property, a list of the proposed ward's monthly expenses, and a list of the individual's income from all sources. "If the financial information about the respondent is unknown to the petitioner, a request that the court enter an order authorizing the petitioner to investigate the respondent's property" (§34-13-104[9][B]) must be included in the petition.

A physician's or psychologist's written report must be presented to the court as medical evidence.

> If the respondent has not been examined within ninety (90) days of the filing of the petition, cannot get out to be examined or refuses to be voluntarily examined, the court shall order the respondent to submit to examination by a physician or, where appropriate, a psychologist identified in the petition as the respondent's physician or psychologist or, if the respondent has no physician or psychologist, a physician or psychologist selected by the court" (§34-13-105[a]).

The proposed ward has the right to demand a hearing on the issue of disability, to present and confront and cross-examine witnesses, to appeal the court's final decision, to attend any hearing, and to have an attorney ad litem appointed to advocate for his or her interests. If the court determines that a conservator is needed, the court shall "enumerate the powers removed from the [new ward] and vested in the conservator" (§34-13-107[2]). The disabled person or any interested person may petition the court at any time for a modification or termination of the conservatorship. (See Tennessee Code, Title 34: Guardianship—Estates of Incompetents, Chapter 11: Guardianships and Conservatorships Generally, §34-11-101 et seq. for conservatorship laws; see Tennessee Code §34-11-108(b) for emergency temporary conservatorships.)

*Texas.* Jurisdiction over the appointment of guardians for the person and/or estate of incapacitated people is vested in county, probate, and district courts. " 'Incapacitated person' means: (A) a minor; (B) an adult individual who, because of a physical or mental condition, is substantially unable to provide food, clothing, or shelter for himself or herself, to care for the individual's own physical health, or to manage the individual's own financial affairs; (C) a missing person; or (D) a person who must have a guardian appointed to receive funds due the person from a governmental source" (Texas Probate Code §601[13]). The proposed ward must be personally served with a copy of the notice and citation concerning the guardianship petition (§111). As of September 1, 1993, age cannot be the sole factor used in determining whether or not a guardian should be appointed over any adult (§602).

Ample notice of the hearing must be given. In its discretion, however, the court may appoint a temporary guardian with no notice at all if "substantial evidence" suggests the targeted individual is incapacitated and in need of immediate protection to prevent personal or financial harm (§875). Although a written application for the temporary appointment may be filed before the court assigns a temporary guardian, it must be filed not later than the end of the next business day following the court's emergency appointment. Once a filing is made for a temporary guardianship, the court will appoint an attorney to represent the proposed ward in all subsequent guardianship proceedings if independent counsel has not been retained by or for the allegedly incapacitated individual.

The court is required to determine during a pretrial hearing whether a proposed permanent guardian has an interest adverse to that of the respondent. Also before a hearing is held for the appointment of a guardian, "current and relevant medical, psychological, and intellectual testing records of the proposed ward must be provided to the attorney ad litem appointed to represent the proposed ward unless . . . the court makes a finding on the record that no current or relevant records exist and examining the proposed ward for the purpose of creating the records is impractical" (§686[a]). The judge may appoint a guardian *ad litem* to represent the interests of the allegedly incapacitated person in the guardianship hearing and a court visitor to evaluate the proposed ward and file a written report. The person filing an application to create the guardianship must give the court a document written by a licensed physician that is based on an examination performed "not earlier than the 120th day before the date of the filing of the application" (§687[a]). The medical document must describe the nature and degree of incapacity, provide a prognosis concerning the severity of the incapacity, state how or in what manner the proposed ward is affected by his or her physical health, "describe the precise physical and mental conditions underlying a diagnosis of senility, if applicable" (§687[a][5], and include any other information requested by the court.

A proposed ward in an involuntary guardianship proceeding may request a trial by jury. Unless the court determines that a personal appearance is not necessary, the proposed ward must be present at the hearing on issues of his or her incapacity (§685[a]). The standard of proof is a preponderance of the evidence (§684[b]). Costs of the proceeding, including the cost of the guardian *ad litem* or court visitor, are to be born by the new ward's estate. The ward or any interested person may petition the court informally to discontinue or modify the guardianship.

Powers and duties of guardians of the person include the right to physical possession of the ward and to establish the ward's legal domicile; the duty of protect, control, and care for the ward; the duty to provide food, clothing, shelter, and medical care for the ward; and the power to consent to all medical, psychiatric, and surgical treatment for the ward other than in-patient psychiatric commitment. Among other powers and with the approval of the court, the guardian of the estate may "compound a bad or doubtful debt due or owing to the estate" (§774[a][3]), settle disputed claims or litigation concerning the estate, and purchase or exchange property. The operation of a farm, ranch, factory, or other business is addressed in Section 779 of the Texas Probate Code:

> If the ward owns a farm, ranch, factory, or other business and if the farm, ranch, factory, or other business is not required to be sold at once for the payment of debts or other lawful purposes, the guardian of the estate on order of the court shall carry on the operation of the farm, ranch, factory, or other business, or cause the same to be done, or rent the same, as shall appear to be the best interests of the estate. In deciding, the court shall consider the condition of the estate and the necessity that may exist for the future sale of the property or business for the payment of a debt, claim, or other lawful expenditure and may not extend the time of renting any of the property beyond what appears consistent with the maintenance and education of a ward or the settlement of the estate of the ward.

"A guardian is entitled to be reimbursed from the guardianship estate for all necessary and reasonable expenses incurred in performing any duty as a guardian" (§666). As amended in 1993 and 1995, the following rules guide compensation for guardians and temporary guardians:

> a. The court may authorize compensation for a guardian or a temporary guardian serving as a guardian of the person alone from available funds of the ward's estate. The court shall set the compensation in an amount not exceeding five percent of the ward's gross income. In determining whether to authorize compensation for a guardian under this section, the court shall consider the ward's monthly income from all sources and whether the ward receives medical assistance under the state Medicaid program.
> b. The guardians or temporary guardian of an estate is entitled to a fee of five percent of the gross income of the ward's estate and five percent of all money paid out of the estate on a court finding that the guardian or temporary guardian has taken care of and managed the estate in compliance with the standards of this chapter. In this section, the term "money paid out" does not include any money loaned, invested, or paid over on the settlement of the guardianship or a tax-motivated gift made by the ward. If the fee is an unreasonably low amount, the court may authorize reasonable compensation to a guardian or temporary guardian for services as guardian or temporary guardian of the estate. (§665)

When the estate of a ward becomes exhausted, the guardianship of the estate of a ward will be settled and closed. (See Texas Probate Code, Chapter XIII: Guardianship, Part 1, Subpart A, §601 et seq. for guardianship laws; Texas Probate Code §875 et seq. for emergency temporary guardianship laws.)

*Utah.* The Uniform Probate Code, with 1975 Official Amendments, was adopted with modifications; 1977, 1979, 1982, 1984, and 1987 amendments were not adopted. Guardianships are appointed in district courts over the person of an incapacitated individual. An "incapacitated person" is

> any person whose decision-making process is impaired by reason of mental illness, mental deficiency, physical illness or disability, chronic use of drugs, chronic intoxication, or other cause, except minority, or the person has unusually bad judgment, highly impaired memory, or severe loss of behavior control, to the extent that the person is unable to care for his or her personal safety or is unable to attend to and provide for such necessities as food, shelter, clothing, and medical care, without which physical injury or illness may occur. (Utah Uniform Probate Code §75-5-201[18]).

Protective proceedings can be held to appoint a conservator of the estate and affairs of a person if the court determines that the person

> a. is unable to manage the person's property and affairs effectively for reasons such as mental illness, mental deficiency, physical illness or disability, chronic use of drugs, chronic intoxication, confinement, detention by a foreign power, or disappearance; and
> b. has property which will be wasted or dissipated unless proper management is provided or that funds are needed for the support, care, and welfare of the person or those entitled to be supported by the person and protection is necessary or desirable to obtain or provide funds. (§75-5-401[2])

When the petition for appointment is filed with the court, the court shall set a date for a hearing on the issues of incapacity. The court may appoint a temporary guardian or conservator with no notice at all if an emergency is believed to exist. The appointment of the temporary guardian will continue for a specified period "not to exceed thirty days pending notice and hearing" (§75-5-310[1]), and a hearing will be held within five days on the issues raised in the petition.

Unless the allegedly incapacitated person has counsel of his/her own, the court shall appoint an attorney to present him/her in the protective proceeding. The cost of this attorney will be paid by the proposed ward, "unless the court determines that the petition is without merit, in which case the attorney fees and court costs shall be paid by the person filing the petition" (§75-5-303[2]). A court-appointed physician or court visitor (described as "a person who is trained in law, nursing, or social work and is an officer, employee, or special appointee of the court with no personal interest in the proceedings" (§75-5-308) may examine the person alleged to be incapacitated and submit a written report to the court.

The proposed ward has the right to be present at the hearing, to present evidence, to cross-examine witnesses (including the court-appointed physician and the visitor), and to a trial by jury. Courts must prefer limited guardianships or conservatorships as opposed to full guardianships or conservatorships, and may grant the full guardianship/conservatorship only if no other alternative exists.

If the incapacitated person made a nomination of guardian prior to his or her incapacity, the nomination will guide the court's appointment "unless that person is disqualified or the court finds other good cause why the person should not serve as guardian" (§75-5-311[3]). A guardian of the person has the following powers and duties, except as modified by order of the court: to determine the ward's place of abode within or without the State of Utah; to provide for the care, comfort, and maintenance of the ward, including the ward's clothing, furniture, vehicles, and other personal effects; to give consents and approvals needed to enable the ward to receive medical or other professional care, counsel, treatment, or service; and to attend to the ward's financial matters (as described in §75-5-312[d]) if a conservator for the estate has not been appointed.

> Upon receipt of a petition for appointment of a conservator or other protective order for reason other than minority, the court shall set a date for hearing. . . . If the alleged disability is mental illness, mental deficiency, physical illness or disability, advanced age, chronic use of drugs, or chronic intoxication, the court may direct that the person to be protected be examined by a physician designated by the court, preferably a physician who is not connected with any institution in which the person is a patient or is detained. The court may send a visitor to interview the person to be protected. The visitor may be a guardian ad litem or an officer or employee of the court. (§75-5-407[2])

Having determined that the proposed ward is an incapacitated adult, the court has the power (either directly or through a conservator) to make gifts, convey or release his or her interests in property including marital property rights, exercise or release powers as trustee, enter into contracts, create revocable or irrevocable trusts of property of the estate which may extend beyond the ward's disability or life, exercise options to purchase securities or other property, and change beneficiaries under insurance and annuity policies and surrender the policies for their cash value. The court may also, "without appointing a conservator, . . . authorize, direct, or ratify any contract, trust, or other transaction relating to the [newly] protected person's financial affairs or involving his estate if the court determines that the transaction is in the best interests of the protected person" (§75-5-409[2]). If a conservator or corporate fiduciary "is guilty of gross impropriety in handling the property of the ward" (§75-7-302[4]), the court may impose a fine in an amount not to exceed $5,000. (See Utah Uniform Probate Code, Title 75, Chapter 5: Protection of Persons Under Disability and Their Property, §75-5-301 et seq. for guardianship/conservatorship laws; Utah Uniform Probate Code §75-5-310 for emergency temporary guardianship/conservatorship laws.)

*Vermont.* Guardianships may be appointed in probate court over the person and property of mentally disabled adults (eighteen and above). A "mentally disabled person" is "a person who has been found to be . . . unable to manage, without the supervision of a guardian, some or all aspects of his or her personal care or financial affairs" (Vermont Statutes §3061[1]). " 'Unable to manage his or her personal care' means the inability, as evidenced by recent behavior, to meet one's needs for medical care, nutrition, clothing, shelter, hygiene or safety so that physical injury, illness or disease has occurred or is likely to occur in the near future" (§3061[2]). A mentally disabled person who is unable to manage his or her financial affairs has demonstrated "gross mismanagement, as evidenced by recent behavior, of one's income and resources which has led or is likely in the near future to lead to financial vulnerability" (§3061[3]).

Guardianships may also be requested to control "spendthrifts," defined by §2681 as "every person who is liable to be put under guardianship on account of excessive drinking, gambling, idleness or debauchery."

> When a person by excessive drinking, gambling, intemperate habits, idleness or debauchery, spends, wastes or lessens his estate and exposes himself or his family to want or suffering and requires or is likely to require aid or assistance from the department of social welfare for himself or his family, the commissioner of social welfare or a member of the family may present a complaint to the probate court setting forth the facts and asking to have a guardian appointed. (§2682)

A hearing will be held not less that fifteen nor more than thirty days after a petition is filed, although the hearing may be continued for up to fifteen additional days "for good cause shown." This requirement for notice may be dismissed by the court to address an emergency situation threatening harm to the targeted elder. Legal counsel will be appointed for the respondent in involuntary guardianship proceedings, although such counsel may withdraw after a guardian is appointed. The court-appointed attorney will be compensated from the allegedly disabled person's estate. If the proposed ward is unable to communicate with or advise counsel, the court may also appoint a guardian *ad litem*. The court will require an examination of the allegedly disabled person (to be paid for out of his or her estate) by a qualified mental health professional within thirty days of the filing of the petition.

The respondent and petitioner "may attend the hearing and testify" (§3068[a]), and may subpoena, present, and cross-examine witnesses, including those who prepared the evaluation. "The court shall not be bound by the evidence contained in the evaluation, but shall make its determination upon the entire record" (§3068[c]). If the court finds the respondent is not mentally disabled, it will dismiss the petition and seal the records of the entire proceeding.

If the court rules by clear and convincing evidence that the proposed ward is mentally disabled, a guardian will be appointed whose powers include choosing or changing the new ward's residence; approving or disallowing the ward's request to sell or encumber personal or real property; receiving, investing, and spending all wages, compensation, public benefits, and pensions and liquidating resources "for the benefit of the ward"; and consenting to surgery or other medical procedures (§3069). At its discretion, the court may appoint a guardian who is not a resident of the state of Vermont. In an "emergency," the guardian may move his or her ward out of the ward's private home and into a nursing home, group home, or similar facility without petitioning the probate court for prior permission.

Grounds for the termination or modification of the guardianship include:

1. the death of the guardian;
2. the failure of the guardian to file an annual report;
3. the failure of the guardian to act in accord with an order of the court;
4. a change in the ability of the ward to manage his or her personal care or financial affairs;
5. a change in the capacity or suitability of the guardian for carrying out his or her powers and duties; . . .
6. Marriage shall not extinguish a guardian's authority. (§3077)

(See Vermont Statutes, Title 14: Decedents' Estates and Fiduciary Relations, Part IV: Fiduciary Relations, Chapter III: Guardian and Ward, Subchapter XII: Total and Limited Guardianship for Mentally Disabled Adults, §3060 et seq. for guardianship laws; Vermont Statutes §3081 for code regarding temporary guardians.)

*Virginia.* Circuit courts have general jurisdiction for the appointment of guardians over the person and conservators of the estate of an incapacitated person. An "incapacitated person" is defined as

> an adult who has been found by a court to be incapable of receiving and evaluating information effectively or responding to people, events, or environments to such an extent that the individual lacks the capacity to (i) meet the essential requirements for his health, care, safety, or therapeutic needs without the assistance or protection of a guardian or (ii) manage property or financial affairs or to provide for his or her support or for the support of legal dependents without the assistance or protection of a conservator. A finding that the individual displays poor judgment, alone, shall not be considered sufficient evidence that the individual is an incapacitated person within the meaning of this definition. A finding that a person is incapacitated shall be construed as a finding that the person is "mentally incompetent" as that term is used in Article II, Section 1 of the Constitution of Virginia and Title 24.2 unless the court order entered pursuant to this chapter specifically provides otherwise. (Virginia Code §37.1-134.6)

Once a petition is filed, the court will set a date, time, and location for a hearing. The person alleged to be incapacitated must be served "reasonable notice" prior to the hearing. The notice to the proposed ward or conservatee must include the following statements in conspicuous, bold print:

WARNING

AT THE HEARING YOU MAY LOSE MANY OF YOUR RIGHTS. A GUARDIAN MAY BE APPOINTED TO MAKE PERSONAL DECISIONS FOR YOU. A CONSERVATOR MAY BE APPOINTED TO MAKE DECISIONS CONCERNING YOUR PROPERTY AND FINANCES. THE APPOINTMENT MAY AFFECT CONTROL OF HOW YOU SPEND YOUR MONEY, HOW YOUR PROPERTY IS MANAGED AND CONTROLLED, WHO MAKES YOUR MEDICAL DECISIONS, WHERE YOU LIVE, WHETHER YOU ARE ALLOWED TO VOTE, AND OTHER IMPORTANT RIGHTS. (§37.1-134.10[D], effective January 1, 1998)

On the filing of every petition for guardianship or conservatorship, a guardian *ad litem* shall be appointed by the court to represent the interests of the proposed ward, and the guardian ad litem will personally appear at all court proceedings and conferences. An evaluation report must be prepared by one or more licensed physicians, psychologists, or licensed professionals "skilled in the assessment and treatment of the physical or mental conditions of the respondent as alleged in the petition" (§37.1-134.11). However, if a report "is not available," the court may either proceed with the hearing or order a report and delay the hearing until the report is completed. The person preparing the evaluation is "immune from civil liability for any breach of patient confidentiality made in furtherance of his duties" (§37.1-134.11[C]).

The court may appoint legal counsel for the respondent if he or she is not represented by an attorney. The allegedly incapacitated person is entitled to a jury trial, and may compel the attendance of witnesses, present evidence on his or her own behalf, and cross-examine witnesses. The respondent is entitled to be present at the hearing, but his or her attendance is not required.

> In determining the need for a guardian or a conservator, and the powers and duties of any needed guardian or conservator, consideration shall be given to the following factors: the limitations of the respondent; the development of the respondent's maximum self-reliance and independence; the availability of less restrictive alternatives including advance directives and durable powers of attorncy; the extent to which it is necessary to protect the respondent from neglect, exploitation, or abuse; the actions needed to be taken by the guardian or conservator; and the suitability of the proposed guardian or conservator. (§37.1-134.13, effective January 1, 1998)

Clear and convincing evidence must guide the court's decision. The guardian need not be appointed for a person who has selected an agent under an appropriate advance directive, nor need a conservator be appointed for a person who has appointed an agent under a durable power of attorney. A guardian may, however, "seek court authorization to revoke, suspend or otherwise modify a durable power of attorney" and may seek the court's permission to "modify the designation of an agent under an advance directive" (§37.1-137.1). The guardian must visit the incapacitated person "as often as necessary" and file an annual report to the local department of social services.

The conservator must take care of and preserve the estate of the incapacitated person and manage it "to the best advantage" (§37.1-137.3[B]). Among other powers, the conservator may without prior court authorization "initiate a proceeding (i) to revoke a power of attorney . . . , (ii) to seek a divorce, or (iii) to make an augmented estate election." (§37.1-137.4[6]). (See Virginia Code, Title 37.1: Institutions for the Mentally Ill; Mental Health Generally, Chapter 4, Article 1.1: Guardianship and Conservatorship, §37.1-134.6 et seq. for guardianship laws; no provisions in code for temporary or emergency guardianships as such, although §37.1-

134.19 makes provisions for situations "when no guardian or conservator [is] appointed within one month of adjudication.")

*Washington.* Superior court of each county has the power to appoint a guardian for the person and/or estate of an "incapacitated person." "[A] person may be deemed incapacitated as to person when the superior court determines the individual has a significant risk of personal harm based upon a demonstrated inability to adequately provide for nutrition, health, housing, or physical safety" (Revised Code of Washington, §11.88.010[1][a]). A person may be deemed incapacitated as to his or her estate "when the superior court determines the individual is at significant risk of financial harm based upon a demonstrated inability to adequately manage property or financial affairs" (RCW §11.88.010[1][b]).

In Washington, a determination of incapacity is a legal rather than medical decision, and age, eccentricity, poverty, or medical diagnosis alone shall not be sufficient to justify a determination of incapacity. The terms "incompetent," "disabled," or "not legally competent," "as those terms are used in the Revised Code of Washington to apply to persons incapacitated under this chapter, those terms shall be interpreted to mean 'incapacitated' persons" (§11.88.010[1][f]).

The court may, in its discretion, appoint limited guardians for people and/or estates of incapacitated people who, while capable of managing some personal and financial affairs, still need protection and assistance. Any interested person or entity may file a petition for appointment of a qualified person as guardian over an incapacitated person "without liability attaching to a petitioner acting in good faith and upon reasonable basis" (§11.88.030). A copy of the petition must be served upon the allegedly incapacitated person and a guardian ad litem not more than five days after the petition is filed, and notice of the hearing must be personally served not less than ten days before the hearing. All petitions shall be heard within sixty days unless an extension of time is requested by a party or the guardian *ad litem* within the sixty-day period and granted "for good cause shown."

Notice to the alleged incapacitated person shall include the following, in capital letters, double-spaced, and in a type size not smaller than ten-point type:

IMPORTANT NOTICE

PLEASE READ CAREFULLY

A PETITION TO HAVE A GUARDIAN APPOINTED FOR YOU HAS BEEN FILED IN THE COUNTY SUPERIOR COURT BY . . . . . . IF A

GUARDIAN IS APPOINTED, YOU COULD LOSE ONE OR MORE OF THE FOLLOWING RIGHTS:

(1) TO MARRY OR DIVORCE;

(2) TO VOTE OR HOLD AN ELECTED OFFICE;

(3) TO ENTER INTO A CONTRACT OR MAKE OR REVOKE A WILL;

(4) TO APPOINT SOMEONE TO ACT ON YOUR BEHALF;

(5) TO SUE AND BE SUED OTHER THAN THROUGH A GUARDIAN;

(6) TO POSSESS A LICENSE TO DRIVE;

(7) TO BUY, SELL, OWN, MORTGAGE, OR LEASE PROPERTY;

(8) TO CONSENT TO OR REFUSE MEDICAL TREATMENT;

(9) TO DECIDE WHO SHALL PROVIDE CARE AND ASSISTANCE;

(10) TO MAKE DECISIONS REGARDING SOCIAL ASPECTS OF YOUR LIFE.

UNDER THE LAW, YOU HAVE CERTAIN RIGHTS.

YOU HAVE THE RIGHT TO BE REPRESENTED BY A LAWYER OF YOUR OWN CHOOSING. THE COURT WILL APPOINT A LAWYER TO REPRESENT YOU IF YOU ARE UNABLE TO PAY OR PAYMENT WOULD RESULT IN A SUBSTANTIAL HARDSHIP TO YOU.

YOU HAVE THE RIGHT TO ASK FOR A JURY TO DECIDE WHETHER OR NOT YOU NEED A GUARDIAN TO HELP YOU.

YOU HAVE THE RIGHT TO BE PRESENT IN COURT AND TESTIFY WHEN THE HEARING IS HELD TO DECIDE WHETHER OR NOT YOU NEED A GUARDIAN. IF A GUARDIAN AD LITEM IS APPOINTED, YOU HAVE THE RIGHT TO REQUEST THE COURT TO REPLACE THAT PERSON. (§11.88.030[4][B])

The proposed ward must be present at the final hearing on the petition unless his or her presence is waived by the court for good cause other than mere inconvenience. The allegedly incapacitated person is entitled to independent legal counsel at the county's expense if necessary. A physician or psychologist (with expertise in incapacity) selected by the guardian ad litem must have examined the proposed ward within thirty days of submitting a report to the court. A jury trial is available, and the standard of proof is clear, cogent, convincing evidence. *"Unless otherwise ordered, any powers of attorney or durable powers of attorney shall be revoked upon appointment of a guardian or limited guardian of the estate"* (§11.88.095[5], emphasis added).

Within three months after his/her appointment and annually thereafter, the guardian of the person and/or estate must file a personal care plan for the incapacitated person and/or a verified inventory of the incapacitated person's property. If, in paying all just claims against the estate from the incapacitated person's assets the estate nears exhaustion and not all bills can be paid, "preference shall be given to (a) the expenses of administration including guardian's fees, attorneys' fees, and court costs. . . ." (RCW §11.92.035[1]). (See Revised Code of Washington (RCW), Title 11—Probate and Trust Law, Chapters 11.88 and 11.92, §11.88.005 et seq. and §11.92.010 et seq. for guardianship laws; a petitioner may move for emergency "temporary relief" under RCW Chapter 7.40.)

*West Virginia.* Circuit courts have jurisdiction over the appointment of guardianships of the person and conservators of the estates of protected persons. "Protected person" means

> an adult individual, eighteen years of age or older, who has been found by a court, because of mental impairment, to be unable to receive and evaluate information effectively or to respond to people, events, and environments to such an extent that the individual lacks the capacity: (A) To meet the essential requirements for his or her health, care, safety, habilitation, or therapeutic needs without the assistance or protection of a guardian; or (B) to manage property or financial affairs or to provide for his or her support or for the support of legal dependents without the assistance or protection of a conservator. A finding that the individual displays poor judgment, alone, will not be considered sufficient evidence that the individual is a protected person within the meaning of this subsection. (West Virginia Code §44A-1-4[3])

The petition for an appointment of a guardian and/or conservator must include a report by a licensed psychologist or physician evaluating the condition of the alleged protected person. The written report must specify the nature of the individual's incapacity, "including the person's specific cognitive and functional limitations" (§44A-2-3), adaptive behavior and social skills, and the type and scope of the guardianship or conservatorship needed. Once the petition is filed, all pleadings, documents, and exhibits contained in the court file will be considered confidential and not available for public inspection.

Upon the filing of the petition, the court will determine the date, hour and location for a hearing to be held within sixty days. Notice of the hearing and a copy of both the petition and the evaluation report must be given to the allegedly mentally handicapped individual fourteen days before the hearing. The notice must contain the following statement in large print about possible consequences of the proceeding:

### POSSIBLE CONSEQUENCES OF A COURT FINDING THAT YOU ARE INCAPACITATED

At the hearing you may lose many of your rights. A guardian may be appointed to make personal decisions for you. A conservator may be appointed to make decisions concerning your property and finances. The appointment may affect control of how you spend your money, how your property is managed and controlled, who makes your medical decisions, where you live, whether you are allowed to vote and other important rights. (§44A-2-6)

A temporary guardian or temporary conservator may be appointed for up to forty-five days (and extended for an additional forty-five days "for good cause shown") upon a court finding that an immediate need exists. The temporary appointment will be made only upon "timely and adequate notice to the protected person after appointment of counsel and after all other protections have been afforded, in accordance with due process of law" (§44A-2-14[c]).

The proposed ward's presence is required in court unless he or she refuses, cannot attend, or his or her presence would be harmful. Counsel is mandated in every case. The alleged protected person has the right to an independent expert of his or her choice to perform an examination and present evidence to the court. The proposed ward's hearing rights include the right to attend the hearing, oppose the petition, present evidence, compel the attendance of witnesses, and to confront and cross-examine all witnesses. The hearing will be closed to the public. The standard of proof required is clear and convincing evidence. The court will make "specific findings of fact and conclusions of law in support of any orders entered" (§44A-2-9[e]), and provide a transcript of the proceedings upon request for the purposes of an appeal.

Once appointed, a guardian is to visit the protected person at least once every six months in order to know of the protected person's capabilities. The guardian must seek prior court authorization to change the protected person's residence to another state, to deviate from his or her living will or medical power of attorney, or to revoke or amend his or her durable power. A conservator of a protected person will apply estate income and principal for the individual's care, and may not revoke or amend the protected person's durable power of attorney without prior court approval. (See West Virginia Code, Chapter 44A, West Virginia Guardianship and Conservatorship Act, §44A-1-1 et seq. for guardianship laws; §44A-2-14 for temporary guardianships and conservatorships.)

*Wisconsin.* Circuit courts have jurisdiction over petitions for guardianship, and incompetent and spendthrift adults (eighteen or older) are subject to guardianship of the person and/or of the estate. " 'Incompetent' means a person adjudged by a court of record to be substantially incapable of managing his or her property or caring for himself or herself by reason of infirmities of aging, developmental disabilities, or other like incapacities. Physical disability without mental incapacity is not sufficient to establish incompetence" (Wisconsin Statutes §880.01[4]). The term "infirmities of aging" means "organic brain damage caused by advanced age or other physical degeneration in connection therewith to the extent that the person so afflicted is substantially impaired in his or her ability to adequately provide for his or her own care or custody" (§880.01[5]). "Other like incapacities" refers to those conditions incurred at any age which are the result of accident, organic brain damage, mental or physical disability, continued consumption or absorption of substances, producing a condition which substantially impairs an individual from providing for the individual's own care or custody" (§880.01[8]).

In Wisconsin law, a spendthrift is a person who is unable to attend to business as a result of the use of intoxicants or drugs or gambling, idleness, or debauchery, or other wasteful course of general conduct. The spendthrift's health, life or property or those of others is likely to be affected, thus endangering the "support of the person and the person's dependents [and exposing] the public to such support" (§880.01[9]). The court may appoint a guardian of the estate of anyone, whether a resident of Wisconsin or not, if any of his or her estate is located within the county.

Any public official, relative or other person may petition the court for the appointment of a guardian of the person or estate. A hearing must be held within thirty days of the date of the filing of the petition. Notice must be given the alleged incompetent, his or her counsel (if any), guardian *ad litem*, and presumptive adult heirs at least ten days before the hearing on issues of incompetency. Where an emergency appointment of a guardian is alleged by the petitioner to be necessary, the court may appoint a temporary guardian with or without notice to the proposed ward.

A written statement furnished by a licensed physician or licensed psychologist must be submitted with the petition, testifying to the mental condition of the alleged incompetent and based upon examination. The proposed ward has the right to counsel, and in all cases an attorney will be appointed as guardian *ad litem*. Additional rights of the proposed ward include: the right to a trial by a jury, the right to present and cross-examine witness including the physician or psychologist reporting to the court, and the right to have the hearing closed. He or she also has the right, at his or her own expense, to secure an independent medical or psychological examination relevant to the issues contested in the hearing. The standard of required proof is clear and convincing evidence. "All court records pertinent to the finding of incompetency are closed" (§880.33[6]).

> Any person other than a minor may, at such time as the person has sufficient capacity to form an intelligent preference, execute a written instrument, in the same manner as the execution of a will under §853.03, nominating a person to be appointed as guardian of his or her person or property or both in the event that a guardian is in the future appointed. Such nominee shall be appointed as guardian by the court unless the court finds that the appointment of such nominee is not in the best interests of the person for whom, or for whose property, the guardian is to be appointed. (§880.09[7]).

Every guardian will be paid for reasonable expenses incurred in the execution of his or her guardianship duties, including necessary compensation paid to accountants, attorneys, brokers, and other professionals, agents and servants. "The guardian shall also have such compensation for the guardian's services as the court, in which the guardian's accounts are settled, deems to be just and reasonable" (§880.24[1]).

A guardianship of the person can be terminated "when the court adjudicates a former incompetent to be competent" (§880.26[c]). A guardianship of the estate will be terminated "when the court adjudicates a former incompetent or a spendthrift to be capable of handling his or her property" (§880.26[c]), or when the estate of the ward falls below $5,000. (See Wisconsin Statutes, Chapter 880: Guardians and Wards, Subchapter 1: General Provisions, §880.01 et seq. for guardianship laws; Wisconsin Statutes §880.15 for temporary guardianship laws.)

*Wyoming*. District courts have jurisdiction over the appointment of guardianships of the person and conservatorships of the estate for incompetent people. An "incompetent person" is "an individual who is unable unassisted to properly manage and take care of himself or his property as a result of the infirmities of advanced age, physical disability, disease, the use of alcohol or controlled substances" (Wyoming Statutes §3-1-101[ix]). A "mentally incompetent person" is "an individual who is unable unassisted to properly manage and take care of himself or his property as the result of mental illness, mental deficiency or mental retardation" (§3-1-101[xii]). As noted in Wyoming's codes, "the appointment of a guardian or conservator does not constitute an adjudication that the ward lacks testamentary capacity" (§3-1-201).

Notice of the competency hearing for a guardianship or conservatorship must be given the proposed ward/conservatee ten days before the hearing, although the notice may be waived "for good cause." A temporary guardian or conservator may be appointed by the court only after a hearing "subject to any notice and conditions the court prescribes" (§3-2-106, §3-3-107), and is limited to not more than ninety days unless the court chooses to extend the temporary guardianship for an additional ninety days. A jury trial may be demanded by the petitioner or the alleged incompetent. The standard of proof required for these proceedings is "a preponderance of the evidence" (§3-2-104[a], §3-3-104[a]).

Within six months of a guardian's appointment, he or she must file a report with the court summarizing the physical condition (including level of disability or functional incapacity), residence, treatment, care and activities of the ward. The report must also describe those actions the guardian has taken on behalf of the ward. A guardianship report must be filed annually within sixty days following the anniversary date of his or her appointment. Subject to the approval of the court, the guardian may commit the ward to a mental health facility or mental health hospital, relinquish the ward's minor child for adoption, and consent to medical treatments for the ward including electroshock therapy, psychosurgery, sterilization, or other long-term or permanent contraception.

A conservator may, without prior order of the court, collect any principal or income, sell and transfer personal property for which there is a regularly established market, and invest the funds belonging to the ward. For good cause shown and under order of court,

> a conservator may make gifts on behalf of the ward out of the assets of the ward to persons or religious, educational, scientific, charitable or other nonprofit organizations to whom or to which gifts were regularly made prior to the appointment of the conservator. (§3-3-801)

When the assets of the estate of the ward no longer cover the charges and claims against them, the court may order the conservator to terminate the conservatorship. When the assets of the ward are insufficient to pay in full all claims against the ward, "priority of payment shall be given to

THE RETIREMENT NIGHTMARE

court costs and other costs of administration of the conservatorship" (§6-3-711). (See Wyoming Statutes, Title 3: Guardians and Ward, §3-1-101 et seq. for guardianship/conservatorship laws; Wyoming Statutes §§3-2-106 and 3-3-107 for temporary guardianships, and §3-3-206 for temporary conservatorships.)

## APPENDIX B

# COSTS INVOLVED IN FIGHTING UNWANTED PROTECTIVE PROCEEDINGS

## *One Example*

The following list itemizes the actual costs incurred during one allegedly incapacitated individual's battle to repel an involuntary conservatorship petition in California's Probate Court. The payments covered all litigation-related expenses incurred by the proposed ward over a period of three years and three months.

| | |
|---|---:|
| Paid to own attorneys: | $632,038.24 |
| Paid to petitioners' attorneys: | $100,000.00 |
| Paid to financial advisor: | $ 19,262.50 |
| Paid to psychologist: | $ 1,606.25 |
| Paid to court-appointed probate volunteer panel attorney: | $ 18,000.00 |
| Paid to court visitor: | $ 610.00 |
| Paid to firm of professional conservators: | $ 7,527.40 |
| Paid to attorney for firm of professional conservators: | $ 48,501.60 |
| Capital gains taxes on assets sold to pay litigation costs: | $350,000.00 |
| **TOTAL:** | **$1,177,645.99** |

# RESOURCES FOR THE ELDERLY

## MAJOR NATIONAL ORGANIZATIONS

Adult Protective Services
Intake, referrals for suspected abuse, neglect, or exploitation
1-800-624-8404

Administration on Aging
Department of Health and Human Services
330 Independence Avenue SW.
Washington, DC 20201
(202) 619-0641
Fax: (202) 619-3759
E-mail: AoAInfo@ban-gate.aoa.dhhs.gov
Website: http://www.aoa.dhhs.gov
Eldercare Locator: 1-800-677-1116

Aging Institute
HHP Building, Room 2367
University of Maryland
College Park, MD 20742
(301) 405-2470

Aging Network Services
4400 East-West Highway, Suite 907
Bethesda, MD 20814
(301) 657-4329
Website: http://www.agingnets.com/

Aging with Dignity
P.O. Box 1661
Tallahassee, FL 32302-1661
(850) 681-2010
Fax: (805) 681-2481
E-mail: fivewishes@aol.com
Website: http://www.agingwithdignity.org

Alliance for Aging Research
2021 K Street, NW, Suite 305
Washington, DC 20006
(202) 293-2856
Fax: (202) 758-8574
Website: http://www.agingresearch.org

American Association for Geriatric Psychiatry
Seventh Floor
7910 Woodmont Avenue
Bethesda, MD 20814-3004
(301) 654-7850
Fax: (301) 654-4137
E-mail: aagpgpa@aol.com
Website: http://www.aoa.dhhs.gov/aoa/dir/16.html

American Association of Homes and Services for the Aging
901 E Street NW, Suite 500
Washington, DC 20004-2037
(202) 783-2242, (800) 508-9442
Fax: (202) 783-2255
E-mail: inform@aahsa.org
Website: http://www.aahsa.org/

American Association of Retired Persons (AARP)
601 E Street NW
Washington, DC 20049
(202) 434-2277, 1-800-424-3410
Website: http://www.aarp.org

American Geriatrics Society
770 Lexington Avenue, Suite 300
New York, NY 10021
(212) 308-1414
Fax: (212) 832-8646
E-mail: info.amger@americangeriatrics.org
Website: http://www.americangeriatrics.org/

APA Committee on Aging
Public Interest Directorate
American Psychological Association
750 First Street, NE
Washington, DC 20002-4242
(202) 336-6050, 1-800-374-2721
E-mail: publicinterest@apa.org
Website: http://www.aoa.dhhs.gov/aoa/dir/53.html

American Society on Aging (ASA)
833 Market Street, Suite 511
San Francisco, CA 94103-1824
(415) 974-9600, 1-800-537-9728
Fax: (415) 974-0300
E-mail: info@asa.asaging.org
Website: http://www.asaging.org

Assisted Living Federation of America (ALFA)
10300 Eaton Place, Suite 400
Fairfax, VA 22031
(703) 691-8100
Fax: (703) 691-8106
Website: http://www.alfa.org/

Catholic Charities U.S.A.
1731 King Street, Suite 200
Alexandria, VA 22314
(703) 549-1390
Fax: (703) 549-1656
Website: http://www.catholiccharitiesusa.org/

Center for the Study of Aging
1331 H Street, NW
Washington, DC 20005
(202) 737-4650, 1-800-221-4272

Children of Aging Parents
1609 Woodbourne Road, Suite 302A
Levittown, PA 19057
(215) 945-6900, 1-800-227-7294
Fax: (215) 945-8720
Website: http://www.careguide.net/

Choice In Dying
1035 30th Street, NW
Washington, DC 20007
(202) 338-9790
Counseling Line: 1-800-989-WILL (9455)
Fax: (202) 338-0242

Clearinghouse on Abuse and Neglect of the Elderly (CANE)
College of Human Resources
University of Delaware
Newark, DE 19716
(302) 831-3525
Website: http://www.aoa.dhhs.gov/aoa/dir/78.html

Concerned Relatives of Nursing Home Patients
3130 Mayfield Road, Suite 209 W
Cleveland Heights, OH 44118
(216) 321-0403

Continuing Care Accreditation Commission (CCAC)
(202) 783-7286
Fax: (202) 783-2255
Website: http://www.ccaconline.org/mail.htm

Eldercare Locator
Washington, DC
1-800-677-1116
Website: http://www.ageinfo.org/elderloc/elderdb.html

Elderhostel
75 Federal Street
Boston, MA 02110-1941
(617) 426-7788, (877) 426-8056 (toll-free)
Website: http://www.elderhostel.org

Elder Support Network
P.O. Box 248
Kendall Park, NJ 08824
1-800-634-7346

Family Caregiver Alliance
425 Bush Street, Suite 500
San Francisco, CA 94108
(415) 434-3388, 1-800-445-810

Family Resource Service
1400 Union Meeting Road, Suite 102
Blue Bell, PA 19422
1-800-847-5437

Gerontological Society of America
1275 K Street NW, Suite 350
Washington, D.C. 20005-4006
(202) 842-1275
Fax: (202) 842-1150
E-mail: geron@geron.org
Website: http://www.geron.org/

Gray Panthers
733 15th Street, NW, Suite 437
Washington, DC 20005
(202) 737-6637, 1-800-280-5362
Fax: (202) 737-1160
E-mail: info@graypanthers.org
Website: http://www.graypanthers.org

Hemlock Society USA
P.O. Box 101810
Denver, CO 80250-1810
(303) 639-1202, 1-800-247-7421
E-mail: hemlock@privatei.com
Website: http://www.hemlock.org

Hospice Association of America
519 C Street, NE
Washington, DC 20002
(202) 546-4759

National Adult Day Care Services Association
c/o National Council on the Aging
409 Third St. SW, Suite 200
Washington, DC 20024
(202) 479-1200

National Aging Information Center (NAIC)
330 Independence Avenue, SW, Room 4656
Washington, DC 20201
(202) 619-7501, (202) 401-7575 (TTY)
Fax: (202) 401-7620
E-mail: naic@aoa.gov
Website: http://www.aoa.gov/naic

National Association for Home Care
228 7th Street SE
Washington, DC 20003
(202) 547-7424
Fax: (202) 547-3540
Website: http://www.nahc.org

National Association of Area Agencies on Aging (N4A)
1112 16th Street NW, Suite 100
Washington, DC 20036-4823
(202) 296-8130
Fax: (202) 296-8134
Website: http://www.n4a.org

National Association of Private Geriatric Care Managers
1604 North Country Club Road
Tucson, AZ 85716
(520) 881-8008
Fax: (520)325-7925
Website: http://www.aoa.dhhs.gov/aoa/dir/135.html

National Association of State Units on Aging
1225 I Street NW, Suite 725
Washington, DC 20005
(202) 898-2578, 1-800-989-6537
Fax: (202) 898-2583
E-mail: staff@nasua.org
Website: http://www.aoa.dhhs.gov/AOA/dir/137.html

National Center for Home Equity Conversion
7373 147th St., West, Suite 115
Apple Valley, MN 55124
(612) 953-4474

National Center for State Long-Term Care Ombudsman Resources
1225 I St., NW, Suite 725
Washington, DC 20005
(202) 898-2578

National Center on Elder Abuse
810 1st Street NE, Suite 500
Washington, DC 20002
(202) 682-2470
Fax: (202) 289-6555
Website: http://www.gwjapan.com/NCEA/

National Council of Senior Citizens
Department of Public Affairs and Legislation
8403 Colesville Road, Suite 1200
Silver Spring, MD 20910-3314
(301) 578-8800
Fax: (301) 578-8911
E-mail: comments@nscerc.org
Website: http://www.ncscinc.org/

National Council on the Aging (NCOA)
409 3rd Street SW, Suite 200
Washington, DC 20024
(202) 479-1200, 1-800-424-9046
Fax: (202) 479-0735
E-mail: info@ncoa.org
Website: http://www.ncoa.org

National Eldercare Institute on Housing and Supportive Services
University of southern California
Andrus Gerontology Center
Los Angeles, CA 90089
(310) 740-1364

National Family Caregivers Association
1-800-896-3650

National Federation of Interfaith Volunteer Caregivers
P.O. Box 1939
Kingston, NY 12402
(914) 331-1358, 1-800-350-7438

National Foundation for Retirement Living
184 Gloucester St.
Annapolis, MD 21403
1-800-626-6767

National Hospice Organization
1901 North Moore St., Suite 901
Arlington, VA 22209
1-800-658-8898, (703) 243-5900
E-mail: drsnho@cais.org
Website: http://www.nho.org

National Institute on Aging (NIA)
Public Information Office
9000 Rockville Pike, Building 31
Bethesda, MD 20892
(301) 496-0216
Fax: (301) 496-2525
E-mail: niainfo@access.digex.net
Website: http://www.nih.gov/nia

National Long-Term Care Ombudsman Resource Center
National Citizens' Coalition for Nursing Home Reform
1424 16th Street NW, Suite 202
Washington, DC 20036
(202) 332-2275
Fax: (202) 332-2949
Website: http://www.nccnhr.org

National Meals on Wheels Foundation
2675 44th Street SW, Suite 305
Grand Rapids, MI 49509
(616) 531-0090

National Resource and Policy Center on Rural Long-Term Care
Center on Aging
University of Kansas Medical Center
3901 Rainbow Boulevard
Kansas City, KS 66160-7117
(913) 588-1636
Fax: (913) 588-1464
E-mail: lredford@kumc.edu
Website: http://www.kumc.edu/instruction/medicine/NRPC

National Support Center for Families of the Aging
(215) 544-5933

Nursing Home Information Hotline
Washington, DC 20005
(202) 347-8800

Older Women's League
666 11th Street NW, Suite 700
Washington, DC 20001
(202) 783-6686, (202) 783-6689, 1-800-825-3695
Website: http://www.ncoa.org/lcao/members/owl.htm

Psychologists in Long-Term Care
261 Mack Boulevard
Detroit, MI 48201
(313) 745-9763

Resource Directory for Older People
1-800-677-1116
Website: http://www.aoa.dhhs.gov/aoa/dir/toc.html

Retired and Senior Volunteer Program (RSVP)
1201 New York Avenue
Washington, DC 20525
1-800-424-8867

Senior Connection
1-800-350-6065

SeniorNet
Third Floor
One Kearny Street
San Francisco, CA 94108
(415) 352-1210, 1-800-747-6848
E-mail: seniornet@aol.com
Website: http://www.seniornet.org

Senior Options
Website: http://www.senioroptions.com

Senior Resource
Website: http://www.seniorresource.com

Setting Priorities for Retirement Years (SPRY Foundation)
10 G Street, NE, Suite 600
Washington, DC 20002-4215
(202) 216-0401
Fax: (202) 216-0779
Website: http://www.spry.org

Social Security Administration
Office of Public Inquiries
6401 Security Boulevard
Baltimore, MD 21235
(410) 965-7700, (800) 772-1213
Fax: (410) 965-0695
Website: http://www.ssa.gov

Visiting Nurse Associations of America
3801 East Florida, Suite 900
Denver, CO 80210
(303) 753-0218, 1-800-426-2547
Fax: (303) 753-0258
Website: http://www.aoa.dhhs.gov/aoa/dir/26.html

Volunteers of America
110 S. Union Street
Alexandria, VA 22314
(703) 548-2288
FAX: (703) 687-1972
Website: http://www.voa.org

Well Spouse Foundation
610 Lexington Avenue, Suite 814
New York, NY 10022
1-800-838-0879, (212) 644-1241

Widowed Persons Service
601 E Street, NW
Washington, DC 20049
(202) 434-2260

# NATIONAL LEGAL ORGANIZATIONS

Adult Protective Services
Intake, referrals for suspected abuse, neglect, or exploitation
1-800-624-8404

American Bar Association
750 North Lake Shore Drive
Chicago, IL 60611
1-800-285-2221, (312) 988-5000
Website: http://www.abanet.org

American Bar Association Commission on the
Legal Problems of the Elderly
740 15th Street NW
Washington, D.C. 20005-1009
(202) 662-8690
Fax: (202) 662-1032
E-mail: abaelderly@attmail.com
Website: http://www.abanet.org/elderly

Kansas Elder Law Network (KELN)
Website: http://www.ink.org/public/keln

Legal Counsel for the Elderly (LCE)
601 E Street NW
Washington, D.C. 20049
(202) 434-2120, 1-800-262-5297
TTY: (202) 434-6562
Fax: (202) 434-6464
Website: http://www.aarp.org

Legal Services for the Elderly (LSE)
17th Floor
130 West 42nd Street
New York, NY 10036
(212) 391-0120
Fax: (212) 719-1939
E-mail: hn4923@handsnet.org
Website: http://www.aoa.dhhs.gov/aoa/dir/118.html

National Academy of Elder Law Attorneys
1604 North Country Club Road
Tucson, AZ 85716
(520) 881-4005
Fax: (520) 325-7925
Website: http://www.naela.com/

National Clearinghouse for Legal Services
205 West Monroe Street, Second Floor
Chicago, IL 60606-5013
(312) 263-3830
Fax: (312) 263-3846
E-mail: ncls@interaccess.com
Website: http://www.povertylaw.org

National Senior Citizens Law Center (NSCLC)
(National Eldercare Legal Assistance Project)
1815 H Street NW, Suite 700
Washington, DC 20006
(202) 887-5280
Fax: (202) 785-6792
Website: http://www.nsclc.org

SeniorLaw
Website: http://www.seniorlaw.com/index.htm

# CONGRESSIONAL COMMITTEES, ISSUES OF AGING

House Select Committee on Aging
712 House Office Building Annex #1
Washington, D.C. 20515-6361
(202) 226-3375

United States Senate Special Committee on Aging
G31 Dirksen Senate Office Building
Washington, DC 20510-6400
(202) 224-5364
Fax: (202) 224-8660
E-mail: mailbox@aging.senate.gov
Website: http://senate.gov/~aging/

# STATE OFFICES OF AGING

For updates, see: http://www.aoa.dhhs.gov/aoa/pages/state.html

**Alabama**
Alabama Commission on Aging
RSA Plaza, Suite 470
770 Washington Avenue
Montgomery, AL 36130
(334) 242-5743
Fax: (334) 242-5594

**Alaska**
Alaska Commission on Aging
Division of Senior Services
Department of Administration
P.O. Box 110209
Juneau, AK 99811-0209
(907) 465-3250
Fax: (907) 465-4716

**Arizona**
Aging and Adult Administration
Department of Economic Security
1789 West Jefferson, Site Code 950A
Phoenix, AZ 85007
(602) 542-4446
Fax: (602) 542-6575

**Arkansas**
Division of Aging and Adult Services
Arkansas Department of Human Services
P.O. Box 1437, Slot 1412
7th and Main Streets
Little Rock, AR 72201-1437
(501) 682-2441
Fax: (501) 682-8155

**California**
California Department of Aging
1600 K Street
Sacramento, CA 95814
(916) 322-5290
Fax: (916) 324-1903

**Colorado**        Aging and Adult Services
                    Department of Social Services
                    110 16th Street, Suite 200
                    Denver, CO 80202-5202
                    (303) 620-4147
                    Fax: (303) 620-4189

**Connecticut**     Community Services
                    Division of Elderly Services
                    25 Sigourney Street, 10th Floor
                    Hartford, CT 06106-5033
                    (203) 424-5274
                    Fax: (203) 424-4966

**Delaware**        Delaware Department of Health and Social Services
                    Division of Services for Aging and Adults
                    with Physical Disabilities
                    1901 North DuPont Highway
                    New Castle, DE 19720
                    (302) 577-4791
                    Fax: (302) 577-4793

**District of**     District of Columbia Office on Aging
**Columbia**        One Judiciary Square, 9th Floor
                    441 Fourth Street, NW
                    Washington, DC 20001
                    (202) 724-5622
                    Fax: (202) 724-4979

**Florida**         Department of Elder Affairs
                    Building B, Suite 152
                    4040 Esplanade Way
                    Tallahassee, FL 32399-7000
                    (904) 414-2000
                    Fax: (904) 414-2002

**Georgia**         Division of Aging Services
                    Department of Human Resources
                    2 Peachtree Street NE, 18th Floor
                    Atlanta, GA 30303
                    (404) 657-5258
                    Fax: (404) 657-5285

**Guam**

Division of Senior Services
Department of Public Health and Human Services
P. O. Box 2816
Agana, Guam 96932
011-671-475-0263
Fax: (671) 477-2930

**Hawaii**

Hawaii Executive Office on Aging
250 South Hotel Street, Suite 107
Honolulu, HI 96813
(808) 586-0100
Fax: (808) 586-0185

**Idaho**

Idaho Commission on Aging
3380 Americana Terrace, Suite 120
Boise, ID 83706
(208) 334-3833
Fax: (208) 334-3033

**Illinois**

Illinois Department on Aging
421 East Capitol Avenue, Suite 100
Springfield, IL 62701-1789
(217) 785-2870
Chicago Office: (312) 814-2630
Fax: (217) 785-4477

**Indiana**

Division of Disability, Aging
and Rehabilitative Services
Family and Social Services Administration
Bureau of Aging and In-Home Services
402 West Washington Street, #W454
P.O. Box 7083
Indianapolis, IN 46207-7083
(317) 232-7020
Fax: (317) 232-7867

**Iowa**

Iowa Department of Elder Affairs
Clemens Building, 3rd Floor
200 Tenth Street
Des Moines, IA 50309-3609
(515) 281-5187
Fax: (515) 281-4036

**Kansas**
Department of Aging
New England Building
503 S. Kansas Avenue
Topeka, KS 66603-3404
(785) 296-4986
Fax: (785) 296-0256

**Kentucky**
Kentucky Division of Aging Services
Cabinet for Human Resources
275 East Main Street, 6 West
Frankfort, KY 40621
(502) 564-6930
Fax: (502) 564-4595

**Louisiana**
Governor's Office of Elderly Affairs
P.O. Box 80374
412 N 4th Street, 3rd Floor
Baton Rouge, LA 70802
(504) 342-7100
Fax: (504) 342-7133

**Maine**
Bureau of Elder and Adult Services
Department of Human Services
35 Anthony Avenue
State House - Station #11
Augusta, ME 04333-0011
(207) 624-5335
Fax: (207) 624-5361

**Maryland**
Maryland Office on Aging
State Office Building, Room 1007
301 West Preston Street
Baltimore, MD 21201-2374
(410) 225-1102
Fax: (410) 333-7943
E-mail: sfw@mail.ooa.state.md.us

**Massachusetts**
Massachusetts Executive Office of Elder Affairs
One Ashburton Place, 5th Floor
Boston, MA 02108
(617) 727-7750
Fax: (617) 727-9368

**Michigan**        Michigan Office of Services to the Aging
P.O. Box 30026
Lansing, MI 48909-8176
(517) 373-8230
Director: (517) 373-7876
Fax: (517) 373-4092

**Minnesota**      Minnesota Board on Aging
444 Lafayette Road
St. Paul, MN 55155-3843
(651) 296-2770
Fax: (612) 297-7855

**Mississippi**    Division of Aging and Adult Services
750 State Street
Jackson, MS 39202
(601) 359-4925
Fax: (601) 359-4370
E-mail: ELANDERSON@msdh.state.ms.us

**Missouri**       Division on Aging
Department of Social Services
P.O. Box 1337
615 Howerton Court
Jefferson City, MO 65102-1337
(314) 751-3082
Fax: (314) 751-8493

**Montana**        Senior and Long Term Care Division
Department of Public Health and Human Services
P.O. Box 4210
111 Sanders, Room 211
Helena, MT 59604
(406) 444-4077
Fax: (406) 444-7743

| | |
|---|---|
| **Nebraska** | Department of Health and Human Services<br>Division on Aging<br>P.O. Box 95044<br>301 Centennial Mall, South<br>Lincoln, NE 68509-5044<br>(402) 471-2307<br>Fax: (402) 471-4619 |
| **Nevada** | Nevada Division for Aging Services<br>Department of Human Resources<br>State Mail Room Complex<br>340 North 11th Street, Suite 203<br>Las Vegas, NV 89101<br>(702) 486-3545<br>Fax: (702) 486-3572 |
| **New Hampshire** | Division of Elderly and Adult Services<br>State Office Park South<br>115 Pleasant Street, Annex Building #1<br>Concord, NH 03301-3843<br>(603) 271-4680<br>Fax: (603) 271-4643 |
| **New Jersey** | Department of Health and Senior Services<br>Division of Senior Affairs<br>101 South Broad Street, CN 807<br>Trenton, NJ 08625-0807<br>(609) 588-3141, (800) 729-8820<br>Fax: (609) 588-3601 |
| **New Mexico** | State Agency on Aging<br>La Villa Rivera Building, 4th Floor<br>224 East Palace Avenue<br>Santa Fe, NM 87501<br>(505) 827-7640<br>Fax: (505) 827-7649 |
| **New York** | New York State Office for the Aging<br>2 Empire State Plaza<br>Albany, NY 12223-1251<br>(518) 474-5731, (800) 342-9871<br>Fax: (518) 474-0608 |

**North Carolina**   Division of Aging
CB 29531
693 Palmer Drive
Raleigh, NC 27626-0531
(919) 733-3983
Fax: (919) 733-0443

**North Dakota**   Department of Human Services
Aging Services Division
600 South 2nd Street, Suite 1C
Bismarck, ND 58504
(701) 328-8910
Fax: (701) 328-8989

**North Mariana**   CNMI Office on Aging
**Islands**   P. O. Box 2178
Commonwealth of the Northern Mariana Islands
Saipan, MP 96950
(670) 233-1320/1321
Fax: (670) 233-1327/0369

**Ohio**   Ohio Department of Aging
50 West Broad Street, 9th Floor
Columbus, OH 43215-5928
(614) 466-5500
Fax: (614) 466-5741

**Oklahoma**   Services for the Aging,
Department of Human Services
P.O. Box 25352
312 N.E. 28th Street
Oklahoma City, OK 73125
(405) 521-2281 or 521-2327
Fax: (405) 521-2086

**Oregon**   Senior and Disabled Services Division
500 Summer Street NE, 2nd Floor
Salem, OR 97310-1015
(503) 945-5811
Fax: (503) 373-7823

| | |
|---|---|
| **Palau** | State Agency on Aging<br>Republic of Palau<br>Koror, PW 96940<br>9-10-288-011-680-488-2736<br>Fax: 9-10-288-680-488-1662 or 1597 |
| **Pennsylvania** | Pennsylvania Department of Aging<br>Commonwealth of Pennsylvania<br>555 Walnut Street, 5th Floor<br>Harrisburg, PA 17101-1919<br>(717) 783-1550<br>Fax: (717) 772-3382 |
| **Puerto Rico** | Governor's Office of Elderly Affairs<br>Call Box 50063<br>Old San Juan Station, PR 00902<br>(787) 721-5710, 721-4560, 721-6121<br>Fax: (787) 721-6510<br>E-mail: rubyrodz@prtc.net |
| **Rhode Island** | Department of Elderly Affairs<br>160 Pine Street<br>Providence, RI 02903-3708<br>(401) 277-2858<br>Fax: (401) 277-2130 |
| **American Samoa** | Territorial Administration on Aging<br>Government of American Samoa<br>Pago Pago, American Samoa 96799<br>011-684-633-2207<br>Fax: 011-684-633-2533 |
| **South Carolina** | Office on Aging<br>South Carolina Department of<br>Health and Human Services<br>P.O. Box 8206<br>Columbia, SC 29201-8206<br>(803) 253-6177<br>Fax: (803) 253-4173<br>E-mail: Rinehart@dhhs.state.sc.us |

**South Dakota**  Office of Adult Services and Aging
Richard F. Kneip Building
700 Governors Drive
Pierre, SD 57501-2291
(605) 773-3656
Fax: (605) 773-6834

**Tennessee**  Commission on Aging
Andrew Jackson Building, 9th Floor
500 Deaderick Street
Nashville, TN 37243-0860
(615) 741-2056
Fax: (615) 741-3309

**Texas**  Texas Department on Aging
4900 North Lamar, 4th Floor
Austin, TX 78751
(512) 424-6840
Fax: (512) 424-6890

**Utah**  Division of Aging and Adult Services
Box 45500
120 North 200 West
Salt Lake City, UT 84145-0500
(801) 534-3910
Fax: (801) 534-4395

**Vermont**  Vermont Department of Aging and Disabilities
Waterbury Complex
103 South Main Street
Waterbury, VT 05676
(802) 241-2400
Fax: (802) 241-2325
E-mail: dyaco@dad.state.vt.us

**Virginia**  Virginia Department for the Aging
1600 Forest Avenue, Suite 102
Richmond, VA 23219-2327
(804) 662-9333
Fax: (804) 662-9354

**Virgin Islands**    Senior Citizen Affairs
Virgin Islands Department of Human Services
Knud Hansen Complex, Building A
1303 Hospital Ground
Charlotte Amalie, VI 00802
(809) 774-0930
Fax: (809) 774-3466

**Washington**    Aging and Adult Services Administration
Department of Social and Health Services
P.O. Box 45050
Olympia, WA 98504
(360) 586-8753
Fax: (360) 902-7848

**West Virginia**    West Virginia Bureau of Senior Services
Holly Grove, Building 10
1900 Kanawha Boulevard East
Charleston, WV 25305-0160
(304) 558-3317
Fax: (304) 558-0004

**Wisconsin**    Bureau of Aging and Long Term Care Resources
Department of Health and Family Services
P.O. Box 7851
Madison, WI 53707
(608) 266-2536
Fax: (608) 267-3203

**Wyoming**    Office of Aging
Department of Health
117 Hathaway Building, Room 139
Cheyenne, WY 82002-0480
(307) 777-7986
Fax: (307) 777-5340

# STATE LONG-TERM-CARE OMBUDSMAN PROGRAMS

For updates, see: http://www.aoa.dhhs.gov/aoa/pages/ltcomb.html

**Alabama**
State LTC Ombudsman
Commission on Aging
770 Washington Avenue
RSA Plaza, Suite 470
Montgomery, AL 36130
(334) 242-5743
Fax: (334) 242-5594

**Alaska**
State LTC Ombudsman
Older Alaskans Commission
3601 C Street, Suite 260
Anchorage, AK 99503-5209
(907) 563-6393
Fax: (907) 561-3862
E-mail: fran purdy@admin.state.ak.us

**Arizona**
State LTC Ombudsman
Aging and Adult Administration
Department of Economic Security
1789 West Jefferson, Site Code 950A
Phoenix, AZ 85007
(602) 542-6452
FAX: (602) 542-6575

**Arkansas**
State LTC Ombudsman
Arkansas Division of Aging and Adult Services
1417 Donaghey Plaza South, Slot 1412
Little Rock, AR 72203-1437
(501) 682-2441
Fax: (501) 682-8155
E-mail: alice.ahart@mail.state.ar.us

**California**              State LTC Ombudsman
                           California Department of Aging
                           1600 K Street
                           Sacramento, CA 95814
                           (916) 322-5290
                           Fax: (916) 323-7299
                           E-mail: cda.phealth@hwl.cahwnet.gov

**Colorado**               State LTC Ombudsman
                           The Legal Center
                           455 Sherman Street, Suite 130
                           Denver, CO 80203
                           (303) 722-0300
                           Fax: (303) 722-0720
                           E-mail: CHGin28@aol.com

**Connecticut**            State LTC Ombudsman
                           Elderly Services Division
                           25 Sigourney Street, 10th Floor
                           Hartford, CT 06106-5033
                           (860) 424-5200
                           Fax: (860) 424-4966
                           E-mail: ltcop@po.state.ct.us

**Delaware**               State LTC Ombudsman
                           Delaware Services for the Aging-Disabled
                           Oxford Building, Suite 200
                           256 Chapman Road
                           Newark, DE 19702 (x 46)
                           (302) 453-3820
                           Fax: (302) 453-3836

**District of**            National Ombudsman Resource Center
**Columbia**               c/o NCCNHR
                           1424 16th Street NW, Suite 202
                           Washington, DC 20036-2211
                           (202) 332-2275
                           E-mail: nccnhrl@erols.com

**Florida**            State LTC Ombudsman
                       Florida State LTC Ombudsman Council
                       Holland Building, Room 270
                       600 South Calhoun Street
                       Tallahassee, FL 32301
                       (850) 488-6190
                       Fax: (850) 488-5657
                       E-mail: FLOmbuds@juno.com

**Georgia**            State LTC Ombudsman
                       Division of Aging Services
                       2 Peachtree Street NW, 18th Floor
                       Suite 18-129
                       Atlanta, GA 30303-3176
                       (404) 657-5319
                       Fax: (404) 657-5285
                       E-mail: bkurtz@mail.doas.state.ga.us

**Hawaii**             Office of the Governor
                       State LTC Ombudsman
                       Executive Office on Aging
                       250 South Hotel Street, Suite 107
                       Honolulu, HI 96813-2831
                       (808) 586-0100
                       Fax: (808) 586-0185
                       E-mail: jgmcderm@mail.health.state.hi.us

**Idaho**              State LTC Ombudsman
                       Office on Aging
                       P.O. Box 83720
                       700 West Jefferson, Room 108
                       Boise, ID 83720-0007
                       (208) 334-3833
                       Fax: (208) 334-3033
                       E-mail: chart@icoa.state.id.us

**Illinois**

State LTC Ombudsman
Illinois Department on Aging
421 East Capitol Avenue, Suite 100
Springfield, IL 62701-1789
(217) 785-3143
Fax: (217) 524-9644
E-mail: browley@age084rl.state.il.us

**Indiana**

State LTC Ombudsman
Indiana Division of Aging and Rehabilitation
Services
P.O. Box 7083-W454
402 West Washington Street, #W-454
Indianapolis, IN 46207-7083
(317) 232-7134
Fax: (317) 232-7867
E-mail: afranklin@fssa.state.in.us

**Iowa**

State LTC Ombudsman
Iowa Department of Elder Affairs
Clemens Building
200 10th Street, 3rd Floor
Des Moines, IA 50309-3609
(515) 281-4656
Fax: (515) 281-4036
E-mail: debi.meyers@dea.state.ia.us

**Kansas**

State LTC Ombudsman
Office of the State LTC Ombudsman
610 SW 10th Avenue, 2nd Floor
Topeka, KS 66612-1616
(785) 296-3017
Fax: (785) 296-3916

**Kentucky**

State LTC Ombudsman
Division of Aging Services
State LTC Ombudsman Office
275 East Main Street, 5th Floor West
Frankfort, KY 40621
(502) 564-6930
Fax: (502) 564-4595

**Louisiana**           State LTC Ombudsman
                        Governor's Office of Elderly Affairs
                        State LTC Ombudsman Office
                        412 N. 4th Street, 3rd Floor
                        Baton Rouge, LA 70802
                        (504) 342-7100
                        Fax: (504) 342-7133
                        E-mail: Hchiang@aol.com

**Maine**               State LTC Ombudsman
                        21 Bangor Street
                        P.O. Box 126
                        Augusta, ME 04332-0126
                        (207) 621-1079, (800) 499-0229
                        Fax: (207) 621-0509
                        E-mail: BGallant@maineombudsman.org

**Maryland**            State LTC Ombudsman
                        Office on Aging
                        State Office Building, Room 1004
                        301 West Preston Street
                        Baltimore, MD 21201
                        (410) 767-1091
                        Fax: (410) 333-7943
                        E-mail: plb@mail.ooa.state.md.us

**Massachusetts**       State LTC Ombudsman
                        Executive Office of Elder Affairs
                        1 Ashburton Place, 5th Floor
                        Boston, MA 02108-1518
                        (617) 727-7750
                        Fax: (617) 727-9368
                        E-mail: mary.e.mckenna@state.ma.us

**Michigan**            State LTC Ombudsman
                        Citizens for Better Care
                        State LTC Ombudsman Office
                        416 North Homer Street, Station 101
                        Lansing, MI 48912-4700
                        (517) 886-6349
                        Fax: (517) 336-7718
                        E-mail: Hturnham@aol.com

| | |
|---|---|
| **Minnesota** | State LTC Ombudsman<br>Office of Ombudsman for Older Minnesotans<br>444 Lafayette Road, 4th Floor<br>St. Paul, MN 55155-3843<br>(612) 296-0382<br>Fax: (612) 297-5654<br>E-mail: sharon.zoesch@state.mn.us |
| **Mississippi** | State LTC Ombudsman<br>Division of Aging and Adult Services<br>750 North State Street<br>Jackson, MS 39202<br>(601) 359-4929<br>Fax: (601) 359-4970 |
| **Missouri** | State LTC Ombudsman<br>Missouri Division of Aging<br>Department of Social Services<br>P.O. Box 1337<br>Jefferson City, MO 65102-1337<br>(573) 526-0727<br>Fax: (573) 751-8687<br>E-mail: cscott@mail.mo.us |
| **Montana** | State LTC Ombudsman<br>Office on Aging<br>Department of Family Services<br>P.O. Box 8005<br>Helena, MT 59604-8005<br>(406) 444-4077<br>Fax: (406) 444-7743<br>E-mail: bbartholomew@mt.gov |
| **Nebraska** | State LTC Ombudsman<br>Department on Aging<br>P. O. Box 95044<br>301 Centennial Mall South<br>Lincoln, NE 68509-5044<br>(402) 471-2307<br>Fax: (402) 471-4619<br>E-mail: ckadavy@agel.ndoa.state.ne.us |

**Nevada**
State LTC Ombudsman
Division for Aging Services
Department of Human Resources
340 North 11th Street, Suite 203
Las Vegas, NV 89101
(702) 486-3545
Fax: (702) 486-3572
E-mail: dasvegas@govmail.state.nv.us

**New Hampshire**
State Long-Term Care Ombudsman
Health and Human Services
Office of the Ombudsman
129 Pleasant Street
Concord, NH 03301-6505
(603) 271-4375, 1-800-443-5640 (in-state only)
Fax: (603) 271-4771
E-mail: Jgriffin@dhhs.state.nh.us

**New Jersey**
State LTC Ombudsman
101 South Broad Street
CN808, 6th Floor
Trenton, NJ 08625-0808
(609) 588-3614
Fax: (609) 588-3365

**New Mexico**
State LTC Ombudsman
State Agency on Aging
State LTC Ombudsman Office
228 East Palace Avenue, Suite A
Santa Fe, NM 87501
(505) 827-7640
Fax: (505) 827-7649
E-mail: ajsilva@nm-us.campus.mci.net

**New York**
State LTC Ombudsman
Office for the Aging
2 Empire State Plaza
Agency Building #2
Albany, NY 12223-0001
(518) 474-0108
Fax: (518) 474-7761
E-mail: faith.fish@ofa.state.ny.us

**North Carolina**    State LTC Ombudsman
Division of Aging
693 Palmer Drive
Caller Box Number 29531
Raleigh, NC 27626-0531
(919) 733-3983
Fax: (919) 733-0443
E-mail: wendy.sause@ncmail.net

**North Dakota**    State LTC Ombudsman
Aging Services Division, DHS
600 South 2nd Street, Suite 1C
Bismarck, ND 58504-5729
(701) 328-8915
Fax: (701) 328-8989
E-mail: 88funk@state.nd.us

**Ohio**    State LTC Ombudsman
Department of Aging
50 West Broad Street, 9th Floor
Columbus, OH 43215-5928
(614) 466-7922
Fax: (614) 466-5741
E-mail: M blaubert@msn.com

**Oklahoma**    State LTC Ombudsman
Aging Services Division, DHS
312 NE 28th Street, Suite 109
Oklahoma City, OK 73105
(405) 521-6734
Fax: (405) 521-2086
E-mail: eehouser@hotmail.com

**Oregon**    State LTC Ombudsman
Office of the LTC Ombudsman,
3855 Wolverine NE, Suite 6
Salem, OR 97310
(503) 378-6533
Fax: (503) 373-0852
E-mail: ombud@teleport.com

**Pennsylvania**       State LTC Ombudsman
                       Department of Aging
                       555 Walnut Street, 5th Floor
                       Forum Place
                       Harrisburg, PA 17101-1919
                       (717) 783-7247
                       FAX: (717) 772-3382
                       E-mail: jobrien@aging.state.pa.us

**Puerto Rico**        State LTC Ombudsman
                       Governor's Office for Elder Affairs
                       Call Box 50063
                       Old San Juan Station
                       San Juan, Puerto Rico 00902
                       (787) 725-1515
                       Fax: (787) 721-6510

**Rhode Island**       State LTC Ombudsman
                       Alliance for Better Long-Term Care
                       42 Post Road, Suite 204
                       Warwick, RI 02888
                       (401) 785-3340
                       Fax: (401) 785-3391

**South Carolina**     State LTC Ombudsman
                       Division on Aging
                       202 Arbor Lake Drive, Suite 301
                       Columbia, SC 29223-4535
                       (803) 253-6177
                       Fax: (803) 253-4173
                       E-mail: cook@dhhs.state.sc.us

**South Dakota**       State LTC Ombudsman
                       Office of Adult Services and Aging
                       Department of Social Services
                       700 Governors Drive
                       Pierre, SD 57501-2291
                       (605) 773-3656
                       Fax: (605) 773-6834
                       E-mail: jeffa@dss.state.sd.us

**Tennessee**

State LTC Ombudsman
Commission on Aging
Andrew Jackson Building, 9th Floor
500 Deaderick Street
Nashville, TN 37243-0860
(615) 741-2056
Fax: (615) 741-3309
E-mail: awheeler@mail.state.tn.us

**Texas**

State LTC Ombudsman
Department on Aging
P. O. Box 12786 Capitol Station
Austin, TX 78711
(512) 424-6875
Fax: (512) 424-6890
E-mail: john@tdoa.state.tx.us

**Utah**

State LTC Ombudsman
Division of Aging and Adult Services
Department of Social Services
P. O. Box 1367
Salt Lake City, UT 84103
(801) 538-3910
Fax: (801) 538-4395
E-mail: hsadm2.cbloswic@email.state.ut.us

**Vermont**

State LTC Ombudsman
Vermont Legal Aid, Inc.
264 North Winooski
P.O. Box 1367
Burlington, VT 05402
(802) 863-5620
Fax: (802) 863-7152
E-mail: jmajoros@vtlegalaid.org

**Virginia**

State LTC Ombudsman Program
Virginia Association of Area Agencies on Aging
530 East Main Street, Suite 428
Richmond, VA 23219-2327
(804) 644-2923
Fax: (804) 644-5640
E-mail: Elderrights@aol.com

**Washington**      State LTC Ombudsman
Washington State Ombudsman Program
1200 South 336th Street
Federal Way, WA 98003-7452
(253) 838-6810, 1-800-422-1384
Fax: (253) 874-7831

**West Virginia**   State LTC Ombudsman Office
Commission on Aging
1900 Kanawha Boulevard East
Charleston, WV 25305-0160
(304) 558-3317
Fax: (304) 558-0004

**Wisconsin**       State LTC Ombudsman
Board on Aging and Long-Term Care
214 North Hamilton Street
Madison, WI 53703-2118
(608) 266-8944
Fax: (608) 261-6570
E-mail: george.potaracke@ltc.state.wi.us

**Wyoming**         State LTC Ombudsman
Wyoming Senior Citizens Inc.
953 Water Street
P.O. Box 94
Wheatland, WY 82201
(307) 322-5553
Fax: (307) 322-3283

# RELATED WEBSITES

Administration on Aging (AoA)
http://www.aoa.dhhs.gov

Administration on Aging's Directory of Web Sites on Aging
http://www.aoa.dhhs.gov/aoa/webres/craig.htm

American Association for Homes and Services for the Aging Files
http://www.spry.org/aahsa.htm

American Association of Retired Persons (AARP)
http://www.aarp.org

American Bar Association
http://www.abanet.org

Bureau of Elder and Adult Services
http://www.state.me.us/dhs/beas/

Bureau of Elder and Adult Services Aging Resources Directory
http://www.state.me.us/beas/resource.htm

Catholic Charities USA
http://www.catholiccharitiesusa.org/

Community Transportation Association of America
http://www.ctaa.org

Disability Resources on the Internet
http://www.aamr.org/DisRes.html

Eldercare Locator
http://www.aoa.dhhs.gov/aoa/dir/91.html

Elderhostel
http://www.elderhostel.org

International Association for Financial Planning
http://www.iafp.org

Joint Commission on Accreditation of Healthcare Organizations
http://www.jcaho.org

Leadership Council of Aging Organizations (LCAO)
http://www.ncscinc.org/lcao/memdir.htm

National Academy of Elder Law Attorneys
http://www.naela.com/

National Aging Information Center (NAIC)
hppt://www.aoa.gov/naic/

National Association for Home Care
http://www.nahc.org

National Council of Senior Citizens
http://www.ncscinc.org

National Council on the Aging
http://www.ncoa.org

National Hospice Organization
http://www.nho.org

National Senior Citizens Law Center
http://www.nsclc.org.

Senior Com
http://www.senior.com

SeniorLaw
http://www.seniorlaw.com

Senior Net
http://www.seniornet.org

Senior Options
http://senioroptions.com/

Social Security Online
http://www.ssa.gov

U.S. Department of Health and Human Services
http://www.os.dhhs.gov

# REFERENCES FOR APPENDIX C

Abeles, N. Ph.D., *What Practitioners Should Know About Working With Older Adults.* Washington, D.C.: American Psychological Association, 1997.
Brown, R. N. *The Rights of Older Persons: A Basic Guide to the Legal Rights of Older Persons under Current Law,* 2d ed. Carbondale, Illinois: Southern Illinois University Press, 1989
Loverde, J. *The Complete Eldercare Planner: Where to Start, Questions to Ask, and How to Find Help.* New York: Hyperion, 1997.

*Resource Directory for Older People*, March 1996. National Institutes of Health Publication Number 95-738. Cooperative effort of the National Institute on Aging (NIA) and the Administration on Aging (AoA). Shelved in research sections of public libraries under: R362.6025.

# GLOSSARY

**ad hoc.** "For this"; for this particular purpose.

**ad litem.** For the suit; for the purposes of the suit; pending the suit. A guardian *ad litem* is a guardian appointed to prosecute or defend a suit on behalf of a party incapacitated by infancy or otherwise. *See* **guardian** *ad litem*.

**adversary proceeding.** One having opposing parties; contested, as distinguished from an *ex parte* hearing or proceeding. One of which the party seeking relief has given legal notice to the other party, and afforded the latter an opportunity to contest it. *Compare* **ex parte**.

**aged person.** One advanced in years; refers to his or her chronological, not mental age. Lawrence Frolik and Alison Barnes[2] subcategorized the elderly or aged into three groups: "the young old, age sixty-five to seventy-five; the old, age seventy-five to eighty-five; and the old old, age eighty-five plus."[3] They are quick to comment, however, that categorizing the aged this way has little functional value and suggest that they be grouped by physical and mental capability (e.g., the well elderly, the frail elderly, and so on).

**ageism.** A negative perception of individuals due solely to their chronological age; systematically stereotyping and discriminating against people because they are old.

**allegation.** The assertion, claim, declaration, or statement of a part to an action, made in a pleading, setting out what he expects to prove (see, for example, Fed.R. Civil P. 8).

**allege.** To state, recite, claim, assert, or charge; to make an allegation. *See* **allegation**.

**Americans With Disabilities Act of 1990 (ADA).** The ADA bans discrimination based on a person's disability. The act gives disabled individuals protections similar to those provided on the basis of race, sex, national origin, and religion. It extends to employment, public accommodations, transportation, and state and local government services. "Disability" under the ADA is defined differently than under other federal programs.

**amicus curiae.** Literally means "friend of the court." A person with a strong interest in or views on the subject matter of an action but not a party to the action may petition the court for permission to file a brief, ostensibly on behalf of a party but actually to suggest a rationale consistent with its own views.

**autonomy.** Independence from outside or surrogate decision-makers.

**average man test.** Used to determine bias of a prospective juror who asserts that he or she is without prejudice but who is so connected with case that an ordinary person under the circumstances would be biased without recognition of his or her prejudice (see *U.S.* v. *Haynes, C.A.Conn.*, 398 F.2d 980, 984).

**beyond a reasonable doubt.** In evidence means fully satisfied, entirely convinced, satisfied to a moral certainty; the phrase is the equivalent of the words clear, precise, and indubitable. In criminal cases, the accused's guilt must be established "beyond a reasonable doubt," which means that facts proven must establish guilt by virtue of their probative force.

**bias.** Inclination; bent; to incline to one side; prepossession; a preconceived opinion; a predisposition to decide a cause or an issue in a certain way, which does not leave the mind perfectly open to conviction. Condition of mind that sways judgment and renders judge unable to exercise his or her functions impartially in particular case. As used in law regarding disqualification of judge, bias refers to mental attitude or disposition of the judge toward a party to the litigation, and not to any views that he or she  may entertain regarding the subject matter involved (see *State ex rel. Mitchell* v. *Sage Stores Co.*, 157 Kan. 622, 143 P.2d 652, 655).

**burden of proof.** In Latin, *onus probandi*. Burden of proof is a term which describes two different concepts; first, the "burden of persuasion," which under traditional view never shifts from one party to the other at any stage of the proceeding, and second, the "burden of going forward with the evidence," which may shift back and forth between the parties as the trial progresses. *See* **standard of proof**; **clear and convincing proof**; **beyond a reasonable doubt**; **preponderance of evidence**.

**capacity.** Competency, power, or fitness; mental ability to understand the nature and effects of one's acts. *See also* **competency**; **disability**; **incapacity**; **mental capacity** *or* **competence**; **testamentary capacity**.

**clear and convincing proof.** The proof which results in reasonable certainty of the truth of the ultimate fact in controversy. Proof which required more than a preponderance of the evidence but less than proof beyond a reasonable doubt. Clear and convincing proof will be shown where the truth of the facts asserted is highly probable (see *In re Estate of Lobe*, Minn.App., 348 N.W.2d 413, 414). *See also* **beyond a reasonable doubt**; **burden of proof**.

**community property.** A system of marital property ownership in which each spouse owns a one-half interest in the property acquired during the marriage. Property acquired by gift or inheritance is generally not included, nor is property acquired before the marriage. The federal estate tax and gift tax both recognize community property ownership. The nine states with community property systems are Louisiana, Texas, New Mexico, Arizona, California, Washington, Idaho, Nevada, and Wisconsin (with adoption of Uniform Marital Property Act). The rest of the states are classified as common-law jurisdictions. The difference between common-law and community property systems centers around the property rights possessed by married people. In a common-law system, each spouse owns whatever he or she earns. Under a community property system, one-half of the earnings of each spouse is considered owned by the other spouse.

**competency.** In the law of evidence, the presence of those characteristics, or the absence of those disabilities, which render a witness legally fit and qualified to give testimony in a court of justice; applied, in the same sense, to documents or other written evidence.

**competency proceedings.** Hearings conducted to determine a person's mental capacity. Such may be held in civil context to determine whether a person should be committed for treatment.

**competent.** Having sufficient capacity, ability, or authority; possessing the requisite physical, mental, natural, or legal qualifications; capable; suitable; sufficient; legally fit. A testator may be said to be "competent" if he or she understands (1) the general nature and extent of his or her property, (2) his or her relationship to the people named in the will and to any people he or she disinherits, (3) what a will is, and (4) the transaction of simple business affairs.

**conservatee.** An incompetent or incapacitated person placed by the court under the care and supervision of a conservator. *See also* **conservator**.

**conservator.** A guardian; protector; preserver. A person appointed by court to manage the affairs of an incompetent person or to manage the estate of one who is unable to manage property and business affairs effectively. *See also* **guardian**.

**county.** The largest territorial division for local government in a state. Its powers and importance vary from state to state, and within the given state as well. In certain New England states, it exists mainly for judicial administration. In Louisiana, the equivalent unit is called a parish.

**court of appeals.** In those states with courts of appeals, such courts are usually intermediate appellate courts (with the highest appellate court being the state Supreme Court). In New York, Maryland, and the District of Columbia, however, courts of appeals are the highest appellate courts. In West Virginia the Supreme Court of Appeals is the court of last resort. Alabama, Oklahoma, Tennessee, and Texas have courts of criminal appeals, with those in Oklahoma and Texas being the highest appellate courts for criminal matters. Alabama, Oklahoma, and Texas have courts of civil appeals, which are intermediate appellate courts. *See also* **Supreme Court, courts of appeals**.

**court of chancery.** A court administering equity and proceeding according to the forms and principles of equity. In some of the United States, the title "court of chancery" is applied to a court possessing general equity powers, distinct from the courts of law. Courts of chancery (equity courts) have been abolished by all states that have adopted Rules of Civil Procedure. *See also* **court of equity**.

**court of civil appeals.** Such exist as intermediate appellate courts in Alabama, Oklahoma, and Texas. The Texas Court of Civil Appeals has appellate jurisdiction of cases decided in district and county courts.

**court of common pleas.** Courts in Pennsylvania wherein all civil and criminal actions are begun (except such as are brought before courts of inferior jurisdiction). Most such courts have been abolished, however, with their jurisdiction being transferred to district, circuit, or superior courts.

**court of equity.** A court which has jurisdiction in equity, which administers justice and decides controversies in accordance with the rules, principles, and precedents of equity, and which follows the forms and procedure of chancery; as distinguished from a court having the jurisdiction, rules, principles, and practice of the common law. Equity courts have been abolished in all states that have adopted Rules of Civil Procedure; law and equity actions having been merged procedurally into a single form of "civil action" (see Fed.R. Civil P. 2.).

**court of last resort.** Court which handles the final appeal on a matter; e.g., the U.S. Supreme Court for federal cases.

**court of original jurisdiction.** Courts where actions are initiated and heard in first instance.

**court of ordinary.** In Georgia such courts formerly had exclusive and general jurisdiction over probate of wills; granting letters testamentary, or of administration, and revocation of same; management, disposition, and distribution of estate of decedents, idiots, lunatics, and insane people and of all such other matters and things as appertain or relate to same; appointment and removal of guardians of minors and people of unsound mind and all controversies as to right of guardianship; receiving and hearing applications for homestead and exemption and granting same; and concurrently with judge of the county court, jurisdiction in binding out of orphans and apprentices, and all controversies between master and apprentice. The probate court now has jurisdiction over such matter.

**court of orphans.** In Maryland and Pennsylvania, a court, elsewhere known as a "probate" of "surrogates" court, with general jurisdiction over matters of probate and administration of estates, orphans, wards, and guardians.

**court of probate.** A court existing in many states having jurisdiction over the probate of wills, the grant of administration, and the supervision of the management and settlement of the estates of decedents, including the collection of assets, the allowance of claims, and the distribution of the estate. In some states the probate courts also have jurisdiction over divorce, custody, adoption, and change of name matters and of the estates of minors, including the appointment of guardians and the settlement of their accounts, and of the estates of lunatics, habitual drunkards, and spendthrifts. And in some states these courts possess a limited jurisdiction in civil and criminal cases. They are also called in some jurisdictions "orphans' courts" (e.g. Maryland, Pennsylvania) and "Surrogate's courts" (e.g. New York).

**courts of appeals, U.S.** Intermediate appellate courts created by Congress in 1891 and known until 1948 as United States Circuit Courts of Appeals, sitting in eleven numbered circuits, the District of Columbia, and the Court of Appeals for the Federal Circuit. Normally cases are heard by divisions of three judges sitting together, but on certain matters all the judges of a circuit may hear a case. Courts of appeals have appellate jurisdiction over most cases decided by United States District Courts and review and enforce orders of may federal administrative bodies. The decisions of the courts of appeals are final except as they are subject to discretionary review on appeal by the Supreme Court (28 U.S.C.A. §§41, 43, 1291).

**courts of record.** Those courts whose proceedings are permanently recorded, and which have the power to fine or imprison for contempt.

**curator.** A temporary guardian or conservator appointed by the court to care for the property or person or both of an incompetent, spendthrift, or a minor. This term has been adopted in a number of common-law jurisdictions, as in several American states. In Louisiana, a curator is a also person appointed to take care of the estate of an absentee.

**custodial care.** This is care in a nonmedical facility that provides room, board, limited supervision, and very limited nursing services that are usually restricted to passing out medications. Residents do not qualify for Medicare or Medicaid reimbursement. These facilities can provide safe and comfortable daily care such as assistance with dressing and bathing, maintenance of a special diet, and the like. They have no official name but are commonly referred to as personal care boarding homes, rest homes, and old age homes. Most are subject to state licensing regulations.

**defendant.** The person defending or denying.

**De Prerogativa Regis.** "The royal prerogative," this fourteenth-century English statute permitted the king to manage the land and property of "lunatics" who had been declared incurably incompetent by an inquisition. The statute also permitted the king to hold property and land in trust for those considered to be "temporarily incompetent."

**developmental disability.** An illness or condition that interferes with normal mental or physical development. The most prevalent developmental disabilities are mental retardation, learning disorders, cerebral palsy, deafness, and autism.

**disability.** The want of legal capability to perform an act. The term is generally used to indicate an incapacity for the full enjoyment of ordinary legal rights; thus, people under age, insane individuals, and convicts are said to be under legal disability. Under the Uniform Probate Code, an incapacitated person is one who is impaired by reason of physical disability.

**disabled person.** A person who lacks legal capacity to act *sui juris* or who is physically or mentally disabled from acting on his own behalf or from pursuing occupations.

**discrimination.** In constitutional law, the effect of a statute or established practice which confers particular privileges on a class arbitrarily selected from a large number of people, all of whom stand in the same relation to the privileges granted and between whom and those not favored no reasonable distinction can be found. Unfair treatment or denial of normal privileges to persons because of their race, age, sex, nationality or religion.

**dismissal without prejudice.** Term meaning dismissal without prejudice to the right of the complainant to sue again on the same cause of action. The effect of the words "without prejudice" is to prevent the decree of dismissal from operating as a bar to subsequent suit.

**dismissal with prejudice.** Term meaning an adjudication on the merits, and final disposition, barring the right to bring or maintain an action on the same claim or cause. It is res judicata as to every matter litigated. *See* **res judicata**.

**double (or multiple) hearsay.** Hearsay statements which contain further hearsay statements within them. A statement made outside of court is hearsay when introduced in court to prove the truth of the statement. However, certain exceptions permit the introduction of hearsay if the out-of-court statement was made on the personal knowledge of the declarant as in the case of a declaration of a deceased person. If such a statement of the deceased person was not made on his personal knowledge, the hearsay would be double or totem pole hearsay.

**double jeopardy.** A Fifth Amendment guarantee enforceable against states through the Fourteenth Amendment, double jeopardy protects against second prosecution for the same offense after acquittal or conviction, and against multiple punishments for the same offense (see *North Carolina* v. *Pearce*, 395 U.S. 711, 89 S.Ct. 2072, 23 L.Ed.2d 656).

**due influence.** Influence obtained by persuasion and argument or by appeals to the affections (see *In re Chamberlain's Estate*, Cal.App., 109 P.2d 449, 452).

**due process of law.** Law in its regular course of administration through courts of justice. Due process of law implies the right of the person affected thereby to be present before the tribunal which pronounces judgment upon the question of life, liberty, or property, in its most comprehensive sense; to be heard, by testimony or otherwise, and to have the right of controverting, by proof, every material fact which bears on the question of right in the matter involved. If any question of fact or liability be conclusively presumed against him, this is not due process of law. An orderly proceeding wherein a person is served with notice, actual or constructive, and has an opportunity to be heard and to enforce and protect his rights before a court having power to hear and determine the case (see *Kazubowski* v. *Kazubowski*, 45 Ill.2d 405, 259 N.E.2d 282, 290).

**due process rights.** All rights which are of such fundamental importance as to require compliance with due process standards of fairness and justice. Procedural and substantive rights of citizens against government actions that threaten the denial of life, liberty, or property. *See* **due process of law**.

**durable power of attorney.** Exists when a person executes a power of attorney which will become or remain effective in the event he or she should later become disabled. Uniform Probate Code §5-501. Unlike a traditional power of attorney, a durable power does not lapse if and when the creator of the power becomes incapacitated or incompetent. The concept of the durable power was first promulgated in 1969. In 1979, the Uniform Probate Code adopted the language of the Uniform Durable Power of Attorney Act, and all states now allow durable powers. However, not all states allow *standby* (or *springing*) durable powers. *See* **standby durable power of attorney**.

**ecological relevancy.** Refers to the applicability of a test to the abilities and skills an individual requires for successful transactions with the everyday world.

**elderly.** Under most government and related programs and under most sections of the Internal Revenue Code, an individual's status as elderly is triggered on reaching age sixty-five.

**estate.** The total property of whatever kind that is owned by a decedent prior to the distribution of that property in accordance with the terms of a will, or, when there is no will, by the laws of inheritance in the state of domicile of the decedent. It means, ordinarily, the whole of the property owned by anyone, the realty as well as the personality. As used in connection with the administration of decedents' estates, the term includes property of a decedent, trust, or other person as such property exists from time to time during the administration, and hence may include probate assets as well as property passing by intestacy (Uniform Probate Code, §1-201[11]). *See* **community property**.

**et seq.** Short for *et sequentes*, "and the following ones." Et seq. also serves as the abbreviation for the singular *et sequens*, "and the following one." It is most commonly used in denominating page references and statutory section numbers.

**evidentiary.** Of or relating to evidence.

**exclusionary rule.** A constitutional rule of law which provides that otherwise admissible evidence may not be used in a criminal trial if it resulted from illegal police conduct. This rule is based upon court interpretation of the constitution's prohibition against unreasonable searches and seizures. The rule does not apply in civil proceedings as such, but statutes may specifically provide for the exclusion of such evidence.

*ex parte.* On one side only; by or for one party; done for, in behalf of, or on the application of, one party only. A judicial proceeding, order, injunction, and so forth, is said to be *ex parte* when it is taken or granted at the instance and for the benefit of one party only, and without notice to, or contestation by, any person adversely interested.

**ex parte hearing.** Hearings in which the court or tribunal hears only one side of the controversy.

**ex parte proceeding.** Any judicial or quasi judicial hearing in which only one party is heard as in the case of a temporary restraining order.

**ex rel.** Abbreviation of "ex relatione," meaning "upon relation or report." In legal matters, an *ex rel.* proceeding is brought in the name of the state but at the instigation and on the information of a private individual, or "relator," who has a private interest in the outcome of the case.

**fiduciary.** "A person having a [legal] duty, created by his undertaking, to act primarily for the benefit of another in matters connected with his undertaking" (34 N.E. 2d 68, 70). The person functions in position of trust, or holds a confidence. For example, an attorney has a fiduciary relationship with his or her client.

**expert testimony.** Opinion evidence of some person who possesses special skill or knowledge in some science, profession, or business which is not common to the average person and which is possessed by the expert by reason of his or her special study or experience.

**expert witness.** One who by reason of education or specialized experience possesses superior knowledge respecting a subject about which individuals having no particular training are incapable of forming an accurate opinion or deducing correct conclusions. A witness who has been qualified as an expert and who thereby will be allowed (through his or her answers to questions posted) to assist the jury in understanding complicated and technical subjects not within the understanding of the average lay person. One skilled in any particular art, trade, or profession, being possessed of peculiar knowledge concerning the same, and one who has given subject in question particular study, practice, or observation. If scientific, technical, or other specialized knowledge will assist the trier of fact to understand the evidence or to determine a fact in issue, a witness qualified as an expert by knowledge, skill, experience, training, or education may testify thereto in the form of an opinion or otherwise (see Fed.Evid. Rule 702).

**freedom.** The state of being free; liberty; self-determination; absence of restraint; the opposite of slavery. The power of acting, in the character of a moral personality, according to the dictates of the will, without other check, hindrance, or prohibition than such as may be imposed by just and necessary laws and the duties of social life.

**functional incapacities.** Refers to inabilities that are observable through conduct or behavior; that which an individual cannot do or accomplish. Some statutes require evidence of functional deficits or incapacities for the appointment of a guardian.

**guardian.** A person lawfully invested with the power, and charged with the duty, of taking care of the person and managing the property and rights of another person, who, for defect of age, understanding, or self-control, is considered incapable of administering his own affairs. One who legally has responsibility for the care and management of the person, or the estate, or both, of a child during its minority. A general term for a court-appointed surrogate (substitute) decision maker. A *general* guardian is one who has the general care and control of the person and estate of a ward, while a *special* guardian is one who has special or limited powers and duties with respect to a ward, e.g., a guardian who has the custody of the estate but not of the person, or vice versa, or a guardian *ad litem. See* **guardian** *ad litem*.

**guardian** *ad litem*. A special guardian appointed by the court in which a particular litigation is pending to represent an infant, ward or unborn person in that particular litigation, and the status of guardian ad litem exists only in that specific litigation in which the appointment occurs. *See* Ad litem.

**guardian (or conservator) of the estate.** A guardian (or conservator) of the estate is limited to control of the incompetent ward's assets. The guardian has no decision-making rights with respect to the ward's personal care or medical needs or wishes.

**guardian (or conservator) of the person.** A guardian (or conservator) of the person is limited to authority over the ward's personal care decisions, including at times medical care decisions. The guardian has no control over the ward's assets, but has complete control over his or her personal and healthcare needs.

**guardianship (or conservatorship).** Guardianship (or conservatorship) is a formal, court-appointed method of substitute decision making on behalf of an individual who has been declared legally incompetent. Some use the term "incapacitated" in place of "incompetent." The terms mean the same thing. Guardianships can be of the person, of the estate, or plenary (both). They can be public, limited, or temporary. The term "guardian" also describes an adult who is legally responsible for a minor.

Parents are the natural guardians of their children. Guardianship of minors operate under separate rules. *See* **guardian**; **ward**.

**habeas corpus.** Latin, "you have the body." The name given to a variety of writs having for their object to bring a party before a court or judge. The primary function of the writ is to release from unlawful imprisonment (see *People ex rel. Luciano* v. *Murphy*, 160 Misc. 573, 290 N.Y.S. 1011). A form of collateral attack. An independent proceeding instituted to determine whether a defendant is being unlawfully deprived of his or her liberty.

**healthcare standby durable power of attorney.** This is a standby durable power for healthcare decisions only. It is recommended for those who are concerned about a potential future loss of capacity due to a life-threatening or terminal illness, especially where state law does not allow a regular durable power of attorney to be used for medical and related lifecare decisions. Healthcare powers allow their creators to designate agents in whom they have complete trust to make critical and life-and-death decisions. Many states have adopted statutes allowing the creation of healthcare powers giving agents authorization to make substituted medicalcare decisions and to terminate life support systems.

**hearing.** A proceeding of relative formality (though generally less formal than a trial), generally public, with definite issues of fact or of law to be tried, in which witnesses are heard and evidence presented. It is a proceeding where evidence is taken to determine issue of fact and to render decision on basis of that evidence (see *People* v. *Ivenditti*, 276 C.A.2d 178, 80 Cal.Rptr. 761, 762). The parties proceeded against or otherwise involved have the right to be heard, in much the same manner as a trial and such proceedings may terminate in a final order. It is frequently used in a broader and more popular significance to describe whatever takes place before magistrates clothed with judicial functions and sitting without jury at any state of the proceedings subsequent to its inception, and to hearings before administrative agencies as conducted by a hearing examiner or Administrative Law Judge.

**hearsay.** A term applied to testimony given by a witness who relates not what he knows personally but what others have told him, or what he has heard said by others. Hearsay includes any statement made outside the present proceeding which is offered as evidence of the truth of matters asserted in the hearing. Also included as hearsay is nonverbal conduct which is intended to be the equivalent of a spoken assertion. Because the credibility of hearsay evidence rests upon the credibility of the out-of-court asserter and not solely on the credibility of the witness in court, hearsay evidence is generally inadmissible unless it falls within one of the many exceptions which provides for admissibility (see, for example, Fed.R.Evid. 803, 804). *See also* **double** (or **multiple**) **hearsay**.

**incapacitated person.** Any person who is impaired by reason of mental illness, mental deficiency, physical illness or disability, advanced age, chronic use of drugs, chronic intoxication, or other cause (except minority) to the extent that he or she lacks sufficient understanding or capacity to make or communicate responsible decisions concerning his or her person (Uniform Probate Code, §5-101).

**incapacity.** Want of legal, physical, or intellectual capacity; want of power or ability to take or dispose; want of legal ability to act. Inefficiency; incompetency; lack of adequate power. The quality or state of being incapable; want of capacity, lack of physical or intellectual incapability, disability, incompetence (see *Bole* v. *Civil City of Ligonier,* 120 Ind.App. 362, 161 N.E.2d 189, 194). *See also* **incompetency**.

**incompetency.** Lack of ability, knowledge, legal qualification, or fitness to discharge the required duty or professional obligation. A relative term which may be employed as meaning disqualification, inability, or incapacity and it can refer to lack of legal qualifications or fitness to discharge the required duty and to show want of physical or intellectual or moral fitness (see *County Bd. of Ed. of Clarke County* v. *Oliver,* 270 Ala. 107, 116 So.2d 566, 567). Legally, incompetency is the inability to properly care for one's property and/or person, or to make or communicate rational decisions concerning one's person. A person can only be labeled "incompetent" if declared incompetent by a court. Most "incompetent" adjudications are the result of mental illness, mental retardation, or other mental disabilities or diseases (e.g., from drug or alcohol abuse or from advancing age, as in Alzheimer's disease). *See also* **incapacity**. *Compare* **competency**.

*in limine.* On or at the threshold; at the very beginning; preliminarily. Any motion, whether used before or during a trial, by which exclusion is sought of anticipated prejudicial evidence. *See* **motion** *in limine.*

*in re.* "In the matter of," usually used to indicate a legal proceeding where there is no opponent; rather, there is a judicial disposition of a matter.

**insanity.** This term is a social and legal term rather than a medical one, and indicates a condition which renders the affected person unfit to enjoy liberty of action because of the unreliability of his behavior with concomitant danger to himself and others. The term is more or less synonymous with mental illness or psychosis. In law, the term is used to denote the degree of mental illness which negates the individual's legal responsibility or capacity.

**interdiction.** *French law*: Every person who, as a result of insanity, has become incapable of controlling his own interests can be put under the control of a guardian, who shall administer his affairs with the same effect as he might himself. Such a person is said to be *"interdit,"* and his *status* is described as "interdiction." In civil law, the term describes a judicial decree by which a person is deprived of the *exercise* of his civil rights.

*inter vivos*. Between the living; from one living person to another. Where property passes by conveyance, the transaction is said to be *inter vivos*, to distinguish it from a case of succession or devise. This is a trust that becomes effective during the lifetime of the trustor.

*inter vivos trust*. Trust created by an instrument which becomes operative during the settlor's lifetime as contrasted with a testamentary trust which takes effect on the death of the settlor. *See also* **living trust**.

**irrevocable trust.** Trust which may not be revoked after its creation as in the case of a deposit of money by one in the name of another as trustee for the benefit of a third person (beneficiary). This is a trust created for purposes of irrevocably transferring assets to another. The trust creator loses all control over the trust assets. Therefore, trust assets are not included in his or her estate on death.

**limited guardianship.** Some states have limited guardianship statutes that allow a guardian only as much power as is required to care for the needs of the incompetent. A limited guardianship is used in cases of situational incompetency, whereby an individual is incompetent to make decisions in only certain area of his or her life. The guardianship is tailored to the ward's needs.

**living trust.** An *inter vivos* trust created and operative during the lifetime of the settlor and commonly for the benefit or support of another person.

**living will.** A living will is a document provided for by a state's "natural death" statute that gives the declarant's physician and family an advance directive that the declarant's life is not to be prolonged in the event it is medically determined that he or she (1) is in a terminal condition that will result in imminent death (under some statutes), or (2) has an irreversible injury or illness that results in a persistent vegetative state (under other statutes). "Imminent death" is a more narrow concept than "irreversible injury or death." States have varying requirements that determine the validity of a living will.

**mental capacity** *or* **competence.** Term contemplates the ability to understand the nature and effect of the act in which a person is engaged and the business he or she is transacting (see *Jones* v. *Traders & General Ins. Co.,* Tex.Civ. App., 144 S.W.2d 689, 694). Such a measure of intelligence, understanding, memory, and judgment relative to the particular transaction (e.g. making of a will or entering into contract) that will enable the person to understand the nature, terms, and effect of his or her act (see *Conley* v. *Nailor,* 118 U.S. 127, 6 S.Ct. 1001, 30 L.Ed. 112).

**mental incapacity; mental incompetency.** Such is established when there is found to exist an essential privation of reasoning faculties, or when a person is incapable of understanding and acting with discretion in the ordinary affairs of life. *See* **incapacity**; **insanity**.

**motion** *in limine.* A pretrial motion requesting court to prohibit opposing counsel from referring to or offering evidence on matters so highly prejudicial to moving party that curative instructions cannot prevent predispositional effect on jury (see *Messler* v. *Simmons Gun Specialties, Inc.,* Okl., 687 P.2d 121, 127). Purpose of such motion is to avoid injection into trial of matters which are irrelevant, inadmissible, and prejudicial and granting of motion is not a ruling on evidence and, where properly drawn, granting of motion cannot be error (see *Redding* v. *Ferguson,* Tex.Civ.App., 501 S.W.2d 717, 714).

**onus probandi.** Burden of proving; the burden of proof. The strict meaning of the term "onus probandi" is that, if no evidence is adduced by the party on whom the burden is cast, the issue must be found against him.

**opinion evidence** *or* **testimony.** Evidence of what the witness thinks, believes, or infers in regard to facts in dispute, as distinguished from his personal knowledge of the facts themselves. The rules of evidence ordinarily do not permit witnesses to testify as to opinions or conclusions. An exception to this rule exists as to "expert witnesses." Witnesses who, by education and experience, have become expert in some art, science, profession, or calling, may state their opinions as to relevant and material matter, in which they profess to be expert, and may also state their reasons for the opinion.

***parens patriae.*** Literally "parent of the country"; refers traditionally to the role of the state as sovereign and guardian of people under legal disability, such as juveniles or the insane. The rationale used to justify stripping an individual of his or her personhood and property; doctrine that the state has the inherent power and duty to protect those of its citizens who are unable to care for themselves. It is a concept of standing utilized to protect those quasi-sovereign interests such as health, comfort, and welfare of the people. *Parens patriae* originates from the English common law where the king had a royal prerogative to act as guardian to persons with legal disabilities such as infants. In the United States, the *parens patriae* function belongs with the states. The use of this power to deprive a person of freedom has been limited by recent laws and decisions; for example, *Kent* v. *U. S.*, 383 U.S. 541, 554-555, 86 S.Ct. 1045, 1054, 16 L.Ed.2d 84.

**parish.** In Louisiana, a territorial governmental division of the state corresponding to what is elsewhere called a "county."

**paternalism.** Relating to groups or individuals in a manner suggesting a father's relationship with his children.

**petition.** An application made to a court *ex parte*, or where there are no parties in opposition, praying for the exercise of the judicial powers of the court in relation to some matter which is not the subject for a suit or action, or for authority to do some act which requires the sanction of the court, as for the appointment of a guardian. A formal written request or prayer for a certain thing to be done. It "connotes an application in writing addressed to a court or judge, stating facts and circumstances relied upon as a cause for judicial action, and containing a prayer (formal request) for relief" (110 S.E.2d 909, 911).

**petitioner.** An adult who presents a petition to a court in order to initiate an equity proceeding or to appeal from a judgment. The adverse party is called the respondent.

**plaintiff.** A person who brings an action.

**plenary.** A formal word for full, complete, or entire.

**plenary guardianship.** This type of guardianship gives the guardian decision-making powers with respect to personal care, health care, and estate and asset management. It combines the authority of a guardianship of the estate and of the person. Often a bank will act as a plenary guardian.

**power of attorney.** An instrument in writing whereby one person, as principal, appoints another as his agent and confers authority to perform certain specified acts or kinds of acts on behalf of principal(see *Complaint of Bankers Trust Co.*, C.A.Pa., 752 F.2d 874, 885). An instrument authorizing another to act as one's agent or attorney. The agent is attorney in fact and his power is revoked on the death of the principal of law. Such power may be either general (full) or special (limited). This power is a written authorization that grants the decision-making power of the principal (the creator of the power) to an agent, or attorney-in-fact, who is designated in the power instrument. A traditional power remains valid only as long as the principal has the ability to terminate it (i.e., remains legally competent to do so). A traditional power may be general, special (rights with respect to a specialized activity), or limited (a general power with limitations). *See* **durable power of attorney**.

**prejudice.** A forejudgment; bias; partiality; preconceived opinion. A leaning towards one side of a cause for some reason other than a conviction of its justice. *See also* **average man test**; **bias**; **discrimination**.

**preponderance of evidence.** As a standard of proof in civil cases, it is evidence which is of greater weight or more convincing than the evidence which is offered in opposition to it; that is, evidence which as a whole shows that the fact sought to be proved is more probable than not. With respect to the burden of proof in civil actions, it means greater weight of evidence, or evidence which is more credible and convincing to the mind. That which best accords with reason and probability. The word "preponderance" means something more than "weight"; it denotes a superiority of weight, or outweighing. The words are not synonymous, but substantially different. There is generally a "weight" of evidence on each side in case of contested facts. The preponderance of evidence may not be determined by the number of witnesses, but by the greater weight of all evidence, which does not necessarily mean the greater number of witnesses, but opportunity for knowledge, information possessed, and the manner of testifying determines the weight of testimony.

**pro persona.** Latin, "for one's own person"; used in some jurisdictions as an equivalent of *pro se* ("on one's own behalf") and *in propria persona.* The phrase is sometimes shortened to *pro per*, for example, a *pro per* litigant.

**public guardianship.** A public guardian is an employee of the state who is available to be appointed as guardian of either the person or the estate, for an incompetent who would otherwise lack a guardian (perhaps because his or her estate will not support a bank to act as guardian). Public guardians are ready to provide substituted consent if no one else is available to do so or if the state considers them the best choice as guardian. The function of the public guardian is to make decisions for the ward concerning management of assets and institutionalization, and for securing entitlements and other benefits. A public guardian is also sometimes called a public trustee, public fiduciary, or state guardian.

**Quia Emptores.** Passed by Parliament in 1290, this act abolished the restraint upon transfer of land that had been imposed under the feudal system. The effect of this statute on both ownership and land transactions was that once the land was sold, the seller had no further connection to it.

**reasonable man doctrine** *or* **standard.** The standard which one must observe to avoid liability for negligence is the standard of the reasonable man under all the circumstances, including the foreseeability of harm to one such as the plaintiff.

**res judicata.** A matter adjudged; a thing judicially acted upon or decided; a thing or matter settled by judgment. Rule that a final judgment rendered by a court of competent jurisdiction on the merits is conclusive as to the rights of the parties and their privies, and, as to them, constitutes an absolute bar to a subsequent action involving the same claim, demand or cause of action (see *Matchett* v. *Rose*, 36 Ill.App.3d 638, 344 N.E.2d 770, 779).

**respondent.** In legal proceedings commenced by petition, the person against whom action or relief is prayed, or who opposes the prayer of the petition. *See* **defendant**. *Compare* **petitioner**.

**revocable trust.** This is a trust that a grantor can later revoke. The primary potential advantage for the elderly and disabled is that a revocable trust provides for professionally management of their assets, while giving them the power to terminate or change trustees or to take the assets back into their own control, if warranted.

**sanction.** Penalty or other mechanism of enforcement used to provide incentives for obedience with the law or with rules and regulations. That part of a law which is designed to secure enforcement by imposing a penalty for its violation or offering a reward for its observance.

**senility.** Quality of being senile; an infirmity resulting from deterioration of mind and body experienced in old age. Feebleness of body and mind incident to old age, and an incapacity to contract arising from the impairment of the intellectual faculties by old age.

**settlement.** Act or process of adjusting or determining; an adjusting; an adjustment between people concerning their dealings or difficulties; an agreement by which parties having disputed matters between them reach or ascertain what is coming from one to the other. To fix or resolve conclusively; to make or arrange for final disposition (see *Wager* v. *Burlington Elevators, Inc.*, 116 N.J.Super. 390, 282 A.2d 437, 441).

**sexism.** The social domination and economic exploitation of members of one sex by the other, specifically, of women by men. Systematically stereotyping and discriminating against people because of their gender.

**shall.** As used in statutes, contracts, or the like, this word is generally imperative or mandatory. In common or ordinary parlance, and in its ordinary signification, the term "shall" is a word of command, and one which has always or which must be given a compulsory meaning; used to denote obligation. The word in ordinary usage means "must" and is inconsistent with a concept of discretion (see *People* v. *Municipal Court for Los Angeles Judicial Dist.*, 149 C.A.3d 951, 197 Cal.Rptr. 204, 206). But it may be construed as merely permissive or directory (as equivalent to "may"), to carry out the legislative intention and in cases where no right or benefit to any one depends on its being taken in the imperative sense, and where no public or private right is impaired by its interpretation in the other sense (see *Wisdom* v. *Board of Sup'rs of Polk County*, 236 Iowa 669, 19 N.W.2d 602, 607, 608).

**show cause order.** Court order, decree, execution, and so on, to appear as directed, and present to the court such reasons and considerations as one has to offer why a particular order, decree, and so forth, should not be confirmed, take effect, be executed, or as the case may be.

**sound mind.** The normal condition of the human mind—that state in which its faculties of perception and judgment are ordinarily well developed, and not impaired by mania, insanity, or other mental disorder. In the law of wills, "sound mind" means that the testator must have been able to understand and carry in mind, in a general way, the nature and situation of his property, his relations to those having claim to his or her remembrance, and the nature of his act.

**spendthrift.** One who spends money profusely and improvidently; a prodigal; one who lavishes or wastes his estate. By statute, a person who by excessive drinking, gaming, idleness, or debauchery of any kind shall so spend, waste, or lessen his estate as to expose himself or his family to want or suffering, or expose the government to charge or expense for the support of himself or of his family, or is liable to be put under guardianship as a consequence of such excesses.

**standard of proof.** The burden of proof required in a particular type of case, as in a criminal case where the prosecution has the standard (i.e., burden) of proof beyond a reasonable doubt, and in most civil cases where proof by a fair preponderance of the evidence is required. *See* **burden of proof**.

**standby durable power of attorney.** This is a power of attorney that comes into effect and gives the attorney-in-fact the power to act on a formal finding of the principal's (creator of the power) incapacity. If and when the principal regains capacity the power is suspended. *See* **durable power of attorney**.

**sui juris.** Latin, "of his own right"; possessing full social and civil rights; not under any legal disability, or the power of another, or guardianship. Having the capacity to manage one's own affairs; not under legal disability to act for one's self.

**supreme court.** An appellate court existing in most of the states. In the federal court system, and in most states, it is the highest appellate court or court of last resort. In others (such as New York) the supreme court is a court of general original jurisdiction, possessing also (in New York) some appellate jurisdiction, but of the court of last resort. *See also* **court of appeals.**

**Supreme Court of the United States.** The U.S. Supreme Court comprises the Chief Justice of the United States and such number of Associate Justices as may be fixed by Congress.

**Supreme Judicial Court.** Highest appellate court in Maine and Massachusetts.

**surrogate.** The name given to some of the states to the judge or judicial officer who has jurisdiction over the administration of probate matters, guardianships, and so on. In other states he is called judge of probate, register, judge of the orphans' court, and the like. He is ordinarily a county officer, with a local jurisdiction limited to his county. *See* **surrogate court.**

**surrogate court.** Name of court in certain states with jurisdiction similar to that of probate court. In New York, the surrogate's court has jurisdiction over all actions and proceedings relating o the affairs of decedents, probate of wills, administration of estates and actions and proceedings arising thereunder or pertaining thereto, guardianship of the property of minors, and such other actions and proceedings, not within the exclusive jurisdiction of the supreme court, as may be provided by law.

**temporary (emergency) guardianship.** A temporary or emergency guardianship is used in cases in which a disabled individual needs immediate medical treatment but is unable to give informed consent due to a life-threatening or severely incapacitating condition. The distinguishing feature of a temporary guardianship is that it gives medical providers the ability to obtain a guardian quickly when an emergency arises that calls for quick substituted decision making. Normal guardianship procedures are too extended to provide emergency guardian services.

**testamentary capacity.** That measure of mental ability which is recognized in law as sufficient for the making of a will. A testator may be said to be competent or have testamentary capacity if he or she understands (1) the general nature and extent of his property, (2) his relationship to the people named in the will and to any people he disinherits, (3) what a will is, and (4) the transaction of simple business affairs.

**testamentary disposition** (or **transfer**). A gift of property that takes effect at the time of the death of the individual who has made the disposition or bequest (by will, by *inter vivos* transaction, or by deed).

**testator.** One who makes or has made a testament or will; one who dies leaving a will. This term is borrowed from the civil law.

**testatrix.** A woman who makes a will; a woman who dies leaving a will; a female testator.

**trust.** A legal entity created by a grantor for the benefit of designated beneficiaries under the laws of the state and the valid trust instrument. For tax purposes, a trust is an independent entity required to file a tax return. *See inter vivos* **trust**; **irrevocable trust**; **living trust**.

**undue influence.** Persuasion, pressure, or influence short of actual force, but stronger than mere advice, that so overpowers the dominated party's free will or judgment that he or she cannot act intelligently and voluntarily, but acts, instead, subject to the will or purposes of the dominating party. Any improper or wrongful constraint, machination, or urgency of persuasion whereby the will of a person is overpowered and he is induced to do or forbear an act which he would not do or would do if left to act freely. Influence which deprives person influenced of free agency or destroys freedom of his will and renders it more the will of another than his own. Misuse of position of confidence or taking advantage of a person's weakness, infirmity, or distress to change improperly that person's actions or decisions. The term refers to conduct by which a person, through his power over mind of testator, makes the latter's desires conform to his own, thereby overmastering the volition of the testator (see *Parrisella* v. *Fotopulous*, 111 Ariz. 4, 522 P.2d 1081, 1083). *See also* **due influence**.

**Uniform Durable Power of Attorney Act (UDPAA).** The UDPAA provides for the creation of durable powers of attorney and standby durable powers, which are powers that spring into effectiveness only when the power's creator becomes incapacitated.

**Uniform Probate Code (UPC).** With respect to guardianship, the UPC defines "incompetency" and governs certain acts of the guardians of incompetent wards. On obtaining court approval, a guardian may engage in estate planning for the ward, but the UPC stipulates that a guardian may not execute or modify a ward's will. It also contains provisions for proper representation at an incompetency hearing. The UPC model of incompetence connects a physical or mental condition to cognitive functioning: the condition renders the individual incapable of understanding, communicating, or making responsible decisions (i.e., "lacking sufficient understanding or capacity to make or communicate responsible decisions"). Note that the court (judge) must still make a value judgment about whether the defendant can make *responsible* decisions.

**unsound mind.** Nonlegal term referring to one who from infirmity of mind is incapable of managing himself or his affairs. The term, therefore, includes insane people (*see* **insanity**). It exists where there is an essential deprivation of the reasoning faculties, or where a person is incapable of understanding and acting with discretion in the ordinary affairs of life (see *Oklahoma Natural Gas Corporation* v. *Lay*, 175 Okl. 75, 51 P.2d 580, 582). But eccentricity, uncleanliness, slovenliness, neglect of person and clothing, and offensive and disgusting personal habits do not constitute unsoundness of mind. *See also* **capacity**.

**villein.** In feudal England, any class of serfs who, by the thirteenth century, had become freemen in their legal relations to everyone except their lord, to whom they remained as slaves.

**ward.** A person, especially a child or incompetent, placed by the court under the care and supervision of a guardian or conservator. *See* **guardian**; **guardianship**.

# NOTES

1. The primary sources for these definitions is Henry Campbell Black's *Black's Law Dictionary,* 6th ed. (St. Paul, Minn.: West Publishing Co., 1990), and Steven H. Gifis's *Law Dictionary* (Hauppauge, N.Y.: Barron's Educational Series, Inc., 1996). When using any law dictionary, be mindful of the fact that the language of law is not static. Rather, it evolves over time as legal terms and words are defined, redefined, and expanded through usage. The secondary source is Lawrence A. Frolik and Melissa C. Brown's *Advising the Elderly or Disabled Client: 1994 Cumulative Supplement* (Boston, Mass.: Warren, Gorham & Lamont, 1994).

2. L. A. Frolik and A. P. Barnes, "An Aging Population: A Challenge to the Law," *The Hastings Law Journal* 42 (1991): 683–718.

3. Ibid., p. 690.

# BIBLIOGRAPHY

"Advice for Family Caregivers." *Families of the Aged*. Silver Spring, Md.: CD Publications, 1988.

Alexander, G. J. "On Being Imposed Upon by Artful or Designing Persons—The California Experience with the Involuntary Placement of the Aged." *San Diego Law Review,* 14, no. 5 (1977): 1083–1099.

————. "Remaining Responsible: On Control of One's Health Needs in Aging." *Santa Clara Law Review* 20 (1980): 13–47.

Alexander, G. J., and T. H. D. Lewin. *The Aged and the Need for Surrogate Management*. Syracuse, N.Y.: Syracuse University Press, 1972.

Anderer, S. J. *Determining Competency in Guardianship Proceedings*. Washington, D.C.: American Bar Association, 1990, p. 11.

Atkinson, G. "Towards a Due Process Perspective in Conservatorship Proceedings for the Aged." *Journal of Family Law* 18 (1980): 819–45.

Bank, L., and Poythress, J. (1982). "The Elements of Persuasion in Expert Testimony." *Journal of Psychiatry and Law* (summer 1982): pp. 173–85.

Barnes, A. P. "Beyond Guardianship Reform: A Reevaluation of Autonomy and Beneficence for a System of Principled Decision-Making in Long Term Care." *Emory Law Journal* 41, no. 3 (1992): 633–760.

Baron, J. B. "Empathy, Subjectivity, and Testamentary Capacity." *San Diego Law Review* 24 (1987): 1043–1080.

Barry, J. "Redefining Aging: 'Golden Years' Now an Extension of Middle Age." *Santa Barbara News-Press*, 16 February 1998, p. D4.

Bayles, F., and S. McCartney. "Minnie Monoff Didn't Want Protection; She Wanted Freedom." *Los Angeles Times*, 27 September 1987, p. A2.

————."If You're Old, You Can't Be Foolish." *Los Angeles Times*, 27 September 1987, p. A2.

————. "Stewards of Elderly Beset with Cases." *Los Angeles Times*, 27 September 1987, p. A28.

————. "Guardianship: Few Safeguards." *Los Angeles Times*, 27 September 1987, p. A2.

Benton, F. C. "The Courts." *Guardianship of the Elderly: Psychiatric and Judicial Aspects*. Edited by G. H. Zimny and G. T. Grossberg. New York: Springer Publishing Company, 1998.

Beyette, B. "So, Do You Have a Strategy for Handling the New Longevity?" *Los Angeles Times*, 2 November 1997, p. E5.

Birnbaum, R., and J. Stegner. "Source Credibility in Social Judgment: Bias, Expertise, and the Judge's Point of View." *Journal of Personality and Social Psychology* 37 (1979): 48.

Boyd, R. S. "Death With Dignity Still Eludes the Nation's Dying." *Santa Barbara News-Press*, 22 November 1995, p. A2.

Brock, J. "Judicial Decisions in Guardianship Cases." In *Guardianship of the Elderly: Psychiatric and Judicial Aspects*. Edited by G. H. Zimny and G. T. Grossberg. New York: Springer Publishing Company, 1998, pp. 86–101.

Brown, R. N. *The Rights of Older Persons: A Basic Guide to the Legal Rights of Older Persons Under Current Law.* 2d ed. Washington, D.C.: ACLU, 1989.

Bulcroft, K., M. R. Kielkopf, and K. Tripp, "Elderly Wards and Their Legal Guardians: Analysis of County Probate Records in Ohio and Washington." *The Gerontologist* 31, no. 2 (1991): 156–64.

Cook, C. M. "The Role and Rights of the Expert Witness." *Journal of Forensic Sciences* 9 (1964): 456–60.

Daly, Eugene J. *Thy Will Be Done: A Guide to Wills, Taxation, and Estate Planning for Older Persons.* 2d ed. (Amherst, N.Y.: Prometheus Books, 1994).

Deets, H. B. "It's Time to Smash Stereotypes about Aging." *AARP Bulletin*, 36, no. 2 (1995): 3.

"Disguised Oppression of Involuntary Guardianship: Have the Elderly Freedom to Spend?" *Yale Law Journal* 73 (1964): 676–92.

Drane, J. F. "Competency to Give an Informed Consent: A Model for Making Clinical Assessments." *JAMA* 252, no. 7 (1984): 925–27.

Easterlin, R. A., C. MacDonald, and D. J. Macunovitch. "Retirement Prospects of the Baby Boom Generation: A Different Perspective." *The Gerontologist* 30 (1990): 776.

Evans, S. "Lax Guardianship Rules Frighten Va. Elderly." *The Washington Post*, 18 July 1988, p. A1.

Emmons, S. "Conservators' Reach Can Be a Surprise." *Los Angeles Times*, 23 November 1997, p. A29.

Felsenthal, E. "Judges Find Themselves Acting as Doctors in Alzheimer's Cases." *Wall Street Journal*, 20 May 1994, p. B1.

Friedman, L., and M. Savage. "Taking Care: The Law of Conservatorship in California." *Southern California Law Review* 61 (1988): 273–90.

Frolik, L. A., and A. P. Barnes. "An Aging Population: A Challenge to the Law." *Hastings Law Journal* 42 (1991): 683–718.

Frolik, L. A., and M. C. Brown. *Advising the Elderly or Disabled Client: Legal, Health Care, Financial, and Estate Planning.* Boston, Mass.: Warren, Gorham & Lamont, 1994.

Gorman, T. "Conservators Suspected of Bilking the Frail." *Los Angeles Times,* 25 April 1999, pp. A1, A29, A31, A32.

Hallman, G. V., and J. S. Rosenbloom. *Personal Financial Planning.* New York: McGraw-Hill, Inc., 1993.

Hurme, S. B. *Steps to Enhance Guardianship Monitoring.* Washington, D.C.: American Bar Association, 1991.

Iris, M. A. "Editorial: New Directions for Guardianship Research." *The Gerontologist* 31, no. 2 (1991): 148–49.

Kalb, C. "Focus on Your Health: Caring From Afar." *Newsweek,* 22 September 1997, pp. 87–88.

Kapp, M. B. "Legal Basis of Guardianship." In *Guardianship of the Elderly: Psychiatric and Judicial Aspects.* Edited by G. H. Zimny and G. T. Grossberg. New York: Springer Publishing Company, 1998, pp. 16–24.

Keith, P. M., and R. R. Wacker. "Implementation of Recommended Guardianship Practices and Outcomes of Hearings for Older Persons." *The Gerontologist* 33, no. 1 (1993): 81–87.

Kirkendall, J. N. "Judicial Decisions in Guardianship Cases." In *Guardianship of the Elderly: Psychiatric and Judicial Aspects.* Edited by G. H. Zimny and G. T. Grossberg. New York: Springer Publishing Company, 1998, pp. 61–73.

Kritzer, H. M., H. M. Dicks, and B. J. Abramson. "Adult Guardianships in Wisconsin: How Is the System Working?" *Marquette Law Review* 76 (Spring 1993): 549–75.

Laucks, E. C. "People Shouldn't Be Denied Selfhood Because They've Aged." *Santa Barbara News-Press,* 27 March 1994, p. A2.

Loverde, J. *The Complete Eldercare Planner: Where to Start, Questions to Ask, and How to Find Help.* New York: Hyperion, 1997.

Lustbader, W., and N. R. Hooyman. *Taking Care of Aging Family Members.* New York: The Free Press, 1994.

Madoff, R. D. "Unmasking Undue Influence." *Minnesota Law Review* 81 (1997): 571–629.

Margulies, P. "Access, Connection, and Voice: A Contextual Approach to Representing Senior Citizens of Questionable Capacity." *Fordham Law Review* 62 (1994): 1073–1099.

Marshall, A., and A. S. Garb. "California Probate Procedure," 5th ed. Los Angeles: Parker & Son, section 709.

Mitchell, A. M. "The Objects of Our Wisdom and Our Coercion: Involuntary Guardianship for Incompetents." *Southern California Law Review* 52 (1979): 1407.

Moore, D. L. "The Durable Power of Attorney as an Alternative to the Improper Use of Conservatorship for Health-Care Decisionmaking." *St. John's Law Review* 60, no. 4 (1986).

Nixon, E. S. "A Consolidated Legal Capacity Standard." *Santa Clara Law Review* 27 (1987): 787–804.

390 THE RETIREMENT NIGHTMARE

Ostrom, C. M. "Who Guards People from the Guardians Watching Over Them?" *Seattle Times*, 25 September 1995, p. A2.

Parry, J. W., and S. B. Hurme. "Guardianship Monitoring and Enforcement Nationwide." *Mental and Physical Disability Law Reporter* 15, no. 3 (1991): 304–309.

Peden, J. M. "The Guardian Ad Litem Under the Guardianship Reform Act: A Profusion of Duties, a Confusion of Roles." *University of Detroit Law Review* 68 (1990): 19–35.

Perr, I. N. "Wills, Testamentary Capacity, and Undue Influence." *Bulletin of the American Academy of Psychiatry and Law* 9 (1981): 16.

Pipkin, W. E. "Expert Opinion Testimony: Experts, Where Did They Come From and Why Are They Here?" *Law and Psychology Review* 13 (1989): 103–18.

"Psychiatric Assistance in the Determination of Testamentary Capacity." *Harvard Law Review* 66 (1953): 1116–24.

Reece, T. "Private Geriatric Care Managers Fill a Real Need." *Santa Barbara News-Press*, 3 February 1997.

Rembar, C. *The Law of the Land: The Evolution of Our Legal System*. New York: Harper & Row, 1980.

Rein, J. E. "Preserving Dignity and Self-Determination of the Elderly in the Face of Competing Interests and Grim Alternatives: A Proposal for Statutory Refocus and Reform." *The George Washington Law Review* 60, no. 6 (1992): 1818–87.

Rein, J. E. "Clients with Destructive and Socially Harmful Choices—What's an Attorney to Do? Within and Beyond the Competency Construct." *Fordham Law Review* 62 (1994): 1101–76.

"Resource Guide: Serving Your Needs." *Modern Maturity* (March/April 1996): 89.

Robinson, D. N. *Psychology and Law*. New York: Oxford University Press, 1980.

*Santa Barbara County Senior Resource Directory, 97–98 Edition*, Area Agency on Aging for San Luis Obispo and Santa Barbara Counties.

Schmidt, W. C. "Guardianship of the Elderly in Florida." *Florida Bar Journal* 55 (1981): 189.

Schwartz, S. J. "Abolishing Competency as a Construction of Difference: A Radical Proposal to Promote the Equality of Persons with Disabilities." *University of Miami Law Review* 47 (1993): 867–82.

Schwitzgebel, R. L., and R. K. Schwitzgebel. *Law and Psychological Practice*. New York: John Wiley & Sons, 1980.

Shellenbarger, S. "Work & Family: Planning Ahead For the Inevitable, An Elder's Illness." *Wall Street Journal*, 22 March 1995, p. B1.

Silberfeld, M., and A. Fish. *When the Mind Fails: A Guide to Dealing with Incompetency*. Toronto: University of Toronto Press, 1994.

Spar, J. E., and A. S. Garb. "Assessing Competency to Make a Will." *American Journal of Psychiatry* 149, no. 2 (1992): 169–74.

Starkman, D. "Guardians May Need Someone to Watch Over Them." *The Wall Street Journal*, 8 May 1998, pp. B1, B2.

Strauss, P. J. "Before Guardianship: Abuse of Patient Rights Behind Closed Doors." *Emory Law Journal* 41 (1992): 761–71.

Tomlinson, T. et al. "An Empirical Study of Proxy Consent for Elderly Persons." *The Gerontologist* 30, no. 54 (191988): 54–64.

Tor, P. "Finding Incompetency in Guardianship: Standardizing the Process." *Arizona Law Review* 35 (1993): 739–64.

von Stange, N., and G. von Stange. "Guardianship Reform in New York." *Hofstra Law Review* 21 (1993): 755–99.

"When You Need A Lawyer." *Consumer Reports* (February 1996): 34–39.

Wilbur, K. H. "Alternatives to Conservatorship: The Role of Daily Money Management Services." *The Gerontologist* 31, no. 2 (1991): 150–55.

"Will Contests on Trial." *Stanford Law Review* 6 (1953): 91–103.

Willot, J. "Neurogerontology: The Aging Nervous System." *Gerontology: Perspectives and Issues* 77 (1990).

Winick, B. J. "The Side Effects of Incompetency Labeling and the Implications for Mental Health Law." *Psychology, Public Policy, and Law* 1, no. 1 (1995): 6–42.

Zimny, G. H., and G. T. Grossberg. *Guardianship of the Elderly: Psychiatric and Judicial Aspects*. New York: Springer Publishing Company, Inc., 1998.

# SUBJECT/AUTHOR INDEX

Adult Protective Services (APS)
  and State Office of Aging, 175
  role of, 175–76
advanced age. *See* old age
advance directives
  convenience joint tenancy accounts,
    217
  durable power of attorney for
    healthcare decisions, 217
  durable powers of attorney for prop-
    erty management, 213–16
  example, Oregon State, 218–25
  for healthcare decisions, 217–28
  for property management, 213–17
  living wills, 225–28
  need to review and update, 209, 215,
    218
  preselection and disqualification of
    conservator or guardian, 228–32
  preventing challenges to, 232–34
  revocable living trusts, 216
adversarial nature of proceedings, 37.
  *See* statutory reform
ageism, 17, 36, 181, 184, 187, 197,
  234. *See also* statutory reform
ageist bias, East versus West, 234–35

"aging in place," 169
Aging Society Project, 18
Aging with Dignity, 227–28
alcoholism as basis of conservator-
  ship/guardianship, 160–61
Alexander, George, 16, 21, 199
alternatives to conservatorships and
  guardianships
  avoiding incompetence/incapacity
    determinations, 168
  home care, 168–69
  mandated by court, 133
  overview of, 167–76
  planning, importance of, 174–75
  Section 8 Federal rent subsidy, 133
alternatives to probate courts. *See*
  statutory reforms
Alzheimer's and the elderly. *See*
  dementia and the elderly
American Association of Retired Persons (AARP), 227
American Bar Association, 33, 199,
  211
American Bar Association Commission on the Mentally Disabled,
  199–200

Americans with Disabilities Act, 40
Annas, George, 226
appealing unfavorable decisions
    concurrent improvement of pro-
        posed ward, 151
    difficulties in, 105–10, 202–203
    evidentiary basis of reversible errors
        for appeal, 44, 109
    expensive and time-consuming, 45,
        110–13, 147–49, 196
    few cases appealed, 45, 117
    incorrect standard of proof used in
        lower court, 144–45
    nonexpert opinion of judge used as
        evidence, 151
    successful appeals, 117–52
    unacceptable grounds for appoint-
        ment, 122, 148
    unsuccessful appeals, 77–113
    use of writ of habeas corpus, 128
    See also statutory reform compro-
        mise of due process rights and
        constitutional protections, 122–30
Area Agencies on Aging
    Eldercare Locator, 173
    Senior Connection, 173
    Senior Resource Directory, 173
    services provided, 172–73
artist's failure to sell artwork as incom-
    petence, 132–34
assessing incompetence, 186–87, 190,
    194
assessment services, 171
Atkinson, Gregory, 18, 53, 77, 181
attendance at competency/capacity
    hearings, 39, 40–41, 195
attorney
    court-appointed, 39–40
    for petitioners, 37
    for proposed ward, 39, 195–96
    for ward or conservatee, 100–101
    importance of in planning for inca-
        pacity, 207–209
    low cost or pro bono, 213
    Martindale-Hubbell legal directory,
        211
    need for up-to-date specialist,
        148–49
    questions to ask, 211–12
    selecting the right attorney, 210–13
autonomy
    artificial standard for the elderly,
        189–90
    destroyed by court, 53
    endangered by vague codes, 186–90
    financial autonomy and the state,
        185
    need to redefine, 189–90
    negated by state use of parens
        patriae, 180–81
    See also statutory reform

Barnes, Alison P., 16, 19, 27, 59, 187,
    196, 197
Baruch, Bernard M., 15, 33
Bayles, Fred, 51–52, 99, 154
Beecher, Henry Ward, 179
Benton, Senior Judge Field C., 45
Bill of Rights, violation of, 126–27.
    See also due process rights
Birnbaum, R., 72
Birren, Dr. James, 18
blindness as proof of incompetence,
    147–49
Brandeis, Judge, 51
Brock, James, 91, 118
Bront, Lydia, 18
Brookings Institution, 20
Brown, Robert, 39, 40, 47, 202, 214,
    218
Bulcroft, Kris, 46, 89
burden of proof
    born by petitioner, 42
    shifts in court, 35–36, 193–94
    standards unmet in court, 135–46
    suggested level of proof, 182
    unrealistic standards of proof, 44

California Lawyer, 155
Callahan, Kate, 227

Card, Emily W., 20

caregivers in America, 167

cases, involuntary/unwanted proceedings

pre-20th century, 60–63, 102–103

Case of Glen Hawkins, California, 23–25, 32, 208

Conservatorship of Earl B., California, 86–87

Conservatorship of Sanderson, California, 136, 143–45

*Cornia* v. *Cornia*, Utah, 85–86

*Cummings* v. *Stanford*, Georgia, 9–10, 25, 80–81, 140, 208

*Epperson* v. *Epperson*, Georgia, 97–98

*Estate of Galvin* v. *Galvin*, Illinois, 136, 141–42

*Goldman* v. *Krane*, Colorado, 122, 125–26

*Grant* v. *Johnson*, Oregon, 122–23, 129–30

Guardianship of Billie, 99–100

Guardianship of Lander, Maine, 105–107

Guardianship of Mr. S., 89–90

*Harvey* v. *Meador*, Mississippi, 112–13

*In re Conservatorship of Lundgaard*, Minnesota, 107–10

*In re Bolander*, Ohio, 147–49

*In re Estate of Liebling*, Illinois, 87–88

*In re Estate of Porter*, Pennsylvania, 136, 142–43

*In re Estate of Wagner*, Nebraska, 119–22

*In re Guardianship of Bockmuller*, Florida, 100–101

*In re Guardianship of Gallagher*, Ohio, 135–36, 138–40

*In re Lecht*, Ohio, 136, 140

*In re McDonnell*, Florida, 131–32

*In re Serafin*, Illinois, 147, 149–50

*In re Tyrell*, Ohio, 84–85, 187

*Interdiction of Dobbins*, Louisiana, 135, 137–38

*Interdiction of Haggerty*, Louisiana, 136, 145–46

*In the Matter of Wurm*, Indiana, 94–97

*Katz* v. *Superior Court, Etc.*, California, 122–25

*LeWinter* v. *Guardianship of LeWinter*, Florida, 150–51

*Matter of Conservatorship of Goodman*, Oklahoma, 122, 126–27

*Matter of Grinker*, New York, 131, 132–33

*Matter of Guardianship of Larson*, North Dakota, 100, 102–103

*Matter of Estate of McPeak*, Illinois, 135–37

*Matter of Nelson*, Missouri, 91–94

*McCallie* v. *McCallie*, Alabama, 131, 134–35

*Rice* v. *Floyd*, Kentucky, 81–82, 215, 131, 215

*Roberts* v. *Powers*, Arkansas, 81, 83

*Smeed* v. *Brechtel*, Oregon, 111

*Smith* v. *Smith*, Pennsylvania, 100, 103–105

*Stangier* v. *Stangier*, Oregon, 90–91

*West Virginia ex rel. Shamblin* v. *Collier*, West Virginia, 122, 127–29

cases, guardianship abuse

*Bryan* v. *Holzer*, 156–57

Conservatorship of Helen Conrad, 162

Conservatorship of John Nagle, 157

Conservatorship of Nelta Bradner, 155–56

Guardianship of Beulah Holt, 164–65

Guardianship of Florence Peters, 154

Guardianship of Jessie Linthicum, 162–63

Guardianship of Marguerite Van Etten, 158–59
Guardianship of Maverick, 157–58
Guardianship of Minnie Monoff, 154–55
Guardianship of Sarah, 160
Guardianship of Violet, 161, 175
*In re Interdiction of Ronstrom*, 159–60
*Matter of Guardianship of Renz*, 160–61
*U.S.* v. *Young*, 163
Census Bureau, United States, 17
Center for Social Gerontology, 15
challenges to legal directives, preventing. *See* advance directives
changes needed in codes. *See* statutory reform
changing roles of court officials, 192–93
Chinello, Judith, 153
Choice in Dying, 227
Churchill, Sir Winston, 117
competing motives of petitioners. *See* statutory reform
complexity/confusion of legal paperwork and proceedings, 193–94
Confucius, 167, 207
consequences of being declared incompetent or incapacitated, 12, 46
conservatorships and guardianships, involuntary
and civil commitment, 39, 130
as antemortem will contests, 43
as civil death, 146
assumption underlying petitions, 83
"compelling state interest" and, 127, 182
competing economic interests, 182
definition, 28–29
distinctions drawn in some states, 29–30
for the mentally ill, 46–47, 199–200
financial burden, 197–98
fundamental liberty interests lost, 182
ninety-four percent of all cases lost by elderly, 45
numbers of, 10–11, 15
"of the person" and "of the estate," 29–30
origins in *Statute De Prerogativa Regis*, 59
plenary, 29
reports required, 33, 199–200
rights lost, 52–53, 186
second petition filed 18 months after first is dismissed, 134–35
statistics on cases won/lost by elderly, 45
stigma of, 145
undue influence and, 63–64, 188–89
*See also* incompetence and incapacity; statutory reform
conservatorships and guardianships
as last choice, 134
for impoverished elderly, 51–52
of the mentally and developmentally disabled, 46–47, 132–134
use of the two terms, 28–29
voluntary, benefit of, 11, 126
conservatorship/guardianship tribunal, suggestions form 197
conservatorship to permit deprogramming, 123–25
constitutional rights. *See* due process and constitutional rights
Consumer Reports, 211–13
convalescent facilities. *See* nursing homes and institutionalization
convenience accounts, 217. *See also* advance directives
costs in one unwanted conservatorship proceeding, 323
Coté, M. J., 65
court investigator, 38. *See also* visitors, court-appointed
Court of Proxies, 187–88
court setting, alternative to, 196
court system in America, 79
courts used as "slow courts of the dead," 112–13, 196–97
cronyism in courts, 40

cult, family defined in court as, 189–90

Currey, Louise, 170

daily money management services for the elderly, 171

decision-making
bad choice made by competent or incompetent mind, 187
competent, suggested definition, 187–88
"deliberate decision-making" standard, 185, 187–88
disabled person directing his care through others, 142
lost via *parens patriae*, 180–81
judicial determinations on, 167, 187
lack of neutral criteria for evaluation, 184
"reasonable" or "responsible" decisions as value judgments, 35–36, 97–98, 183–84
right to be eccentric or different, 141–42, 180–81, 194
right to be irrational, 62
right to make foolish or imprudent decisions, 79, 131–32, 180–81, 184
poor decisions as proof of incompetence or incapacity, 36, 43, 184–86
unrealistic or artificial standard of autonomy, 91, 189–90

definitions, legal, 363–86
definitions vague or lacking, 88–97, 186–90
"deliberate decisions" standard, 184. *See also* decision-making

statutory reform

demeanor evidence in court, 84–85

dementia
and the elderly, 19
diagnosis of in court, 99–100
"normal senility," used in court, 85–86

demographics on the elderly in America
caregiving and, 167–68
general, 17–18
men vs. women, 22
racial, 22

demonstrating competence or capacity, 30

Denver Department of Social Services, 125–26

*De Prerogativa Regis*, 59

deprivation of fundamental liberty interests, 31, 34, 125, 128–29

deprivation of property rights, 125

designing persons, 103–105

disqualifications in advance directives, 229

Donnelly, Elise, 35

double jeopardy protection, lack of, 52

"Dr. Fox" test, 72–73

due process and constitutional rights
compromised in hearings, 39, 45, 100–105, 128, 190–91, 192
constitutional rights circumvented, 30, 34, 37–38, 39, 52, 73–74, 101, 102–103, 124, 125, 126–27, 129–30
for criminals, 30, 100
for the elderly, 28, 30, 100, 118
right to an attorney, 39
*See also* rights lost by ward; statutory reform

Duke, Joy, 164

durable powers of attorney
defined, 214–15
disregarded by court, 81–82, 214–15
immediately effective or standby, 214
in conjunction with revocable living trusts, 213, 216
need for renewal of, 215–16
practical considerations, 215–16
supported by court, 134–35
use of, 213–16
*See also* power of attorney

elder abuse
   defined, 175–74
   lengthy litigation as, 112–13
   reporting, 176
   *See also* Adult Protective Services
Eldercare Locator. *See* Area Agencies
   on Aging
elder law attorney, need for, 41, 211.
   *See also* attorney
emotional burden of proceedings, 45,
   46, 53, 74, 121, 154–55, 164
Emmons, Steve, 32
entitlement applications, 171
epidemic, legal, 11, 16
Evans, Sandra, 162
evidence used in court. *See* incompetence and incapacity; statutory
   reform
ex parte hearings
   allegation of emergency, 34, 191
   conservatorship/guardianship estab-
      lished without a hearing, 34, 102,
      125–26, 129–30
   held incommunicado, 125, 130
   right to adequate notice disregarded,
      37–38, 190–91
expert witnesses
   as "liars," 67
   bias among, 69–70
   "Dr. Fox" test, 72–73
   effectiveness of, 71–72
   expert testimony, history of, 67
   Federal Rules of Evidence, 67
   influence of, 72–74
   mental health expert witnesses,
      70–71
   on competence, testamentary ca-
      pacity and undue influence,
      232–34
   opinion evidence, 34, 68–69
   purpose of, 42, 69–70
   qualifications, 70–71
   use in conservatorship/guardianship
      proceedings, 41–42, 66–67

factors driving conservatorship/guar-
   dianship proceedings
   assisting the incompetent or inca-
      pacitated, 21
   financial interests of third parties,
      21–22, 23, 182–83
   preservation of inheritances, 10,
      11–12, 21, 46, 63–66, 86–87,
      87–88, 119–22, 182–83
Fifth Amendment rights, violation of,
   52
filed by social workers, social welfare
   agencies and neighbors, 208
filing of conservatorship/guardianship
   petitions, 331, 36–37
financial abuse, potential for. *See*
   cases, guardianship abuse; statutory reform
financial burden of proceedings. *See*
   payment for proceedings
financial decisions as proof of incom-
   petence/incapacity, 43, 79–81
financial penalty for intentional abuse
   of elderly, 198
First Amendment rights, violation of,
   103–105, 124–25
fiscal mismanagement, 184–86
Five Wishes living will, 227–28
flawed nature of conservatorship/
   guardianship codes, 16, 179–203.
   *See also* statutory reform
Fourth Amendment rights, violation
   of, 102–103
freedom from involuntary physical
   confinement, 31
freedom of association, 124–25
Friedman, Lawrence, 27, 87
Frolik, Lawrence A., 16, 19, 27, 52
functional definitions of capacity and
   competence, 187–88, 194

Garb, Andrew S., 64, 66, 233
geriatric care management, 169–72. *See
   also* National Association of Professional Geriatric Care Managers

geriatric experts, assessments by, 194, 195–96

Gorman, Tom, 162

Grand Jury counterpart for protective proceedings, 194

Green, Don, 33, 153

guardian *ad litem*
  decisions based on intuition or opinion, 127–28, 192
  redefinition needed, 192
  representing ward in appeal, 125
  role of, 191–93
  testifying against proposed ward, 127–28

guardians/conservators
  lack of licensure, 32–33, 153
  lack of supervision or accountability, 153–65, 198–201
  *See also* cases, guardianship abuse

guarding the guardians. *See* statutory reform

Guttmacher, 40

Hallman, G. Victor, 217, 226

health as evidence of incompetence/incapacity, 33–34, 36

health care decisions
  differences between, 226
  durable power of attorney for, 217–25
  living wills, 217, 225–28
  problems with living wills, 226–28

hearsay evidence, used in court, 44, 193–94

hereditary property rights in feudal society, 57–59

Hibbard, Frank, 158

home care
  at a distance, 173
  need for advance planning, 174–75
  preferred to nursing home care, 168
  range of options, 167–75
  *See also* alternatives to conservatorships and guardianships

Holmes, Oliver Wendell, Jr., 57

Hooyman, Nancy R., 167, 174

House Subcommittee on Health and Long-Term Care, 198

Hugo, Victor, 153

Hurme, Sally Balch, 33, 39, 199, 200

incompetence and incapacity
  blindness and, 147–49
  criteria lacking, 42
  danger of being labeled, 77–78
  definitions, 35
  demeanor evidence of, 84–85, 141
  evidence of in support of unpopular causes, 103–105
  evidence of in property management, 80–81, 84–85, 107–109, 112–13, 119–22, 131–32, 184–86
  eccentricity and, 141–42, 188
  functional deficits and, 194
  gift transactions used as evidence of, 185
  impaired health as proof, 89–90, 136–37, 137–38, 142–43
  individual interpretations, 34
  legal rather than medical concept, 35
  need for objective standards, 187–88
  partial insanity and will contests, 59–63
  personality disorder and, 103–105
  physical illness or disability and, 97–98, 127–29, 138–39, 141–42, 182
  planning for, 207–35
  presumption of, 20, 181
  proof vague or lacking, 33–34, 35, 42, 127–29, 129–30, 135–46
  subjective determinations, 187. *See also* judicial opinions subjective in nature
  use of preprinted findings in court, 110

inheritance and disinheritance of property in English law, 58–59

institutionalization. *See* nursing homes and institutionalization insufficient notice. *See* notice of incompetency/incapacity hearing

insufficient or incorrect proof of incompetency in courts, 135–46

intact decision-making, importance of, 180–81, 183–84

*inter vivos* gifts, 185

involuntary intervention absent a finding of mental incompetence, 126

involuntary petitions and the poor, 48–49

Jagiello, Barbara, 156

joint deposits, 217

judge as trier of fact, 41, 66

judicial decisions hard to appeal, 202–203

judicial determinations of statutory standards, 28, 34. *See also* decision-making

judicial opinions, accountability, 203

judicial opinions subjective in nature, 34, 118, 129, 150–51, 187, 202–203. *See also* statutory reform

judicial reports, requirement for, 203

jurisdiction of trial court, 83, 146

Kahn, Robert L., 208

Keith, Dr. Pat, 39

Kielkopf, Margaret, 46, 89

Knaus, William, 227

lack of beneficial outcome, 197

language in codes harmful to elderly. *See* statutory reform

Lanterman-Petris-Short Act, 47

LaRouche organization, 103–105

legal language, added burden of, 191

Legal Counsel for the Elderly (LCE), 227

legal representation, 195

Legal Services Corp., 213

Lewin, Travis, 16, 21, 199

licensing of professional conservators and guardians, 32–33, 153. 158, 165

limited guardians, use of, 199

living wills, 209, 225–28

"loser pays" suggestion for change, 198

losses suffered by conservatee or ward, 46, 52–53, 144–45, 186, 207–208

Loverde, Joy, 174

lunacy determinations, 59

Lustbader, Wendy, 167, 174

mandatory retirement age, 18

Martindale-Hubbell legal directory, 211

McCartney, Scott, 51–52, 99, 154

McNeely, Suzanne, 169

medical evaluations, 195–96

mental illness and property management, 132–34

mental impairment linked to physical disability, 147–49. *See also* incompetence and incapacity

Mill, John Stuart, 27

Miller, Adam L., 20

Mitchell, Annina M., 78

misuse of parens patriae. *See* statutory reforms

money and the elderly, 10, 20–22

"Moonies." *See* Unification Church of Rev. Sun Myung Moon

Mother Teresa, 227

National Academy of Elder Law Attorneys, 41

National Association of Professional Geriatric Care Managers, 171

National Council on the Aging, 174

New York Department of Social Services, 132–34

nomination of conservator/guardian. *See* advance directives; preselecting conservator or guardian

notice of incompetency/incapacity hearing disregarded in "emergency" situations, 129–30

insufficient, 190–91
legalese in, 191–92
requirement for, 37–38
warnings given the proposed ward, 38
nursing homes and institutionalization
conservatorships/guardianships as "price of admission," 182
elderly population in, 19–20
fear of, 168
placement by guardians/conservators, 47, 154–55, 162–63
survival rates in, 50–51

"old age"
age-related physical illnesses used in court, 36, 127–29
basis of incompetence or incapacity in court, 35–36, 73, 79–81, 94–97, 128–29
decision-making and, 36
definitions of, 18–20, 34–35
financial decisions and, 43, 80–81
inability to manage property and, 119–22, 126–27, 127–29
"normal senility," used in court, 85
undue influence and, 63–66
weight as issue of incompetence, 127
opinion evidence, 68–69

*parens patriae*
definition, 30–31, 180
misused by states in involuntary proceedings, 81–83, 131–35, 180–81
negating personal autonomy, 179–80
use in protective proceedings, 30–31
Parry, John W., 33, 39, 199, 200
paternalism, 36, 131, 132, 181, 184, 197
payment for proceedings, 31–32, 37, 40, 44–45, 110–11, 149–50, 197–98

payment for dismissed temporary guardianship, 149–50. *See also* statutory reform
Peden, James M., 192, 193
Perr, I. N., 63
petitions
allegations in, 33–34
evidence required, 33–34
preparing paperwork, 37
where filed, 36–37
petitions, filed by
adopted son, 150
adult children, 80, 81, 85, 86, 87, 90, 94, 97, 119, 126, 127, 131, 134, 136, 140, 143, 149, 158, 161, 162, 164
family (parents and siblings together), 103
former husband, 129
friend, 141
neighbors, 145
nephews and nieces, 112, 137, 147, 156
parents, 123, 129
siblings, 83, 100, 102, 142
sister-in-law, 84
spouse, 154, 159
stepson, 89
social workers/institutions, 23, 99, 105, 107, 111, 125, 132, 138, 154, 155, 157, 157–58, 160, 160–61, 162, 163
petitioners' motives not evaluated, 31, 37, 84–88, 117–18. *See also* statutory reforms
physical disabilities as incompetence, 36, 147–49 *See also* incompetence and incapacity
physical examination mandated by court, challenge to, 145–46
Pipkin, W. E., 72
placement of new ward/conservatee, involuntary
general, 47
in adult child's home, 161, 164–65

in boarding home, 99–100
in cheaper facility, 162
in congregate care facility, 160, 160–61
in locked psychiatric ward, 129–30
in nursing home, 50–51, 97–98, 125, 154–55, 155–56, 162–63
planning for possible incapacity
  discussions with attorneys during initial planning, 209
  discussions with significant others, 209
  See also advance directives
plenary conservatorships and guardianships, 29
power of attorney, 214. See also durable powers of attorney
power of conservator or guardian, 29, 47–50, 78
preselecting conservator or guardian
  example of form, Texas, 229–32
  importance of, 228–32
  selecting and disqualifying individuals, 229
presence of proposed ward or conservatee at hearing, 40–41, 129–30
presumption of incompetence in court, 193–94
preventing challenges to advance directives. See advance directives
probate courts
  alternative to, 196–97
  courts hearing conservatorship and guardianship cases, 36–37, 78
  "courts of the dead," 196–97
  pace too expensive and too slow for the elderly, 112–13
Probate Volunteer Panel Attorney, 192–93
problems with codes
  lack of common legal language, 28–29
  lack of federal policy/oversight, 27
  lack of precise functional definitions of terms, 34–35, 88–97, 118

mischaracterized as nonadversarial, 31, 37, 42, 119–22.
power of individual judges in interpreting codes, 118, 129–30, 244–47
See also statutory reform
procedural safeguards, need for, 192
proceedings as "nonadversarial," 37, 42. See also statutory reform
professional conservators, 24
progressive state codes, problems with, 183–84. See also decision-making
property management.
  and advanced age, 119–22, 126–27
  as proof of incompetence or incapacity, 79, 184–86
  convenience joint tenancies, 217
  durable powers of attorney, 213–16
  revocable trusts, 216
  See also old age; statutory reform; decision-making
prospective reports, court-mandated, 200
public guardians, 51–52, 105–107

Quia Emptores, 58

Rein, Jan Ellen, 31, 34, 81, 97, 165, 167, 182, 184, 186, 203, 234–35
Repensek, Frank, 160
reports, court-mandated, 33, 199–200
reports, judicial, 203
resources for the elderly, 325–62
  congressional committees on issues of aging, 337
  major national organizations, 325
  national legal organizations, 335
  related websites, 358
  state long-term-care ombudsman programs, 348
  state offices of aging, 338
"responsible" or "reasonable" decisions, 183–84. See also statutory reform; decision-making

restoration hearing, 45, 100–101, 131–32, 142–43
revocable living trust, 216
rights at hearing, 39, 191
  rights lost by ward, 29–30, 38, 52–53, 186, 208
  *See also* due process rights; conservatorships and guardianships, involuntary
right to be irresponsible, 17, 143, 183–84. *See also* decision-making
Robert Wood Johnson Foundation, 226, 228
Robinson, D. N., 63
role ambiguity in court, 192
Rosenbloom, Jerry S., 217, 226
Rowe, John W., 208

sale of ward's home and/or automobile by conservator/guardian, 47–49, 160–61
"sandwich generation," 167
Savage, Mark, 27, 87
scam artists and predators of the elderly, 185–86
Schafer, Doug, 158
Senior Connection. *See* Area Agencies on Aging
sexism, 197
Shakespeare, William, 9
Shellenbarger, Sue, 170
shifting roles of court-appointed officials, 191–93
Sinclair, Molly, 158
sound mind, presumption of, 64
Spar, James E., 64, 66, 233
standard of proof required, established in California, 143–45
state codes and statutes, individual, 237–322
state codes and statutes, problems
  lack national oversight, 27
  no common legal language, 28–29
  statutory guidelines disregarded, 125

statutory reform, suggestions for
  ageist bias in tests of property mismanagement, 94–97, 184–86
  ambiguous roles of court officials, 99–100, 191–93
  appeal process difficult and expensive, 202–203
  attendance at hearing, 195
  automatic provisions for termination lacking, 201–202
  complexity of court proceedings, 147–49
  confusion of changing roles, 192–93
  court-appointed visitors, 200–201
  court setting, 196–97
  due process not protected, 126–27, 192, 195–96
  evaluation for functional deficits only, 194
  examining petitioners' motives, 37, 84–85, 117–18, 181–83
  financial abuse, potential for, 155–57, 162, 163
  hearing inequities, 195–96
  guarding the guardians, 153–65, 198–201
  insufficient notice, 190–91
  judicial opinions not published, 203
  limited guardians, use of, 199
  medical evaluations, 195–96
  need to define terms used in proceedings, 186–90
  payment for dismissed temporary guardianship, 149–50
  payments for proceedings required of ward, 197–98
  probate courts as "slow courts of the dead," 112–13, 196–97
  reports required, 199–200
  shifting burden of proof, 193–94
  States' misuse of parens patriae, 180–81
  subjective judgments made by judges, 150–51
  undue influence claims, 188–90

value judgments in language of codes, 97–98, 183–84

Stegner, J., 72

stereotypes and aging, 19–20, 235

supervision of guardians and conservators lacking, 32–33

supportive services, 174–75

susceptibility of testator, 64–65

termination of conservatorships and guardianships
at death of ward or conservatee, 45, 105
for want of timely prosecution, 149
lack of automatic provision for, 105–107, 201–202
statistics on, 105
See also restoration hearing; statutory reform

testamentary capacity
California standards of, 62, 64
challenging wills over, 63
development of concept of, 63–66
legal standard of, 62, 66
Massachusetts standards, 62
Minnesota standards, 62
Missouri standards, 62

testamentary rights in feudal society, 58–59

threat of future competency lawsuits, 52, 132, 134–35

Towey, Jim, 227

Tripp, Kevin, 46, 89

unconstitutional use of presigned blank guardianship petitions, 125–26

undue influence
as proof of incompetence or incapacity, 43–44, 64
Catch-22 created in court, 96
circumstantial evidence of, 64–66
coercion, compulsion or restraint, 66
disposition and opportunity to exert, 65

example of use in court, 188–90
family relationships and, 189–90
in will contest or involuntary protective proceeding, 62, 85–86, 94–97, 119–23, 188–90
mental illness and, 43–44
relationship issues and, 65
misuse of, 64
required elements of, 63–66, 189
use of wills as proof, 66

Unification Church of Rev. Sun Myung Moon, case involving, 123–25

Uniform Guardianship and Protective Procedures Act (UGPPA), 28

Uniform Probate Code (UPC), 28, 35

UCLA Center on Aging, 18

U.S. Administration on Aging, 15

vagueness in codes unconstitutional, 123–25

Vagrancy Act of 1714, 59

value judgments in language of codes. See statutory reform

victimization by artful or designing persons, 123

videographic/photographic evidence, used without consent, 102–103

videotaping advance directives
purpose, 232–34
use of forensic or geriatric psychiatrists, 233

visitors, court-appointed, 200–201. See also court investigator

von Bismarck, Chancellor Otto, 18

Wacker, Dr. Robbyn, 39

Wagner, Donna, 174

Weeks, Linda, 160

Weihofen, 40

Weisfeld, Vicki, 228

Wigmore, I. J., 67, 68

Wilbur, Kathleen, 15

will contests
antemortem, 58

partial insanity in, 59–60
postmortem, 59–63
preventing, 232–34
use of expert witnesses in, 66–73
women's roles
control of wealth, 22

majority of elderly wards and conservatees, 22

Zimmy et al., 45